UNIVERSI

E. M.

Series of yearbooks, each a collection of representative intercollegiate debates on important questions of the day. Constructive and rebuttal speeches for both sides. Each debate is accompanied by selected bibliography and briefs.

Vol. XXXI. 1944-1945.

The Partition of Germany; World Peace Settlement; Admission of All Races to State Universities; Cartels; Compulsory Military Training; Permanent Government Economic Controls; Settling Labor Disputes by Legislation.

Vol. XXX. 1943-1944. o.p.

Vol. XXIX. 1942-1943.

The Value of the College Woman to Society; A Planned Economy for the United States After the War; A Universal Draft of Man- and Woman-power; The War Marriage; A Federal World Government; A Permanent Federal Union; Blueprints for a Better World (Burton-Ball-Hatch-Hill Resolution); A Russian-United States Alliance.

Vol. XXVIII. 1941-1942.

Federal Incorporation of Labor Unions; A League of Nations; Military Training; Failure of Colleges to Meet Student Needs; A Federation of Democracies Based on the Churchill-

Roosevelt Principles; A Federal Sales Tax; Compulsory Saving; Postwar Reconstruction; Western Hemisphere Solidarity; Freedom of Speech in Time of National Emergency.

Vol. XXVII. 1940-1941.

Industry Can Solve the Employment Problem; Conscription of Capital for Defense; Preservation of Democracy Through Decreased Government Control; Interstate Trade Barriers; Japanese Aggression; Union of United States and British Commonwealth of Nations; Regulation of the American Press; Compulsory Military Training; Strikes in Defense Industries; Western Hemisphere Defense.

Vol. XXVI. 1939-1940.

The Basis of a Lasting Peace; Shall the United States Enter the War?; Government Ownership and Operation of Railroads; Neutrality of the United States; Extension of Reciprocal Trade Agreements; The Third Term for President; Should the Roosevelt Administration Be Approved?; The Dies Committee; Civil Liberties; Labor; Foreign Affairs; Government and Business.

WITHDRAWN

THE REFERENCE SHELF

Vol. 18   No. 6

PALESTINE:
JEWISH HOMELAND?

Compiled by
JULIA E. JOHNSEN

THE H. W. WILSON COMPANY
NEW YORK   1946

PREFACE

Palestine has been prominently before the public for some years, in headlines, writings and public discussions. This Eastern Mediterranean country, of interest to a large part of the world by reason of its religious associations, its international importance to the great powers, and the racial questions involved, has long been marked by recurrent outbreaks of terrorism, conflict and other disorder. To the United States it has been considered of such importance and concern as to be included in the platforms of the two leading political parties in the last presidential election, to be subject to discussions and hearings in Congress, and to have led finally to the appointment of a joint Anglo-American Committee of Inquiry on Palestine which is now engaged in an investigation of the situation.

The Palestine problem has its roots in the racial urge and strivings of a people standing high in cultural and other advancement, for a homeland of its own. The attempt to realize this hope was quickened after World War I, but under conditions that gave rise to controversy which has lasted to the present time. The homeland sought in Palestine has been visualized as ranging from a cultural and spiritual center, based on the status so far attained, to that of a free Jewish state with full rights as to autonomy, immigration and expansion. Sympathizers with the latter aim have tended to keep alive and intensify the problem and subject it to recurring periods of international concern. Conditions have been investigated from time to time, but no feasible solution has yet been found. Among proposals suggested are a bi-national state, partitioning, the opening of other areas for the expansion or transfer of populations, immediate independence and self-government, the growth toward a Jewish majority and state, and recently, a trusteeship of the United Nations. Especially intense has been the problem of refugees left by the late war, both in its humanitarian aspects and as a means of bringing about a Jewish majority in Palestine, with the ultimate outcome of a Jewish commonwealth or state.

The Arabs in Palestine, whose claim to the country is an indigenous one, and whose hopes for independence were subject to disappointment after the First World War, have steadily opposed the influx of another and alien people. Conscious of a glorious historical past, and subject to the same intensified influences that have wrought momentous changes elsewhere throughout the world, they have visualized far-reaching possibilities of a more advanced future. They are backed by the moral support of an immense Arab and Moslem population in the Near East, Asia and Africa, and by the more specific strength of the Arab League, which was formed in Cairo in March 1945 to represent the united interests of this people.

Palestine is more than a problem of its principal contending races, it is a world problem; a problem of the British Empire, of Russian interests, of the Near East, of the Mohammedan Orient, of America, of the United Nations and more. Today the nations are striving to attain a greater world unity and peace; the welfare and stability of a section may well affect the welfare and stability of all, and the need is ever manifest for resolving dissensions and disunities with greater understanding, comity, justice and trust, among peoples and nations in the great regions of East and West.

The compiler has attempted to set forth, without bias, and with full appreciation of the deep interests at issue to the peoples most closely involved in the Palestine problem, some of its more fundamental background and outstanding aspects. Extensive writings have appeared on the subject during the last quarter century and more; some of the representative, up-to-date discussions are reprinted here. Other phases and viewpoints are covered by materials in the bibliography, which will facilitate further investigation. The list of organizations is selective and is based both on a relative balance of interests, and upon sources of materials that have been available and helpful in this study.

Grateful acknowledgment is made for courtesies extended in granting the use of copyright materials and in otherwise facilitating the preparation of this book.

JULIA E. JOHNSEN

February 25, 1946

CONTENTS

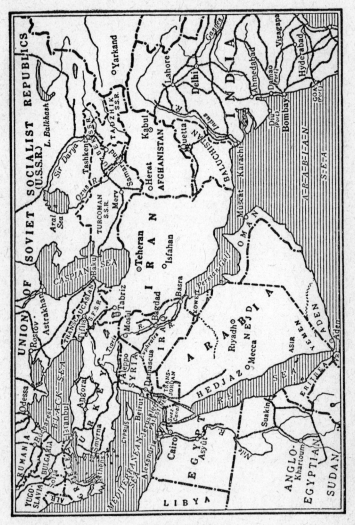

THE NEAR EAST
From *Europe Since 1914*, by F. L. Benns, by permission of the publishers.
F. S. Crofts & Co.

THE BACKGROUND AND PROBLEM

CONFLICT OVER PALESTINE [1]

During the First World War the British Government, finding Turkish aid to Germany imminent and American aid to the Allies still doubtful, made certain promises to Arab nationalists and to Jewish leaders of the Zionist movement. Out of the diametrically opposed aims of the recipients of those pledges the conflict in Palestine arises. The Zionist aim is the conversion of the land of Judaism's origin into a national home for the Jewish people. The Palestinian Arabs' objective is independent sovereignty in their ancestral home, preferably as part of a reunited Syria.

Today in Palestine 1,200,000 Arabs and 560,000 Jews face each other, practically *en bloc,* in bitter enmity. The Palestine Royal Commission, sent from London in 1936 to "ascertain the underlying causes" of Arab-Jewish disturbances, reported:

> There is no common ground between them. The Arab community is predominantly Asiatic in character, the Jewish community is predominantly European. They differ in religion and in language. Their cultural and social life, their ways of thought and conduct, are as incompatible as their national aspirations. These last are the greatest bar to peace. . . . Neither Arab nor Jew has any sense of service to a single state.

The application of the Mandate System to Palestine and the stated objectives of the Palestine Mandate indicate a belief on the part of the British Government, and presumably of the League of Nations Council which approved the mandate, that the building of a Jewish homeland and the fostering of Arab national independence were objectives not mutually incompatible in Palestine. They seem to have expected much from the conciliatory effect of the material prosperity which Jewish immigra-

[1] *Information Service* (Federal Council of the Churches of Christ in America). 53:1-6. October 7, 1944.

tion would bring to the country, and from the impetus offered
to general Arab development by Jewish enterprise, technology
and intellectual achievement. In consequence of the inclusion
of the Balfour Declaration, the text of which will be quoted
later, in its preamble the Palestine Mandate differed from the
other Class A Mandates for ex-Turkish territories in the omission of that "provisional independence" which was specified
by the League of Nations Covenant. The British construe the
Covenant in this respect to be permissive rather than obligatory.

With Arab realization of ultimate Zionist aims conflict has
grown steadily more bitter and seems likely to intensify. As
the Arab community grows in number and improves in economic
status and education its demand for independence is likely to
grow, together with its resentment toward the obstacle—evidently and admittedly the only obstacle—to that independence, the
Jewish national home. The rise to independence of Saudi
Arabia, the Yemen, Iraq, Egypt, and Transjordan and the progress of Syria and Lebanon spur the ambition and intensify the
sense of injustice of the Palestinian Arabs. The Arabs throughout the Middle East are consolidating. . . . At the same time,
the cruelties of the Nazi regime put an unbearable pressure upon
the Jews in Palestine and abroad to assure a haven for those who
can escape and to preserve a core of Jewish culture which may
flourish in independent security.

The Crown Colony type of government under the mandate
is admittedly unsuitable for governing either educated Arabs
or democratic Jews, each separately capable of full self-government. It cannot evolve into self-government without cooperation between the two elements of the population. With the
close of world hostilities only force is likely to keep the uneasy
balance between these two communities. The dilemma of the
British Government is a very real one. The British people are
strongly sympathetic toward ideals of independence; they have
old and strong ties with the Arab people as well as deep commitments in the Moslem world; British friendship for the Jewish people is of long standing and is at present intensified by
sympathy in their great agony.

The first of the British promises already referred to was made early in 1916 to leaders of the Arab Nationalist Movement, which was seeking possible assistance in turning to account the opportunity for successful revolt offered by Turkey's imminent involvement in the war as an ally of Germany. The Arabs were to strike at Turkish power in conjunction with the Allied attack. In return Britain agreed to support the claim to national independence of the Arab peoples within a specified area. The pledge consisted mainly of correspondence between Sir Henry McMahon, High Commissioner of Egypt, acting for the British Government, and the Grand Sherif of Mecca, later King Hussein of the Hejaz, acting for the Arab Nationalists.

A point which has been ever since in dispute is whether or not Palestine was included in the sections of territory excepted by Great Britain from the area of Arab independence. The British Government has maintained that it was certainly intended to be and definitely was excluded. The Arabs contest this interpretation. In 1939 a committee appointed by the United Kingdom and Arab delegates in London to consider the documents reported that they had been "unable to reach agreement upon an interpretation." Still maintaining that "on a proper construction of the correspondence Palestine was in fact excluded" the United Kingdom delegates had nevertheless informed the Arab delegates that certain of the latter's contentions had "greater force than has appeared hitherto" and that the language "was not so specific and unmistakable as it was thought to be at the time."

The British promise in the McMahon-Hussein correspondence referred to "those regions lying within those [proposed] frontiers *wherein Great Britain is free to act without detriment to the interests of her ally, France,*" and ended with the warning that maintenance of French good-will would be paramount. The absence of definite delimitation of excepted areas apparently arose from a disinclination to supply the French with a basis for claims greater than fortune might otherwise produce. The Sherif's reply postponed the point for postwar decision and warned that there would be no concession whatever of Arab land to France. Careful reading suggests less a misunderstanding than strategic preparation for later moves, with fair warning given by either side.

In view of international interests in the area at the time and the existence there of Russian, Italian, French and American missions of the Orthodox, Roman Catholic and Protestant Christian churches, it seems doubtful that Britain would have assumed it feasible summarily to settle the future of that part of Syria now called Palestine. The French claim to all Syria, including Palestine, was very much alive and Russia's interest was keen. It should, moreover, be remembered that the victory over the Ottoman Empire was not a British but an Allied victory. In point of fact, unknown to Arab leaders, Britain, France and Russia in the Sykes-Picot Agreement (April-May 1916) arranged for internationalization of the area roughly corresponding to Palestine as now constituted.

In January 1918, the "Hogarth Message" assured Hussein that the British Government was "determined that the Arab race shall be given full opportunity of once again forming a nation in the world" and urged Arab unity as prerequisite. Also, His Majesty's Government was "determined that in so far as is compatible with the freedom of the existing population, *both economic and political,* no obstacle should be put in the way of the realization" of the ideal of "a return of Jews to Palestine." The "Declaration to the Seven" (a reply to inquiry from prominent Arabs in Cairo) in the following June stated that it would be the policy of the British Government that the future government of the regions formerly under Turkish dominion, occupied by the Allies, "should be based upon the principle of the consent of the governed."

The committee above referred to concluded its report with the judgment that it was

evident from these statements that His Majesty's Government were not free to dispose of Palestine without regard for the wishes and interests of the inhabitants of Palestine, and that these statements must all be taken into account in any attempt to estimate the responsibilities which —upon any interpretation of the correspondence—His Majesty's Government have incurred towards those inhabitants as a result of the correspondence.

On November 2, 1917, the British Government made the following statement, through Arthur J. Balfour, then Foreign Secretary, in a letter addressed to Lord Rothschild:

His Majesty's Government view with favor the establishment in Palestine of a national home for the Jewish people, and will use their best endeavors to facilitate the achievement of this object, it being clearly understood that nothing shall be done which may prejudice the civil and religious rights of the existing non-Jewish communities in Palestine, or the rights and political status enjoyed by Jews in any other country.

This declaration was the result of much consultation and its meaning has been as hotly debated as that of the McMahon letters. A Zionist draft had read "that Palestine should be reconstituted as the national home of the Jewish people." The phrase "a national home" was an innovation in diplomatic language and it has been urged that the coining of this new expression indicates that the familiar terms "commonwealth" and "state" had been weighed and considered inapplicable. The use of the word "national" seems, nevertheless, significant. The description of the 91 per cent Arab majority of the Palestine population as "non-Jewish communities" suggests that a special position was being accorded the Jewish minority. The difference between the "civil and religious rights" reserved to Arabs and the "rights and political status" guaranteed to Jews in other countries was later pointed up by the Italian endorsement of a "Jewish national center" which, in contrast, stipulated "that no prejudice shall arise through it to the *legal and political* status of existing religious communities and to the civil and political rights already enjoyed by Israelites in any other country." (Italics ours.)

The Declaration has been interpreted as authorizing only a Jewish cultural center. However, in many countries such Jewish centers flourished at the time. In Palestine itself settlements— some primarily religious—existed which might readily have been expanded. The Royal Commission says of the oft-quoted 1922 Churchill Memorandum defining the "national home" that "though the phraseology was clearly intended to conciliate, as far as might be, Arab antagonism to the national home, there is nothing in it to prohibit the ultimate establishment of a Jewish state, and Mr. Churchill himself has told us in evidence that no such prohibition was intended." The Commission concluded:

Thus His Majesty's Government evidently realized that a Jewish state might in course of time be established, but it was not in a position to say that this would happen, still less to bring it about of its own motion.

It records the Jewish understanding that "in the course of time" the national home might develop into a Jewish state if the experiment of establishing it should succeed and a sufficient number of Jews should go to Palestine. This suggests the core of British optimism about results. Nothing in Britain's long experience, and indeed in the history of colonization—including Jewish projects—forecast the rate at which Jewish settlement has gone forward.

The strategic position at the Eastern end of the Mediterranean was an important factor in the British course of action. German influence had penetrated the Ottoman Empire to an extent that caused serious concern to the British Government. In 1968 control of the Suez Canal will revert to the independent Egyptian Government. A proposal to build a supplementary canal from the Palestinian coast to the Gulf of Aqaba had been broached. Roads, railways and airlines were contemplated that would make the country a hub of east-west communications important commercially, politically and militarily. An oil pipeline runs from the Mosul field to Haifa. The security of such a confluence of strategic routes could not be left to chance. A strong, modern community which would owe its very existence to Great Britain would bolster the defense of the new and inexperienced Arab states. Britain's backing for the Zionist venture would disallow that of Germany or Turkey, both of whom were ready in 1917 to deal with Zionist leaders.

It was doubtless argued that the two Semitic-language peoples in time would coalesce. Anticipation that arrangements agreeable to the Arabs would be feasible is implicit in the economic arguments used with Hussein. The Allies had publicly repudiated all conqueror's rights and an arrangement that would too closely resemble a protectorate was likely to meet with opposition from British liberals. The circumstances of the Dreyfus case and the suffering of Jews in Eastern Europe had evoked much sympathy in England. The British public would receive with approval a project to relieve the oppression of the Jewish people.

In the early stages a definite effort was made by Zionist leaders to moderate the public expression of their expectations, under admonition from British Government officials. The Report of the American (King-Crane) Commission to the American Secretariat at the Peace Conference in 1919 pointed out that "a national home for the Jewish people is not equivalent to making Palestine into a Jewish state." In the Churchill Memorandum of June 3, 1922, the British Government drew attention to "the fact that the terms of the Declaration referred to do not contemplate that Palestine as a whole should be converted into a Jewish national home, but that such a home should be founded *in Palestine.*" Moderate leaders among Zionists have recognized the advantages of deliberation and have stressed caution and conciliation. But the enthusiasm of the Diaspora, Zionist propaganda, the Polish depression, and Nazi persecution have combined to rush the project. The inconclusiveness of the British Government's attitude, due to internal disagreement, has left the situation open to conflicting interpretations.

The Zionist Organization was established in 1897 by the first Jewish Congress held at Basle under the leadership of Theodor Herzl. The Basle Program stated: "The aim of Zionism is to create for the Jewish people a publicly recognized and legally secured home in Palestine." ✕

In accordance with Herzl's plan for colonial development an "appropriate Jewish agency" was authorized by the Palestine mandate to advise and cooperate with the Administration of Palestine "in such economic, social and other matters as may affect the establishment of the Jewish national home and the interests of the Jewish population in Palestine," and "to assist and take part in the development of the country." "Close settlement by Jews on the land" was to be encouraged; the Administration might arrange with the Jewish agency to construct or operate public works, services and utilities, and to develop any of the natural resources of the country. English, Arabic and Hebrew were to be official languages. Each community might maintain its own schools.

The Zionist Organization was later superseded as the colonizing agent in Palestine for the Jewish people by the Jewish Agency in whose membership non-Zionists were included, although they have been inactive in recent years. The Jewish Agency represents the Jewish people in all matters affecting the national home, and the National Council of Jews in Palestine acts for Jews in that country in all phases of Jewish relationships with the Administration. The elected General Assembly and the National Executive Council (Va'ad Leumi) chosen by the Assembly constitute the responsible government of the national home, and its religious affairs are administered by the Rabbinical Council. The Royal Commission states that the Va'ad Leumi and the elected committees of towns and villages were entitled by law to levy taxation by annual budgets and to maintain social services, especially in the fields of public health and education. The regulations provided, of course, for their control by the government of Palestine, especially with regard to finance.

A Jewish population of 9 per cent in 1919 had risen in October 1943 to 35 per cent of Palestine's total. Zionist colonization was characterized by extensive successful soil reclamation and crop substitution as well as industrial expansion, and development of commerce and shipping. One third of the Jewish population is organized in cooperatives of one kind or another. The Jewish National Fund has invested $30,000,000 in land acquisition, land improvement, afforestation and water supply. Land owned by the Fund is inalienable and is leased, never sold, to Jewish settlers, who must agree to cultivate it themselves. The total Jewish investment since the end of World War I has been $400,000,000. The social services have made a magnificent and successful attack upon ignorance, poverty, and especially disease. The whole project has called forth the most extraordinary devotion and enduring labor.

Concessions for development of the power resources of the two main rivers of Palestine were awarded to Zionist enterprise, and projects of electrification and irrigation are in some cases completed, in others still in plan. Use of the mineral resources of the Dead Sea is already fairly well developed. Sustained immigration is the crucial feature of the program. It is of the essence of the Zionist concept that Palestine shall offer a permanent solution for the Jews, marked by an integration of physical, psychological and social factors.

The Arabs' case is fundamentally that of the right of an indigenous population to its home soil. Since the Arab conquest in 640 A.D. Arabs have been settled in Palestine. They claim uninterrupted occupation by their fathers from times antedating the Hebrew invasion which is related in the *Old Testament.*

For the past 20 years Arab representatives have made unremitting appeal to the right of self-determination as publicized by President Wilson and authenticated in the Covenant of the League of Nations. With the British Government and before world opinion they argue that Article 22 of the Covenant specifically applied this right to them. It reads in part:

> Certain communities formerly belonging to the Turkish Empire have reached a stage of development where their existence as independent nations can be provisionally recognized subject to the rendering of administrative advice and assistance by a mandatory until such time as they are able to stand alone. The wishes of these communities must be the principal consideration in the selection of the mandatory.

By this clause the Turkish territories were differentiated from other, less advanced, mandated areas. Article 20 of the same document required that

> The Members of the League severally agree that this Covenant is accepted as abrogating all obligations or understandings *inter se* which are inconsistent with the terms thereof, . . .

and the Arabs are convinced that the Balfour Declaration and the Sykes-Picot Agreement—are thus inconsistent and should therefore have been cancelled.

The Arabs argue that the mandate itself is an injustice and a betrayal; that it contravenes the stated purpose of the League by first depriving them of control of immigration and then imposing alien settlement with privileged status which aims at eventual control by majority rule, reducing them to a minority in their own land. No machinery exists for appeal from the mandate by a mandated population. The Permanent Mandates Commission's supervisory role is advisory only. There is no court before which the Arab case can be brought except by the mandatory itself. The British Government has refused to go back of the mandate in response to appeals. The disillusion, exasperation and bitterness engendered in the Arab population of Palestine by this situation developed into violence against the Jews and at length, in 1933, into attack upon the government, and in 1936 into open rebellion.

Beyond the fundamental injustice which they charge, the Arabs contend (1) that a remote historical connection terminated over 18 centuries ago cannot now confer any right to territory; (2) that, except for an 80-year period of the reigns of Kings David and Solomon, during Israel's existence as a nation in Palestine its territory was confined to the hill country, whereas the main Zionist settlement is in the fertile coastal plain; (3) that the land cannot support such heavy immigration and that Arabs are being and increasingly will be dispossessed; (4) that Arab prosperity is due largely to the release of Arab initiative following the removal of Turkish domination. Possible material benefit has no weight in the balance against their independence and desire to determine their own culture pattern. They recall the "golden age" of the Arab peoples and they intensely desire to share in the Arabic renaissance. They claim that Islam has shown religious tolerance toward the Jews throughout its history. And they resent what they consider a Western attempt to right at Moslem expense a situation originally created by Christian intolerance.

The Zionist argument that the Emir Feisal committed the Arabs to cooperation with reference to the Jewish homeland is rejected on the ground that the pact with Dr. Weizmann signed in January 1919, was invalidated by the Emir's proviso making its implementation contingent on full realization of Arab independence; and further that he had no authority to sign away Palestine's independence. The General Syrian Congress on July 2, 1919, with Palestinian delegates participating, adopted its Damascus Program which repudiated the Sykes-Picot Agreement, the Balfour Declaration, and any plan for partition of Syria or for a Jewish commonwealth in Palestine.

There seems to be no doubt that Axis encouragement and aid were accepted by Arab nationalist leaders. Such action was, of course, exceedingly objectionable to the British Government and constituted a serious danger to United Nations interests. However, the part played by Axis interests in the present Palestine situation can be over-emphasized.

The Christian Arabs of Palestine have taken the side of their Moslem brethren, with certain reservations. Other sects in the country are, on the whole, willing to accept a Moslem state. To some extent this is due to their weakness as small minorities. A prominent member of the Protestant community, since deceased, stated that his people felt the economic and cultural pressure of Zionism feared a materialistic domination unsympathetic to Christianity.

There appears to have been a sincere effort on the part of the Mandatory Government in Palestine to maintain impartial administration. Vacillation between conciliation and repression, however, has brought upon the administration the censure of the Permanent Mandates Commission. Its unenviable position under the mandate is described by the Royal Commission thus: "poised . . . above two irreconcilable communities, compelled to follow a path between them marked out by an elaborate, yet not very lucid, legal instrument, watched at every step it takes by both contending parties inside the country and watched from outside by experienced critics on the Permanent Mandates Commission and by multitudes of Jews throughout the world."

From 1922 to 1941, inclusive, 315,985 Jews entered Palestine. Between 1932 and 1938, according to British official figures, the number was 219,115. Between 1922 and 1938 imports rose from £7.2 millions to £13.6 millions, exports from £1.6 millions to £5.0 millions. Of the exports some 80 per cent were citrus fruits, and Arab orange groves were nearly as extensive as Jewish. During the 'thirties, with the influx of refugees from Germany, Austria and Czechoslovakia, industry developed. The population in 1942 was 1,613,376 of whom 992,063 were Moslems, 126,501 Christians and 481,706 Jews.

Arabs, both Moslem and Christian, totaled approximately
1,110,000.

Of the 350,000 increase in the Arab population of Palestine
between 1920 and 1937 roughly nine tenths is attributable to
natural increase. Regarding the economic effect on the Arab
community of Jewish immigration the Royal Commission said
that the import of Jewish capital had had a "general fructifying
effect on the economic life of the whole country," making possible the expansion of Arab industry and citriculture and the
improvement of methods of cultivation, and giving employment to Arab labor. The reclamation and anti-malarial work of
the Jewish colonies has benefited the whole population of the
affected areas, and Jewish social services have aided the general
population to a certain extent. A beneficial result is attested
by the disproportionate increase in the Arab population of the
urban areas most affected by Jewish development. The Commission warned, however, that such benefits depend on the
homeland's continued prosperity and are endangered by a continued widening of the political gulf between Jew and Arab.
The war has brought an extension of Palestine's prosperity and
its industry. Jewish enterprise has taken an active part in the
industrial development, and contributed largely to the success
of the Middle East Supply Center's activities.

Repeated efforts to associate Palestinians, Jewish and Arab,
with the administration in representative capacities in such
manner as to develop "self-governing institutions" for the country as a whole have been wrecked by the impossibility, on the
one hand, of reconciling Jews to minority representation, because Arab preponderance would preclude the national home,
and on the other hand, of reconciling Arabs to less than majority
representation, because it would eliminate hope of Arab independence.

In the spring of 1918, with the war still in progress, the
military administration still governing and the mandate still
under consideration, a Zionist Commission empowered by the
British Government to travel in Palestine, investigate and report
on the prospects for a national home, and develop friendly
relations with the Arabs, visited the country. The Royal Com-

mission reports that this Zionist body desired that Jews "should at once participate in the military administration: that there should be a land commission, with experts nominated by the Jewish organization 'to ascertain the resources of Palestine.' " Among other things, "they desired to select and supplement the pay of Jewish candidates for the police. They demanded and began to train their own military defense force." At that early stage "there was in effect a separate Jewish judicature," and "it was obvious that the Jews had created a very efficient intelligence department, from which (as is indeed the case today [1937]) the administration could keep little secret."

In 1920 the Chief Administrator recommended to the Home Government that the Zionist Commission be eliminated. The privileges accorded the Commission, he said, had "firmly and absolutely convinced the non-Jewish element of our partiality," and there would be danger of revolution if exclusively Jewish labor were employed on government projects and government lands were handed over to the Zionist organization. He urged, further, that great works of electrification, road and port building ought properly to be carried out by the government and not by one section of the population.

In 1937, however, the Royal Commission said of the Jewish Agency: "In fact there is no branch of the administration with which the Agency does not concern itself." But

we do not think the Agency is open to criticism on this ground. . . . The words of Article 4 [of the Mandate] entitle the Agency to advise the Government and cooperate with it in almost anything that may affect the interests of the Jewish population in Palestine.

. . . The Agency is obviously not a "governing" body: it can only advise and cooperate in a certain wide field. But, allied as it is with the *Va'ad Leumi,* and commanding the allegiance of the great majority of the Jews in Palestine, it unquestionably exercises, both in Jerusalem and in London, a considerable influence on the conduct of the Government."

. . . This powerful and efficient organization amounts, in fact, to a government existing side by side with the Mandatory Government.

The Supreme Moslem Council was later established in an effort to equalize this situation.

The unequal economic status of the two communities is a source of embarrassment to the Administration. The Jewish section is a highly developed Western society set down in the midst of a predominantly primitive—while not lacking in intellectual potential—Asiatic community. The Jewish immigrants come from different countries and represent all classes and activities, "a complete society in miniature," according to Sir Herbert Samuel. They are selected, trained, controlled and financed. Young, enthusiastic idealists predominate. The average in education is very high. They already possess "an elaborate social and political organization." The community has the added advantage of a highly integrated, scientifically organized educational system, well financed and supplied with trained personnel. The Arabs depend largely on government educational effort, hampered as it is by lack of trained teachers and by an insufficiency of funds.

Serious complications grow out of the problems already existing in the feudal type of Arab economy and the incredibly involved medieval system of land tenure. The latter places almost unparalleled difficulties in the way of land title verification, survey and registration. Popular resentment arises from the fact that sale of land to Jews displaces the *fellah,* who under the Arab tenure has always remained on the land regardless of changes in ownership.

Temporary and partial restrictions upon Jewish immigration have proved insufficient to allay Arab violence. The criterion of "economic absorptive capacity" for control of immigration was supplemented by that of "the political high level," which inevitably led to cessation of immigration. The Royal Commission's suggestion of partition into a Jewish and an Arab state was considered by the Palestine Partition Commission, upon examination, to be unworkable, as well as unacceptable to both factions. No feasible boundaries were found for the Jewish state that would be suited to defense. Nor could any be discovered that would not leave a small Jewish minority in the Arab state and a relatively large Arab minority in the Jewish state. Population resettlement offered no solution since the land necessary for compensation on any large scale was unavailable.

In May 1939, the British Government made a public state ment of policy (popularly called "The White Paper"). The three "main obligations" under the mandate were reviewed: (1) to cultivate "such political, administrative and economic condi- tions as will secure the establishment in Palestine of a national home for the Jewish people," facilitate Jewish immigration under suitable conditions, and encourage close settlement by Jews on the land; (2) to safeguard the civil and religious rights of all in- habitants and insure that the rights and position of other sections are not prejudiced and (3) to advance the development of self- governing institutions. The Government stated its belief that "the framers of the mandate . . . could not have intended that Palestine should be converted into a Jewish state against the will of the Arab population of the country" and declared "un- equivocally that it is not part of their policy that Palestine should become a Jewish state" or "that the Arab population should be made the subjects of a Jewish state against their will." Since the Government could "not agree that the McMahon correspond- ence forms a just basis for the claim that Palestine should be converted into an Arab state" and since a Jewish national home had been definitely established, an independent Palestine state would be established within ten years, Arabs and Jews sharing in the government. Jewish immigration must cease on March 31, 1944, and would not be resumed except with Arab consent. (An indefinite time extension has been given for the uncompleted immigration quota of Jews and an extra 25,000 European ref- ugees.) Transfer of Arab land to Jews was prohibited in some areas; in others it was restricted. It was pointed out that for the establishment of an independent state and relinquishment of the mandatory the first requisite was such relations between Arabs and Jews as would make good government possible.

Several of the numerous investigating commissions sent to Palestine by the British Government have reported on the eco- nomic absorptive capacity of the land. Concentration of land ownership was already a cause for concern prior to Jewish settle- ment. Land surveys have been and are being made, together with extensive search for subsoil water and study of possible reform of the land tenure system, preparatory to planned agricultural development under Government auspices.

The shortage of land was attributed by the Partition Commission not so much to the sale of land to Jews, in view of their extensive reclamation of areas held to be uncultivable, as to the high Arab birth rate, the cessation of Turkish conscription and growing restrictions abroad on immigration—particularly in the Western countries. It would, however, be increasingly aggravated by the rapid natural increase of the indigenous population. The 1931 Report of the Census of Palestine pointed out that "nearly a quarter of the agriculturists would be unable to maintain their present standard of life if they were unable to find a secondary means of subsistence." The Commission concluded that if the Arab rural population continues to increase at its present rate, the demand for such supplementary employment, and even the pressure to leave the land and seek for whole-time employment in the towns, will be intensified—quite apart from any further acquisition of land by the Jews. The future for the Arab population is therefore already menacing and since, in the main, available capital is Jewish, they could be faced with the prospect of greater economic hardship if Jewish immigration should be completely closed down. The Commission recommended that alienation of land be permitted only in districts where extensive cultivation could be replaced by intensive farming. The only basis for expansion was found to be in the coastal plain, where land transfer is still permitted.

The strength of the movement in America for a Jewish homeland in Palestine results from the traditional role of that tiny strip of land in the life of the Jewish people. Palestine to the religious Jew is not merely a place: it is an idea. Dr. Louis Finkelstein, president of the American Jewish Theological Seminary, has put the matter in a way to give to non-Jews the "feel" of this deathless attachment to that ancient land:

For the Jewish religion, Palestine is the land of the Lord, set aside from the beginning as a unique sanctuary for distinctive forms of communion with God. A large part of Jewish ritual law was formulated especially for life in Palestine. The sanctity of Palestine . . . derives from the fact that the land shares forever the holiness of the Temple. Just as it is possible for a Jew to worship in private, and yet preferable that he do so in the synagogue; and as he may pray in any language, but is enjoined to do so in Hebrew; so, while Judaism can be practiced and followed with devotion anywhere, especial merit attaches to those "who dwell in the Holy Land, reading the *Shema* morning and evening, and speaking the Hebrew tongue." . . .

Zionist opposition to the White Paper is based in the main on the fact that stoppage of immigration renders the achievement of a Jewish state practically impossible by placing the attainment of a majority beyond reach. It is charged . . . that this is a nullification of the mandate, and of the Balfour Declaration endorsed by 52 national governments. The judgment of the Permanent Mandates Commission is cited, that the new policy does not accord with previous interpretations of the mandate or with any possible interpretation.

Anti-Zionist opposition to the White Paper is based on the "fundamental fact" that proposals which exclude Jews as Jews, from right of entry and acquisition of land "do violence to the fundamental concept of democratic equality and thus to the very purposes and ideals to which the United Nations are pledged."

In considering the Zionist problem it is well to keep in mind that the welfare and economic health of Palestine and of the Jewish colonies there are separate questions from the rescue of war refugees. It has been urged that a slower and steadier expansion might produce a more stable future.

In view of Arab predominance in the region it would seem that Arab compliance in the Zionist plan is a prerequisite to be secured at any cost. The Royal Commission noted that the Arabs "detected, too, in some of those young newcomers an arrogance which seemed to suggest that they felt themselves to be members of a superior race, destined before long to be masters of the country."

Raphael Straus, a Jewish social historian for some years resident in Palestine, speaks of a "preponderant" urban population which "obviously upsets the entire program of agricultural colonization" and exaggerates the cost of public works, education and public security. Further comment on the economic phase appears in the following passage from the Report of the Royal Commission:

> Much of the expenditure has been uneconomic. For some of the capital provided no return could be expected; for the rest only a small and possibly long-delayed return. . . . But, if it was to realize its promoters' dreams within measurable time, it would need a more normal economic basis; it would need to be regarded as a "sound proposition" and attract investment in the usual way of business.

For that purpose the welding of the population into a unit, and the lessening of the economic, social and intellectual distance between groups is primary. An obstacle to effective government action toward reconciliation was erected in the sanctioning of separate systems of education on different levels of financial support and supply of trained personnel. As was inevitable, both are schools of nationalism which perpetuate the conflict. The Jews have hoped to see a greater part of the Jewish population cultivate the land and a larger part of the Arab population engage in trade and industry. Although recent trends show increased industrial occupation among Arabs, a heavy proportion of urban workers appears among Jewish immigrants.

THE NEAR EAST: YESTERDAY AND TODAY [2]

At the outset of a discussion of the Near East it is necessary to define the lands that are covered by this general geographical term, since there is some want of uniformity in its application. The Oxford Dictionary defines the Near East as the southeastern part of Europe, i.e., the Balkan states together with Asia Minor; it defines the Middle East as the southwestern countries of Asia. This definition reflects the point of view and the usage in the political language of Europe. But on this side of the Atlantic the practice is to follow the universal usage of students of Eastern cultures and languages in defining the Near East as those lands contiguous to the southeastern shores of the Mediterranean

[2] By William Robert Taylor, Professor of Oriental Languages, University of Toronto. In Anderson, Violet, ed. *The United Nations Today and Tomorrow.* p.83-100. Ryerson Press. Toronto. 1943.

along with Asia Minor and Arabia, while the term, Middle East, is applied to Iraq, Persia, and Afghanistan.

It has to be allowed, however, that the distinction between Near East and Middle East, as thus defined, is often very fluid, since the cultural factors that bind, for example, Iraq with Egypt transcend the geographical conditions of distance and desert that on the map seem to divide them. For the same reason it is difficult to determine where the western bounds of the Near East should be marked. The history of Egypt has been affected by invasions from Libya at intervals for several thousands of years; and since the days of Caliphs all the lands on the south shore of the Mediterranean have shared a common heritage of language, literature, religion, and custom. Practical recognition of the basal unity of the culture of these Levantine countries is seen in the recent transference of certain British civil officials from Transjordania to Benghazi for the administration of Libya and the adjoining districts, their acquaintance with the one country fitting them for service in the other.

The area of the Near and Middle East exclusive of the countries west of Egypt is about 2,500,000 square miles—roughly, the area of Canada with British Columbia and the Yukon left out. The population is now over 65,000,000, of which 35,000,-000 belong to the Arab-speaking peoples, or 50,000,000, if we include the countries west of Egypt. This Near-East population, unlike that of most occidental regions, is gathered in foci or islands of habitation. In the Arab-speaking area there is a fairly continuous strip of green stretching in a great arc or crescent from the Delta of the Nile to the head of the Persian Gulf. Within this crescent are three river valleys. The two greatest are the Nile, at one end, and the Tigris-Euphrates, at the other; the third is that which lies between the Lebanon ranges and is watered by the Orontes and Litani rivers and the rains which these mountains cause to fall. In Arabia proper there are the moist fringes of the coast lands, and the rare fertile spots in the interior which together form the Nejd. Between these cultivable areas provided by rivers and rainfall lie the great deserts and steppes, which like great seas offer formidable barriers against intercourse. It is because of these geographical conditions that the Arab-speaking population falls into blocks. The 17,000,000 of Egypt are concentrated in 3 per cent of its area; the 3,500,000 of Syria-Lebanon are shut up in 50 per cent of its 58,000 square miles; 80 per cent of Transjordania is arid; in Arabia less than 2 per cent of the land is cultivable. Since the wastes of the Near East are unchangeable because waterless, it is obvious that these natural features must be viewed as fixed and inescapable. Even if by more scientific methods of irrigation and cultivation and by the introduction of industry the population of this area might be increased, the elemental facts would not be altered; the population would still be distributed as in times past.

The influence of geography has gone further and made it impossible in the long history of these lands to effect stable political unity. Each region developed inevitably its own life, with its own economic order and social structure, and with its particular relations with foreign peoples and cultures. And within each of the larger divisions smaller ones existed. In Syria there have always been Damascenes and Alepins, in Mesopotamia Baghdadis and Mosulis, and in Egypt the communities of Upper, Middle, and Lower Egypt with Cairenes over against Alexandrians. Politically there is always this centrifugal tendency in the East, an inherent dislike of large overriding authority. And, socially, these parts have at no time up to the present shown any uniformity; tribalism, feudalism, and monarchism of one form or another have persisted alongside one another. And to these contrasts must be added the eternal conflict between the Bedouin and the settled people, between the desert and town. . . .

The Pan-Arab knows, what we all know, that there are other factors which in large measure transcend these socio-geographical forces that work against unity in their world. Ninety-two per cent of the Arab-speaking peoples are Moslems, which means that a common pattern of religious practice, law, buying and selling, contracts, marriages, domestic institutions, private conduct and public relations, holds them together by bonds that are akin to those of patriotism. Nearly 100 per cent of them use the same language in their daily affairs, and, though the dialect of one region may differ from that of another, an Iraqi and a Miṣri understand one another as well as a Glaswegian and a Cockney; Mecca and Tunis listen to the same Arabic broadcasts. The journals and books which pour from the presses from Algiers to Baghdad are governed by one literary standard, that set by the Koran. The Holy Cities of Iraq, Syria, Palestine, and Arabia, where in the annual pilgrimages thousands of Moslems commingle, quicken powerfully their sense of a community of interests and loyalties. Then, we must not forget that a basis for the unity of these peoples lies in *a common pride in their history.* They have not forgotten that for several centuries (from the eighth to the fifteenth century) they were the dominant world power; that their sway, extending from India to the Pyrenees, exceeded that of any earlier empire. Their history has had a more impressive glory and continuity than that of any European power. When they fell apart under the rule of the later Caliphs, they were brought together again in the Ottoman Empire, which, in its turn, continued to emphasize the importance of the Near East in the affairs of the world. And with the recollection of this past political significance there remains also their memory of their cultural leadership. When Europe was involved in the darkness and ignorance of the Middle Ages, they preserved, extended, and in due course transmitted to the West, not only the accumulated stores of the science and the philosophy of the Graeco-Roman civilization but much of the best of Byzantine and Persian art, architecture, and literature. They founded the earliest universities in Europe. Their works in medicine, astronomy, chemistry, physics, geography, theology, ethics, logic, metaphysics, history, and poetry, became the first textbooks of the West. They had even to teach us chivalry and good manners. "When the Crusading Knights were settling their differences by personal combat in the arena, the more civilized Near East was using law courts and fixed legal codes." They remember this legacy of their former glory. A modern Egyptian addressed a group of students who were setting out to Europe for study in these words:

> The parting prayers of your parents will cry out in your ears that you belong to a people who have a great past, and this past lays on you the charge that while you may change it, you may not despise it.

11048

Then there is another powerful factor which effects a sense of unity in the Near East, the general belief that the Western powers have not dealt fairly with them. They argue that, after the collapse of the Turkish Empire, a greater measure of freedom and independence should have been accorded to them and that the mandatory powers, in violation of their pledges, resisted political development in the occupied countries. Skilful leaders and organizations supported by ample contributions from native and Axis sources, and by the broadcasts from Berlin and Bari, and, more recently, from the "Free Arabia" radio station in Athens, have steadily fomented these grievances, however real or unreal in fact. Since 1939 the catchword of this propaganda is "Freedom from the Anglo-Jewish joke." We may not complain of the methods of the agitators since they follow the techniques employed by us against the Turks in the last war, but we cannot overlook the results. No leading Near Eastern power, with the questionable exception of Iraq, has declared war against the Axis countries. Despite the correct attitude of the government of Egypt in the fulfilment of its treaty obligations to Great Britain, and despite the influence of the pro-British premier Mustapha Nahas Pasha, Egypt has given no active military assistance to the Allies. In every country in the Near East there are powerful groups hostile to the Allied cause, the designs of which are at present countered more by the sheer indifference of the populace than by any positive enthusiasms for the United Nations. The sum of our argument is that the Near East is, in spite of its social and geographical handicaps, awake with a new sense of its common heritage and interests, but this awakening is in these days accompanied by suspicion of and hostility to the democracies of the West.

The analysis of this situation is complex. Some of the contributory causes are imperialism, commercialism, the administration of the mandates, and, ironically, the growing Westernization of the East.

The entrance of Western imperialism into the Near East dates from the time of Napoleon. The plan of the French was to open up again Western trade with the whole of the East through the southeastern Mediterranean ports and so destroy

British trade supremacy through the British control of the routes around the Cape. . . .

From that time Turkey became "the sick man" of the political world. By two major strokes the death of "the sick man" was brought about. The first was delivered by Mohammed Ali, pasha of Egypt and friend of France. In two battles between 1831 and 1833 this vassal of Turkey drove the Turks out of Syria, and sent his son, Ibrahim, into Asia Minor on a victorious march against Constantinople. For various reasons the European powers, with the exception of France, feared that this Moslem leader might split up the Turkish Empire and precipitate unpredictable rises. They conspired, therefore, by threats and by promises to force him back into Egypt; and they gave a sop to his pride by recognizing him as a quasi-independent ruler with dynastic rights within the Turkish Empire.

The consequences of Mohammed Ali's successful challenge of Turkish power followed thick and fast. The powers in various ways sought for spheres of influence in Syria and Palestine. The English, for example, in 1841 assisted in the establishment of a bishopric in Jerusalem, although there were no Anglicans in the country. The Jews in 1878 initiated a scheme of colonization along the coast of Palestine, and the English assumed the role of protector of Jews in Palestine and Syria. Later, both the Russians and the Germans built large hospices and imposing cathedrals in Jerusalem. In 1860 French troops were landed in the Lebanon to protect the Christian minorities and restore order, thus giving reality and emphasis to her so-called *"droit historique"* in Syria which she based on French holdings there in the time of the Crusades, and on her claim from 1535 to be the natural protector of all Christian minorities throughout the Levant —a claim which so far as Palestine is concerned she gave up or suspended only in 1922, four years after the English occupation, at the insistence of the Pope. The quarrel between Russia and France in 1850 over the relative rights of Latin and Orthodox priests at the Holy Places in Bethlehem and Jerusalem was only a prelude to a demand in 1853 by Russia that the orthodox clergy in the Ottoman Empire be given extraterritorial rights.

which was tantamount to a demand for an official right to interfere in the internal affairs of Turkey.

The Crimean War, which followed, seemed to be a triumph
for Turkey's cause; in reality, it put Turkey under the protection
of all the great powers, who solemnly swore to guarantee the
integrity of the Ottoman Empire. This formal engagement,
however, did not prevent Russian political manoeuvres in the
Balkan area and in 1878 Serbia, Rumania, and Bulgaria, declared
their independence of Turkey. In the same year Cyprus was
ceded to Britain, and Bosnia to Austria. France, which had
taken over Algeria in 1830, added Tunisia to her African dominion in 1881. Italy, coming later on the scene of international politics, forced Turkey in 1912, after a brief war, to surrender Tripoli and Libya, the last of its African possessions.

The helplessness of Turkey in the face of the steady dis-
memberment of her territory showed that "the sick man" was
near to death. The *coup de grace* to the Ottoman Empire was
delivered through the events of the First Great War. In the
Treaty of Sèvres (1920), the Sultan renounced sovereignty over
Mesopotamia, Palestine, Syria, and Arabia, and formally recognized the loss of Egypt, Cyprus, and North Africa. Those
clauses of the ill-fated treaty were not scrapped in its later revision at Lausanne. The conference at San Remo (1920) par-
celled out the mandates, which were duly confirmed later by
the League after the adjustments recognized by the Treaty of
Lausanne in 1923.

In order to understand the course of the peace settlements
in the Near East we must keep in mind the broad understanding of the Triple Entente into which Russia, France and Great
Britain jointly entered shortly before the First World War. The
building of the Suez canal had made both Egypt and the region
east of the canal a vital concern of the British Empire. After
the Russo-Japanese War the rivalries between the three powers
became more tense in the Near East. The Russians, after their
ambitions in the Far East had been checked, sought room for expansion in southwest Asia, particularly, to provide Siberia an unrestricted outlet to an open sea, and they crowded the interests
of the Austro-German group as well as those of the British and

French. The conclusion of the Triple Entente eased the tension so far as the contracting powers were concerned. The region of the Caucasus and Persia was recognized as Russia's sphere of influence with due allowance for British interests in Persia; Syria, i.e., the region west of a line drawn through Damascus, as France's; Egypt, the Suez region, and Mesopotamia, as Great Britain's. The conception of the Berlin-Baghdad railway was the counter stroke of the Austro-German group.

The much discussed Sykes-Picot Agreement in 1916, entered into by Great Britain, France, and Russia, followed the lines of the Triple Entente so far as the allocation of the Ottoman Empire was concerned, except that the distributions were on an ampler scale: Russia, in addition to Eastern Anatolia, was to receive Constantinople plus territory on either side of the Bosphorus; France was to receive a large part of southern Anatolia and territories east of Damascus as far as Mosul; Great Britain was to take, over and above the Iraq, all that lay between the Euphrates and the Suez, and in addition the two ports of Acre and Haifa. Palestine was to be under a regime of international control. This agreement was a secret arrangement. It was made by the British after, and presumably on the strength of, the conversations which Sir Henry McMahon had initiated with the Sherif Hussein. Knowledge of its terms came to Hussein only in 1917, after the Bolsheviks had published it along with other secret documents in the archives of the Czarist Ministry of Foreign Affairs. In their dealings with the Sherif, the British had made vague references to understandings with France, and they had explicitly informed him that the region west of Damascus was not to be a part of the projected Arab Free State. The failure to specify at the same time the status of Palestine in relation to Arab territory may charitably be explained as due to the vagueness of the Sykes-Picot Agreement with respect to its administration. Their lack of frankness, however, is inexcusable. The contention of Mr. Churchill, speaking as a Minister of the Crown in 1922, that Palestine was excluded by implication, since it was a part of the vilayet of Syria, is not convincing. The British, at the best, were thinking, absurdly, that the Arabs would be satisfied with an independent state consisting of Arabia and the steppes and wastes of the Syrian Desert.

The San Remo Conference in 1920 was simply an open ratification of the Sykes-Picot Agreement, with such adjustments as were made necessary by the demise of Czarist Russia. Syria and the Lebanon were to be placed under a single mandate to be entrusted to France; Great Britain was to hold two mandates, one for Iraq and another for Palestine. Also, France agreed to transfer the Mosul district with its oil to Great Britain in return for a quarter interest in the then known Turkish Petroleum Company, and for a free hand in Syria inclusive of Damascus in which Feisal, a friend of Britain, was ruling. A rider was added to the Mandate for Palestine, that the mandate would carry with it the obligation on the part of Great Britain to give effect to the Balfour Declaration relative to the establishment of a national home for the Jews there. This rider was doubtless a factor in reconciling France to the relinquishment of her claims to Palestine, as the southern section of Syria.

The proceedings of the San Remo Conference were justly open to criticism on several grounds. The San Remo Conference met in April 1920, some three months after the Treaty of Versailles had been ratified (January 10, 1920); the Covenant of the League of Nations, being a part of the Treaty, was then the only legal instrument through which mandates might be assigned and defined. Further, Article 22 of the Covenant stipulated that the wishes of the populations concerned were to be taken into account in the selection of the mandatories. In this respect, neither the Resolutions of the General Syrian Congress (July 2, 1919) which pronounced against France in favor of the United States or Great Britain as a temporary mandatory and which expressed a desire that the government of Syria be a constitutional monarchy, that Syria be undivided, and that its right to independence be recognized, nor the Recommendations of the King-Crane Commission with regard to Syria and Iraq (August 28, 1919), were respected. The spirit of the Conference was, in the words of Admiral Farragut,

"Damn the torpedoes, full speed ahead." In the political gamble at the conclusion of the last war the stakes were serious and the stakes were high, and the diplomats involved played the game according to the ancient rules.

There is an old saying, "The proof of the pudding is in the eating." As soon as San Remo became an inescapable fact of history, the test of the sincerity of the parties to it was to be the character of the administration of the mandates. At the outset the functioning of the mandates was complicated by factors that emerged with special force in the postwar period in the Near East. The first was that to which we have already made some reference, the Arab Movement. It had its beginnings about one hundred years ago in Syria with the arrival of Mohammed Ali and his son, Ibrahim. The most effective contributors to its rise were the Catholic and Protestant Mission Schools, and, in particular, the American Presbyterian Mission at Beirut, with their ideas and with their printing presses. As it got under way it developed centres and means of agitation against Turkish oppression. Secret societies were banded into the rising Arab Movement, which for a very brief period cooperated in an unnatural alliance with the Young Turk Committee of Union and Progress. Egypt gave asylum to the bolder spirits who had to flee Turkish territory. Up to the Great War, however, the Arab Movement was chiefly negative—anti-Turkish. But by one of the ironies of history, the British by dangling before the Arabs the idea of a free Arab state and by defeating the Turks touched it off almost overnight into a positive force. It took shape first as Pan-Arabism. Later, the Grand Mufti in Jerusalem tried to transform it into Pan-Islamism. This phase of it failed because Persia and Turkey held aloof, and Egypt would not warm up to it. Today both Pan-Arabism and Pan-Islamism are, in their earlier forms dead issues. Since Ibn Saud captured Mecca on October 13, 1924, no one has been proposed as Caliph to claim universal Moslem allegiance; and the vital elements of Pan-Arabism have been taken up by Arab Nationalism. The steady and impressive progress of Egypt towards national stature and the independence achieved by Persia and Turkey have been powerful influences in this direction.

This nationalism in the East is a highly eruptive thing. In the first place, it runs counter to Islam, which set itself to supplant national and racial divisions by a theocratic hegemony. In the second place, it implies a concept of the social order which is new and exotic in the East. In short, it signifies the arrival in the East of the ideas which have been agitating the West since the eighteenth century. Its mature fruitage is seen in the new Turkey and the new Iran. It expresses itself in violent opposition to the political control of foreign powers and in the restriction of foreign exploitation. But along with this, it does the West the doubtful compliment of adopting its manner of dress, its jazzy amusements, its vices, and its salacious literature. More seriously and creditably, it is marked by the rise of the middle classes in participation in the affairs of the state, and by the eclipse of the power of the sheiks, pashas, princes, and first families. This is followed by extensive programs of education and of social betterment. Egypt spends 11 per cent of her national income, that is, $20,000,000 annually, on education (Great Britain, 7 per cent). As an example of the westernizing of the East, we may cite the astonishing fact that more copies of *Maria Chapdelaine* were sold in Egypt than in Quebec: 100,000 as against 6,000 copies. But, in the final analysis, the Near East means to Arabacize what it adopts from the West, since it is conscious of its own intrinsic values, which it wishes to preserve.

In the face of such a ferment in the Near East the mandatories needed an endowment of large supernatural gifts for the peaceful discharge of their commissions. But, unfortunately, they had only human qualities, and those were not always the highest. It is to be remembered, also, that they were caught in what for them was a vicious circle. The more they applied themselves to their tasks, the more they westernized the people; and the more they westernized the people, the more they reaped criticism and hostility; the more they increased the facilities for radio communication, the more they opened the way for Axis propaganda; the better they made the roads, the easier they made the spread of discontent. In an honest estimate of their performances it must be admitted that they conferred great benefits on the mandated territories. They built excellent highways and railroads; maintained law and order; set up efficient courts of justice and police systems; improved sanitary conditions and water supplies in towns and cities; raised the health standards by regulations for the control of malaria, typhus, trachoma, leprosy, and other endemic diseases; reformed and graded taxation; undertook in certain instances public works for the improvement of economic conditions; established good postal systems; and modernized the currency and the fiscal systems. The best evidence of the success of these policies is seen in the rapid increases in population and income that followed their introduction, according to the statistical reports of the several mandates. On the other hand, they were open to criticism on several counts. They were occupying countries that did not want them, and they had entered these countries by the questionable San Remo Conference, rather than by assignment through the League of Nations. Also, in the administration of the mandates, they were weak in their agricultural and industrial policies, in the promotion of the economic independence of the mandates at the expense of British and French imports, but vigorous in the exploitation and distribution of oil and in the development of airways related to their imperial interests. And neither the British nor the French did full justice to the advancement of education. Egypt and Turkey have each about 1,000,000 students in the public schools—5 per cent of the population. Syria ought on the same percentage basis to have over 150,000 in the state schools, but in 1934 there were only 75,000. In Palestine in 1922 there were 303 government schools with an attendance of 18,000; in 1932 there were still 303 schools, though the attendance had risen to 25,000, which was still only 2.5 per cent of the population.

Politically, the performances of the mandatories were quite unequal, the British far surpassing the French in observing the intention of the provisions in the Covenant of the League governing the exercise of the mandates in Arab countries. George Antonius, an intelligent Arab writer who has published a trench-

ant criticism of western policies in the Near East in which he
plays no favorites has this to say:

> The British contribution to the building up of Iraq is one of the
> most remarkable instances of postwar construction. Just as hard things
> may legitimately be said of the British Government's piratical attempt
> to grab Iraq after the War so it can without exaggeration be said that
> the modern state of Iraq owes its existence largely to the efforts and the
> devotion of its British officials.

After a stormy beginning in 1920, marked by a revolt which
cost the British Treasury $250,000,000, and after ten years of
patient political tutelage, the British crowned their efforts by
the model Anglo-Iraqi Treaty (June 30, 1930), by which Iraq
was to be recognized as a sovereign independent state and to be
sponsored by Great Britain for admission to the League of Nations; and in exchange for the use of certain stations for Air
Force bases and of the existing means of communication, the
British were to give Iraq assistance in the building up of a
national army. The Permanent Mandates Commission feared
that the British had been too forward in the matter, but on the
assurances of the British admitted Iraq to the League in 1932.

In Syria the French made a series of blunders, apparently
through the notion that the mandate was a certificate for indefinite occupation. They struck at the unity of the country
by dividing it into three separate states; they tied the currency
to the French franc with its instability, and put the manage-
ment of the currency in the hands of a French Bank; they encouraged the use of the French language at the expense of
Arabic by the compulsory teaching of French in all state schools
and by putting French on a basis of equality with Arabic in
the law-courts. For the first seven years the country was under
a form of martial rule exercised by three successive generals,
Gouraud, Weygand, and Sarrail, which terminated in the Druze
revolt of nearly two years' duration. Later, in 1930-32, the
attempt to set up a Republic in Syria, was followed by another
upheaval. The real benefits of French rule were regularly
eclipsed by their errors and general lack of *savoir faire*. Finally
they were driven to draw up the Franco-Syrian and Franco-
Lebanon treaties on the model of the Anglo-Iraq treaty. But
before it could be ratified the War broke out. . . .

The British experiment has been far less happy in Palestine than in Iraq. The difficulties in this instance, as we all recognize, emerge primarily out of the problems created by Jewish immigration. Three major factors have contributed to the unrest which periodically leads to armed violence and revolt in one or another part of the country. The first factor is the Balfour Declaration. Its terms are vague. What is meant by "a national home for the Jews" or by "the civil and religious rights of existing non-Jewish communities"? It can be said in defense of Balfour in this respect that he did not anticipate the recent political developments in Europe which caused tens of thousands of Jews to be suddenly compelled to seek entrance to Palestine. The second factor is the presence of inflammatory leaders among both parties to the issue. And the third and most serious factor is the failure of the British Government to give effect to the sound report of the Sir John Simpson Commission of 1930. We cannot turn back the hands of the clock and annul the Balfour Declaration. Britain is committed to it irrevocably. She has time to apply it, for there is no mention in the terms of the mandate for Palestine of its eventual independence. And with firmness an equitable solution is possible.

All these facts which we have been covering make it clear that there is much unfinished business in the Near East, business to which Great Britain is committed and business in which the whole world has a stake. The Near East is the link between three continents, and it stands at the bottleneck of the world's highways. Points like the Suez Canal and the Dardanelles, and the major air bases and air routes, are of vital concern to every nation. The Near East is the heart of the Moslem faith; what happens in it affects the mind and attitudes of 250,000,000 Moslems. But in spite of its strategic significance, it is one of the most open and defenseless regions in the world. It has no coal and no iron, the materials from which men forge the instruments of war. Its chief resources are cotton and oil, and, in South Anatolia, some chrome—one sixth of the world's supply. It produces some grain, wool, olive oil, and fruit. In none of these products does it lead the world, yet in the possession of an ambitious world power it could provide enough of an economic margin to give victory. The command of its air, land, and waterways could, as we have recently seen, throttle the free intercourse of the nations. It is not a question, therefore, whether we shall stay in the Near East or get out of it. We are in it irrevocably by history and by geography. The question is how and in what spirit we shall relate ourselves to it.

In the postwar period there are concrete situations already marked out for solution. One of these was outlined by Mr. Anthony Eden in his speech on May 29, 1941:

> The Arab world has made great strides since the settlement reached at the end of the last War, and many Arab thinkers desire for the Arab peoples a greater degree of unity than they now enjoy. . . . It seems to me both natural and right that the cultural and economic ties between the Arab countries and the political ties, too, should be strengthened. His Majesty's Government will give their full support to any scheme that commands general approval.

In other words, full support is to be given to Arab ambitions to promote a federation of the Arab states. In Palestine, likewise, the solution lies in the direction of the creation of a binational or confederated state under the sponsorship of an international guaranty. The eclipse of the Axis powers will change the atmosphere in which the Arabs and the Jews can begin to compose their differences. But besides helping new states to birth, there is also an obligation to protect the interests of others that have already reached independence and some stability. In 1968 Egypt, by agreement, takes over the possession of the Suez Canal. By what conventions will she be protected in her rights, and how will she adjust her rights to the interests of other nations? Will her rights be less sacred than those of the Americans in the Panama Canal? Also, there is the problem of her mounting population. To feed her millions more areas for irrigation must be made available by more dams, barrages, and basins along the Nile. The sources of the Blue Nile lie in Lake Tana in Abyssinia. The control of these sources and territories are of vital importance to Egypt and the Sudan. How, then, shall the integrity of Abyssinia and her borders be guaranteed? If we go beyond the Arab-speaking regions, we meet other concerns of international magnitude. How stable and secure is the infant Republic of Turkey? Since the Persian railroad from Bandar Shapur to the Caspian has been extended first to Tabriz, and now to Russia, will she be absorbed into the Russian congeries of Republics at the cost of her national identity?

In the interest of future world peace these problems must be solved in accordance with the trends of modern public opinion. The old theory of diplomacy is being superseded at length by the Wilsonian idea. The Atlantic Charter contemplates the establishment of an international organization with competent powers to effect an ordered world society; it bespeaks the termination of predatory imperialism, and the recognition of the rights of peoples, minorities, and classes. The application of the principles enunciated in its eight articles of the Near East would introduce an era of peace, prosperity and security unprecedented for centuries. We must never forget that peace is one.

> There is no separate place where men are free,
> No justice measured by geography;
> If one chain grips a heel, one heart knows fear,
> Peace is betrayed, not only there, but here.

THE GEOGRAPHICAL REGIONS OF PALESTINE [3]

Palestine is a well defined geographical entity. It lies, a narrow, dissected, karstic upland, between the Mediterranean, which it borders with a narrow coastal plan, and the deep rift of the Jordan Valley, to which it declines steeply on the east; to the south is the desert of Sinai, to the north are the mountains of Lebanon. Although so well set off from its surroundings as to have almost an insular character, the land is far from uniform; in fact, it is best described as a geographical mosaic. The purpose of this article is to break up the mosaic into its components —in other words, to essay a classification of the geographical units of Palestine. Only one serious attempt at such classification has appeared hitherto—that by Schwöbel, and his work suffered through the lack of a sufficiently good map. Today the 1:100,000 map of the Survey of Palestine provides us with an adequate base.

[3] By D. H. Kallner in charge [1939] of editorial work on an Atlas of Palestine in behalf of the Hebrew University; Geomorphological Explorer; and E. Rosenau, Climatologist with the Meteorological Section of the Department of Civil Aviation, Government of Palestine, at Lydda Airport. *Geographical Review.* 29:61-80. January 1939.

It is scarcely necessary to point out the significance of a comprehensive geographical classification in political considerations. It is important to emphasize the fact that, although the boundaries between the smaller geographical units are not fixed and rigid, the cores of the units are well differentiated and the main geographical boundaries are clear enough on the terrain.

The usual morphological division of Palestine is into coastal plain, mountains, and Jordan Valley (see Fig. 1). The coastal

KEY TO REGIONS

COASTAL PLAIN

1 Dunes
2 Galilean Plain
3 Haifa Bay
4 Carmel Shore
5 Hadera Plain
6 Sharon Plain
7 Longitudinal passage of Qalqiliya
8. Ramle-Lydda Plain
9 Southern Plain
10 Hills of the SE Plain

MOUNTAIN BLOCK GALILEE

11 Western Foothills
12 Central Upper Galilee
13 NE Upper Galilee
14 NE Tiberian Highlands
15 Basin Region
16 Nazareth Hills
19 Mt. Nabi Dahi

EMEK

20 Emek (Esdraelon) Plain
21 Valley of Jezreel and Beisan Plain

CARMEL REGION

22 Main Carmel
23 SW Carmel
24 Megiddo Pass
25 Umm el Fahm Hills
26 Arraba Plain

MAIN MOUNTAIN BLOCK

27 Mount Gilboa
28 West Samarian Hills
29 Central Samaria
30 East Samarian Mountains
31 NE Samarian Wilderness
32 Shephelah
33 Judean Mountains
34 Judean Desert

JORDAN RIFT VALLEY

35 Lake Tiberias
36 Eastern Slopes
37 Hule Plain
38 Basaltic Threshold between Hule and Tiberias
39 Western Slopes
40 Samakh Plain
41 Jericho Plain
42 Dead Sea

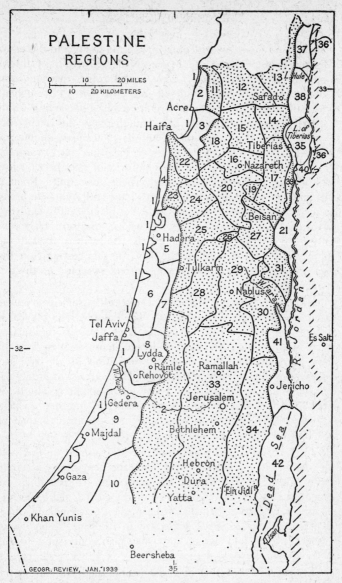

FIG. I—The geographical regions of Palestine. The regions are grouped by three major divisions—the coastal plain, the highland block (stippled), the Jordan valley. Note that the eastern limit (diagonal-ruled line), the western slope of the Trans-Jordan plateaus, is not coincident with the political boundary. Scale approximately 1:1,600,000.

plain is a narrow strip widening toward the south. In the north it begins at the frontier near Ras en Naqura where the Galilean mountains reach the coast. The Carmel ridge, running from southeast to northwest, divides it into two parts. Throughout practically the whole extent a cordon of dunes of varying width borders the sea, interrupted here and there by the steep cliffs of old dunes. The coastal plain, with its 2900 square kilometers, comprises 70 per cent of the plains of Palestine and 21 per cent of its total area, exclusive of the subdistrict of Beersheba. Geologically the coastal plain is a fairly young formation. Even in the Pliocene the coast, according to Picard and Avnimelech, lay at the border of the mountains, and the plain itself is built up from Pliocene and Quaternary sediments. Seaward it is continued by a submarine shelf, which also widens toward the south. The coast, exposed in the winter to surf beating from the southwest and to the accompanying current sweeping northward, is regular.

Almost everywhere the coastal plain has sufficient underground water at moderate depths. The dune barriers prevented natural drainage, so that originally large areas of the surface were swampy. In the last few decades most of these swamps have been drained, and intensive cultivation of the soil has become possible, notably in the Bay of Haifa area, which only ten years ago was a vast swamp. Today in the southern suburbs of Haifa we find an intensive horticulture and industry—cement factories, mills, iron foundries—and here the main branch of the Iraq oil pipe line ends.

In the main coastal plain, south of Mt. Carmel, we first note the region about Hadera. The landscape here shows a certain spaciousness. In the west chiefly oranges are cultivated, in the east corn and grapes. As in most of the coastal plain, the predominant type of settlement is the medium-sized village: there is practically no dispersed settlement in Palestine. The Jewish villages are all laid out on a regular plan; only some of the Arab villages show any design.

In contrast with this open landscape, the plain of Sharon presents a rolling aspect, owing to the well defined old dunes lying parallel to the coast. Where there is Jewish colonization, this region is intensively cultivated: the large citrus groves are most important. To the east, between the old dunes and the mountains, is a longitudinal passage, in which the railway runs. In this zone there is no underground water at moderate depth, but the heavy soil makes it the main center of Arab corn growing.

To the south is the plain through which runs the ancient Jerusalem-Jaffa road. There also are the Lydda airport and the main railway junction of the country, at the point where the lines from Egypt to Haifa and from Jaffa to Jerusalem cross. The plain here is open, with large cornfields (mainly wheat), on which the bordering citrus groves are already encroaching. The part poorest in water—around the towns of Ramle and Lydda— has the largest olive grove of the Palestinian plains.

Westward is practically one vast citrus grove, reaching to the dunes. Citrus culture began here about twenty-five years ago and has transformed a former grape-growing region. The wine cellars of Rishon le Zion have declined considerably during the last twenty years, but a brewery has now been added to its activities. Some of the Jewish settlements have grown into small country towns, the largest of which is Rehovot, with 7000 inhabitants (1936). In these places a modest industry has developed, favored by the seasonal character of the work in the orange groves and by a sufficiency of water and benefiting by the development of traffic for shipment of the citrus fruits. Another factor—and a not unimportant one—is the lower price of land compared with the prices about Jaffa and Tel Aviv. A ridge of dune sandstone one kilometer wide and 40 meters high runs through this region from Rehovot to Gedera. Its slopes are preferred for settlement, which thus not only leaves the valuable soil of the plain for cultivation but also utilizes a more healthful site for dwelling places.

Beyond the cornfields crossed by the Wadi Rubin the undulating plain continues. This southernmost part, scarcely touched as yet by Jewish colonization, presents a typical picture of Arab agriculture. The plain broadens considerably toward the south and rises to 200-250 meters eastward to the foot of the mountains. It is divided longitudinally by three ranges of old dunes, which rise above the surrounding country to an altitude of 80 meters and reach a width of 5 kilometers. These, too, are preferred places of settlement and travel. The mean annual amount of precipitation in this steppe country is 300-400 millimeters, all of which falls between November and April, mainly in heavy showers in January and February. Corn is grown in spring and early summer in rotation with barley and wheat in winter and durra and fallow alternately in summer. Trees are found only at the inner border of the dune belt. Here are large settlements, whose size increases toward the south as their number decreases. Most of the villages of this region have 300 to 1200 inhabitants, but the inner border of the dune belt shows places such as Majdal, with 6400 inhabitants, and Khan Yunis, with 7200. The conurbation of Gaza, with 25,000 inhabitants, also depends on agriculture almost exclusively. Here the density of population is on an average of 50 to 75 to a square kilometer, but it decreases toward the southeast, where the sedentary population is replaced by seminomads and the density is only 20 to 35 to a square kilometer. In the economy of these half-nomadic tribes agriculture is still more important than cattle breeding, a relation that becomes inverted as one goes farther south.

The uplands are divided into the Galilean mountains and the main block of the Palestinian mountains by the lowland passage of the Emek. East of the narrow strip of the northern coastal plain rise the longitudinal karstic ridges of the mountains of Galilee. There is scattered macchia vegetation, and in the valleys and lowlands olive groves are common. Galilee is thus covered with a verdure unknown in the rest of the country. Here are numerous basins enclosed by parallel ridges, some of them true karst *poljes* [upland hollows].

Galilee—such is its morphology—has always been a preferred place of retreat. It shelters a great number of religious and national fragments of population, some in mixed communities, some in separate villages: Moslems and Christian Arabs, Druses, Matawilahs (Moslems of the Shiah persuasion), Circassians, Algerians, and Jews form this population mosaic. It is interesting that here we find the only Jewish community of peasants who have uninterruptedly been living in Palestine since ancient days.

The usual division into Upper and Lower Galilee is justified geographically. Upper Galilee is mountainous; its central part, a series of parallel ridges, culminates in the peak of Mt. Jermaq, 1208 meters; the relief of eastern Upper Galilee, however, is less marked. Lower Galilee does not reach either the absolute or the relative altitudes of Upper Galilee: its highest peak is Mt. Hazzur, 584 meters. The difference in altitude between the mountains near Safad and the Lake of Tiberias is about 1150 meters; the greatest relative altitude of Lower Galilee, east of the village of Ulam, is only 580 meters. In contrast with the ridges of Upper Galilee, the hill country of Lower Galilee has an "incoherent aspect," as Abel puts it—karstic basins in the north-central part and basaltic plains in the east.

In human geography also there are pronounced differences between Upper and Lower Galilee. As a whole, Galilee has a relatively low density of population (a rural population of 13 to 50 to a square kilometer), but Upper Galilee has a distinctly larger number of villages than Lower Galilee.

Of the regions of Lower Galilee, the basins of the center and the basaltic regions of the southeast deserve special attention. The Sahl al Battauf, a well defined *polje* mostly inundated in spring, with an area of 44 square kilometers, is by far the largest of the basins of this type scattered over the country. The present drainage does not conform to this basin topography. For example, the basin of Ash Shaghur, along the road from Safad to Acre, is drained by three different wadies, and the basin of Sakhnin is even crossed by the main divide of Palestine.

The dark basalt, in contrast with the light-gray limestone, gives to eastern Galilee a gloomy appearance, which is heightened by the use of the basalt as building material. The "Horns of Hittin" are remains of former focuses of basaltic eruptions. South of Tiberias the country rises to the hills of Nazareth by three steps, with respective altitudes of 220, 350, and 430 meters. Between are plains on the flat basalts, where corn is grown in fields, whereas in the rest of Galilee and on the main upland masses corn is grown on sloping terraces and on the valley floors. The southeastern part of this basaltic land is relatively backward and is the only region of Palestine in which the population decreased between 1922 and 1931.

The Galilean hills fall southward in a steep scarp, 200 meters or more, to the Plain of Emek, or Esdraelon. The plain has an area of 276 square kilometers. Numerous small springs on the southern border formerly made it highly malarial. Jewish postwar colonization drained the plain and established a flourishing agriculture on the deep alluvial and basaltic soils. To the east, between Mt. Gilboa in the south and the basalt slopes in the north, is the valley of Jezreel, below sea level. The Emek and the valley of Jezreel together make up 9 per cent of the plains of Palestine.

In the northwest Mt. Carmel, with its terracelike rise and its extensive pinewoods, is a typical Mediterranean mountain country. Beyond the hills of the Umm el Fahm the mountains of Samaria begin, lower in the northwest. In the northeast Gilboa rises like a pulpit above the Emek. Along the Jordan Valley is a high, karstic, mountainous country, consisting of parallel ridges running in a northwestern direction and presenting in many places the appearance of the tropical "conical" karst. In the east they are steeply dissected along the border of the rift valley. These uplands are distinctly barer than those of Galilee.

Central Samaria has the densest population. The preferred areas for settlement are the borders of the numerous basins, particularly the Sahl Mukhnah, the meridional furrow through which runs the Jerusalem-Nablus road, and the western border of the region where a 200-meter meridional step leads to the lower mountains of northwestern Samaria. As elsewhere in the uplands, the preferred sites are the slopes, terraces, ridges, and summits of the hills ("acropolis sites"), because of ease of travel, better air drainage, and, in former times, the important factor of safety.

In northwestern Samaria and northern Judea the olive is the most characteristic tree. Its spread well defines the boundaries of the different regions. The olive is carefully cultivated on sloping terraces, often together with corn; close to the settlements vegetables are raised.

The mountains of Judea constitute the highest and southernmost part of the main mountain block. They can be divided into three longitudinal strips. In the west the limestone foothills of the Shephelah rise above the soft sediments of the coastal plain to a height of 300 meters. The main block of the Judean mountains rises steeply above the foothills to 700 meters. Even steeper is the fall in the east, toward the Judean desert. The highest peak of Judea in the north is 1016 meters (east of Silwad), in the south 1017 meters (near Hebron, in the vicinity of Halhul). Bailey Willis describes the relief as the "Judean matureland." It is not a peneplain but a morphological system with only slight relative relief compared with the deep valleys and regions with a large relative relief on the eastern and western borders. The slopes of the gorgelike valleys are artificially terraced, in many places to their whole extent. For the most part, the terraces are not wholly utilized today, and they suggest a former higher degree of cultivation.

Population is fairly dense in the Judean mountains. The northern part is the main olive-growing region of Palestine, and near Ramallah and Hebron are the largest grape-growing districts of the country. Around Jerusalem and along the roads in its vicinity there is a large cultivation of vegetables, which find a good market in the towns: The greatest density of population is around Jerusalem; but even here there is still much land that is not used. There are neither woods nor fruit trees on the slopes; and if economic conditions were favorable, the soil could be cultivated to a far greater extent. A prerequisite, however, would undoubtedly be the removal of the numerous flocks of goats, which prevent any kind of reforestation.

The farther south we go, the fewer and, as on the coastal plain, the larger are the settlements: Dura has 7255 inhabitants and Yatta 4034. Toward the south the mountains decrease in altitude, and we reach what Picard and Solomonica call the Beersheba Basin. Here is the town of Beersheba (2959 inhabitants), the only permanent settlement; except for this, the region is inhabited by seminomadic tribes.

The Judean desert, which forms the slope of the Judean mountains to the Jordan Valley, has been described as "without exception the wildest and most desolate district in Syria." The rainfall decreases markedly . . . through the Judean mountains, the Jordan Valley, and the plateau of Transjordan. The small amounts fall mostly in a few heavy showers in the rainy period. The torrents they feed accomplish a vast amount of erosion, so steep are the slopes—a relief of as much as 1100 meters in a tract 20 kilometers wide (5½ per cent)—and so greatly are they weathered by the intense insolation of summer. The evaporation crust found in certain parts of the desert gives little protection. As a result the land, which declines to the Jordan Valley in three great steps, is widely dissected. There are no permanent settlements except some monasteries, police posts, and the oasis 'Ein Jidi, on the Dead Sea.

The Jordan rift valley is a deep furrow 10 to 20 kilometers wide and 1100 to 1700 meters deep separating the originally connected tablelands of Transjordan and Palestine. The terraces cut in the steep walls furnish proof of former higher levels of the valley lakes. Three lakes divide the valley into natural units, Lake Hule, the Lake of Tiberias, and the Dead Sea; their present levels are +70, —209, and —395 meters respectively. The two upper lakes contain fresh water; the Dead Sea is a relict lake with a high salt content.

Above Lake Hule are large swamps, the drainage of which is being begun to reclaim what should become one of the richest districts of Palestine. Beyond Lake Hule the Jordan breaks through the basaltic threshold in a deep gorge with a gradient of 1¾ per cent. It opens into the storied landscape of the Lake of Tiberias, the dark-blue oval of its waters enclosed by bare shores backed by steep mountains. Toward the east the plateau of Transjordan rises to 600 meters; toward the west are the spurs of the Galilean mountains and the basaltic plains. The basaltic slopes of the southwestern part of the shore (400 meters high) are barely covered with a crust of weathered material; the bedrock is exposed and gives a gloomy appearance to the whole landscape. A few plantations scattered oasislike about the lake add a touch of green, particularly in the southwest and northwest.

Between the Lake of Tiberias and the point where the valley of Jezreel meets the Jordan the valley floor is fairly wide; but it narrows southward, and for a space the river hugs the western wall. Its course is irregular, abounding in meanders, and there are many rapids. The climate is extremely dry, and the gallery forest alongside the river contrasts sharply with the elsewhere arid valley. South of the Wadi el Far'a, along which runs the road from Nablus to Salt, the valley floor widens again. Here it is composed entirely of Lisan marls, deposits of a diluvial lake rich in salt and gypsum. The marls erode into typical badlands, owing to their easy weathering, the more marked the nearer they are to the river. The undissected part of the valley floor, near the mountain border, furnishes the largest yields—in the oasis of Jericho, for instance, famous of old for its date palms and now for its banana plantations; and in the young oases of Duyuk and Nu'eima, north of Jericho.

The landscape of the Dead Sea can be called without exaggeration one of the most magnificent and peculiar in the world. In the oppressive heat of summer vapors rise almost visibly from the dark, heavy mirror of the water. Sheer precipices border the sea; in many places there is no room for even a narrow beach. Near 'Ein Jidi the almost vertical cliff rises 650 meters above the sea, and in the southeast the peak of Mt. Khanzire, only 7¾ kilometers from the shore, rises 1626 meters above it (21 per cent). The high walls and the great dry valleys of tributaries cut into them give a rugged relief to the scene, the more magnificent because of the almost total absence of life.

Reference has already been made to the steps by which the desert of Judea rises to the Judean mountains. These steps are markedly dissected at their borders but elsewhere have remained level. This whole region, in the main built up of horizontal strata, is furrowed by numerous valleys leading to the Dead Sea. The larger ones are deep-cut canyons, which open with pebbly floor to the shore; the most famous is that of the Arnon, on the east side. More than one kilometer from the border of the rift valley the Lisan marls fill these valleys to an undetermined depth (125-meter borings north of the Dead Sea did not reach the bottom of the marls); hence even before the marls were deposited the valleys were as wide as they are at present, and even more deeply cut. The wide, pebbly floors, which support some scattered tamarisks, are vertically cut in the Lisan-marl walls, 100 meters high. Tributary valleys, and the smaller main valleys also, open as hanging valleys.

The absolutely barren Lisan Peninsula, consisting almost exclusively of the marls, which derive their name from it, divides the Dead Sea into two basins. The northern one is known to be 400 meters deep; the southern, however, is a shallow pan, in no place deeper than six meters. The southern shore line of the southern basin varies, as is natural in a lake without outlet in a dry climate. On the shore of this great evaporating pan and on the north shore of the sea are the two factories of the Palestine Potash Company. The southern basin continues into the Sabkha, a salt pan with halophytic bush vegetation, above which, in the south, the Lisan marls rise in a wall about 40 meters high, penetrating into the Wadi el 'Araba, the southernmost part of the Jordan rift valley between the Dead Sea and the Gulf of 'Aqaba.

The Wadi el 'Araba runs southward, furrowed by wide wadies, down which the rare, torrential showers pour sheet floods and which have only occasional patches of sparse vegetation. The high walls, which make the 'Araba an oven in summer, are formed of limestone and marls on the west, of Nubian sandstone and the red crystalline rocks of the "Sinai granite" on the east. The floor of the valley rises to 200 meters above mean sea level and then gradually declines toward the south.

The Jordan Valley thus extends $1\frac{3}{4}$ degrees of latitude farther south than the other two major regions of Palestine. The region between the Jordan Valley and the western boundary of the mandatory territory of Palestine is the subdistrict of Beersheba, often called the Negeb. It contains 46.6 per cent of the area of Palestine and 5 per cent of the population. Geographically it belongs not to Palestine but to the Sinai Peninsula. The lack of regular precipitation, the marked aridity, the absence of a housed population, and the low population density distinguish it sharply from the rest of Palestine.

This territory can be divided into the deeply dissected eastern decline to the Jordan Valley and the Gulf of 'Aqaba and the plains and mountainous parts (400-1000 meters high), which form the spurs of the corresponding regions of the inner portion of the Sinai Peninsula. The broad, sandy region in the north forms a continuation of the dunes of the northern coastal desert of Sinai.

THE PALESTINE QUESTION, A CHRISTIAN POSITION [4]

The problems of the Jews who are now emerging in Europe from terrible experiences under Nazi tyranny concern every Christian. The urge to succor the suffering wells in our hearts. The question of the Jewish homeland in Palestine troubles our conscience. Both these concerns call for deep human understanding, for wisdom and cool judgment. Under both lies the old and ugly fact of anti-Semitism with its tragic and indelible imprint on all Jewish minds and hearts.

One thing we are moved to ask: Does not the linking of the problem of rescue with the issue of Palestine create confusion and militate against solution of either? The refugee problem is immediate. It is complicated in Europe and elsewhere by national attitudes, the difficulties of property restoration and general uncertainty regarding the nature of the re-emerging world. The number of the Jewish remnant is not yet definitely known but estimates have been sharply reduced. The emotional attitudes of those who remain, their desires with reference to their future, have yet to be learned. Some may wish to go to their former homes, some to other countries. How many may prefer Palestine is not yet clear. Insistence by Jewish nationalists that Palestine is the only possible haven for Jewish refugees, in the face of the political impasse in that country, seems to us definitely to obstruct their rescue by all other means. And does it not appear, further, that the presentation of Zionism as philanthropy obscures the real issue of Jewish nationalism? For the welfare of the sufferers, for the psychological health of the Jewish community throughout the world, and for the future relationship of Christians, Jews and Moslems it seems to us imperative that effective decisions on these two questions be reached. . . .

Jews as a group have been characterized as a race, but the term does not cover Chinese Jews, Indian Jews, and other non-Europeans. The term "culture" seems to have a more generally accurate quality but the many and diverse sub-cultures of Judaism

[4] Statement prepared by Protestant Church leaders, adopted September 28th, 1945, by the Committee of Reference and Counsel (the executive group of the Foreign Missions Conference of North America). Foreign Missions Conference of North America. New York. 1945. 8p. mim.

inject some uncertainty. Significant argument among Jews themselves at present centers on whether Jews are essentially a national group or a religious group. Zionists maintain that national elements basic in Judaism are crippled by the lack of a national home and the autonomy that should provide an environment in which an integrated Jewish culture might develop naturally according to its own genius. They believe the Jewish spirit to be hampered by "homelessness" and a lack of that psychological security they believe political independence would confer. Jewish anti-Zionists define the Jews as primarily a religious entity, a character which is neither disturbed by nor disturbing to their different national affiliations. Judaism's future is for them inextricably bound up in the development of full and true democracy throughout the world.

To many persons, both Jews and non-Jews, Jewish nationalism appears to be a philosophy of defeatism. They see security for Jews only in the sharing of democratic equality, enduring, sincere and real, in the United States, in Poland, in Germany—in Palestine, and everywhere. From this point of view it seems to be a contradiction of the whole trend of Jewish life and thought for centuries that Jews should seek a solution in nationalism—and especially in a nationalism that so closely resembles racism at a time when the dangers of such nationalism have been uniquely dramatized in Jewish tragedy. The *Judenstadt* ideal originated by Theodor Herzl did not spring from the universal religious ideal of Judaism but from a desire for group security.

Only Jews can know the Jewish heart, its memories and its needs. Jews alone can decide which ideal they must follow. A nation is not constructed from outside. It is born of a people's will toward cohesion. It requires a common home. It cannot be accomplished in dispersion, by groups scattered throughout the world, speaking different languages, obeying different laws, observing different customs and living under different social conditions.

It is for Jews to decide whether they shall or shall not be a nation. But Judaism is divided on the question. A unity that is maintained by disregarding a cleavage so fundamental must be spurious. It seems to us that a cleancut decision is needed. A

choice by which those Jews who believe in a Jewish nation would
adhere to the national entity and those who recognize Judaism
as primarily a religion would abstain unfortunately would, to be
sure, split Judaism. But it should not prejudice the position in
the lands of their choice of those who elect not to participate in
the Jewish national establishment. The position which advocates
Jewish nationalism and abstains from personal identification with
the nation is equivocal. Jewish nationalists who themselves
remain Americans, Britons, Frenchmen, compromise all Jews
enfranchised abroad as well as those now resident in Palestine.

After this choice has been made (and many Jews will choose
nationalism) a question remains which has been evaded—in the
Balfour Declaration, in the mandate for Palestine, and in almost
all discussion of the issue. What temporal right is conferred by
religious nostalgia? And what relation does it bear to the rights
ordinarily assumed to inhere in continuous habitation?

World peace may depend on equitable solution of the conflict
over Palestine. Tensions are mounting in the Near East which
involve France, Great Britain, Russia, most of the Moslem states
and the United States of America. An incipient cultural renaissance is working in Islam. Nationalism has been reborn in the
Arab world. Independence is demanded in Moslem India, in
Syria and Lebanon, and in Palestine. Iraq, Iran and Egypt are
restive under foreign "influence" and tutelage. The League of
Nations principle of "self-determination of peoples" and its
dictum that the independence of certain former sections of the
Turkish Empire could be "provisionally recognized" have not
been forgotten. With the coming of the airplane the Near East
is more than ever the hub of world communications. Its importance as the world's richest source of oil has been enhanced
by recent discovery. In the heart of this politically and militarily
strategic area with its great commercial potentialities and growing
industry lies the small country of Palestine. It is peopled by a
majority of Syrian Arabs, whose business men are probably as
clever as any in the world, and a large minority of Jews enthusi-
astically devoted to the building there of their national sovereignty and an authentic Jewish culture. A non-Arabic Palestine
controlling the best East Mediterranean ports and cutting the

slender fertile crescent of Arabia would isolate the Arabs' infant industry and its hinterland from Europe.

The Soviet Union has opposed Zionism as being out of line with her own policy of giving complete equality in law and opportunity to Jews. In view of the fact that many Soviet citizens are Moslem, and in consideration of Russia's strategic and economic interests in the Middle East, it appears unlikely that this attitude will materially change in the near future. It seems to us that careful thought must now be given to a situation which, if it is allowed to drift, may place the Soviet Union and the United States on opposite sides in a dangerous international issue. . . .

With the rise of Hitlerism and the ominous echoing of anti-Semitism in many parts of the world, under the tightening of immigration controls everywhere, Zionist pressure upon the gates of Palestine increased and Zionist moderation with reference to Jewish status there declined. Arab opposition sharpened. And anti-Semitism spread, in Palestine and neighboring Arab lands and also in other countries where Jews might wish to settle.

As the surviving Jews are found in liberated Europe they prove to be a pitifully small remnant. Estimates of four million to be absorbed in Palestine alone prove to have been excessive. Recent estimates have run as low as one million Jews surviving in Europe. The actual total may be about one and a half million.

Much support in money and political influence for the Jewish colony in Palestine has come from the United States and Great Britain. The bulk of the actual immigration, however, has been from the countries of Eastern Europe. Much of this area is now under Soviet occupation or influence. Jews have not been allowed to emigrate to Palestine from Soviet territory. Jews resident in France, Belgium, Holland, Czechoslovakia, Yugoslavia and Italy will probably elect to remain there. Others may go to these countries, where the Jewish communities have been decimated. That European emigrants to Palestine may prove to be few is suggested also by Dr. Weizmann's call for American Jewish settlers. In these circumstances there appears to be little likelihood that Jews can ever achieve a majority in Palestine, even if all restrictions upon entry should be abandoned.

Jewish objections to the White Paper restrictions upon their entry take three main forms:

1. It is the Zionist claim that the Balfour Declaration and the mandate guaranteed their right to colonize and did not provide for any cessation of that right. It should be remembered in this connection that renunciation of conqueror's rights by the principal Allied powers preceded the establishment of the mandate system by the League of Nations. The right of self-determination, moreover, was a basic principle of the League itself. The mandate system was an effort to implement a "trust" for dependent peoples. Before the Armistice with Germany which ended World War I the twelfth of Woodrow Wilson's famous Fourteen Points published the specification that "the other nationalities" then "under Turkish rule should be assured an undoubted security of life and an absolutely unmolested opportunity of autonomous development." If, therefore, Arab opposition to the establishment of the Jewish homeland continues and Arab consent to Jewish immigration is not forthcoming, no basis is provided by the League for coercion. Prosecution of the project, if continued, would in reality rest on those repudiated conqueror's rights. If this was understood by the Jewish people, it seems doubtful that they would be willing to ask that Great Britain exercise in their behalf a type of imperialist power which she once abjured.

Quite aside from all consideration of British interests in the area, we cannot believe that the safety and the future of the Jewish settlement would be advanced by a policy which would undermine Britain's own influence among the Arab peoples. It is upon British solidarity with the Arabs that the homeland, in the last analysis, is built. With momentum of change rapidly increasing throughout the Near East it seems highly unlikely that Britain or any other power or combination of powers will undertake to coerce the Arabs in Palestine. And under the new Charter of the United Nations it would be anomalous to attempt to care for Jewish need at the cost of a small and unwilling ward of its own self-government.

2. Zionists and Anti-Zionists alike demand for Jews everywhere equal rights with other citizens. Nothing could be more

just. In addition, Zionists insist that Jewish immigration into Palestine should be "unrestricted" and that its control should be placed in Jewish hands. This double appeal, at one and the same time to "equality" and to "preferred status," seems to us contradictory and has been far from reassuring to the Arab population. Moreover, immigration policies throughout the world— like controls on foreign capital investment—are directed toward the maintenance of desirable conditions for existing populations, such as standards of living, the social character of the population, political serenity. No country in the world could safely become committed to "unrestricted" immigration of any one group.

3. Anti-Zionists object to immigration restriction only as it bears upon Jews as Jews, citing the mandate bar upon discrimination on grounds of "race, religion or languages." If in Palestine it had been ordinary immigration that was involved this argument would seem more relevant than it does in the present circumstances. It was not ordinary immigration, however, but a unique project in colonization, controlled and to a considerable extent financed from outside the country, and imposed against the expressed wishes of the native population. Its cessation is an attempt to redress an imbalance, caused by earlier discrimination in favor of Jewish entry, which has produced an explosive situation. In view of the feeling caused and in furtherance of the fight against anti-Semitism we think it highly desirable that, if it is at all possible, some less invidious arrangement or formula should be devised.

A comprehensive plan for the resolution of the conflict between the old Arab population of Palestine and the new community of Jewish settlers can be devised only by those who carry responsibility therefor and are in possession of all relevant information. We think, however, that appeal to variously interpreted historical pledges and commitments should no longer be allowed to obstruct settlement of the status of the two communities now living within the borders of Palestine. And we venture to suggest several principles which we think should be controlling in any arrangement concluded for their future.

1. The rescue and rehabilitation of surviving European Jews is a separate question from the welfare of Palestine and can be secured only if so dealt with. Neither Jewish nationalist aspira-

tions nor Arab nationalist objections should any longer obstruct their rehabilitation. Study and restudy of all possibilities of permanent and temporary haven should be vigorously pursued and every feasible prospect acted upon. We shall recur to this later.

2. The primary aim should be the progressive development of understanding and friendly relations among all communities in Palestine and their cooperation, on a basis of personal equality, in the advancement of the whole country's welfare.

3. Sympathetic account should be taken of the religious sensibilities of all communities within the limits of justice to all and the reasonable welfare of all.

4. So far as is possible without impeding a workable setup the legitimate expectations of Jews and Arabs alike should be incorporated in the Palestine settlement. Government on the principle of unrestricted majority rule may not be feasible in the situation. The principle, in any case, cannot be only unilaterally valid. If it would be valid with a Jewish majority it is valid when the majority is Arab.

5. The rights of all groups and individuals, along the line indicated in the American Bill of Rights, should be safeguarded.

It appears to us that the working of any arrangement must depend on confidence and the good will of the communities. Without these the best plan will be futile. With them no insurmountable barrier appears to the early granting of independence to Palestine, as a country consisting of several autonomous communities, all cooperating in a central government on a basis of representation equal or proportional as may be decided. The rights, religious, civil and political, of minorities should be guaranteed by treaty between the new state and the United Nations, and the legitimate interests of Great Britain safeguarded by treaty with the British Government. Under such an arrangement immigration could safely be put on a normal basis. We believe that postwar developments will, in any case, remove it as a point at issue.

If, in spite of the discipline of events, sufficient cooperation is still not forthcoming for this desirable outcome, we believe the only alternative is the establishment of a mandate under the United Nations. Such a mandate should involve closer supervision and encouragement than did the mandates system of the League of Nations.

We feel, however, that the world's responsibility in this matter is not wholly, or even primarily, political. For the refugees that responsibility is humanitarian. We feel that appeal, in humane terms that could not be disregarded by Christian peoples, should be made by the interim authority of the United Nations organization asking the member states to accept for immigration certain special quotas, sharing the total immigration in proportion to their existing Jewish communities. This would apply the American quota system to this special problem. Such an arrangement could well provide for choice by the entrant so that each might reach a community in which he could feel himself to be among his own. The share of any one country would be a contingent too small to be an economic burden. . . .

We must remember that it was not with the Arabs that anti-Semitism originated nor in their culture that it rooted and flourished. Are we Christians ready to confess that Christianity has no more certain cure to offer than geographical concentration of the Jewish people, and that questionable good, national sovereignty? We believe that the future of Christianity depends upon the heart with which Christians now attack this menace to all that we have put our faith in for nineteen centuries. We believe that a demonstration of Christian justice toward the Arabs would do much to stem the anti-Jewish tide in Moslem lands. We call upon Christian leaders here and now to initiate a more positive and vigorous program to eradicate anti-Semitic feeling in our own country. Can we ourselves claim the name of Christian if we are not ready to share suffering and to carry some of the weight of the heavy cross that bears down upon Israel, the people of whom Jesus was born?

MUST THE JEWS QUIT EUROPE? [5]

Ideologies apart, let us face up practically to the Jewish problem in Europe in the light of the exodus proposal. And

[5] From article by Zachariah Shuster, Editor of the American Jewish Committee publication, the *Committee Reporter*, and writer for other publications. *Commentary*. 1:9-16. December 1945.

we can do this without involving ourselves in any discussion of the absorptive capacity of Palestine, which would require too lengthy a consideration of political and economic problems. The crux of the exodus argument is a difference of opinion, not as to the possibilities of life in Palestine, but as to the possibilities of Jewish life in Europe.

About the basic facts of the situation of the surviving Jews of Europe there can be little debate. The situation is extremely bad. No less than six out of every ten Jews in Europe are in need of assistance. In every liberated country the remaining and returning Jews have to start from scratch. They have to find homes; they have to fight to get back their property; they have to adjust themselves to following new occupations. Large numbers of them want to get away from the places where their nearest and dearest were slaughtered and from which they were violently uprooted. Emigration is certainly a vital necessity for many of the Jews who have survived Nazism. The discussion, however, is not about emigration; nor is it about Palestine as a destination for substantial numbers of Europe's Jews. No other country received so many Jews immediately after liberation from the German concentration camps. The Jewish community in Palestine eagerly awaits the survivors from Europe and gives them all physical and moral support. The crucial question remains whether all this must imply the total evacuation of Jews from Europe.

Let us hear what some of the survivors themselves have to say. Chaplain Ernst M. Lorge, after a visit to Jews in the German concentration camps, reports that "if asked what their plans for the future were, their reply would run approximately like this: 99.5 per cent of the Jews originating from Poland have the definite and unchangeable desire to go to Palestine. About one half of the Jews of Hungary, Rumania and Slovakia want to return home, while the other half want to go to Palestine. About two thirds of the Jews coming from Western countries want to return, and only one third plan to go to Palestine directly" (*Jewish Frontier*, August 1945). Even accepting the interpretation of Chaplain Lorge, that those who want to return to their former countries do not intend to stay in Europe, but contemplate emigration at a later date, the fact remains that total exodus is not an immediate desire of *all* European Jews.

Earl G. Harrison, in his report to President Truman on the condition of the displaced Jews in Germany, states that "the great majority of the Jews now in Germany do not wish to return to those countries from which they came" and that "Palestine is definitely and pre-eminently the first choice." He adds, however, that "Palestine, while clearly the choice of most, is not the only named place of possible emigration. Some, but the number is not large, wish to emigrate to the United States, where they have relatives, others to England, the British Dominions, or to South America."

Even more significant is the testimony of two leaders of the Jews of Poland. One is Dr. Emil Sommerstein, Chairman of the Central Committee of the Jews in Poland, a veteran Zionist, devoted to the ideal of a Jewish state. At the recent World Zionist Conference in London, after restating his Zionist convictions, Sommerstein spoke of "the duty of Jews as citizens of Poland to participate in the new economic and democratic rebuilding of the country" (*Zionist Review,* London, August 10, 1945).

The same idea was echoed even more strongly by another Polish Jewish leader at the World Zionist Conference. Dr. Adolf Berman, in an address to the Conference, said,

Parallel with the struggle for free immigration into Palestine, it is our duty to help rebuild the economic, social and cultural life of the Jewish communities. Immigration is not a speedy process. It is hard to believe that it will include *all* Jews. Meanwhile life goes on and the new Jewish life after liberation must become productive and creative. The opinion that there is nothing more to do in the destroyed Jewish communities and that it is not worth building anything there is both false and dangerous (*Proletarisher Gedank,* September 1, 1945).

Recent information from Poland tells of the first beginnings of reconstruction there. The Central Committee of Polish Jews, with the help of the J.D.C. [Joint Distribution Committee], has undertaken the task, not only of opening homes for Jewish chilren, providing medical aid and public dining rooms, but also of economic reconstruction. It has started twenty-two industrial cooperatives and workshops. The Cracow Jewish Committee has established an amber workers' cooperative, while in Tarnow a cooperative factory for the manufacture of men's and women's clothing has been set up. Similar information has reached us from other liberated countries.

The scope and importance of all this should not be exaggerated. Jews remaining in Europe face tremendous difficulties. Anti-Semitism has not vanished with the disappearance of the Hitler regime, and pogroms are still on the order of the day in the new Poland. The Jews of Europe will need all the help of all democratic forces, as well as of their fellow-Jews in the United States, to lay new foundations for their future. Yet rebuilding is going on and will continue to go on, in the words of Sommerstein, in accordance with the law of life itself.

This is admitted even by those who preach exodus. In July Dr. Arieh Tartakower, one of the leaders of the World Jewish Congress and of the Labor Zionist movement, said: "The Jews of Europe do not want the bliss of the 'new democratic' Europe; they want to leave that continent, and almost all want to go to Palestine" (*Jewish Frontier,* July 1945). But only a few weeks later, writing from London after the conference of the World Jewish Congress, which was attended by delegates from Poland, Bulgaria, Greece, Czechoslovakia, Finland and all Western European countries, Dr. Tartakower stated that, besides the immediate questions of restoration of rights, the struggle against anti-Semitism and restitution of property, there was also discussion of the future "and primarily of rebuilding a new Jewish life in Europe for those who desire and are able to remain. . . . He stated,

It was rightly underscored by a number of speakers that there are no ideologies of emigration among us today—Jewish migration to Palestine cannot be considered emigration in the usual sense of the word. We are not ready to give up any single position in the countries of the Diaspora and as long as there are Jews there we shall fight for their rights and for a dignified life for them. This was the principle of reconstruction conceived and adopted by the conference. . . . If any evidence was needed that, despite the hell through which European Jewry has passed, it is alive and determined to continue to live and to fight and create, this conference produced the evidence (*The Day,* September 6, 1945).

Dr. Leon Kubowitzki, another leader of the World Jewish Congress, recently returning from a visit to Western Europe, stated definitely that anti-Semitism there is on the wane and that "much of the reported anti-Semitism is the work of small groups or individuals who acquired confiscated Jewish property and want to hold on to it, rather than spontaneous mass reaction."

There is still another aspect of the new Europe that should give pause to the exodus adherents. Most of the remaining Jews of Europe today live in countries in the so-called Soviet sphere of influence. Dominating these countries are regimes that follow anti-emigrantionist policies. Hungary, with its nearly 400,000 Jews, has now the largest Jewish community of Europe. Next comes Rumania, with its more than 300,000 Jews. Poland, Yugoslavia, and Bulgaria have between them another 200,000 Jews.

Most of these countries have already made known their opposition to mass emigration by any group of their population, including Jews. Rumania has forbidden young Jews of military age to leave for Palestine. The premier of Bulgaria, Kimon Gheorghieff, while expressing sympathy for a Jewish national home in Palestine, stated that the attitude of the Bulgarian government would have to be defined in accordance with the "general policy of the country" and that it was not desirable for "young and healthy Jews to leave Bulgaria for Palestine, because the new government is based on a program which practices equal treatment of all citizens." The Rumanian propaganda minister, Professor Constantinescu, declared that "for all democrats, the Jewish problem has never existed." They know only of a "so-called anti-Semitic problem and a Zionist problem; for they have never regarded the Jews as separate from the population at large." It has been known that the Rumanian government looked with disfavor on plans for Jewish emigration to Palestine. The new Polish government, it is presumed, will not put any obstacles in the way of Jewish immigration, while not encouraging it.

These countries in Southeastern Europe, in their passive or active opposition to emigration of any large group of their citizens, are following in the footsteps of the U.S.S.R., which has always prohibited any group of its citizens from leaving its territory.

All this adds up to the fact that among the European countries that have most of the Jewish population and where Jewish misery is the greatest, governmental policy will strongly oppose mass exodus. This is a matter not to be taken lightly.

At the same time there is an apparently contradictory tendency in some of these countries to eliminate their minorities, presumably as a result of experiences with their German minorities. Transfers of populations are now taking place on a vast scale. The Czechs are determined to get rid of their three million Sudeten Germans and seven hundred thousand Magyars, and the mass expulsion of these unfortunate minorities has been going on since the liberation of Czechoslovakia. The Poles are expelling the twelve million Germans living in the territories ceded to them after the Nazi surrender. The U.S.S.R. and the new Poland are exchanging populations as a result of the establishment of new boundaries between them. All these states seem determined to make nationality and religion synonymous with citizenship.

Edward Beneš, president of Czechoslovakia, has even applied this principle to the Jewish minority. In a recent statement he declared that those Jews "who would not leave for Palestine ought to get assimilated completely into the people of the country in which they want to live, or reside there as citizens of a foreign state." Some of the exodus adherents point out that if this policy were to become general Jews would be confronted with three choices—to leave those countries, to disappear as Jews, or to be in the anomalous position of being the lone and single minority in a large section of Europe. None of these possible choices augurs well for the future, they assert.

Certainly this represents a serious problem. But it should be pointed out that the western world is far from being in agreement with this policy. It runs completely counter to the modern concept of the state. To make the state and the ethnic group synonymous is, in a sense, to return to the medieval principle that imposed the religion of the rulers upon the entire community. To base the structure of the state on a single racial or religious group is surely contrary to the spirit of interdependence among all peoples and groups in the world.

Lord Acton stated as long ago as 1862 that "the combination of different nations in one state is as necessary a condition of civilized life as the combination of men in society. . . . Where political and national boundaries coincide, society ceases to advance, and nations relapse into a condition corresponding to that of men who renounce intercourse with their fellow men."

It should be understood and underscored that the controversy pro and contra exodus is not a pro and anti Zionist argument. Many Zionists do not accept the exodus argument, and some non-Zionists do. There is no basic incompatibility between the building up of Palestine as a Jewish center for those who wish to go there and the continuance of Jewish life on a secure basis in other countries. No one will ignore the great and special contribution of Palestine to the Jewish life of our generation or its potentialities for the future. The argument is whether the reconstruction of Palestine must be accompanied by the disappearance of Jewish life from any large section of the world.

Dr. S. Rawidowicz points out in *Hadoar* that the notion of many Zionists that the Jews in Palestine live there by right, while they live in all other countries as if on sufferance, is a dangerous one. He stresses that both Zionism and emancipation are products of the modern era and that neither can be realized in an undemocratic world. He speaks out vigorously against the artificially simplified dilemma—either Palestine or extinction—posed by some sections of the Zionist movement, and proclaims the idea of Jewish "unconditional survival." He says:

In the face of the unconditional extermination of Israel by one of the biggest and most "cultured" countries in Europe before the eyes of the entire world, we must ask ourselves and everyone else that every thought and action in Israel shall, from now on, be rooted in a belief in the unconditional existence of Israel. . . . Our duties now and in the future are:

To continue building Palestine, and with greater vigor than in the past three generations, but not make it the condition of Jewish existence which implies the denial of the future of the Jews in other countries; to love Palestine, but not to turn this love into abuse or hostility toward Jewish people in other countries; to love Palestine and love Israel wherever it is; Israel even more than Palestine. . . . Let not the Zionists go around as the healers of all diseases, as though mocking the Jews who suffer from anti-Semitism and as though they, the Zionists, have the magic pill. . . . They haven't got it. . . .

A sober evaluation of all the arguments on both sides and of the actual Jewish situation in the contemporary world must, in this writer's opinion, lead to the conclusion that no either-or proposition can solve the Jewish problem. Jews cannot and must not escape from the modern world. They are part of it; they helped create it; and their destiny is interwoven with it. In this atomic age, to envisage the future and safety of Jews as a thing completely separated and isolated from the rest of the world is an illusion that flies in the face of reality. We live in One World. Jews in Western civilization are here to stay, not as guests and tolerated exiles, but as permanent and equal members of a society which is struggling to evolve a way of life based on individual liberty and social justice.

What is urgently needed in Jewish life today is a recognition of the full compatibility of Palestine with Jewish life elsewhere. Such a balanced view is certainly not easy to achieve. The simple formula of the extremist always sounds more logical and consistent. But Jewish life cannot be imprisoned in any single viewpoint or slogan. Jews will live in Europe. Jews will live in Palestine. Jews will live in the United States. Each Jewish group in the world will have its own opportunities. Each will suffer, in one degree or another, from limitations and disabilities. From the interplay of complex and various factors, each may hope to evolve its own pattern combining Jewish distinctiveness with full participation in the life of the surrounding peoples. In each, Jewish group life and the Jewish heritage will continue and be carried forward.

SOVIET RUSSIA, THE JEWS, AND PALESTINE [6]

The recrudescence of anti-Semitism on the one hand, and the natural desire of the more Orthodox Jews to practice their

[6] From article by John G. Hazam, Professor of History, College of the City of New York. *Arab World*. 1, no3:65-72. 1945.

faith and preserve their traditional culture without undue, extra-
legal harassment, on the other, caused them to yearn for the
establishment, somewhere in the U.S.S.R., of a separate self-
governing Jewish community—a kind of Russian Palestine. The
first community of this nature to be founded was that in the
Crimea, but did not prove successful. Then, in 1928, Jewish
groups began to migrate to eastern Siberia and settle in the area
around the town now called Biro-Bidjan, not far from the Man-
churian frontier. In 1934 the Soviet Government made the area
a Jewish Autonomous Region with the promise that when this
region became sufficiently populated and acquired a numerical
Jewish majority, it would be accorded the status of a Soviet Republic.

The country, as described in a brochure printed in Moscow,
is a veritable paradise, nearly twice the size of Palestine. It has
everything that Palestine has not—wide expanse of fertile land,
"meadows of succulent grasses," vast virgin forests, the largest
iron and coal deposits in the Far East, rivers teeming with fish,
and woodlands swarming with game—truly "a land of milk and
honey."

However, although shortly after its founding it was hailed
everywhere with great satisfaction, the Biro-Bidjan enterprise has
so far by no means prospered. First of all, the tremendous
amount of arduous labor required to clear the raw soil and the
primitive conditions under which the urban colonists had to live
discouraged not a few of them. At its inception, the region was
open only to Russian Jews, but, later, carefully selected Jews
from foreign countries were also admitted.

In the second place, at least some, if not most, of the funds
for the plan came from contributions collected outside of Russia,
mainly from organizations in Great Britain and the United States
who employed distributing agencies in the Soviet Union. Shortly
after the notorious Stalin-Hitler Pact of 1939, these agencies
discreetly liquidated their affairs and withdrew entirely from the
country.

Due, doubtless, to the inimical position taken by the Soviet
Union on Zionism, the Zionist bodies throughout the world consequently evinced an obvious coldness towards her Siberian

scheme. If they did not actually disapprove of it, they gave it the merest lip service, and that grudgingly. It was feared that Stalin was conspiring to set up a rival state to compete with their own pet project in Palestine. Some were convinced that he was bent on sabotaging that project; they even thought they saw his hand inciting and aiding the Arabs in their riots against the Jews. In any case, the Zionists were more concerned with cramming more and more Jews into Palestine than in steering them off to the Soviet "paradise."

Zionist criticism of the Biro-Bidjan experiment became more outspoken and vehement immediately after 1939 when Moscow was collaborating with the Axis camp. Biro-Bidjan was described as a subtle devise for exiling the Jews to Siberia. Others inquired sarcastically: "How can you have Jewish culture without free synagogues and the right to teach the Hebrew language?" One called Biro-Bidjan just another "racket" by which the Soviet sought to secure much needed foreign exchange. And there were many who charged that Moscow had deliberately planted the colony near Manchukuo so that in the event of a Japanese invasion of Siberia, the Jews would serve as "cannon fodder" and their propaganda appeal would command for Russia the support of world Jewry.

Be that as it may, by the beginning of the present war Biro-Bidjan, after a decade of existence and the expenditure of millions of dollars, had acquired a Jewish population of only 20,000—still constituting a minority in the region. For its failure up to this point, the Kremlin is inclined to blame the Zionists who, it believes, had deliberately boycotted the settlement.

With respect to the European Jews outside of Russia, there is another indication of the Soviet position. In the critical years just before the war, Russia at once became acutely aware of the need of populating the wide open spaces of her vast, continental dominions. In an effort to increase her birthrate, she tightened up the lax laws governing the family relationships. Besides that, she displayed a reluctance to permit any of her citizens, gentiles or Jews, to migrate to foreign lands, whether to Palestine or anywhere else. Mindful of the years of suffering perpetrated on the Jews under Nazi tyranny, one would expect that the Soviet Union would be only too eager to welcome such refugees into her own borders. Yet, with negligible exceptions, such has not been the case. In the emergency the Kremlin and its usually articulate press have been conspicuous by their strange taciturnity.

Today, however, Russia is primarily concerned with what she regards as much bigger issues, issues which are bound to determine ultimately her destiny as a dominant world power. When Hitler turned his panzer divisions on Russia in June 1941, a great change came over the total Soviet outlook, domestic as well as foreign. Sorely beset, she appealed urgently for all-out aid, both material and moral, and from all quarters, both Communist and capitalist.

In the course of the war since that date she has experienced a sweeping ideational conversion which seems to put Marxism into reverse. She has found it expedient, as in the old Romonov days, to readopt and make full use of the policies of theism, nationalism, and imperialism. In order to assure for the U.S.S.R. the absolute unity and whole-hearted support of all the people, she has abolished the Comintern and resurrected the venerable Orthodox Church as an indispensable adjunct of the Soviet state.

Also as a result of this gigantic struggle, Russia has been rapidly transformed into a highly industrialized nation which is now abandoning its doctrine of economic self-sufficiency and gearing its expanded factories for the postwar world market. She is seeking strategic areas for her airfields, oil for her machines, and spheres of influence for her security. And that usually means imperialism.

As previously explained, Russia has had a long-standing interest in the Middle East. In the last few years she has displayed an unmistakable desire to make her influence felt throughout the Arab world. She has already established diplomatic relations with nearly every one of the independent Arab states. Palestine, which does not enjoy sovereign status, has acquired a Soviet consul general. Russia is also reported to be seeking air facilities and a share in some of the oil concessions. It is even rumored that she has contrived to purchase some private shares in the company which operates the Suez Canal. These are but few of the many moves that are indicative of the direction which the new Soviet policy is taking in this highly strategic center of the globe.

But the Near East, and particularly Palestine, is an area in which religion and politics have usually been inextricably intertwined. Alert to this situation the U.S.S.R. has shrewdly taken steps to gain the confidence and cooperation of all religious factions, both in Russia and abroad—the loyal followers of the Prophet Mohammed, the pious members of the Orthodox Church, and the much-maligned Children of Israel. By the dissolution of the Comintern and its antagonizing program of militant atheism the Soviet removed one of the chief barriers to such a rapprochement.

Russia's own Moslem citizens, who have been rendering valiant services in sacrificing their lives and fortunes for the Red cause, have been encouraged to organize and make their voices heard among their multitudinous brethren in the Arab countries and elsewhere. Last year a Shaikh al-Islam was appointed and officially recognized as the spiritual head of all his coreligionists in the U.S.S.R.; also a Moslem Board of the Transcaucasus was set up under his direction.

Evidently, his activities on behalf of Moscow are already bearing desired fruit. In Nablus, Palestine, for instance, a group of young Arabs are reported to have formed a society of Friends of the Soviet Union for the purpose of promoting a more intimate understanding between the Arabs and Russia. On her side, Russia recently reciprocated by permitting, for the first time, large numbers of her Moslems to make the annual pilgrimage to Mecca, and, further, facilitated their journey by granting them special transport arrangements.

The U.S.S.R. is also attempting to recover lost ground and to woo those who are of the Orthodox persuasion in Syria and Palestine. The politically opportune revival of the Russian Orthodox Church opened the way for this effort. In Palestine, as has been recounted, the Tsars had a material as well as a moral stake. After the Bolshevik Revolution the institutions and lands owned by the Moscow Patriarchate in Jerusalem fell into the hands of the local Orthodox clergy, who refused to submit to the

Soviet regime. The British mandate authorities, who jointly administered these properties, proceeded to use the vacant spaces for the purpose of constructing various public buildings.

Last year, Premier Stalin, apprized of the situation, acted to reacquire these holdings. After making representations to the British Government, he not only got his claims recognized but also gained the resubmission of the ecclesiastics who occupied these premises. Thus, in the event of future disorders in Palestine, the Soviet would have specific interests to protect.

Similarly, a few weeks ago, on the occasion of the crowning of the new Patriarch of All the Russians in Moscow, the Patriarchs of Antioch, Jerusalem, and Alexandria were cordially invited to attend, which they did. The close link which formerly bound them to Moscow is being carefully reforged, and all the schismatic congregations who, after 1917, detached themselves from the mother church, are being brought back into the fold. Communist Russia, no less than the capitalist states, is able to utilize the prestige of its church as an important instrument of national and imperialistic policy.

But the Kremlin is too realistically astute to court the Arabs exclusively and remain obstinately at loggerheads with the Zionists. After all, Russia is now in military and political alliance with England and must avoid any display of her habitual anti-British bias. Moreover, in America as well as in Britain the well-knit and well-fed Zionist organizations, in contrast with the Arabs, wield so powerful and inordinate a weight in the affairs of state that it is well not to disregard or disrespect them.

The Zionists, on their part, have become better disposed towards the Soviet, especially since the heroic stand at Stalingrad. Realizing that Russia has borne the major brunt of the bloody battles against the Fascist tormentors of the Jews, the Zionists have expressed their sympathy and gratitude by making large contributions to the Russian war relief.

These circumstances have recently resulted in the exchange of mutually friendly gestures between the Zionists and the Kremlin. In the autumn of 1943, Ivan Maisky, the then Soviet ambassador in London, while en route for the famed Moscow Conference, stopped off in the Near East and in particular visited

Palestine. Here he made a personal investigation of the Jewish-Arab problem; he made a tour of the Jewish settlements and talked with a number of Zionist and Arab leaders. Of course, he was careful not to commit himself to either party, but he must have made a comprehensive report to Stalin. The fact that he was the first ranking Soviet diplomat to go to the Holy Land for purposes of inquiry is indeed a measure of Russia's awakening attentiveness to the wider significance of the problem.

There is, of course, no way of knowing the precise nature of the Palestine appraisal which Maisky presented to his superiors, but a few subsequent actions by Moscow indicate that there was a partial suspension of the stringent restraints which had previously frustrated the Russian Zionists. Not long afterwards, a Jewish Soviet delegation left for England and the United States, where they attended meetings of the Zionist leaders. The U.S.S.R. also relaxed its interdict on the entry of Zionist literature and Palestinian exhibits. Soon, a bureau on Jewish Religious Affairs was established in Moscow. Nevertheless, the government continued to maintain its reticence. When, a few months ago, representatives of both the Zionists and the Arabs approached Soviet official circles in Cairo on the question of Palestine, the Russians refused to be drawn into any expression of opinion on the matter.

That Soviet frigidity towards the Zionists has tended to thaw out does not necessarily signify that the Kremlin had jettisoned altogether its former notions. Events of the last several weeks in the Balkans amply demonstrate this fact. Ever since the Nazi occupation of the Balkan region anti-Semitic laws have either been introduced or made more severe. The situation was made all the more difficult when hordes of Jewish refugees from central and eastern Europe straggled into the area in the hope of reaching neutral Turkey, where they might be able to secure British visas for Palestine. Indeed, the sorry plight of these refugees has been the mainstay of Zionist propaganda for the abrogation of the British White Paper of 1939, which puts definite limits on Jewish immigration into the Holy Land.

As the Red Army swept over Rumania, Bulgaria, and Hungary, these marooned unfortunates thought that their liberation would mean a resumption of their journey to Palestine. But they reckoned without the Balkan, Russian and British authorities. In the first place, the reorganized, Communist-controlled Balkan governments announced the removal of all legal disabilities on the Jews and also promised to restore, or compensate them for, their confiscated properties. However, unsettled conditions and empty national treasuries rendered these assurances valueless. And Bulgaria's Communist Minister of the Interior proceeded to ban all Jewish emigration from the country.

The Russians, too, instead of expediting the movement of the Balkan refugees to Palestine, actually took measures to prevent it. Since most of these Jews came from districts lately conquered and annexed by the U.S.S.R. (Poland, Bukowina, Bessarabia, etc.), they thereby became Soviet citizens, and Russia needs all her manpower for the huge task of postwar reconstruction.

As for England's viewpoint in the matter (now that Churchill and Stalin understand each other here), London stated that since the critical situation which menaced the Jews in the Balkans had been happily alleviated by Russia, there was no longer any reason for them to leave those countries; therefore, Britain hereafter would not grant Palestine visas to all Jews arriving in Turkey. Thus, abetted by the Balkan and British authorities, the Kremlin does not appear to have altered substantially its negative stand on Zionist aspirations.

In summary, it may be said that despite the fact that the Jews have been accorded identical status with all others of her citizens, the U.S.S.R. has neither been able to stamp out anti-Semitism entirely nor to dispose wholly of her Jewish problem. Even the project of establishing a special Jewish community at Biro-Bidjan has fallen far short of expectations. To add to the embarrassment of the Soviet, Zionism, which is abhorrent to communism, has persisted, in defiance of official censure.

Meanwhile, the exigencies of the war and her alliance with the two chief capitalist nations have prompted Russia to revise Marxism towards the right and to embark on a new career of positive, if not aggressive, interest in the outside world, especially in the strategic and oil-bearing lands of the Middle East.

As a consummate realist who thinks primarily in terms of the Soviet's paramount concerns, Stalin (no less than Churchill) is most unlikely to sacrifice the loyalty of his own numerous Moslems and the good-will of the countless other Moslems, who live in the lands where he is seeking economic preferment, in order to appease a comparative handful of vociferous Zionists, however wealthy and influential they might be.

Recent events have made it abundantly clear that, at the conclusion of hostilities, the Palestine problem is not going to be settled unilaterally by England, but will be decided by the Big Three in concert. At such a conference one may be certain that the triumphant voice of Soviet Russia—the only major power that is an immediate neighbor of the Moslem world—will be listened to with more than ordinary respect. And whatever ring that voice might have, almost certainly it will not be pro-Zionist.

JEWISH-ARAB COOPERATION IN PALESTINE [7]

Is there any way out? There are many in Palestine who think there is, and that the way out is Arab-Jewish understanding and cooperation. This is a difficult way out. It has become more and more difficult year by year, one may almost say, day by day. But it is the one way that is far-seeing and that offers some ray of hope. It would require enormous, systematic, unrelenting effort on the part of all concerned. It cannot be achieved by political formulas alone, although these are of fundamental importance. If only the tiniest fraction of the thought and effort being put into the Indian situation today—also a last-minute effort—might be given to Palestine, positive, constructive results could be achieved. The Palestine problem is much less complicated. But to bring about Arab-Jewish understanding requires no less a degree of intelligence and of determined effort and good-will than Moslem-Congress understanding in India.

There are, it seems to many of us, two primary conditions which require first to be met. These are:

7 By Judah Leon Magnes, President, Hebrew University, Palestine. *Political Quarterly* (London). 46:297-306. October 1945.

1. That the basis for policy in Palestine be the creation of a binational Palestine, in which both peoples, Jews and Arabs, are to have equal rights and duties. Conversely this means that there is to be no Jewish state and no Arab state of Palestine.

2. That the international background of Palestine be emphasized and reinforced, and that to this end Great Britain declare its readiness, under suitable conditions, to bring Palestine under the Trusteeship System of the United Nations, and that Palestine thus become a Trust Territory instead of a mandated territory.

To take the second point up first. It is generally recognized that the mandatory system has not been very successful in Palestine. One of the chief objectives of the mandate was to develop self-government. There was considerable upper-class self-government under Turkish rule; and under the mandate there has been some progress in a democratic direction, but not much. There is more estrangement than ever before, and the sense of frustration is almost universal.

Although this is a tiny country, there are considerable numbers of men and women of ability among both the Jews and the Arabs. Yet there are hundreds of British officials in posts which could be filled by Jews and Arabs. No Jew or Arab is a member of the Executive Council, or the head of any department, or a district commissioner, or the president of a court. As is well known, there is no legislative council—legislation is by administrative decree. The points of contact between government and the population are in large measure police contacts. It is authoritarian, colonial administration pushed to an extreme. Britain has been the virtual ruler of Palestine. The Mandates Commission of the old League of Nations, which was only advisory, was ineffective.

Under the Charter of the United Nations, the trusteeship terms for each territory to be placed under the Trusteeship System are to be agreed upon by the states directly concerned including the mandatory of a territory held under mandate (Article 79). This means in effect that it is dependent upon Great Britain if Palestine is to become a Trust Territory, and that the terms of the trusteeship agreement must meet with Great Britain's approval first of all.

We would propose that a trusteeship agreement be concluded without undue postponement and that it include the following provisions:

1. That a Regional Trusteeship Board be set up under the Trusteeship Council for the purpose of working out policy for Palestine, of guaranteeing its security and of being responsible for the achievement of the basic objectives of the Trusteeship System as defined in Article 76 of the Charter of the United Nations.[8]

2. That the Regional Trusteeship Board consist, in the first instance, of representatives of Great Britain, the Arab League, and the Jewish Agency for Palestine. Great Britain represents the Christian world, the Arab League represents the Arab world, and the Jewish Agency the Jewish world, at least in reference to Palestine.

It is a matter for further consideration as to whether and when the United States, Russia and France, who are to be members of the Trusteeship Council, should also sit on the Regional Board. Theoretically speaking that would be advisable. But that might increase rather than lessen the practical difficulties, at least for the moment. In any event the Charter is fortunately very elastic in permitting the creation of different forms of "specialized international bodies" and in encouraging "individual agreements."

3. That Great Britain be designated under Article 81 as the "Administering Authority."

4. That the main political directive to be given by the Trusteeship Council to the Regional Board be the achievement

[8] Article 76 reads:
The basic objectives of the Trusteeship System, in accordance with the purposes of the United Nations, laid down in Article 1 of the present Charter, shall be:

(*a*) To further international peace and security;
(*b*) To promote the political, economic, social and educational advancement of the inhabitants of the Trust Territories, and their progressive development towards self-government or independence as may be appropriate to the particular circumstances of each territory and its peoples and the freely expressed wishes of the people concerned, and as may be provided by the terms of each trusteeship agreement;
(*c*) To encourage respect for human rights and for fundamental freedoms for all without distinction as to race, sex, language, or religion, and to encourage recognition of the interdependence of the peoples of the world; and
(*d*) To insure equal treatment in social, economic and commercial matters for all members of the United Nations and their nationals, and also equal treatment for the latter in the administration of justice without prejudice to the attainment of the foregoing objectives and subject to the provisions of Article 80.

of Arab-Jewish cooperation in a binational Palestine based upon equal rights and duties for both peoples.

It is not suggested that these are to be the only terms of trusteeship agreement. But they do give expression to the basic fact that for millions of persons throughout the world Palestine is a land *sui generis,* the Holy Land of three monotheistic religions, an international land in the peace of which all the world is interested. "Seek the peace of Jerusalem."

Moreover, one of the very greatest advantages of a Regional Trusteeship Board of this kind would be the fact that here Arab representatives and Jewish representatives would meet and discuss Palestine with each other before the public opinion of the interested world. Jews and Arabs no longer meet. They must meet face to face. It is only thus that "the general principle of good neighborliness" can be encouraged. Before this forum of the Regional Board they would bring all their arguments. Policy would be adopted, in so far as possible, through agreement; otherwise, through the procedures laid down by the Trusteeship Council or some other appropriate organ of the United Nations. The fact that the Board was not a temporary body, or merely advisory, but permanent and authoritative as to policy and security, and had on it both Arab and Jewish representatives, would give all contending parties the opportunity of again and again bringing forward issues the answers to which, to the mind of any of them, had not worked out satisfactorily.

The Regional Trusteeship Board does not yet exist, nor do I pretend that the outline I have given is the only possible way for it to work. My main contention is merely that there should be an authoritative regional body on which Great Britain (perhaps also, later, the other three great powers?), as well as Arabs and Jews sit, for the purpose of working out a policy for Palestine and of being responsible for its security, and in the last analysis for its administration.

As to the basic policy for Palestine, there are three proposals which more or less hold the field. The one is that Palestine become an Arab state with guarantees for the present Jewish minority. The second is that Palestine become a Jewish state or commonwealth with guarantees for the Arab minority resulting from a very large and rapid Jewish immigration. Trying to put either of these proposals into effect would probably mean armed conflict within Palestine and perhaps beyond.

The third proposal is that of partition—dividing the tiny land into three parts and giving one part to the Arabs and the other to the Jews and the third to the British. There are Jews who are ready for this solution, and it is said that there are some Arabs who might become reconciled to it. In so far, it is a better solution than Palestine an Arab state, which no Jews are ready for, or Palestine a Jewish state, which no Arabs are ready for.

Yet partition is an illusory, superficial solution. Aside from the difficulty of establishing half-way satisfactory boundaries, it does not work in the direction of Arab-Jewish understanding and cooperation, but rather the opposite. It seems simple, yet it is only facile, and it is shortsighted. It creates two Balkan-like irredentas on both sides of the borders. It is an invitation to the rearing of a generation of intransigeant, chauvinistic Jewish and Arab youth. It creates two petty, economically impossible units. It destroys any hope of markets for Jewish industry in neighboring countries. It narrows the borders for possible Jewish immigration. It mangles the conception of the Holy Land. It refuses to face the necessity of working hard and long, perseveringly and systematically, day by day, year by year, towards Jewish-Arab rapprochement and peace. Palestine an Arab state, Palestine a Jewish state, would probably lead to warfare almost at once. Partition may not result in this at once. But it makes warfare none the less probable.

The way of Arab-Jewish understanding is the longer but the one effective way, if there is to be peace and development in Palestine. This cannot be achieved simply by decree, as through the declaration for a Jewish state or an Arab state. It cannot be brought about through a surgical operation, as with partition. The idea of an Arab-Jewish binational state based upon parity is difficult to work out in practice, but it is not impossible. Switzerland gives the lead.

I cannot be expected here to outline all of the implications of this idea. A committee appointed by the Jewish Agency gave this problem intensive consideration over a period of years, and came to a number of constructive conclusions. Unfortunately their report, although submitted to the Jewish Agency in August 1943, has been left unpublished as being out of accord with official Zionist policy, which stands for Palestine a Jewish state or commonwealth.

But I should like to deal somewhat with the implications of this binational state as to Jewish immigration. Immigration remains the crux of the matter. One of the first results of a firm policy favoring a binational state based on parity would be a lessening of Arab tension concerning Jewish immigration. Many Arabs, I should say most Arabs, do not oppose Jewish immigration because it is Jewish. There is not much Arab anti-Judaism, for the present at least. Arabs object to Jewish immigration chiefly because of their fear that it will lead to a Jewish state and the domination of the Arabs by the Jews. If, however, *ex hypothesi,* there is not to be a Jewish state, one of the main psychological obstacles to Jewish immigration is, if not removed, at any rate reduced.

That should open the way to an immediate immigration of homeless Jewish refugees. One does not know how many there are. The Hitler massacres have exterminated perhaps 5,000,000 Jews, more war casualties than the British, Americans, and French combined. There are thousands of refugees who are homeless at this very moment and who are eager for the opportunity of settling in Palestine. Many of them are the remnants of the unspeakable concentration camps. Many of them are young. There are orphans. There are bereaved fathers and mothers.

Suppose it were said at once and in the same breath:

First, the main objective of British policy in Palestine is to be Arab-Jewish cooperation in a democratic, progressive Palestine within a progressively democratic and independent Arab world, and

Second, it is an act of common humanity that a generous step be taken speedily to enable those refugees who are now waiting homeless to come to the Jewish national home *now.*

What an exclamation of approval would arise from the throats of millions in the Christian world. What a deep feeling of relief would surge up within the stricken Jewish people.

And the Arab world? Of course, you could stir up considerable excitement over this first contingent of homeless refugees. But no Jewish state is intended; and let us assume further that the political and economic interests of the various Arab states are to be advanced. Under such circumstances, I submit, not even the most extreme Arab nationalist leader could provoke the Arabs in Palestine or elsewhere to rise in revolt on *that* issue. On the contrary, I am convinced that many of the leaders of the Arab states represented in the Arab League, who have thus far given an impressive demonstration of their moderation and political sagacity, would themselves realize that by acquiescing in this immigration of the homeless they would be performing a humane act, in accordance with the best traditions of the Arab peoples, and they would be adding appreciably to their own political stature and prestige.

How the future after that would shape itself is the problem which the Regional Trusteeship Board, when established, would have to concern itself with. The Regional Board would have its relevant committees unremittingly at work, and with Jewish and Arab representatives on them. One of the immediate tasks of the Regional Board would be to prepare a plan for the development of Palestine for the benefit of all its inhabitants. Working together on such a plan would be a chief means of promoting Arab-Jewish cooperation looking towards a binational state based upon the equality of the two peoples.

On the assumption that there were additional Jews ready for immigration, and if there was room for the further absorption of immigrants, and there certainly would be, particularly if the Negeb (the Southland) could be opened up, this process of Jewish immigration could go on over the years, thus giving the Jews the chance of catching up with the Arabs in population, i.e., up to parity in number. At present there are over a

million Arabs and over half a million Jews. This would give
the Jews the opportunity of an immigration of an additional
500,000; and even more, because the Arab birth-rate is higher
than the Jewish (2.7 : 1.3). Immigration figures would be
fixed by the Regional Trusteeship Board upon the basis of the
capacity of the country to absorb new immigrants. The determination of the capacity would be one of the chief functions
of the Regional Trusteeship Board.

There are those who are greatly worried as to what would
take place after the elapse of the years required to achieve
parity in population. Our answer is that this will depend
upon what happens during the process of reaching this parity.
It depends upon the ability of the two peoples to keep the
peace with one another over a protracted period. But if they are
wise enough to keep the peace—these two Semitic peoples—not
only Palestine but this whole Semitic world will benefit.

There is another point of importance for Jewish-Arab understanding, and therefore for Jewish immigration—Palestine's relation to the newly formed Arab League. The closer the binational
Palestine can be brought to the League generally, and more
particularly to the idea of freer economic and political cooperation between Palestine, Transjordan, Syria, and the Lebanon,
the closer will be the relations between Jews and Arabs. Meanwhile the Arab League will doubtless raise various questions
with the British Government relating to the Arab world, such as
treaty revision for some of the Arab states, and the Arab League
would thus be capable, as no other body can be, of giving the
Arabs the assurance that the Arab world is in for a new deal
generally; and, as a member of the Regional Trusteeship Board,
the Arab League could guarantee to the Arabs of Palestine that
they are not to be dominated by a Jewish state. The Arab
League can help the Palestine Arabs to lift the Palestine question
out of the sphere of purely local politics and put it where it
belongs, on to a high international plane. The more such understandings can be reached with the Arab League, the more chance
there is for peaceful Jewish immigration, and the more chance
for the peaceful development of Palestine and the Middle East.

PALESTINE INQUIRY [9]

His Majesty's Government have been giving serious and continuous attention to the whole problem of the Jewish community that has arisen as a result of Nazi persecution in Germany, and the conditions arising therefrom. It is unfortunately true that until conditions in Europe become stable the future of a large number of persons of many races, who have suffered under this persecution, cannot finally be determined. The plight of the victims of Nazi persecution, among whom were a large number of Jews, is unprecedented in the history of the world. His Majesty's Government are taking every step open to them to try and improve the lot of these unfortunate people. The Jewish problem is a great human one. We cannot accept the view that the Jews should be driven out of Europe, and should not be permitted to live again in these countries without discrimination and contribute their ability and talent towards rebuilding the prosperity of Europe. Even after we have done all we can in this respect, it does not provide a solution of the whole problem. There have recently been demands made upon us for large scale immigration into Palestine. Palestine, while it may be able to make a contribution, does not by itself provide sufficient opportunity for grappling with the whole problem. His Majesty's Government are anxious to explore every possibility which will result in giving the Jews a proper opportunity for revival.

The problem of Palestine is itself a very difficult one. The mandate for Palestine required the mandatory to facilitate Jewish immigration, and to encourage close settlement by Jews on the land, while ensuring that the rights and position of other sections of the population are not prejudiced thereby. His Majesty's Government have thus a dual obligation, to the Jews, on the one side, and to the Arabs on the other.

The lack of any clear definition of this dual obligation has been the main cause of the trouble which has been experienced in Palestine during the past twenty-five years. His Majesty's

[9] Text of statement by Ernest Bevin, British Secretary of State for Foreign Affairs, in the House of Commons, November 13, 1945. 5p. mim. British Information Services. New York.

Government have made every effort to devise some arrangement which would enable Arabs and Jews to live together in peace and to cooperate for the welfare of the country, but all such efforts have been unavailing. Any arrangement acceptable to one party has been rejected as unacceptable to the other. The whole history of Palestine since the mandate was granted has been one of continual friction between the two races, culminating at intervals in serious disturbances.

The fact has to be faced that since the introduction of the mandate it has been impossible to find common ground between the Arabs and the Jews. The differences in religion and in language, in cultural and social life, in ways of thought and conduct, are difficult to reconcile. On the other hand, both communities lay claim to Palestine, one on the ground of a millenium of occupation and the other on the ground of historic association coupled with the undertaking given in the First World War to establish a Jewish home. The task that has to be accomplished now is to find means to reconcile these divergencies.

The repercussions of the conflict have spread far beyond the small land in which it has arisen. The Zionist cause has strong supporters in the United States, in Great Britain, in the Dominions, and elsewhere; civilization has been appalled by the sufferings which have been inflicted in recent years on the persecuted Jews of Europe. On the other side of the picture, the cause of the Palestinian Arabs has been espoused by the whole Arab world and more lately has become a matter of keen interest to their 90,000,000 co-religionists in India. In Palestine itself, there is always serious risk of disturbances on the part of one community or the other, and such disturbances are bound to find their reflection in a much wider field. Considerations not only of equity and of humanity but also of international amity and world peace are thus involved in any search for a solution.

In dealing with Palestine, all parties have entered into commitments. There are the commitments imposed by the mandate itself, and, in addition, the various statements of policy which have been made by His Majesty's Government in the course of the last twenty-five years. Further the United States Government themselves have undertaken that no decision should be taken in respect to what, in their opinion, affects the basic situation in Palestine without full consultation with both Arabs and Jews. Having regard to the whole situation and the fact that it has caused this world-wide interest which affects both Arabs and Jews, His Majesty's Government decided to invite the Government of the United States to cooperate with them in setting up a joint Anglo-American Committee of Enquiry, under a rotating chairmanship, to examine the question of European Jewry, and to make a further review of the Palestine problem in the light of that examination. I am glad to be able to inform the House that the Government of the United States have accepted this invitation.

The Terms of Reference of the Committee of Inquiry will be as follows:

1. To examine political, economic, and social conditions in Palestine as they bear upon the problem of Jewish immigration and settlement therein and the well-being of the peoples now living therein.

2. To examine the position of the Jews in those countries in Europe where they have been the victims of Nazi and Fascist persecution, and the practical measures taken or contemplated to be taken in those countries to enable them to live free from discrimination and oppression and to make estimates of those who wish or will be impelled by their conditions to migrate to Palestine or other countries outside Europe.

3. To hear the views of competent witnesses and to consult representative Arabs and Jews on the problems of Palestine as such problems are affected by conditions subject to examination under paragraphs 1 and 2 above and by other relevant facts and circumstances, and to make recommendations to His Majesty's Government and the Government of the United States for ad interim handling of these problems as well as for their permanent solution.

4. To make such other recommendations to His Majesty's Government and the Government of the United States as may be necessary to meet the immediate needs arising from conditions subject to examination under paragraph 2 above, by remedial action in the European countries in question or by the provision of facilities for emigration to and settlement in countries outside Europe. . . .

This inquiry will facilitate the finding of a solution which will in turn facilitate the arrangements for placing Palestine under trusteeship.

So far as Palestine is concerned, it will be clear that His Majesty's Government cannot divest themselves of their duties and responsibilities under the mandate while the mandate continues. They propose, in accordance with their pledges, to deal with the question in three stages:

1. They will consult the Arabs with a view to an arrangement which will ensure that, pending the receipt of the ad interim recommendations which the Committee of Inquiry will make in the matter, there is no interruption of Jewish immigration at the present monthly rate.

2. After considering the ad interim recommendations of the Committee of Inquiry, they will explore, with the parties concerned, the possibility of devising other temporary arrangements for dealing with the Palestine problem until a permanent solution of it can be reached.

3. They will prepare a permanent solution for submission to the United Nations and, if possible, an agreed one.

The House will realize that we have inherited, in Palestine, a most difficult legacy, and our task is greatly complicated by undertakings, given at various times to various parties, which we feel ourselves bound to honor. Any violent departure without adequate consultation would not only afford ground for a charge of breach of faith against His Majesty's Government, but would probably cause serious reactions throughout the Middle East, and would arouse widespread anxiety in India.

His Majesty's Government are satisfied that the course which they propose to pursue in the immediate future is not only that which is in accordance with their obligations, but is also that which, in the long view, is in the best interests of both parties. It will in no way prejudice either the action to be taken on the recommendations of the Committee of Inquiry or the terms of the trusteeship agreement, which will supersede the existing mandate, and will therefore control ultimate policy in regard to Palestine.

His Majesty's Government in making this new approach, wish to make it clear that the Palestine problem is not one which can be settled by force and that any attempt to do so by any party will be resolutely dealt with. It must be settled by discussion and conciliation and there can be no question of allowing an issue to be forced by violent conflict.

We have confidence that if this problem is approached in the right spirit by Arabs and Jews, not only will a solution be found to the Palestine question, just to both parties, but a great contribution will be made to stability and peace in the Middle East.

Finally, the initiative taken by His Majesty's Government and the agreement of the United States Government to cooperate in dealing with the whole problem created by Nazi aggression, is a significant sign of their determination to deal with the problem in a constructive way and a humanitarian spirit. But I must emphasize that the problem is not one which can be dealt with only in relation to Palestine: it will need a united effort by the powers to relieve the miseries of these suffering peoples.

EXCERPTS

What is needed is not a "possible way out," but a decent way out.

A decent way out of the Palestine problem envisages a situation larger than the rights of Jews, Arabs, Britons or any other groups related to the country. It calls for something more than a home for the homeless. It demands indeed a world polity of justice, bent upon establishing tranquillity everywhere by wise and humane actions.

Palestine is a most interesting example of the failure of *Realpolitik*. The policy of moral and political compromise adopted by the mandatory government has wrecked the peace of the land for two decades. The Jews have suffered incredible difficulties, while the Arabs have never been given a frank understanding of their opportunities.—*"Palestine, A Decent Way Out." By Rabbi Charles E. Shulman, North Shore Congregation, Glencoe, Ill.; Chaplain, U.S. Navy. Christian Century. F. 17, '43. p. 196.*

The communal problem of the Arab and Jew in Palestine is of the same order as the problem of Moslem and Hindu in India. Neither problem can be solved by majority rule or by the subordination of one group to the other. In both problems, the policy of the British Government is complicated by the tendency of the disputants to take up extreme attitudes and then make them the foundation of their policy. But it is no solution for the British simply to plump for one type of extremism and make it their own. The position today is that neither the Arabs nor the Jews can get everything they want. The Jews cannot have a Jewish Palestine. The Arabs cannot put a complete ban on any more Jewish immigration. It is the British Government's delicate and difficult task to find a way of persuading both sides to accept unpalatable policies. This task will take vision and patience. Above all, it will take time. The last thing the Government should feel at this moment is that quick decisions are either possible or necessary.—*Economist* (*London*). *Ag.* 18, '45. *p.* 223.

Spread through the Arab states of the Middle East are the world's most valuable oil reserves. Deposits around the Persian Gulf alone exceed 20,000,000,000 barrels. No all-weather, global air route can be developed without the use of the Middle East. The same area dominates eastern access to the Mediterranean and to the Red Sea.

The United States, Britain and Russia all came out of the war with new defensive and economic interests in the Middle East.

Russia is paying increasing attention to that part of the world. Her plans are unexplained. They may range from trade to empire expansion. But today her diplomatic agents and missions outnumber those of the British in the Middle East. Russia's railroad link with the Indian Ocean cuts across Britain's land route to India and runs between her richest oil fields in the territory.

Britain, concerned over Russia, naturally fears a Palestine situation which will stir new hatreds in the Arab world. She is aware that either the Arabs or the Jews might turn to Russia if they clash with the British. Consequently, Prime Minister Clement Attlee is determined to go slowly. He is not willing to

meet Mr. Truman's request for the admission of 100,000 Jews
into Palestine. He has offered, instead, to admit fewer than
25,000 a year. Britain may regard the agitation in this country
as nothing but domestic politics unless she is convinced the
United States will back her with military support if necessary.—
*Reprinted from the United States News, an independent weekly
magazine published at Washington, D.C. O. 26, '45. p. 28.
Copyright 1946 by the United States News Publishing Corporation.*

There is no better testing ground of future American foreign
policy than the Middle East. Strategically, politically, economically it is packed with dynamite. Its minor explosions are perhaps not too serious. The massacre of Armenians or Assyrians
is of less importance to United States local politics, of course,
than a race riot in Harlem or St. Louis. And the internecine
feuds of Jews and Arabs can continue without real hurt unless,
for whatever reasons of conceived need, somebody pits Jew
against Arab or vice versa. It is the continued acceptance of
the Middle East as a pawn of empires that is the real danger.
And until our policy recognizes the facts and sets itself against
them, we offer some hundred million people only modest appeasement.

The backbone of a new Middle East policy must be a desire
to deal directly with the Arab world. Economically the policy
must seek to develop resources of oil, raw materials, and manpower while asking as a return only what is commensurate with
the capital employed and the talent lent. The policy must work
to relieve the Middle East of the tribute it pays as well as the
returns it gets from its dependent financial status.

There would have been dangers some decades ago in fashion-
ing such a new policy. Small independent countries, strategically
situated, could always cause difficulty. And with isolationism
rampant, we were forced to allow others to resolve those difficulties until the world slowly set itself for war. But today
independence should hold no terrors. It means only a diffusion
of power and a breaking up of the unnecessary bureaucracies
of the world. Strategically independence carries no dangers

unless we disbelieve in San Francisco and believe that now is the time to build a tacit Anglo-American alliance against the world.

A hundred million Arabs cannot be ignored; an area larger than the United States cannot be left to the casual ministrations of uninstructed diplomats. A policy based on these foundations requires, of course, reorientation in thinking with regard to our place in the world. In foreign affairs it will need not only competence at the top but also manpower all along the line.

It is the Middle East that will first challenge the basic concepts of empire. That challenge is now being offered in Syria and it is in the making in Egypt and Ethiopia and Iraq. That fact we shall have to face whether we like it or not. And as we face it our position with regard to empire will have to be defined. If we could only evolve out of the Middle East a policy that will find, under the superstructure of San Francisco, a substitute for empire we would make a discovery as great as that of democracy. It may perchance be done. But if we would do it, we must see the Middle East directly and not as an adjunct to empire. If Liberia and Bolivia can exist in their own right, so equally can Egypt and the Sudan and even Palestine. But it requires a will on our part to seek new answers to old questions.—*James M. Landis, Dean, Harvard Law School. In "Middle East Challenge." Fortune. S. '45. p. 188. Copyright, Time Inc.*

Two great colonizing experiments have been made by Jews in the past fifty or sixty years, one in the Argentine and the other in Palestine. Colonization in the Argentine was begun under the best possible auspices. Practically unlimited areas of fertile soil were at the disposal of the settlers; a benevolent government placed no obstacles in their way. The price of land was moderate, and the committee conducting the operations had great resources at its disposal (something like £10,-000,000 in gold, which, fifty years ago, represented a vast sum of money.) The Jewish Colonization Association was a body of most competent men, commanding great authority in the

Jewish world, and devoted to their work. They acquired some 1,500,000 acres of land for agricultural settlement. But after fifty years of colonization, no more than 30,000 people have been settled there. Moreover, the younger generation of the settlers shows little disposition to remain on the land.

The first modern settlers to arrive in Palestine, on the other hand, were mostly poor young students who had abandoned Russian universities in search of a free, independent, and simple life. This they intended to make for themselves on the soil of Palestine. They entered upon their task without experience, without funds, unaided and untutored. The leaders of the Jewish communities looked askance at this quixotic undertaking, and prophesied its early and dismal failure. Moreover, the Turkish Government placed every imaginable difficulty in the way of the first pioneers. It was an upstream passage for them. But the men who set out on it were inspired by a sacred faith in a future. They were the men of destiny, called upon to blaze the trail—however narrow and steep—on which later generations were to tread. Their awareness of a great mission sustained them, and gave them the endurance and spirit of sacrifice which laid the foundations of the first Jewish settlements—chiefly in the coastal plain. Small in their beginnings, these villages have grown gradually and continually. They have a place—and a very honorable place—in the development of Jewish life in Palestine, and with them will always be associated the name of their founder—Baron Edmond de Rothschild—a man whose heart and power of vision were as great as his wealth. At first it was a mere trickle of new settlers which came to join them, rising after 1905, and in full tide since 1919.

Today there are in Palestine some 250 Jewish rural settlements, with a population of more than 140,000. Towns have been built up and industries established. The country has been awakened from its age-long neglect. The ancient Hebrew tongue has been revived, and is heard today in the fields and orchards of Palestine, in the streets and workshops, as well as in the schools and the University. The total acreage of land in Jewish hands—acquired by slow degrees by purchase in the open market—is now approximately 400,000 acres. On this land a close-knit, well-organized, modern Jewish community of over half-a-million souls has arisen. It is normal in every way—in its structure, its occupational distribution—and the whole edifice, moral, social, and intellectual, has been built up in a comparatively short space of time by the efforts of the Jews themselves on the neglected land of Palestine. Jewish labor, highly organized and creative, has played a leading part in this performance—*Chaim Weizmann, President, Jewish Agency for Palestine. Foreign Affairs. Ja. '42. p. 327-8.*

Palestine will remain as it has been for these thirteen centuries—a holy land of three great world religions. But if its sanctity to Jews and Christians needs no advocate, its sacredness to Moslems, strangely, still does.

Because the view is often held and expressed by sincere people that the "Arabs are mere interlopers in Palestine," and ought to give way to the "return" of the rightful and historic Jewish "owners" of the land of the Bible, a word may be said regarding the ethnology of the land. The simple fact is that the majority of the "Arab" people of Palestine are not descendants of "new arrivals" with the Islamic-Arab conquest in the seventh century—that event itself being thirteen hundred years ago!—but are a mixed race whose connection with the land goes back into very early history. It is a natural tendency for history to be simplified by the concept that all the Moslems of the conquered lands came in, and assumed control, from the outside. And it is an understandable fancy for all of the Moslem population to believe that their ancestors were of the *conquering race.* But the conquerors, and the settlers who followed in the wake of military success and control, were no doubt only a small minority of the continuing population. On the part of the latter, however, the designation "Arab" was gradually adopted along with the new religion by the majority and along with the Arabic language by all. Further, the change in religion was in most cases voluntary, for the sake of preferment and advantage, and as a natural process of following the predominant environmental influence and practice.

Therefore, the "Arabs" of Palestine are the historic "people of the land," composed of elements of many races inhabiting the country through the past, but, naturally, along with Syria, Egypt, and Mesopotamia of the Bible world, forming a part of the medieval and contemporary Arabo-Islamic cultural area of the Near East. And they, thus, are the rightful owners of Palestine—for it has been their home always. Of the present population of over a million and a half including the more than 400,000 Jews (all but 30,000 of whom have entered since the World War), the majority, over a million, are Moslem. There are also over 100,000 Christian "Arabs"—whose interests and rights are strangely overlooked in discussions!—who have remained loyal to their ancient faith. To both Moslems and Christians, as well as to the non-political-Zionist Jews who with sacrifice have established themselves in Palestine and desire only to live and let live, we must accord that sympathy and understanding which we ourselves desire and demand in connection with love of homeland.

Both Moslems and Jews have inalienable rights and interests in the Holy Land. (And certainly the Christians, the forgotten people of Palestine, have *their* claims to peace, security, and participation in government of their country!) All, as all have done in the past, can make significant contributions to the New Palestine—if all can be content to compromise and work together. It is unfortunate for Jews to overlook the great civilization of the Arabs in past centuries and to point only to the more recent degradation of Palestine—which was due not to the Arabs, but to the calamitous regime of the Ottoman Turks (from whom the present Turks are widely different!). It is unfortunate for the Arabs to exaggerate their animosities resulting from the advantage to the Zionists of British imperialistic aid and of world-wide Jewish financial and political support. It is unfortunate for the Arabs to direct their main struggle negatively—*against* fear of being overwhelmed by Zionist immigration—instead of positively *for* racial and national progress. It is unfortunate as well, for Western Christians to cloud their understanding and sympathies by misinterpreting the Biblical prophets and reading into them predictions of the sure

"return" of all the Jews of the world (about sixteen million,
for a land that is already crowded and taxed in its resources!)
to Palestine without regard for elemental logic, or for elemental
justice, to the non-Jewish population. Each group in Palestine
needs what the others have to contribute to the common welfare—and the welfare can be mutual if no group will seek undue
aggrandizement. And all of them need the informed sympathy
and understanding of the hundreds of millions of adherents of
the three great religions which came from the land.—*Charles
D. Matthews. Birmingham-Southern College, Alabama. Moslem
World. O. '43. p. 252-3.*

Even a superficial observer of the transformation wrought by
the Jews in Palestine is bound to admit that a policy of preserving the status quo in that country would deprive the Middle East
of a much needed stimulus to development. Without benefit of
planning and coordination on a regional scale, the Jewish effort
in Palestine has already produced some of the results anticipated
by T. E. Lawrence when he said:

The Jewish experiment is . . . a conscious effort on the part of the
least European people in Europe, to head against the drift of ages, and
return once more to the Orient from which they came. . . . The success
of their scheme will involve inevitably the raising of the present Arab
population to their own material level, only a little after themselves in
point of time, and the consequence might be of highest importance for
the future of the Arab world. It might well prove a source of technical supply rendering them independent of industrial Europe, and in
that case the new confederation might become a formidable element of
world power. However, such a contingency will not be for the first
or even for the second generation, but it must be borne in mind in
any laying out of foundations of empire in Western Asia. These to a
very large extent must stand or fall by the course of the Zionist effort.

It is in this wider setting that the problems of Palestine are
embedded.

In ancient days the Middle East supported many times its
present population. Since rainfall is insufficient in these regions,
the inhabitants built and maintained artificial systems of irrigation, terracing the hills to prevent erosion and storing the winter
rains in reservoirs. In Iraq traces of canals and dykes go back

to the fifth millennium before Christ; but in the wake of historical disasters these intricate systems were destroyed and the country, once a granary of the ancient world, was reduced to little
more than a wilderness. Today Iraq, though it is the size of
Italy and no poorer than the latter, has a population of three and
a half million. Its main problem is best stated in the words of
one of its former Prime Ministers:—

What Iraq wants above everything else is more population. This is a
necessary condition of progress. . . . In the Nile Valley, from Aswan
to the sea, where you have a riverain population living on irrigated
lands, there are some thirteen million inhabitants. The possible irrigable
area in Iraq is certainly not less than that of Egypt.

According to Sir William Wilcocks, the famous engineer,
Iraq could take some fifty million settlers. It is only the most
glaring example in the Middle East of great potentialities and
enormous neglect. There are three and a half million people
in Syria and the Lebanon, though the area of these two countries is equal to more than a third of prewar Poland. Only a
quarter of the area considered cultivable by the French authorities is actually farmed. Transjordan, three and a half times the
size of Western Palestine, with very large cultivable areas, harbors less than 400,000 people. Even Saudi Arabia has large
areas awaiting cultivation, as well as gold and, like Iraq, oil.
Egypt alone, more westernized than any other Arabic-speaking
country, is densely populated. Here fifteen million people live
on a cultivated area which is one third larger than Western
Palestine.

There has been some progress in all these countries since
the last war, but no planned development on a large scale.
Conscious efforts to break the rule of stagnation in the Middle
East have been made in only two lands, Turkey and Palestine.
Under Mustapha Kemal, modern Turkey increased its national
cohesion as a result of the exchange of population with Greece,
and concentrated on education, agricultural improvement and
industrialization. Unlike the Arab states which had once been
part of the Ottoman Empire, modern Turkey grasped the essential truth that it is impossible to base real independence on
economic poverty and social backwardness.

But in the case of Turkey, as well as that of Palestine, it is a non-Arab people that has been responsible for social progress. Despite some slow and inevitable changes, the social structure of the Arab Middle East is very much what it was a century ago. Patriarchal relations prevail in each little community headed by the Sheik, and outside of the community the individual has no standing. The big land-owning families, controlling wealth, education, and therefore power, have but little interest in the masses of the people except as an object of exploitation. "We keep the people ignorant and oppressed, in order to be able to govern them, for otherwise how could we govern them?" This confession of a leading member of the council at Antioch in the last century still holds good. The state of ignorance and subjection in which the people are held results in a general attitude of indifference and suspicion towards all authority which is ingrained in the Arab mentality and difficult to overcome.— *Ephraim Broido, Palestinian writer, authority on Middle Eastern questions. From his "Jews, Arabs and the Middle East." American Zionist Emergency Council. New York. '44. p. 6-8.*

PALESTINE AS A JEWISH HOMELAND

HISTORICAL BACKGROUND AND
PRESENT STATUS [1]

Jewish historical connection with Palestine goes back some 3,700 years to the time when Abraham first entered Canaan, later known as Eretz Israel. According to Jewish, Mohammedan and Christian tradition, Canaan was promised to Abraham and his descendants by God. Centuries later, Israel's religion and nationhood were born and reared in Palestine, reaching maturity and universal stature there during the Second Commonwealth. Throughout the ages, even in the darkest periods of the Crusades, the protracted wars of the Middle Ages and in modern times, the Jews never entirely left the soil of Palestine. In their wanderings through the countries of the earth, they derived spiritual inspiration—through prayers, religious ideals, festivals, laws and customs—from the prophets and sages of Palestine. The yearning for a return to their ancient homeland has been a constant element in the traditional pattern of Jewish aspiration.

In the modern period, the Jewish resettlement of Palestine (which started in 1878), while driven by economic and political exigencies, has also been motivated by the age-old attachment of the people to the land.

The historical connection of the Jewish people with Palestine and their right to rebuild their national home in that country, were legally recognized in the issuance of the Balfour Declaration (1917), and through the Palestine mandate, endorsed after the First World War by fifty-two nations of the world, including the United States. After the conquest of Palestine by Lord Allenby in 1918 (in which the Jewish Legion took part), and a brief interim of a military administration, Great Britain accepted

[1] American Jewish Conference. Committee on Preliminary Studies. "A Survey of Facts and Opinions on Problems of Post-War Jewry in Europe and Palestine." p. 78-96. The Conference. New York. August 1943.

in 1922 the mandate for Palestine from the League of Nations. A civil Palestine Administration was established, headed by a High Commissioner and a staff of British officials. The mandatory power, as a trustee for the administration of Palestine, is subject to the supervision of the Permanent Mandates Commission of the League of Nations.

The terms of the mandate charged the administration with the responsibility of facilitating the establishment of a Jewish national home in that country. In the course of ensuing events, the British Government issued several official statements, known as White Papers, which presented its views and policies on the implementation of the mandate. The first White Paper, issued on June 3, 1922, even before the mandate was ratified, stated that "the terms of the [Balfour] Declaration do not contemplate that Palestine as a whole should be converted into a Jewish national home, but that such a home should be founded in Palestine." At the same time, it declared that the Jewish community in Palestine "should know that it is in Palestine as of right and not on sufferance, that is the reason why it is necessary that the existence of a Jewish national home in Palestine should be internationally guaranteed, and that it should be formally recognized to rest upon ancient historic connection." With regard to Jewish immigration into Palestine, the White Paper further stated that "this immigration cannot be so great in volume as to exceed whatever may be the economic capacity of the country at the time to absorb new arrivals." . . .

Following the Arab riots of 1929, the British Government sent a commission (known as the "Shaw Commission") to Palestine to investigate conditions there. Upon its recommendation the government issued the Passfield White Paper (in October 1930) declaring that there was no land available for further Jewish colonization. The Paper further sought to regulate Jewish immigration not only on the basis of the economic absorptive capacity of the country, but also on the condition of Arab as well as Jewish unemployment existing at any time.

This statement of policy (the Passfield White Paper) met with protest on the part of Jewish and non-Jewish public opinion.

Consequently, Ramsay MacDonald, then British Prime Minister, addressed a public letter to Chaim Weizmann (February 1931) in which he reaffirmed the intention of his Government to fulfill the obligation assumed in the mandate. He further gave assurance that there would be no ban on land purchase and that Jewish immigration would continue on the basis of the economic absorptive capacity of the country.

The latest statement of policy issued by the mandatory government with regard to Palestine is known as the MacDonald White Paper of May 17, 1939. It came at the end of a three-year period of Arab riots and in the shadow of the approaching Second World War. This White Paper limited Jewish immigration to 10,000 a year for the ensuing five years. In consideration of the plight of Jewish refugees, it granted a bonus immigration of an additional 25,000. . . .

The Paper further granted the High Commissioner "general powers to prohibit and regulate transfers of land," and provided for the establishment of an independent government by the majority in Palestine at the end of ten years. While it praised Jewish achievements in Palestine, it intimated that the British Government had fulfilled its obligations under the mandate.

Vigorous protest against the White Paper of 1939 was voiced not only by Jews throughout the world, but by non-Jewish public opinion and statesmen, including members of the British Parliament and of the United States Congress. In June 1939 Winston Churchill declared in Parliament: "There is much in this White Paper which is alien to the spirit of the Balfour Declaration. . . . I should feel personally embarrassed in the most acute manner if I lent myself, by silence or inaction, to what I must regard as an act of repudiation. . . ."

The Council of the League of Nations, whose consent was required by the terms of the mandate, did not approve the 1939 White Paper. The Mandates Commission of the League, after examining the Paper, and after hearing MacDonald's defense of it, decided unanimously that the policy of curtailing Jewish immigration and land purchase "was not in accordance with the interpretation which the Commission had always placed upon the Palestine mandate."

The Jewish Agency for Palestine has demanded the annulment of the White Paper as an illegal abrogation of Jewish rights. The legal rights of the Jews to Palestine, the Agency maintains, are still derived from the Balfour Declaration and the Palestine mandate, in accordance with the original intent and true purpose of those documents.

The right of the Jews to Palestine has been established not only by historical ties with the land and the legal status accorded by the nations of the world, but also by the energy, labor and enterprise which Jewry has devoted toward developing the country. Since 1920, the Jewish Yishub (settlement) in Palestine has made great progress. The Jewish population has grown from 55,000 (or 9.7 per cent of the total) at the close of the First World War, to over 550,000 (or 33 per cent of the total) in 1942. More than 25 per cent of it is now established in 276 rural settlements (cooperative and private colonies) on land acquired by the Jewish National Fund and other public and private agencies.

A large segment of the Jewish population is engaged in industries, both private and cooperative, comprising about 2,300 factories and 4,000 small shops, which produce building materials, machinery, metalware, utensils, textiles, chemicals, electrical supplies and a variety of other commodities. Two large scale enterprises, the Palestine Electric Corporation and the Palestine Potash Company (the latter extracting minerals from the Dead Sea), have added great impetus to the country's general economic development, and have also attracted British and American capital investments. Jewish industrial production increased from $32,000,000 in 1937 to $80,000,000 in 1942. The cooperative movement, organized by the Histadrut (General Federation of Jewish Labor) and private associations, embraces more than a third of the Jewish population among its members, and is engaged in all branches of agriculture, industry, commerce and transportation. While commerce and shipping absorb a small percentage of gainfully occupied Jews (in comparison with Jewish employment in other countries), there is a flourishing domestic trade and a lively exchange with neighboring states and also with distant lands. In the last two decades, the Jews have invested in Palestine an estimated total of $560,000,000, of which about $105,000,000 came from national and public funds.

Along with its economic development, the Jewish Yishub has promoted social, cultural and religious institutions which not only serve the members of its own community, but also are a source of inspiration to Jewry outside Palestine. There is a progressive elementary school system, there are institutions of intermediate and higher education, research and experimental stations, technical and professional schools, Yeshivahs and other religious institutes, and the Hebrew University in Jerusalem. The Hebrew language and culture as well as the arts, literature, social and natural sciences, have been fostered by these institutions. The Yishub has its medical centers which serve Jews and Arabs alike, its social security and unemployment funds, institutions for financial aid and social service agencies.

In the present war, the Yishub has rendered valuable service to the British armed forces stationed in Palestine, building barracks, supplying a considerable quantity of food, and by developing and expanding war industries which are of great value to the Allied command in the Middle East. About 180 of the new industrial establishments are engaged directly in war work. Without conscription and despite the fact that the Jews have not been permitted to form their own military force in Palestine, 21,000 Jewish men have enlisted in the British fighting forces, and are serving on all fronts. Two thousand Jewish women have volunteered in the Palestine Auxiliary Territorial Service (PATS). In addition, the Yishub has also given many engineers, architects, sailors, airmen, physicians, and nurses, who are serving with valor and distinction in the British and Allied Mediterranean campaigns.

The Jewish community in Palestine is organized on a democratic basis, governed internally by the Asefat Hanivcharim (National Assembly), composed of party representatives elected by popular vote, and which, in turn, elects the Va'ad Leumi, or National Council.

In the decade 1933-1942—the most tragic years in Jewish history—Palestine absorbed 280,000 Jewish immigrants, thereby

more than doubling its Jewish population. It has been pointed
out by those who are engaged in colonizing the country, that
every Jew who settles there prepares the ground for another
Jew to enter. The entire economy of the Yishub, and the policies
of the World Zionist Organization and of the Jewish Agency,
are geared toward the end of expanding opportunities for Jewish immigration. Since the outbreak of the present war, 40,000
Jewish refugees, and some 4,000 children who have escaped
extermination by the Nazis, have found a haven and a permanent home in Palestine.

While the Yishub may be ready and willing to absorb masses
of Jewish immigrants after the war, the question may still be
asked: Will Palestine be able to sustain them, or, what is the
absorptive capacity of that country? Experts who have studied
the agricultural, industrial and commercial possibilities of Palestine, point out the following factors which have to be taken into
consideration.

Palestine (not including Transjordan) has an area of over
10,000 square miles, or 26,000,000 dunams (a little larger than
Sicily), only half of which is at present considered cultivable.
Of the cultivable portion, only half is cultivated to date and
sustains a population of 1,580,000. The Jewish settlement,
comprising about 550,000 souls, occupies 1,457,000 dunams,
or 5.8 per cent of the entire country. Furthermore, about one
third of the Jewish land possession has been reclaimed from
swampy areas. It is therefore maintained that with greater
modernization and intensification of farming in compact settlements (especially of the cooperative and communal types),
through further reclamation work of swampy tracts, and
through irrigation processes of arid lands, the possibilities of
agricultural colonization can be greatly increased. . . .

The Jews have already given ample proof of ability to build
and expand Palestinian industry, which was practically non-
existent before they started their colonization. Many refugees
from Nazi dominated territories, e.g., have brought their technical knowledge and experience to Palestine where they have
reestablished their laboratories, factories and industries. The
war has given additional impetus to new enterprises, especially

in chemistry, pharmaceutics, diamond cutting and machine tooling. Some of these promise future expansion. The textile industry has an especially promising future. Cotton is being cultivated in neighboring Egypt and the Jews have had considerable experience in this industry both as promoters and skilled workers.

Commerce and shipping, it is said, will develop with the continued growth of the Yishub and the general advancement of the neighboring countries in the Near East. Earlier in the present war, closer trade relations were established not only with Syria and Egypt, but also with more distant lands such as South Africa, Singapore, and New Zealand. These relations have possibilities for further developments after the war. Lying at the crossroads of three continents, Palestine has vast opportunities for shipping and air transportation, in which fields the Jewish Yishub has made a promising start.

There is yet another factor, namely, the human element—the enterprise, inventiveness and adaptability of the Jewish immigrant—which turns the wheels and turbines of the industrial and commercial machinery, and creates the facilities for expanded colonization. This is the dynamic view of the absorptive capacity of Palestine. Estimates on the total absorptive capacity of the country vary, ranging from an additional 900,000 souls to a peak estimate of 4,000,000.

There are at present over a million Arabs in Palestine (about two thirds of the total population), the majority of whom are Moslems. About 100,000 are Christians of various denominations. The Moslem Arabs may be divided into six classes, three lower and three upper, the latter forming a small but very strong minority. Of the lower classes there are the fellaheen, which constitute the bulk of the population, the Bedouins and the wage laborers. For generations they have lived in dire poverty and ignorance without possessing the economic strength or political power to influence the course of events in the country. The upper classes comprise the effendis, or big landowners, the Moslem religious hierarchy, and those who are engaged in the liberal professions or in government employment. To the effendi class also belong the rich mer-

chants and money lenders who, in addition to exacting from
the farmer exorbitant rent, take a large share of his income in
the form of interest on loans. The Christian Arabs belong
mostly to the middle class or are engaged in government service.

Before the advent of Jewish colonization, the economic and
social life of the country was primitive, with a very low standard of living. The Jews have introduced modern European
civilization, technological advancement and democratic ideals
of government. The economic, cultural and religious differences between the Jews and the Arabs are thus deeply rooted
in their respective historical developments.

In everyday life, Jews and Arabs have frequently found
common interests. They have established friendly working relations among neighboring villages, between various labor elements, as well as in trade and commerce. It is commonly
known that the Arabs have derived great benefit from Jewish
colonization in Palestine.

The Royal Commission Report of 1937, after reviewing
the progress of the Arab population under the mandate sum-
marizes the evidence of the Jewish contribution as follows:

1. The large import of Jewish capital into Palestine has had a
general fructifying effect on the economic life of the whole country.

2. The expansion of Arab industry and citriculture has been largely
financed by the capital thus obtained.

3. Jewish example has done much to improve Arab cultivation,
especially of citrus.

4. Owing to Jewish development and enterprise the employment
of Arab labor has increased in urban areas, particularly in the ports.

5. The reclamation and anti-malaria work undertaken in Jewish
colonies have benefited all Arabs in the neighborhood.

6. Institutions, founded with Jewish funds primarily to serve the
national home, have also served the Arab population. Hadassah, for
example, treats Arab patients, notably at the Tuberculosis Hospital at
Safad and the Radiology Institute at Jerusalem, admits Arab country-
folk to the clinics of its Rural Sick Benefit Fund, and does much infant
welfare work for Arab mothers.

7. The general beneficent effect of Jewish immigration on Arab
welfare is illustrated by the fact that the increase in the Arab population is most marked in urban areas affected by Jewish development.

The Arab population rose from 664,000 in 1918 to over
1,000,000 in 1940. The Arab death rate fell from 26.83

per 1,000 in 1925 to 17.38 per 1,000 in 1939. Their industrial establishments grew from $3,000,000 worth in 1922 to
$12,500,000 in 1937. Arab land cultivation increased from
4,700,000 dunams in 1921 to 7,400,000 in 1937. Their general standard of living has risen and their cultural life, too,
has advanced considerably. . . .

The Arabs were disappointed with the results of the Peace
Conference, as they did not attain the independence to which
they had aspired even in other territories outside Palestine, particularly in Syria. Extremist elements, notably under the leadership of Auni bey Abdul-Hadi, gained the upper hand in the
Arab nationalist movement. These launched an anti-British
and anti-Jewish campaign which has continued to this day. . . .

Zionist leadership has often repeated its desire to come to an
agreement with the Arabs. . . . In a recent Memorandum of the
Jewish Agency for Palestine, the position of the Agency with
regard to Jewish-Arab relations is summarized as follows:

We are mindful of the difficulties which might arise with the
Arabs and everything possible should be done in order to arrive at a
settlement with them. That may take a long time and would necessarily be a gradual process. An essential element in reaching an understanding would be the attitude of the democratic nations. If they are
ready to make clear to the Arabs that they consider the policy of a
Jewish Palestine as just, while at the same time guaranteeing to the
Arabs their rights in Palestine, the way to an understanding will be
far easier. Certainly under any regime, complete equality must be
guaranteed to all the inhabitants of Palestine, Jews and Arabs, and even
in the interim period both Jews and Arabs should have a larger measure
of self-government in all municipal affairs while educational and religious matters should be left entirely to the respective communities.

Arab opposition has continued unabated. There has been
little evidence throughout the years of the mandate, that the
Arabs have had any intentions of meeting with the Jews on
common ground. Instead, they have organized strikes and
caused disturbances which culminated in the riots of 1936-1939.

Shortly before the start of the war, the Jewish Agency consented to participate in a Round Table Conference of Arab and
Jewish representatives, called in London in 1939 by the British
Government. But the Arab leaders refused to sit at the same
table with the Jewish representatives. Following that Confer-

ence, the British Government issued the MacDonald White Paper in May 1939. While the Yishub withstood the Arab onslaughts and continued its colonizing efforts with even greater tempo, the situation remained tense until the outbreak of the war. It still awaits solution which will have to come from the authority of the United Nations.

The representative body of the Zionist movement which is responsible for the colonization work in Palestine, is the World Zionist Organization (and its Congress), which comprises all Zionist parties, except the Revisionists. According to Article 4 of the Palestine mandate, the World Zionist Organization is recognized as the "appropriate Jewish agency . . . for the purpose of advising and cooperating with the administration of Palestine in such economic, racial and other matters as may affect the establishment of the Jewish national home and the interests of the Jewish population in Palestine. . . ." This was confirmed by the League of Nations and endorsed by the United States Congress in 1922. The same Article in the mandate also empowers the W.Z.O. "to take steps in consultation with his Britannic Majesty's Government to secure the cooperation of all Jews who are willing to assist in the establishment of the Jewish national home." Accordingly, the enlarged Jewish Agency for Palestine was formed in 1929, consisting of a Council in which Zionists and non-Zionists are represented in equal number. The Agency is now the representative "public body" mentioned in the mandate.

VARIOUS CONCEPTIONS OF THE ROLE OF PALESTINE IN JEWISH LIFE

There are differing views and opinions among Zionists as well as non-Zionists about how the Jewish national home shall be built, on its ultimate form of social and political order, on methods of colonization, relations with the Arabs and the mandatory government, and on the place Palestine occupies in the life of world Jewry. Yet all these views converge on one focal point, namely, that the condition of millions of Jews today and the interests of all Jews imperatively require that the achievements of the Jewish Yishub in Palestine must be preserved and its future growth and development assured.

The achievements of the Jewish Settlement (Yishub) in Palestine have been recognized by all factions, whether Zionist, non-Zionist or even anti-Zionist. It is commonly agreed that Palestine is destined to play an important role in the life of the Jews and their struggle for survival. All agree that Palestine can serve as a place of refuge for despoiled and persecuted Jews of devastated Europe. It is also generally accepted (except by left-wing anti-Zionists) that due to the spiritual values created by the Jewish community in Palestine, that country is developing into a cultural-religious center of Judaism.

However, there are different views as to the possible expansion of the Jewish settlement in Palestine and the degree of its influence on Diaspora Jewry. It will be best to present the various conceptions of the role of Palestine in Jewish life, from the points of view of the official Zionist parties, other Jewish organized bodies, and the opponents of political Zionism.

1. *Official Zionist Views*

(a) General Zionists (Zionist Organization of America, Hadassah and Order Sons of Zion) look to Palestine as a future Jewish commonwealth and as the main country to absorb the large masses of Jewish immigrants, wherever they may come from and whatever may be the driving forces of their migration. In Palestine the Jews will have the opportunity to develop a complete and normal life as a people, attain full status of freedom and take their rightful place among the peoples of the world. The General Zionists, although maintaining that the social and economic ideology of the Jewish national home should be determined by Jews who live there and not by those of the Diaspora, hold that Palestine should be built on foundations of social justice and equal opportunity for all.

Without jeopardizing or infringing upon the civic and political status of the Jews in any other country, the Jewish commonwealth in Palestine will exert a wholesome influence on the Diaspora, enhancing cultural and spiritual values, and freeing the Jewish people from the anomalous position of a nation without a state.

This view has been summarized by Dr. Chaim Weizmann in the following statement:

A Jewish state in Palestine would be more than merely the necessary means of securing further Jewish immigration and development. It is a moral need and postulate, and it would be a decisive step toward normality and true emancipation. I believe that after the war Jews everywhere can gain in status and security only through the rise of a Jewish state.

All other Zionist factions concur in the main with this point of view, but each of them adds a concept of its own, which emanates from its specific ideology of Jewish life and the world order.

(b) Labor Zionists (Poale Zion-Zeire Zion, Pioneer Women's Organization of America, Jewish National Workers' Alliance) maintain that the Jewish problem can be solved only by an economic restratification of Jewish life, developing a labor class in all basic industries, as well as a Jewish agrarian population, and by changing the economic and social order of the world on socialist principles.

In Palestine the Jewish people will be able to rebuild their individual and group life on the basis of social and economic justice and equality. In common with the labor movement of the rest of the world, they will help establish a just world order. Palestine is thus the vanguard of the redemption of the Jewish people, not only from the shackles of Galut, but from all the social and economic ills of capitalist society. While Palestine will concentrate the most vital and creative forces of the Jewish people for solving the Jewish problem, the Jews of the Diaspora will also work toward the same end.

(c) Hashomer Hatzair (a faction of the Labor Zionist movement) "see in Zionism the only way to fight for a new social order for the Jews," which can be accomplished only in Palestine. "The larger future of Zionism," it declares, "is inseparably tied to the victory of Socialism. . . . As a chalutz movement, [it] concentrates on the upbuilding of Palestine.

Though it 'negates' the Diaspora with its social, economic and cultural limitations, it does not alienate itself from the masses living therein. Thereby [it is] fighting for the human and national rights of the masses of Israel not yet able to find a solution in the great national enterprise of Zionism under construction in Palestine."

In Palestine, Hashomer Hatzair aims to build a "complete cooperative commune," or the Kibbutz, which it describes as the vanguard for a new society, the absorptive medium for Jewish workers' immigration, the constructive instrument for the Jewish workers' class and a force in the struggle of the general workers' class.

(d) Mizrachi (orthodox religious Zionist organization; and Mizrachi Women's Organization of America) "strives for the upbuilding of the Jewish national home in Palestine on the basis of Israel's religious traditions." It "aims to redeem and develop the land of our fathers, where social and economic problems will be solved in the spirit of the Torah, and where the spiritual and cultural wealth of our people, as preserved in the sacred writings, will not only be restored to its pristine glory, but will develop to even greater dignity and splendor." It regards Palestine as "the only real solution to the homelessness of Jewry . . . or the problems facing the Jewish religion." Its program for the Diaspora is to strengthen orthodox Judaism in every country where Jews live.

(e) Hapoel Hamizrachi (religious labor Zionist pioneer movement, Torah v'Avodah) declares that "the most effective way to realize the religious, national, ethical and social principles of the Torah is to create a religious labor commonwealth in Eretz Israel. . . . For Palestine is not only an excellent haven of refuge for the millions of persecuted Jews but is the complete solution to the Jewish question."

(f) Jewish State Party "believes that the only solution of the age-old Jewish problem, the problem of a stateless minority, is the establishment of a Jewish commonwealth based on a Jewish majority within the historic boundaries of Palestine." Since it believes, further, that the Diaspora is being rapidly liquidated, it has only one ultimate aim, namely, "the reestablishment of the Jewish state."

(g) New Zionism (also called "Revisionism") envisages "Palestine as a Jewish state," on both sides of the Jordan, governed by a "Supreme Council of the Zionist Movement." This being its main task, New Zionism embodies "two principles" of world Jewish action: " 'evacuation' (of the doomed ghettos) and 'policy of alliances' (with those governments whose interests demand the establishment of the Jewish state)."

2. *Views of Other Organized Jewish Bodies on the Role of Palestine*

(a) The Reconstructionists consider a Jewish national home in Palestine as a prerequisite for the survival of the Jewish group, its complete emancipation and the continued development of its historic civilization. In Palestine "a sufficiently large community of Jews must be permitted to lead a full, normal and creative life. With the resulting enrichment of Judaism's cultural and spiritual content, Jews in the Diaspora will then feel themselves members of a minority group that possesses motivation, idea and purpose."

(b) The Rabbinical Assembly of America (Conservative) maintains that "the right of the Jewish people to Palestine as its national home, [is] indispensable to [its] national existence." "The Zionist ideal to establish in Palestine a legally assured and publicly recognized home for the Jewish people, is an integral part of the religious outlook as well as the program of practical activities sponsored by the Rabbinical Assembly of America."

(c) United Synagogue of America (Conservative) expresses its "firm belief that the survival of the Jewish people and their religion is linked with the future of Palestine . . . and [believes] that in Palestine the Jewish people can best fulfill their historic destiny."

(d) The Central Conference of American Rabbis (Reform) "declares that it discerns no essential incompatibility between Reform Judaism and Zionism, no reason why those of its members who give allegiance to Zionism should not have the right to regard themselves as fully within the spirit and purpose of Reform Judaism."

(e) The Union of American Hebrew Congregations (Reform) views the establishment of a Jewish homeland in Palestine as the fulfillment of "an unprecedented need of finding a permanent haven for so many uprooted Jews of Europe." It also recognizes "the fact that Jews have been bound by historic and spiritual ties to the Holy Land," and "that a large portion of Jewry is desperately in need of a friendly shelter and a home where a spiritual, cultural center may be developed in accordance with Jewish ideals."

(f) The American Jewish Committee affirms its "deep sympathy for and [the] desire to cooperate with those Jews who wish to settle in Palestine." It recognizes "that there are now more than half a million Jews in Palestine who have built up a sound and flourishing economic life and a satisfying spiritual and cultural life, and who now constitute substantially one third of the population, and that while this Palestinian immigrant has been a blessed amelioration of the condition of this large number of Jews, and has helped to bring about a great development of the country itself, settlement in Palestine although an important factor, cannot alone furnish and should not be expected to furnish the solution of the problem of postwar Jewish rehabilitation."

(g) The American Jewish Congress endorses the General Zionist view with regard to the role of Palestine in the life of the Jewish people.

(h) B'nai B'rith has always regarded Palestine in a practical light, as "a living, vital and productive community." In America, it has cooperated with the Jewish Agency and the Jewish National Fund in land purchase, colonization work, and the promotion of cultural institutions in Palestine. B'nai B'rith has expressed its "faith in the fulfillment of the Balfour Declaration, which gives assurance to Jews who choose Palestine as their homeland that they may dwell there and enjoy the blessings of life.

(i) A statement by 826 Rabbis [including 217 members of the Central Conference of American Rabbis (Reform); 253 members of the Rabbinical Assembly of America (Conservative); and 356 members of the Rabbinical Council of America (Orthodox) and the Union of Orthodox Rabbis] declares that

"Zionism is an affirmation of Judaism. . . . [It] is not a secularist movement. It has its origins and roots in the authoritative religious texts of Judaism. . . . Nor is Zionism a denial of
the universalistic teachings of Judaism. Universalism is not a
contradiction of nationalism." The political action of the Zionist movement, which culminated in the Balfour Declaration and
the Palestine mandate, has made it possible for half a million
Jews to settle in Palestine. Effective political action will also
be necessary in order to open the gates of Palestine for mass
Jewish immigration after the war.

3. Opposition to Zionism

There has been opposition to the Zionist movement among
Jews ever since its earliest proponents started discussing the return of the Jewish people to their ancient homeland by means
of organized human effort. Opponents to rebuilding Palestine
by "natural" means first were found among orthodox Rabbis
who, in arguing against men like Rabbi Zvi Hirsch Kalischer
(1861), Rabbi Samuel Mohilever, and other early Zionists,
claimed that it was contrary to the will of God to "force" the
redemption of the Holy Land before the coming of the Mes-
siah. Later, when the movement started to engage in practical
colonization in Palestine (1882) and formed an international
political organization—the World Zionist Congress (1897)—
the opposition grew in intensity, coming from various groups
and for different reasons.

In Western Europe, where Jewish emancipation had been
completed, some Jewish communal leaders held that the nationalist tendencies of Zionism would jeopardize the status of the
Jews in the countries in which they were citizens. They were
opposed to designating the Jews as a separate people, nation,
or nationality. They felt that such tendencies would give the
anti-Semites a pretext for segregating Jewish citizens from the
rest of the population. Nor did they consider Palestine as a
solution to the problem of refugees fleeing from Russia and
Rumania in the wake of anti-Jewish excesses in those countries.
Then the gates of the United States and other overseas asylums

were wide open, and the mass emigration of Jews was diverted to these lands. Orthodox Rabbis and lay leadership, both in Western and Eastern Europe, continued their opposition to Zionism not only on the ground that it was contrary to the Messianic hope of Jewish tradition, but also because of the secular political aspect which the movement assumed after the formation of the World Zionist Congress.

Disapprobation came, too, from other groups in Eastern Europe. These considered themselves Jewish nationalists, but were against establishing a Jewish national home or state in Palestine. They were Diaspora-Nationalists who, claiming Yiddish as their national language, sought to organize Jewish life in nationality units within the countries of the Diaspora (Jewish People's Party in Czarist Russia), while others (the Yiddish Territorialists) searched for a country other than Palestine where the Jews would build for themselves a territorial center. Other sources of disapproval were elements in the Jewish Socialist movement in Czarist Russia, especially the "General Alliance of Jewish Workers," known as the Bund (organized 1897), which considered the Zionist movement to be contrary to the interests of the workers' class. They thought the solution to the Jewish question was in a Socialist revolution.

Out of these developments, present day opposition to the Zionist movement still exists among many elements of orthodox Jewry, notably the Agudath Israel which though favoring now the upbuilding of Palestine along orthodox traditional lines, refuses to identify itself with the Zionist movement as such. Among the Jewish socialist groups, the Bund has retained its traditional stand against Zionism.

The expressions of opposition by Jewish Communists to the Zionist movement and the Palestine Yishub, have undergone several changes in form, although the general line has remained the same. Until recently, they opposed Zionism and Zionist settlement in Palestine, on the ground that they were inimical to the interests of the colonial peoples and the Jewish masses. They anticipated the solution of the Jewish problem by the world "social revolution." However, since the summer of 1941, the Communists have "recognized the Jewish community in Palestine as an important part of our people—a community which is building an organized national life in that part of the world." But they make no statement with regard to the future expansion of Jewish colonization there.

In the United States, Reform Rabbis and laymen were among the early opponents of the Zionist movement. However, their opposition diminished in the course of time and today there are many of them who are affiliated with Zionist organizations in America, taking a leading part in the movement. Yet, opposition is still maintained by a considerable number of Reform Rabbis who together with certain laymen have recently formed the American Council for Judaism, which aims "to combat nationalistic and secularist trends in Jewish life." Prior to the formation of this Council ninety reform Rabbis issued a statement presenting their views with regard to Zionism and Palestine as follows:

> Realizing how dear Palestine is to the Jewish soul, and how important Palestinian rehabilitation is towards relieving the pressing problems of our distressed people, we stand ready to render unstinted aid to our brethren in their economic, cultural and spiritual endeavors in that country. But in the light of our universalistic interpretation of Jewish history and destiny, and also because of our concern for the welfare and status of the Jewish people living in other parts of the world, we are unable to subscribe to or support the political emphasis now paramount in the Zionist program. We cannot but believe that Jewish nationalism tends to confuse our fellowmen about our place and function in society and also diverts our own attention from our historic role to live as a religious community wherever we may dwell. Such spiritual role is especially voiced by Reform Judaism in its emphasis upon the eternal prophetic principles of life and thought, principles through which alone Judaism and the Jew can hope to endure and bear witness to the universal God.

Opposition to Zionism also comes from many individual Jews who dissociate themselves from organized Jewish life, though some of them are active in Jewish philanthropy. Their opposition, which is not organized, stems either from indifference to Jewish survival or from a denial of the need to perpetuate the Jewish group and its distinctive character.

MOTIVES BEHIND THE BALFOUR DECLARATION [2]

Since England first occupied India the basis of English political strategy has been the consolidation of her control over that country. India could not be allowed to have common boundaries with regions under the control of any other European power. For that reason Great Britain constituted herself protectress of Turkey, "the Sick Man of Europe" at a time when Turkey seemed destined for disintegration, and the European powers were preparing to divide the booty of Turkey's gigantic Asiatic possessions. Not Turkey, but Czarist Russia was England's enemy. When Russia in 1853 demanded that Turkey accept her as guardian of the Christians within her borders and the holy places in Palestine it became clear to Great Britain that Russia was pressing on to India, and would have to be fought.

All the military conflicts among the European powers in the nineteenth century revolved about the drive to the treasure of Asia, but two great events radically altered the entire course of Britain's strategy. They were the construction of the Suez Canal and the emergence of Germany as a first-class capitalistic power.

The Suez Canal was the most important waterway ever built. According to some authorities it created the most important revolution in the history of humanity since the discovery of America. The Suez Canal made England the greatest Empire in the world. Napoleon with his prophetic eye had foreseen that Egypt and Suez would be the vital points in the struggle for world domination. Hoping to deal England a death blow, he had marched on Egypt in 1793 and at the same time had planned to build the Suez Canal. But he had neither the time nor the means to carry out his plans. It remained for the British to realize his dreams.

Palestine may now be considered even more important than Egypt in Britain's Mediterranean policy, for she has become the terminus of the land and air routes to India. Significant is the

[2] By A. S. Lyrique, for many years leading columnist on the Warsaw *Heini*; authority on the Jewish question. *Jewish Mirror*. 1:11-17. D. '42-Ja. '43.

fact that Haifa is connected with Suez by railroad and is also the terminus of a railroad line traversing Transjordan and Iraq on the way to Bagdad. Haifa promises to be even more important, for England has nearly completed construction of a gigantic encircling railroad line from Capetown to Cairo, to Haifa, to Bagdad, to India. It is intended to protect the sea and land routes from India and Africa. Palestine is a link in the great chain of the Empire and it is thus easy to understand why she has shifted to the center of the stage of world politics.

Why, therefore, did Great Britain present the Jews with the Balfour Declaration? Why promise them a "national home" in Palestine? Great Britain's actual aims have been the subject of contention between the Zionist movement and successive British governments. Sharp disagreement exists to this day among the British themselves as to the correct interpretation of the phrase "national home." Did it mean a Jewish state, or merely free Jewish immigration into Palestine and that only as a minority? The disagreements are not merely a matter of theoretical or juridical discussion, but are part of a bitter political struggle still far from being concluded.

In July 1937, in the heat of the Arab riots, a government commission arrived in Palestine. It was appointed to investigate the situation, to hear the claims of Jews and Arabs, and to work out a "final" solution for this perplexing problem which had already cost much blood.

Lord Peel, a very clever statesman, presided over the commission. A well-informed specialist in Palestinian problems, he frequently upset addresses with his remarks showing up contradictions in the testimony of witnesses, and even at times the inadequacy of their knowledge. This caused Jews to regard him with suspicion, but the thick volume of the Commission's report turned out to be a pleasant surprise. It abounded in praise of the Jewish accomplishments, and displayed considerable understanding and sympathy for the Jewish plight.

In this report, too, it seems to me, you find the best and most impartial reply to the question: What is the intention of the Balfour Declaration?

The fact that the Balfour Declaration of 1917 was published in order to win over Jewish support for the cause of the Allies and the

Jews actually did supply such support is a matter that the Arabs understand very little. Neither do the Arabs appear to comprehend that the present state of the Arab world is in every way due to the sacrifices which the Allies and their supporters made during that period. Nor do the Arabs grasp the truth which is that the *Balfour Declaration, insofar as it aided the Allied victory, also helped to free the Arab lands from Turkish sovereignty* (italics ours). Had the Turks and their Allies, the Germans, won, it is hardly possible that the Arab lands would have become independent countries. . . .

And now we must consider the intent of the Balfour Declaration. We have studied all the protocols dealing with the questions and it is clear to us that the phrase "to establish a national home in Palestine" was the result of a compromise between those ministers who wished to create a Jewish state, and those who opposed it. In any event, it is clear that the English Government could not clearly come out for a Jewish state. She could only pledge herself to facilitate the creation of a Jewish national home. Whether that home would be large enough later to evolve into a Jewish state would depend upon the energy and achievements of the Jews themselves.

Lloyd George, the wartime Prime Minister has stated:

It was our idea, and this interpretation is most pertinent, that a Jewish state must not be founded immediately at the conclusion of the war against the wishes of the majority of the inhabitants of the country, but on the other hand, we thought: If in time Palestine should receive a constitution of her own, and if at that time the Jews should have made full use of the opportunity for a national home in such a manner that they shall have become a responsible majority, then Palestine will become a Jewish state.

This was the thought of the British Government at the time; that the Jewish state was to be established in the future, although the British Government was not to create it. However, it was clear that the terms of the mandate called for cooperation on the part of the British Government, particularly in making possible "close settlement of Jews on the land."

This is confirmed by a statement of President Wilson made on March 3rd, 1919. He said: "I am convinced, that the Allied governments, with the full concurrence of our government and our people, are agreed that the foundation for a Jewish state will be laid in Palestine." General Smuts, who was a member of the war cabinet at the time of the Declaration, declared in a speech in Johannesburg on the third of November, 1919 that "a stream of Jewish migration will soon be flowing into Palestine and in the course of time a great Jewish state will be created there." Lord Robert Cecil, Lord Samuel, and Winston Churchill wrote or spoke in the same tenor.

The Zionist ideal—the founding of a Jewish commonwealth in Palestine—has been for centuries part of Jewish tradition. Since the days of Cromwell and the visit of Menasseh ben Israel to England the idea has persisted among the British reared in the Biblical tradition. At every European conference in the nineteenth century there have been Britishers who pressed the claim of the Jews to Palestine. In 1838 Lord Shaftsbury presented to his government a plan of Jewish colonization in Palestine, and a year later a group of Englishmen presented another petition of like import. Queen Victoria expressed her sympathy; Gordon and Kitchener in their day were at least semi-Zionists. In 1925 Lloyd George gave interesting expression to the attitude of the British people as a whole. He said: "We gained a basic education in the history of your (the Jewish) race in its golden age when the Jews produced those wonderful books which have influenced and educated human character and awakened humane ideas not only among the Jews, but among non-Jews as well, and through which we were nurtured on all that is best in the Christian character. Such being the case, your appeals fell upon responsive ears." The Peel Commission in its report emphasized the fact that the Zionist ideals had this moral basis in English tradition.

The Balfour Declaration, however, was presented from more than idealistic motives. It is certain the British wished to win over Jewish sentiment to their cause, regarding their support of high practical and moral importance.

What the statesmen intended to do is quite clear. On the 17th of February 1919 the Zionist leaders, Weizmann, Sokolow, Ussishkin, were received by the peace conference, which they addressed and upon which they made a profound impression. In reply to a question put by the Secretary of State Robert Lansing, Weizmann said: "By a Jewish national home we mean the creation of such conditions in Palestine as will make it possible to settle from fifty to sixty thousand Jews yearly. We wish to develop our own schools, our own institutions and the Hebrew language. Finally, we wish to create such conditions as will make Palestine as Jewish as America is American and England English." The Zionist leaders had previously advised with the representatives of Great Britain and there was an agreement with them on the Jewish demands to be presented at the conference. Weizmann weighed and measured every word, and his reply to Lansing's question was the result of this previous understanding. The official report of that session quotes Lord Balfour as being "very pleased." Nor did any section of the Balfour press express the slightest dissatisfaction with the interpretation of the Balfour Declaration by the Jewish delegation.

Immediately after the conclusion of the war there was a state of great moral enthusiasm. There was still hope in the creation of a better and finer world in which justice would prevail, for the great and the little peoples alike. At such a moment the ideal of the Jewish state was accepted everywhere, and Weizmann's statement about Palestine becoming as Jewish as America was American did not disturb anyone, not even the American delegates. As Rabbi Wise relates in an article on the new Palestine, President Wilson always felt a deep sympathy for Zionist aims.

But the enthusiasm wore off after a while. There was no unity among the victorious nations. The Zionists, too, soon saw that there would be a long road from the dream to reality. There were too few Jews in Palestine to constitute a Jewish state, and responsible leaders came to the conclusion that this must come about only through gradual development. In 1922 came the Churchill White Paper by the terms of which Transjordan was cut off from Western Palestine. Its acceptance was forced down the throats of the Zionist executives. Nevertheless Weizmann insisted: "We must place our faith in the good will of England; otherwise we shall accomplish nothing."

The fact is that every British Government during the last 25 years has reaffirmed the Balfour Declaration and despite the fact that many Zionist illusions have been shattered during the last 25 years about one-half million Jews have entered Palestine during this period. Without England's consent this would have been impossible. . . .

According to informed opinion the importance of Palestine to Great Britain will be greater than ever, not only because of the use of Haifa as a great naval base but also because Palestine must be the outlet for the sea commerce between India and the Far East. More than ever will Great Britain need a friendly Palestine and it is not likely that even the need of Arab appeasement will create a desire to antagonize the Jews. Several hundred thousand Jews in a country as poor and small as Palestine are a great power with which they will have to reckon. . . .

Some years ago Oxford University issued an interesting brochure on Palestine, written by Dr. James Parker—not a Zionist. In it Dr. Parker says:

To understand the situation in Palestine, one must remember that the entire English policy there hinges on the conflict between the Arabs and the Jews. But, in reality, this conflict is not the expression of a struggle between two nations, but of a struggle between the East and the West. The Jews are Europeans; their standard of living is European; their achievements in Palestine are the result of a technical knowledge based on European and American science. On the other hand, the Arabs are still Orientals, their development proceeds slowly; they live their lives out in blind religious fanaticism, and are fearful that free intercourse with Jews will necessarily leave them the weaker, conquered people. Were the question merely political, one might hesitate for a solution, for the wise Solon has not yet risen to arbitrate the Arab-Jewish conflict. But politics are still not the only consideration, not even in our times, times of chauvinistic nationalism. To understand the future of Palestine one must remember what the Jews have already attained in the course of twenty years regardless of the great difficulties and bloodshed.

The enemies and opponents of Zionism may criticize and find fault, but the Jews can justly reply: Consider the human material with which we have had to work—people from Eastern Europe, middle class, middle aged urbanites. Has anyone excelled us in results? Yet other pioneers received free land, while we have been forced to pay dearly for every foot of ground—often far more than its real value. And yet we made great progress not only in colonization, but also in industry. The Dead Sea alone is now the greatest source for potash and bromide in the world, sufficient to cover the needs of the entire world for the next 5,000 years.

The Jews in Palestine have overcome many economic crises, political conflicts, bitter disappointments. The fact that, in a single year recently, Palestinian economy has been able to absorb a hundred thousand immigrants is the best proof that its economy can adapt itself to any condition and stand firm. Palestine is now becoming the center of a world movement. It is only in its beginnings; it has a remarkable future. It will be the splendid function of the Jews to become spiritually and materially, the mediators between the East and West.

THE CREED OF AN AMERICAN ZIONIST [3]

A generation ago the native-born, homebred American Zionist was a *rara avis* indeed. Some few of the species were about, men of insight and courage—Louis D. Brandeis, for example. But most American Jews were altogether indifferent to the Zionist program. And as for the rabbinate, only the Reform branch was articulate at the time, and that was anti-Zionist almost to the last man.

Now, three decades later, there are still many Jewish anti-Zionists, among them men and women of intelligence and sincerity. . . . When ninety rabbis recently issued an anti-Zionist pronouncement, almost nine hundred rabbis joined in repudiating it. Witness the fact that the Central Conference of American Rabbis—representative of the Reform ministry and once the fountainhead of anti-Zionism—has of late consistently voted pro-Zionist by approximately two to one. Let the American Jewish Conference speak—an assembly of five hundred delegates, appointed one quarter by all important national Jewish organizations, and elected three quarters by popular vote. That body went on record, with only *four* dissenting ballots, in favor of a Jewish homeland and commonwealth in Palestine. And whereas a generation ago anti-Zionists were anti-Zionists with-

[3] By Milton Steinberg, Rabbi of the Park Avenue Synagogue, New York City; author of *The Making of the Modern Jew,* and other works. *Atlantic Monthly.* 175:101-5. February 1945.

out qualification, they tend these days to be anti-Zionist but "pro-Palestinian."

What has happened to the Jews of America in all their varieties and conditions? Have they, as has been suggested, yielded to counsels of desperation? Have they succumbed to the wild chauvinism now sweeping mankind? It would be a most unusual madness that could unhinge so many Jews of deep religious convictions and broad human perspectives. Besides, Jewish chauvinism could scarcely fire non-Jews into incandescence—non-Jews like Jan Smuts, Reinhold Niebuhr, Wendell Willkie, Dorothy Thompson, Henry Wallace, and Walter Clay Lowdermilk.

No, the great transformation in the attitude toward Zionism is neither aberration nor despair. It reflects simply the cogency and practicality of the Zionist idea. What is that idea? Put tersely and in the idiom of official documents, it is that a politically secured, legally recognized Jewish homeland be established in Palestine, in which Jews who so elect may settle as of right; and that this homeland become ultimately a Jewish commonwealth. As for the practicality and cogency of the idea, let me present it as it appears to a typical American Zionist—myself.

Perhaps I ought begin by clearing the ground of a stubborn misconception. It is not true that I am a Zionist because I am not content to be an American, or because I doubt America's future. This land, I am deeply convinced, is on its way to new horizons of freedom and justice. In other words, it is not the fact that, pessimistic about the Jewish prospect in America, I have one eye cocked on Palestine—just in case. And I am no less sanguine about the future of democracy elsewhere. I make this point so explicitly because it has been bruited about by some Jews that to be a Zionist is to be compromised in Americanism and deficient in democratic faith. On behalf of hundreds of thousands of American Jews who, like myself, are Zionists, I wish to affirm that these grave allegations represent, at the best, ignorance and, at the worst, slander.

In part I am a Zionist because of the record of Zionist accomplishment. Inspired by the Zionist ideal, supported by

Zionist funds, operating under conditions made possible by Zionist political effort, thousands of Jews migrated from Europe to Palestine and there set about incarnating an ancient dream. It was from many points of view a grotesque enterprise to which they committed their lives. They were told that the whole business was superfluous—Jews in the West being already free and in Eastern Europe on their way to emancipation; that an emigrant from the Old World had the whole globe open to him; that Palestine was an arid, backward country where Jews could not survive, let alone be creative; and that in any case it could absorb no more than a handful of settlers. Discouraged from all sides, grappling with heartbreaking difficulties, these Jews accomplished the impossible.

What an achievement is theirs! In one generation they built a community of almost 600,000 persons, free and self-reliant. Out of ghetto alleys they took Jews who had lost all rapport with soil and workshop, and made them into farmers, mechanics, sailors, and fishermen. They caused the desert to blossom and sand dunes to hum with the myriad sounds of cities. They evoked a great flowering of Hebraic culture—the greatest perhaps in two millennia. They experimented boldly and idealistically in new forms of social living, in cooperatives, collectives, and communes. They introduced modernity and democracy into the Near East, awakening it from its immemorial medievalism.

When liberty stood with its back to the wall, they rallied to its defense. About 35,000 of them enlisted in the British military forces—the equivalent proportionately of an American volunteer army of seven millions. From their farms they helped to feed Allied armies; in their upstart factories they forged or repaired military matériel. And meantime they gave refuge in ten years to 280,000 of their brethren, who otherwise would now be dead to the last soul.

This is a superb record, achieved, be it remembered by Zionists, not even by pussyfooting "pro-Palestinians." Of and by itself it constitutes a compelling Zionist case. And yet I cannot claim it as the ground of my conviction. For, truth to tell, I was of my present persuasion before that record was achieved. Which brings me to the core of my case.

I am a Zionist in the first place because I am a religious Jew. From my Judaism I have derived a God faith, an ethical code, personal and social, a pattern of observances, but also, interwoven with these, a love for Palestine and the yearning that at least a part of the House of Israel be restored to its soil. That aspiration is written deep in the Bible. It is inscribed boldly in the whole rabbinic tradition, ancient and medieval. And it pervades Jewish ritual. My religious heritage, then, makes me a Zionist.

Does this sound unrealistic? We shall soon see that it is not without common sense. But since at the moment I am in peril of being hanged as a sheep, let me be bold enough to perish as a wolf. Let me confess to an even wilder vision, to the historic confidence of the Jewish religion that something is destined to come out of the reassociation of Israel with Palestine. Twice this people struck foot on its ancestral soil and wonderful events occurred. The first time, prophetism came into being; the second, Rabbinic Judaism, Christianity, and the foreshadowing of Islam. I should be less than candid if I did not admit to a high expectation concerning the third encounter—an expectation of new instruction coming out of Zion, of some fresh word of God sounding in Jerusalem.

But my thinking on Zionism is not altogether so high-flown. I advocate Zionism as the most immediate and practicable answer to a vast, terrible, and very tangible need. Long ago, in the halcyon days of the nineteenth century, Herzl and his associates already perceived the incipient pressures of political reaction, economic constriction, and psychic mass embitterment. They foretold that brute powers might bring down in ruins the centuries-old edifices of European Jewry. They pleaded that, against the evil hour, the Jews should prepare a homeland of their own.

And has not the Old World House of Israel been trampled into blood-drenched splinters? And in all the grim devastation, does not Jewish Palestine shine as a joy-bringing, hope-dispensing beacon? What is more, the need of a haven of refuge will in the future be more, not less, acute.

No Jew, no Zionist, no person of good will and democratic persuasion, can tolerate the thought of any Jew's being denied residence and equality of status in the land of his birth or citizenship. For this objective, among others, the present great war is being waged. The continued abuse of Jews in Europe would mock our professions and sacrifices alike. As I have already intimated, I have warm hopes for the future peace and security of Jews who elect to remain in the Old World. For a time, until mankind returns to sanity and the democratic spirit reroots itself, the United Nations may have to guarantee the rights of all minorities. But in the not too distant future, I expect, every European, regardless of creed or origin, will sit under his own vine and fig tree, and none shall make him afraid.

And yet there will be thousands of Jewish survivors for whom a return to former scenes will be impossible. First, anti-Semitism will not immediately vanish from Central and Eastern Europe. Again, there are those whose last roots have been severed. No person, synagogue, household, or occupation will remain to draw them back. And for still others the very word *home* will be surcharged with unbearably painful recollections. Those who want to go elsewhere must have the full right.

And where, one asks, are they to turn? In the earliest days of Hitlerism, the Evian Conference demonstrated that no government wanted homeless Jews. Now, what with World War II, with demobilization, reconversion, and the dread of mass unemployment, immigration barriers almost certainly will go up, not down. As for undeveloped areas, the earth has been combed for possible havens for Jews. The result—next to nothing. Each suggested territory, it turned out, was either already overpopulated, or unsuited for colonization by Europeans, or closed by political considerations. And all suffered from a common disadvantage—years would be required to prepare them for mass colonization. Meantime, what are the homeless Jews of the world to do with themselves?

I would not be misunderstood. In proposing Palestine as the focus of Jewish migration I do not debar other sites. The position of European Jews is so tragic that they can no doubt use many centers of resettlement. I do mean that we must not lose the bird in the hand for any in the bush. Palestine is assigned by international covenant to large-scale Jewish settlement. It is ready now, without the spadework necessary else-where. Jews *want* to go there—no trivial consideration. Witness how before the war they clamored for visas; witness further the preferences expressed by refugees in Italy.

The country, small though it is, is large enough. It now has a population of about a million and three quarters. How many more can it accommodate? In the first century of our era, according to historians like Baron and Schürer, it contained anywhere from 2,500,000 to 4,000,000 human beings, and that without modern agriculture and industry. In our one genera-tion it has absorbed a half-million Jews, and the saturation point is not even remotely in sight.

What is the maximum? Estimates vary. A group of Jew-ish authorities hold: "Palestine should be capable of absorbing another three million inhabitants." But these are Jews speak-ing; their pleading may be *ex parte*. Consider then the con-clusions of Walter Clay Lowdermilk, Chief of the Soil Con-servation Service of the United States Department of Agricul-ture. After a long study, he has decided that the country is capable of receiving *four million* immigrants beyond its present population. Let us cut his estimate in half. Six years ago, what remains might not have been equal to the needs of Euro-pean Jews. Today, alas, it will suffice.

But I am impelled to Zionism by a more personal considera-tion, by the needs of my own spirit. No tradition can coast along merely on past momentum. Every religion and culture must for its health be constantly regenerated with new elements fashioned after its genius but stamped in the mold of the day. Now, though Judaism is extraordinarily rich in accumulated resources, it too requires infusions of the fresh, novel, and con-temporaneous. Yet it is everywhere a minority religion and culture; even its most devoted adherents expend themselves mainly in the larger civilization. To Judaism they come with the remainder of their time and energy. But people are not normally creative under such circumstances, as the state of Judaism demonstrates. Hence there must be a place where Hebraism will be a first culture, where it can flourish without hindrance, and whence transfusions of new values may emanate.

Nor is this abstruse verbiage. The brilliant renaissance in Palestine, the revival there of Jewish music, art, letters, folkways, the theater, and the Hebrew tongue have invigorated, stimulated, and enriched every Jewry in the world. That too is why I am a Zionist; because, while I would remain a Jew without Jewish Palestine, my Judaism, by virtue of it, is more meaningful to me and my Jewish fellows.

There are other reasons for my Zionism, over which I cannot pause: the contribution it has made to Jewish self-respect at a time when so many forces conspire to break it down; the promise inherent in the social experiments afoot in the Jewish homeland. But tempting as such themes are, I must forgo them to deal with another matter closer to our line of inquiry: How, if all I have said is true, can any Jew be anti-Zionist?

In posing this question I do not have in mind dejudaized Jews, indifferentists, escapists, or psychic rebels against being Jewish. Such negative Jews will all be anti-Zionist. I mean, how can informed professing Jews resist Zionism?

Differing conceptions of the nature of Judaism and the Jewish identity—here is the continental divide where Zionists and non-Zionists part. To the non-Zionists, Judaism is purely a religion, the Jews members of a church. Hence notions of a homeland and commonwealth are altogether inappropriate.

But is this definition valid? Obviously not. For, if it were, no Jew could be irreligious and remain a Jew. And yet there are atheists, agnostics, and skeptics who consider themselves, and are universally considered, Jews. Even some of the leading American anti-Zionists, who are most insistent that Judaism is a communion only, neither profess nor pray, feast not on festivals and fast not on days of penance. A pretty paradox! For how can they be Jews by virtue of a faith they do not possess?

Incontrovertibly, religion is a motif in Jewish living—the major motif, I should say. But other elements are involved also. Race, anthropologically speaking, is certainly not one of these. A culture is. Present in the Jewish patrimony are a large literature, secular as well as sacred, music, folklore, art, mores, and institutions. But many a modern Jew acknowledges the culture no more than the faith, and is yet subjectively and objectively a Jew. Something more remains. That plus is a social identity. It consists in the fact that Jews are a historic entity, an organic group sharing memories, interests, and hopes; that they are in sum a *people*.

The first error of the anti-Zionist is that he misconstrues Judaism. He blunders again for lack of imagination. It escapes him that other Jews live in scenes different from his, and that circumstances alter cases. America is a uni-national and, except for secondary cultures, a uni-cultural land. Judaism here naturally takes the form of a religio-cultural entity. But Poland, Rumania, and the Soviet Union are composed of many peoples, cultures, and nationalities. There Jews also constitute in law and public opinion a *nationality* body.

As for Palestine, there the Jews are a nation in maturation. Being a people as well as a communion, why should Israel not take on various forms with various settings? With these actualities the American anti-Zionist refuses to make peace. He will not allow other Jewries any status but his own. Having misinterpreted Judaism, he compounds his fallacy by generalizing it. Willy-nilly, all other Jews must be what he is, exclusively a member of a sect.

But would not Jewish "nationality" status in Eastern Europe, and especially a Jewish commonwealth in Palestine, affect the political obligations of American Jews? Would Jews not owe allegiance to the Jewish homeland? Did the establishment of Norway or Eire as a self-governing state modify by a hair's breadth the relation of Irish or Norse Americans to America? The American Jew has only one political duty: to America. To Palestine he will be bound by ties of religion, sentiment, and culture, as other Americans are so often related to their lands of origin. But whatever Palestine is or may become, the American Jew remains an American citizen, knowing no political sovereignty save the American.

The anti-Zionist is troubled further lest Zionism contravene the great universalistic motif of Judaism, its glorious doctrine of the primacy of mankind over individual, clan, and nation, its historic ministry as a "kingdom of priests and a holy nation." Is not all this ado about culture, commonwealth, and peoplehood a retreat from the advanced position so long and so nobly maintained? Does not Zionism constrict the wide horizons of the Jewish spirit?

To which my response is that over objectives there is no dispute among us. Where we differ is on method. Anti-Zionists seem to feel that Jewry does best by mankind when it suppresses all distinctiveness except in religion. Zionists hold that Jews can give more to the world by developing their peculiar heritage to the full, provided always that the heart is firmly set on the service of all humanity. This position I accept, first because it is sanctioned by the very prophets who conceived universalism. As Scripture testifies, they loved mankind and the world, but Israel and Zion also, loving them for themselves, and as witnesses to God's Kingdom. Besides, I cannot see how either an individual or a group, possessed of talents, benefits anyone by being less itself. To me the indicated course would appear self-cultivation dedicated to the overarching ideal.

But Judaism, religion and culture alike, needs Jewish Palestine for its fulfillment. Wherefore considerations of universalism, far from negating Zionism, endorse it. For only when enriched and stimulated by a Jewish homeland will Jewry be equal to its destiny.

Anti-Zionists, last of all, exhibit a distaste for certain words. It was Thomas Hobbes who, anticipating semantics, pointed out that words are counters, not coins; that the wise man looks through them to reality. This counsel many anti-Zionists seem to have neglected. They are especially disturbed by the two nouns *nationalism* and *commonwealth,* and by the adjective *political.* And yet these terms on examination are not at all upsetting.

Jewish nationalism means no more than recognition of the peoplehood of Israel, and of the propriety of that people's being a religio-cultural group in America, a nationality in Eastern Europe, and in Palestine an actualized nation.

Nor is the word *political* more horrendous, even when it precedes *Zionism.* For what does it signify? It refers either to methods for realizing the Zionist objective or to the objective itself. If to the former, it denotes the World Zionist Organization, the Jewish Agency for Palestine, and their transactions with the Mandatory Power and others on immigration into Palestine and related problems. If this be *political* Zionism, what can be wrong with it? Anyone wishing Jews to be free to enter Palestine knows that governments must be dealt with and understandings negotiated. Or are there some so naïve as to approve of results but not of the only means for attaining them?

Or is the *politics* in Zionism against which anti-Zionists protest a matter of ends? Is their objection leveled against the ultimate establishment of a Jewish *commonwealth* in Palestine?

If so, let it be noted first that when organized Zionism supplanted its traditional slogan, a "Jewish state," with the formula, a "Jewish commonwealth," it made its program pliable, adaptable to future circumstance. *State* is a very precise concept with clear connotations of unrestricted political sovereignty. A *commonwealth*, on the other hand, can be a state or a dominion or a locally autonomous unit within a federation. The Zionist proposal then is that Jews, when conditions are ripe, be accorded some as yet unspecified type of self-determination. And can any request be more reasonable? If Jewish immigration into Palestine continues, as it must, the Jews some day will constitute the preponderant element in the population. Shall they, just because they are Jews, be forever denied the act or hope of autonomy?

But why do Zionists press their political goals? Why not simply allow immigration to continue? Because without the commonwealth formula there will be no further immigration! On May 17, 1939, Britain issued the notorious White Paper that first repudiated its obligation to establish a Jewish commonwealth, and then, once that was out of the way, limited all future Jewish immigration to 75,000. That policy, the misbegotten child of Chamberlain appeasement, was denounced in Parliament by persons as diverse as Josiah Wedgwood, Sir Archibald Sinclair, the Archbishop of Canterbury, and Herbert Morrison. Winston Churchill called it bluntly "a breach of faith." It was castigated by the Permanent Mandates Commission of the League of Nations. It has contributed to the death of thousands of Jews. So it has engendered the bitterness that recently breached with acts of terrorism the splendid, long-sustained self-discipline of Palestine Jewry. Still it stands. And if it continues to stand, an intolerable paradox will come into being: Palestine, the land assigned by international agreement for Jewish settlement, will be open to all immigrants except Jews.

On what ground is the White Paper assailed? As inhumane? Only in part. After all, Palestine has done its philanthropic share for the Jews. The real bases for protest are public covenants, notably the Balfour Declaration and the Mandate. And these as interpreted by Balfour, Wilson, Lloyd George, and Churchill boil down to a commitment for a Jewish commonwealth in Palestine. This pledge is the writ by virtue of which the abrogation of the White Paper may rightfully be demanded, the lease whereby homeless Jews claim entrance to the land. It is Jewry's *locus standi* in its crucial cause now hanging in the balance. At all times it must be presented in evidence before the bar of humanity's conscience.

One question remains: Where does this leave the Arabs of Palestine? Does it not entail the gravest injustice, moral and physical, to them? Arab-Jewish relationships in Palestine are complex, far too tangled for proper presentation here. But let me at least indicate the chapter headings of the Zionist view on the matter.

First, I think we ought look at the record. What has been the effect of Jewish immigration and achievement on Palestinian Arabs? Whereas in near-by Moslem lands populations have remained static, in Palestine Arab numbers have soared from 664,000 in 1918 to over a million at present. This increase has been due in part to the better living conditions, to the modern hygiene, and to the advanced agriculture Jews have introduced. But in addition Arabs by the thousands have been immigrating into Palestine from all Near Eastern countries. Jewish enterprise has made the land one of promise for them as well as for Jews. Further, the value of Arab industry in Palestine quadrupled between 1922 and 1937, the area of land under cultivation increased by over 50 per cent. Even Arab culture has benefited. Thanks to the taxes paid by Jews, the country has been able to maintain educational facilities such as would otherwise have been impossible.

Nor is there any reality to the notion that Arabs have been driven from the soil. That charge, once noised about widely, is heard no more—at least not in responsible circles. For when the British Government went looking for Arabs made "landless" by Jews, it sought everywhere but found only a corporal's guard. And of these, many had been tenant farmers who had been compensated but had preferred not to invest their reimbursement in farms. But how is this possible? Much of the ground occupied by Jews was not only uncultivated hitherto: it was classed as uncultivable. No one lived where now Tel Aviv stands, and almost no one in the recently drained Huleh Swamps, or in the once malaria-infested valley of Esdraelon. Again, where land under cultivation has been purchased, a portion of it has been given to its former tenants, who, freed from the sharecropper's lot, now get along better than ever.

But if the Arab has not only not been hurt but even helped, why his fierce resistance? In the first place, that opposition is less universal than is supposed. Of what there is, some is the class interest of rich landowners and urban employers of Arab labor whose feudal grandeur is being threatened. Some reflects the natural resentment of any populace over the entrance into its midst of new elements. Some echoes Axis agitation, propaganda, and bribery. Some reflects the weakness of the mandatory administration. But much of it—perhaps most—is straightforward, unexceptionable nationalism. The Palestinian Arabs know that but for the Jews they would some day enjoy autonomy. Now at the best they will have to share political authority with another group; and should Jewish migration continue, they will in the end occupy a minority position. This is a real, in fact *the* real, grievance.

In sum, two legitimate ideals have come into conflict in Palestine. Two peoples are attached to the land. Both have deep aspirations concerning it.

Quite clearly, as Reinhold Niebuhr once put it, neither perfect satisfaction nor perfect justice can be rendered to both sides.

The best to be hoped for is the greater justice, the minimal wrong.

What are the alternatives? One is the freezing of Jewish Palestine in its present dimensions and, if the former Grand Mufti and King Ibn Saud have their way, even the expulsion of the Jews now in the land. The other is the continuance of Jewish immigration, the achieving of a Jewish majority, the establishment of a Jewish commonwealth. In this commonwealth all Arab rights, religious, cultural, economic, civic and political, whether individual or group, would be guaranteed. Arabs would of course vote and hold office, conduct their own school system, follow their own culture and faith.

Now, how do these prospects stack up against each other?

As to urgency: On one side the Palestinian Arabs, injured not a whit, are denied only a political aspiration. On the other side are Jews by the millions to whom entrance to Palestine is truly a matter of survival.

In terms of *Realpolitik*: Which is the safer solution, a Jewish minority in an Arab majority, or an Arab minority in Palestine protected by guarantees and backed up by a deep Arab hinterland?

In the broader view: Has not the Arab world as a whole vast territories on which to realize political autonomy? Is not Palestine a mere 5 per cent of that world? Are not the 95 per cent, often without effort on their part, achieving independence? As for Israel, where else can it incarnate fully its peoplehood and culture?

With still wider vision: Jewish Palestine is the outpost in the Near East of modernity and democracy. Will not the prospect of the entire area be brighter if the Jewish settlement continues to grow?

And for the advantage of universal humanity: The most that mankind can expect from the Arab prospectus is the establishment of another Arab state. The Zionist program means the salvaging of lives, the rebirth of Hebraic culture, the promise of a progressive Jewish Palestine for the Levant and the world, and, let it not be forgotten for a moment, the solution of the centuries-old and otherwise insoluble problem of Jewish home-lessness.

There is, I repeat, an Arab case. But not in anguish, urgency, or import does it begin to equal the Jewish.

How, in conclusion, do I as an American Jew and Zionist envisage the future of Jews and of Judaism in the emerging world? I see a society in which all men are free, politically, economically, culturally, spiritually. I see Jewries at ease and secure in the various lands of their residence, devoted citizens of these lands, and at the same time the bearers and the transmit-ters of a living Hebraism, significant to them and to the world. And I see in Palestine a Jewish commonwealth where the homeless Jews of the world shall have found rest; where the Jewish spirit shall have been reborn; whence shall flow to the Jewries of the Dispersion inspiration and the stuffs on which it feeds.

This dream has been spoken to me in almost every syllable of the religious tradition I cherish. It represents a desperate need, physical and spiritual, for world Jewry. It is fraught with infinite promise for Israel and mankind.

THE CASE FOR A JEWISH COMMONWEALTH IN PALESTINE [4]

In facing the postwar world, the problem of the surviving remnant of uprooted, dispossessed European Jewry cries for a constructive, permanent solution. All are, of course, agreed that those Jews who may desire to remain in or to return to their former dwelling places should be guaranteed their elementary rights of citizenship. But what of those who are unwilling to live as members of a tolerated minority in an atmosphere of hatred, despite paper guarantees of equality? And what of those Jews, wherever they may dwell, who long for freedom and security in that national homeland promised the Jewish people at the end of the First World War?

    [4] By Louis E. Levinthal, Vice President, American Association of Jewish Edu-cation; Author of *Credo of an American Zionist*, and other works. *Annals of the American Academy*. 240:89-98. July 1945.

The Zionists urge that the United Nations declare now that Palestine shall as soon as practicable be established as a free and democratic Jewish commonwealth. They ask that in the meantime large-scale Jewish immigration and colonization be facilitated, and that the Jewish Agency for Palestine be enabled to increase the economic absorptive capacity of the country so that the Jews may speedily become the majority of the population and thus constitute Palestine as their commonwealth, in which all the inhabitants, regardless of race or faith, shall enjoy equal rights.

That this is precisely what is meant by a Jewish commonwealth has been clearly set forth by an authoritative Zionist spokesman who testified last year in support of the Wright-Compton Resolution before the Committee on Foreign Affairs of the House of Representatives:

By a Jewish commonwealth we certainly do not mean a state which is exclusively Jewish. . . . If, then, we are asked what do we mean by the adjective "Jewish" as applied to the future Commonwealth of Palestine, my answer is that it is a short and abbreviated way of saying that through the repatriation of large numbers of European and other Jews the Jewish people will attain a numerical majority in Palestine and thereby permanently guarantee the open door for others who may follow; so that Palestine shall never cease to serve as a sanctuary and homeland for any and all Jews, from whatever part of the world, who may choose to go there in the future. . . . The development of this Jewish commonwealth shall take place under democratic institutions and in a democratic spirit. . . . Jew and Arab devoted to their respective cultures and traditions shall cooperate as free and equal citizens and jointly contribute to the prosperity and welfare of a common single unitary state. The Arab citizens of the Jewish commonwealth will be as favorably situated as are the French-speaking citizens of the British Dominion of Canada. It will be a free and democratic Jewish state composed of Jews, Moslems, Christians and, if there are any, Buddhists, as well—compatriots, all. All shall be eligible to public office, even the highest.

It is to be noted that this Zionist policy does not represent an extremist or intransigent position. On the contrary, it is a moderate and reasonable program, formulated by the Zionist Organization under the leadership of its President, Dr. Chaim

Weizmann, of whom Mr. Sumner Welles wrote in *The Time for Decision*:

> In such conversations as I myself have had with the world's leading figures, I have rarely perceived such qualities of sincerity, real statesmanship, ability, and underlying humanity as I have seen in Dr. Weizmann. If any human being can find a solution for the problems which still beset the final establishment of the National Jewish Homeland, Dr. Weizmann will find it if he is given the chance.

The Wiezmann policy, which is the official Zionist policy and which has the endorsement of the vast majority of the Jews of this country and abroad, is essentially a compromise between two opposing minority views.

On the one hand, there are some Zionists who demand that all of Palestine on both sides of the Jordan (including Transjordan, comprising more than three quarters of the total area of mandated and historic Palestine) should constitute the territory of the Jewish state. They want the state established now, without waiting until the Jews become the majority of the population. Indeed, some few of these "maximalist Zionists" even talk about transferring Arabs from Palestine to neighboring Arab countries. On the other hand, there are the non-Zionists, who profess a desire to promote Jewish immigration and colonization in Palestine and the creation there of a Jewish spiritual and cultural, but not a national, home. Some urge the establishment of a binational state with numerical and political parity as between the Jews and the Arabs. Others would have Palestine continue indefinitely under the present mandate or under some form of international trusteeship, without any provision for genuine self-government.

The policy as formulated by Dr. Weizmann and the Zionist Organization repudiates the views of both these opposing groups. It regards either the conception of a binational state with political parity or the idea of a permanent trusteeship for two equally autonomous or equally nonautonomous communities as unworkable in practice and as sure to act as a constant incentive to deadlock and to bitter strife. It views as artificial and fantastic the notion of numerical parity of population with the annual flow of Jewish immigration dependent on the fluctuating

Arab birth rate. At the same time, the Zionist Organization rejects the demands of the small dissident chauvinistic minority.

It is my profound conviction that the Zionist program is statesmanlike and constructive. It is a genuine good-neighbor policy. It provides for real compromise in Palestine, without, however, compromising Palestine and without compromising the Jewish people. I shall briefly set forth some of the reasons for my belief that it is entitled to the support of enlightened American and world public opinion and to the active assistance of the United Nations.

THE ZIONIST PROGRAM IS JUST

(a) *It asks for the fulfillment of the underlying purpose of the Balfour Declaration and of the Palestine mandate.*

The Zionists propose nothing essentially new or radically different from what was promised the Jewish people during and immediately after the First World War.

In the Report of the British Royal Commission on Palestine of 1936-37, Prime Minister Lloyd George, President Wilson, Winston Churchill, and others are quoted with respect to their interpretations of the Balfour Declaration. According to them it was intended to afford the Jewish people—the Jewish people throughout the world and not merely the Jews in Palestine—the opportunity to build the foundations of a Jewish commonwealth in Palestine. With fewer than 60,000 Jews in the country in 1917, it was obviously premature at that time to speak of a Jewish commonwealth; but it was contemplated that if the Jews took advantage of the opportunities to be offered them and became the majority of the population, a democratic Jewish commonwealth would thus be created.

The Zionists submit that now, with 600,000 Jews in Palestine, the time has come for the fulfillment of the original intent and underlying purpose of the Balfour Declaration, and of the Mandate based upon it, by the early reconstitution of Palestine as a Jewish commonwealth.

(*b*) *The Jewish people have relied upon the international promise given them and, despite overwhelming obstacles, have built strong and enduring foundations for their future commonwealth.*

Dr. Walter C. Lowdermilk, an objective, scientific observer, in his recent book *Palestine—Land of Promise,* describes what has already been, and what can in the future be, achieved by the Jewish pioneers in the Holy Land. He points out that enormous energy, untold sacrifice, and vast sums of money have converted a desolate, derelict area into a thriving, progressive country, and that these miracles wrought by the Jewish people have been due to the inspiration of the Zionist movement.

It is submitted that the equitable doctrine of estoppel requires that the promise relied on by the Jewish people be fully performed. It would be a gross deception of the hundreds of thousands of Jews who have come into Palestine on the basis of that promise if they were now to be doomed to a permanent minority status.

(*c*) *Historic justice calls for the support of the Zionist program.*

It is estimated that five million Jews have already been exterminated by the Nazis and their satellites. Little Palestine has given shelter and asylum to hundreds of thousands of refugees—indeed, to more than has any other country in the world. But thousands who perished might have been saved had it not been for the Palestine White Paper issued in 1939 by the Chamberlain government. It is grossly inaccurate to say, as an official of the British Embassy has publicly declared, that "no Jews who have been able to escape from Nazi-occupied Europe have been refused asylum or safety either in Palestine or somewhere else." Alas, tens of thousands of helpless Jewish refugees have died because immigration visas and certificates were denied them by the British Administration of Palestine. The pitiful fate of the passengers of the S.S. "Struma" and the S.S. "Patria," drowned in the Mediterranean Sea, can never be forgotten. Of course, the Nazis are primarily responsible for these poignant tragedies, but the British Government, whose White Paper drastically restricted Jewish immigration at a time when the national homeland was most urgently needed as a haven of refuge, cannot escape culpability.

Historic justice demands that atonement be made for the needless death of multitudes of innocent victims of bureaucracy and red tape. Historic justice demands the fulfillment, at long last, of the Balfour Declaration and the mandate.

(d) *The Zionist program is not unjust to the Arabs.*

It is sometimes alleged that Zionism is unjust and that the Balfour Declaration itself was unjust. It is contended that Palestine has long been an Arab country, that promises made to the Arabs have been broken, and that the interests of the Arab inhabitants have been ignored by the Jewish Agency for Palestine.

As a matter of fact, there were no promises given by the British to the Arabs which conflicted with those given to the Jews. As a further matter of historic record, the rights of the Arabs in Palestine have been scrupulously safeguarded, and the Arabs have benefited and profited no less than the Jews from the recent colonization of the Holy Land.

It should also be noted that the Arab world as a whole possesses vast underpopulated and underdeveloped territories and numerous national states in which to exercise political autonomy and sovereignty. The Jewish people can claim only little Palestine for its national home, its commonwealth.

Furthermore, as everyone must know, Palestine was the birthplace of the Jewish people, and Palestine gave birth to no other people. Palestine owes its unique place in world history to the Jewish people, and to none other. The Jews never ceased to pray and hope for their return to the Land of Israel, and the fact is that until they did return about a half century ago, Palestine remained barren and desolate.

This "historical connection of the Jewish people with Palestine" is the very basis of the Balfour Declaration and of the mandate. But it was not necessary to confirm that historical connection in international legal documents of the twentieth century. Indeed, as one leading Zionist has said: "The Balfour Declaration is not our Bible. The Bible is our Balfour Declaration."

(*e*) *The Zionist program is in complete accord with the principles of the Atlantic Charter.*

It has sometimes been claimed that the principles of the Atlantic Charter do not permit the realization of the Zionist objectives. The contention is that the Atlantic Charter forbids promoting Jewish immigration into Palestine without the consent of the Arab inhabitants, who constitute a majority in the present population of the land. The answer to this claim should be obvious. It was never intended that the principles of the Atlantic Charter should abrogate existing international obligations. The Balfour Declaration and the Palestine mandate are international commitments and should be respected as such.

Furthermore, the third principle of the Atlantic Charter provides that the countries represented "wish to see sovereign rights and self-government restored to those who have been forcibly deprived of them." It is a well-established historic fact that until the destruction of the Jewish state by the Romans in A.D. 70, the Jewish people exercised sovereignty over Palestine for more than a thousand years. Palestine has never since constituted an independent political entity; it has been a province of some empire, governed from afar. The Romans perished without leaving a legal successor, and according to the principles of international law, as pointed out by an eminent expert, [Ernst Frankenstein] the Jewish people has never lost its right to Palestine. The Atlantic Charter, therefore, fully supports the Zionist claim. In accordance with its explicit provisions, the United Nations should "wish to see sovereign rights and self-government restored to" the Jewish people "who have been forcibly deprived of them."

Moreover, it should be remembered that the idea of self-determination underlying the Atlantic Charter signifies that every people, great or small, should have an equal right to life, liberty, and the pursuit of happiness, and should become the master of its own destiny. The Arabs have a half-dozen states in vast territories in which they may find full expression for their national aspirations. The Jews have only tiny Palestine. That the principles of self-determination and of the Jewish national home are not inconsistent should be clear from the fact that

President Woodrow Wilson and General Jan Smuts, the leading advocates of self-determination, were also among the most ardent supporters of the Zionist ideal.

ZIONIST PROGRAM IS FEASIBLE

(a) *The Zionists have demonstrated that Palestine is fit to become the Jewish commonwealth.*

Reports of reliable experts indicate that the present area under irrigation can be increased tenfold, making room for an additional farm population in Palestine of at least one million. Industrial Palestine, by the further development of its hydroelectric power and the extension of its existing markets in the Near East, can support at least four million additional inhabitants. No one can predict even approximately the number of European Jews who will survive this war and who may desire to go to Palestine. It is, however, well established that Palestine can absorb the survivors from the horror chambers of Europe, and also such other Jews as may seek a new life in the Jewish national home—and all without disturbing a single Palestinian Arab in his present job or possessions.

(b) *The Zionist program has been approved by the overwhelming majority of Jewish religious leaders as well as Jewish laymen, and also has the endorsement of large sections of enlightened American and world public opinion.*

At the American Jewish Conference (August 1943), representing every major Jewish community, organization, and group in the country, 480 out of 502 delegates adopted a resolution in favor of the re-establishment of a Jewish commonwealth in Palestine. With very few exceptions, all rabbis, Orthodox, Conservative, and Reform, have repeatedly manifested their enthusiastic support of the Zionist program.

Leaders of labor and industry, clergymen of all denominations, statesmen, writers, scholars, and philosophers have united in wholehearted advocacy of the Zionist objective. Every American President from Wilson to Roosevelt has voiced the continued American interest in the development of the national home, and in 1944 both American political parties at their national conventions unanimously adopted pro-Jewish-commonwealth planks in their respective platforms.

Furthermore, many of the leading statesmen of the United Nations are sympathetic and understanding friends of the Zionist cause. Zionists were heartened by the fact that Franklin D. Roosevelt had on two recent occasions publicly pledged his best efforts to effectuate the establishment of a free and democratic Jewish commonwealth in Palestine. There is reason to believe that President Truman will carry out his predecessor's pledge, for as Senator he was one of the early members of the American Palestine Committee which, under the chairmanship of Senator Robert F. Wagner, has zealously advocated the Zionist program. Also significant is the fact that the Russian Soviet representative at the recent World Trade Union Conference in London (February 1945) voted in support of a resolution endorsing the Zionist program, a resolution which had previously been adopted by the Latin American Labor Congress at Cali, Colombia (December 1944). General Jan Smuts of South Africa and President Eduard Beneš of Czechoslovakia are veteran proponents of Zionism. Winston Churchill, too, has from the period of the First World War been a consistent and ardent supporter of the Balfour Declaration and of "our dreams for Zionism."

(c) *Arab opposition, though real and troublesome, is not an insurmountable obstacle.*

It is true that most of the Arab politicians, resenting the introduction of progressive social concepts and modern scientific advances into the primitive Near East, and interested to preserve the semifeudal economy of which they alone have been the beneficiaries, are opposed to a Jewish commonwealth. It is also undeniable that fascist-subsidized Arab leaders, like the former Mufti of Jerusalem, when last heard from an "honorary Aryan" in Germany, may be expected to continue to oppose the Jewish commonwealth, or, indeed, any Jewish immigration, even on a minimal basis. But surely in the postwar world in which the Four Freedoms are to prevail, in which there is to be international security based on justice and maintained by force when necessary, such vital questions as the future status of Palestine will not be dependent on the approval of medieval feudal lords or totalitarian tyrants, whether they speak German, Japanese, or Arabic.

It is frequently contended that there is serious danger of constant violent resistance on the part of the Arabs in the Near East if the United Nations should announce their approval of the Zionist program. It is submitted that while the worst of the Arab riots in the past have been instigated by the Axis powers, Arab violence has for the most part been the result of successive acts of capitulation and appeasement by the mandatory power, which has constantly whittled down the provisions of the Palestine mandate. It is irresolution and lack of forthrightness that provoke conflicts. Riots and bloodshed in Palestine have resulted from tension of doubt and uncertainty, rather than from tension of basic hostility. I am confident that when the nations of the world will unequivocally declare their determination to fulfill that which the Balfour Declaration and the mandate were intended to achieve, the ground will be prepared for genuine Arab-Jewish rapprochement—for harmonious relationship and cooperation between the two Semitic peoples, the Arabs and the Jews.

ZIONIST PROGRAM IS ESSENTIAL

(a) *A declaration by the United Nations now of the early creation of a Jewish commonwealth is the only practical way of insuring large-scale Jewish immigration and colonization in Palestine.*

It cannot be stated too often that the plea for a Jewish commonwealth is not motivated by a desire for the external trappings of sovereignty. It is rather urgent necessity that has produced the Zionist program.

Most persons, including many anti-Zionists, seem to agree that the doors of Palestine must be kept open for Jewish mass immigration. James G. McDonald, former League of Nations High Commissioner for Refugees Coming from Germany, recently summed up the situation as follows: "Palestine offers incontestably the primary hope for the solution of the problem of

Jewish refugees. . . . In Palestine, and only there, can the mass of Jewish refugees hope to be welcome and to be assisted to integrate themselves in the life of the community."

It is, however, not sufficiently understood that the basis for the Jewish claim of the right to immigrate, regardless of the opposition or consent of the inhabitants of the land, is the special status of the Jewish people with regard to Palestine, the special status based on "the historical connection of the Jewish people with Palestine," a status recognized by the Balfour Declaration and the mandate. It is because of that special status that Jews are not like ordinary immigrants whose right to enter is subject to the consent of the inhabitants. Jews going to Palestine are *homecomers,* not *immigrants.* They are engaged in the enterprise of rebuilding their commonwealth, and that is why the existing population has no right to prevent their entry and settlement.

Only in a commonwealth where the Jews are in the majority will the absorptive capacity of the land be steadily enlarged. Only in such a commonwealth will an increasing Jewish immigration be made possible by appropriate legislation and administration. Only in such a commonwealth will the social and economic welfare of all the people of the country be successfully promoted.

Justice Horace Stern, of the Supreme Court of Pennsylvania, who is not a member of the Zionist Organization, has recently presented the following argument, though in a different context, on this aspect of the subject:

When, in the case of Palestine, shall the right of self-government be granted? Zionists and non-Zionists cannot but agree that if an independent local government be established while the Jews are still in a minority, there might result legislation in regard to the continuance of immigration and other questions of national policy which would gravely impair, if not wholly liquidate, the entire Palestine project on which the Jews have expended so much wealth and energy and built such eager hopes. Moreover, assuming that the form of self-government will be a democratic one in which all individuals will have equal political rights, it is obvious that the nature of the legislation which will be enacted in Palestine will be determined by the majority of the voting population. It is certain that the Jews must compose that majority if Palestine is to share in the social and economic progress of Western civilization, for the

Jews not only have imbibed the ideals of social justice from their ancient forebears but have acquired, in their more recent European and American environment, experience with modern laws and institutions designed to implement those ideals through practical measures of legislation and government.

It is submitted that if the Jews be denied control over economic policies in Palestine, large-scale Jewish immigration there may not eventuate, for a hostile administration can check immigration by hindering the development of the country. Economic control requires political control, and political control can come only through self-government in a Jewish commonwealth.

(*b*) *The realization of the Zionist program will promote the cultural, spiritual, and religious welfare of Jews throughout the world.*

The Jews are the only people in the world who constitute a minority of the population wherever they dwell. While many Jews are completely at home, as individuals enjoying the blessings of democracy together with their fellow citizens, the Jewish people, as a people, has been homeless since A.D. 70. This national homelessness has prevented the free, normal, and creative development of Jewish cultural, spiritual, and religious values, and has repeatedly exposed the Jews in many lands, and still exposes them today, to hatred, discrimination, and persecution.

A Jewish commonwealth in Palestine will tend to make the status of the Jewish people equal to—no greater and no less than—the status of every other normal people with a national homeland of its own. President Roosevelt summed this up when he wrote in 1936:

> The interest which I have had and have frequently manifested in the rebuilding of the ancient Jewish homeland is, I am persuaded, an interest which is shared by all who recognize that every people has the inalienable right to life, liberty and the pursuit of happiness.

Of course, Zionist political implications would apply exclusively to the Jews living in Palestine, and not at all to Jews in other lands. It never was contemplated that a Jewish commonwealth would represent the interests of Jews throughout the world, as is sometimes erroneously claimed. It is, however, sub-mitted that for the Jews outside Palestine, a publicly recognized and legally secured national home will serve as a cultural, spirit-ual, and religious center, enriching Jewish life wherever Jews live.

Furthermore, the Zionist movement has proved that the Jew-ish people, as a people, can be creative, thus refuting the chief arguments of anti-Semites. The non-Jew has often gone to Pales-tine with the common prejudices against the Jew; but he has come away, his misconceptions removed and in their place a wholesome respect for Jewish creative energy, a respect generated by magnificent achievements in peaceful colonization, in soil reclamation, and in cooperative living.

The contention of some anti-Zionists that the establishment of a national Jewish commonwealth is inconsistent with Jewish religious teachings of universalism is totally unfounded. There is, of course, no contradiction between enlightened nationalism and ethical universalism. To argue that the character of Judaism as a universal religion demands the destruction of Jewish nation-hood is just as absurd as if the command "Thou shalt love thy neighbor as thyself" were interpreted to mean that I should de-stroy myself in order to avoid conflict with my neighbor. It is common knowledge that the prophets of Israel were at the same time universalists and ardent nationalists.

Furthermore, many keen observers and students of Jewish life have come to the conclusion that there is no way of bringing self-respect and dignity to a group situated as are the Jews other than to normalize their status as a people with a national home, a commonwealth of their own. The most notable of all Ameri-can Zionists, the late Justice Louis D. Brandeis, of the Supreme Court of the United States, declared: "Every American Jew who aids in advancing the Jewish settlement in Palestine, though he feels that neither he nor his descendants will ever live there, will be a better man and a better American for doing so."

(c) *The re-establishment of a Jewish commonwealth in Palestine is necessary to aid the redemption of the whole Near East and the establishment of a stable world peace.*

It is a well-known fact that the Near East was once a great world center with populous cities, fruitful soil, and lofty, teeming civilizations. Then came erosion, undernourishment, disease, decay. Some fifty years ago the Jews began to redeem the land of Palestine. They took nothing from the Arabs. The Jews set the Arabs and the whole Near Eastern world a shining example in the recreation of the soil of an ancient land and in the renaissance of the soul of an ancient people. This lesson, not only the Near East but all Europe, all the world, must learn if there is to be a stable, enduring peace.

In Philadelphia in May 1943, Dr. Weizmann delivered an address in the course of which he said that if he were to utter that which he believes stirs in the depths of the conscience of the United Nations, he would speak thus to the Arabs:

You are a people recognized by the world. Palestine is one—and it is among the smallest—of the many countries which you inhabit, but none of which you fill to the extent of one half, one quarter, or one tenth of their capacity.

If the chance is given you to develop in freedom and peace, if you can call your lands your own, remember that this is due to the efforts of the democracies in the last war, and of the United Nations in this war. What you will get out of this war you will owe to the sacrifices of the peoples who have poured out their blood on a score of battlefields for the freedom of the world.

You owe it also in a measure to the Jewish people, to the very soldiers whom Jewish Palestine has furnished—the flower of its manhood—without compulsion, to swell the armies of the United Nations in the Near East.

We think it right and proper that the Jewish people should be restored at last to that small niche which it has cherished through thousands of years of homelessness, that niche in which were born the principles of the civilization for which we fight.

If you and the Jews will cooperate, you will build up, for your mutual benefit, and for the benefit of the world, those tremendous areas which today are a desert and a reproach to humanity. Such an up-building, indeed, is a life and death necessity for you. An empty country, a political and geographical vacuum invites aggression; it invites predatory nations. You and the Jews can make this part of the world safe for yourselves and for us; for all three of us have a stake in this part of the world.

I believe that if the United Nations spoke in the spirit of Dr. Weizmann and followed up such a declaration by definitive action, a just solution would be found to the problem of Palestine for the benefit of the Arabs as well as the Jews—one that would lead to a great advance in the life of the whole Near East. I am firmly convinced that the Zionist program is feasible as well as just, desirable as well as essential. And I am confident that the United Nations, with the full support of Great Britain and our own country, will in the not too distant future declare themselves in favor of the Zionist program and help in the reconstitution of Palestine as the Jewish commonwealth.

Only when justice and security shall have been granted to the weakest and the most wronged of the peoples of the earth will the sign be given that an era of peace and freedom has finally come to bless all mankind.

THE ARABS AND PALESTINE [5]

Both Jews and Arabs are said to stem from a common ancestor, from Abraham, who immigrated into Canaan, i.e. Palestine, and so neither of them seem to have been earlier in the land than the others. Recent views assume that only part of the Israelites migrated to Egypt—as reflected in the Joseph story —and part of them remained in Palestine. So part of the Canaanite population encountered by the Jews when they entered the promised land under Joshua were Israelites, too. Therefore, the Arabs have no priority on the land.

To the Arabs Jerusalem is only the third holy city, to the Jews it is the first and only holy city, and Palestine is the place where their original history, their sacred history took place. Besides, to the Arabs Jerusalem is a holy city only insofar as they trace their tradition back to Jewish origins, insofar as after the Arab conquest of Jerusalem in 637, the "Omar Mosque," the "Dome of the Rock" was erected by the Omayyad Caliph Abd el Malek on the very place where the Jewish Ark of the Covenant and the Temple of Solomon had stood, on a rock *"even shetijah"* (world foundation stone), which was con-

[5] By Albert Einstein, discoverer and exponent of the theory of relativity; Professor Emeritus of the Institute for Advanced Study, Princeton; and Dr. Eric Kahler, Princeton, in answer to testimony given by Philip Hitti before the House Committee on Foreign Affairs, February 15, 1944. *Princeton Herald.* April 14, 1944.

sidered by the Jews as reaching down to the bottom of the cosmic ocean, the navel of the world. And Jerusalem was a *gibah,* a direction of prayer, under Mohammed only as long as he counted on the Jews as the main supporters of his new creed; he changed it, when his hopes failed, together with other institutions established out of pure consideration for his Jewish adherents, as for instance fasting on the Jewish Day of Atonement. The first *gibah,* has, therefore, as much validity for the Arabs as the Jewish Day of Atonement—both are today abolished in their religious significance. It seems a little far-fetched to use this abrogated rite as evidence on which to base the Arab claim to Palestine.

If, finally, the Arab conquest of Palestine is considered holy it would be only fair to admit the corresponding holiness of the peaceful claim and the peaceful reclamation of the country by the Jews. To refer to the legitimacy of a "holy war" sounds rather queer for a people which denounces peaceful immigration as a violation of their rights. . . .

But the Jews do not resort to arguments of power or of priority. One does not get very far with historical rights. Very few peoples of the world would be entitled to their present countries if such a criterion were applied. . . . But by their holy war and their conquest of Palestine the Arabs contributed their share to depriving the Jews of their homeland and so to the making of the Jewish problem, even though one must concede that their share is comparatively smaller than that of other peoples. The stand the Arabs take, however, with regard to the Jews is exactly the one which all peoples of the world are taking. No people, unfortunately, understands why it should contribute anything to the solution of the Jewish problem. The surface of the globe is everywhere occupied, and wherever the Jews could be given a piece of land under fair climatic conditions they would encroach on some property rights and sovereignties and would face friction with a population already firmly established on the spot. No country has been found where the Jews could possibly form an autonomous community, however small.

Every people has a country of its own which it developed with all the care of generations and none of these countries has any connection with a specifically Jewish tradition or concern. The Arabs possess four major countries—Saudi Arabia, which harbors their holy places, Yemen, Iraq, and Transjordan—if we leave aside Egypt, which is only partly Arab, Syria and all the North African colonies and provinces as yet not enfranchised from European rule. And the least and obviously most neglected of their settlements was the part they occupied in the tiny Palestinian country; only nine hundred thousand of fifty million Arabs live there. This tiny Palestinian country, on the other hand, is the only place in the world legitimately and most deeply connected with the Jewish people, its religious foundation and its historic tradition as an independent people.

In order to clarify the Palestinian problem let us compare the situation of the Jews with that of the Arabs. The Jews are and have always been numerically a small people. They have never exceeded fifteen and a half million. Deprived of their homeland through the ancient and medieval conquests of Palestine, they lived dispersed all over the world and what they have suffered since by persecutions, expulsions and tortures of all kinds is far beyond anything the other peoples had to endure. Of the fifteen and a half million computed in 1938 at least two millions [later evidence indicates nearer four millions] have been slaughtered or starved to death by the Nazis in the various European countries during the past few years. So the Zionist movement, or better the striving for a haven in the place of Jewish origin, is by no means an "exotic, artificially stimulated movement," . . . but a movement urged forward by utter need and distress.

The promise held out to the Jews in the Balfour Declaration after the First World War has been whittled down bit by bit in the course of the British appeasement policy yielding to interests partly British, partly Arabian—a policy bitterly denounced by Churchill himself before he became Prime Minister. Palestine is a link in the lifeline of the British Empire between the Near East and India; and the Jewish people, by necessity a dependable ally of the British, have been sacrificed to the

Arabs, who, by their numerical and political strength and the trump of the Islamic portion of the Indian population, were in a position to sell even their neutrality dearly in the present conflict. The final result has been the complete prohibition of Jewish immigration into Palestine at the very moment when more hundreds of thousands of Jews were threatened with annihilation by the Hitler armies occupying Hungary and Rumania.

We invite every fair-minded American to look at the photos in a recent account of the martyrdom of Polish Jewry under Nazi occupation, published by the American Federation of Polish Jews (*The Black Book of Polish Jewry*) and to read the report of an American and non-Jewish eye-witness, Walter Clay Lowdermilk, an expert in land cultivation who travelled through the Near East to study the land record of that region.

Dr. Lowdermilk tells us:

During my stay in Palestine in 1939, I witnessed a tragic by-product of the German advance into Czechoslovakia. In Palestine and Syria we were told of old cargo boats, filled with refugees from Nazi-dominated Central Europe . . . whose miserable passengers were not permitted to land anywhere because of the lack of formal visas. We saw those wretched ships floating about on a steaming sea in unbearable summer heat with refugees packed in holds under intolerably inhuman conditions. The laws governing the transportation of animals for slaughter in the United States do not permit conditions like those which some of the intelligentsia of Central Europe had to undergo in these old boats on the Mediterranean. The revolting slave ships of a century ago were better; for slaves had a slave value and their ships were sped to their destination without delay. But Jewish refugees were kept floating about upon a torrid sea, just out of sight of land, with the desperate hope that the captain . . . would attempt to discharge them illegally on the shores of Palestine.

During our stay in Beirut, an old cargo boat, loaded with 655 refugees . . . was unloaded at the quarantine station for a few days. The ship was so overrun with rats that the passengers had to be removed to exterminate this vermin. We found that they had been floating about for eleven weeks, packed into little wooden shells built around the four cargo holds. The congestion, the ghastly unsanitary conditions and sufferings that these people had undergone aroused our highest admiration for their courage and fortitude. We were astonished to find that these former citizens of Czechoslovakia represented a very high level of European culture . . . 42 were lawyers, 40 were engineers, 26 were physicians and surgeons, in addition to women doctors, professional writers, gifted musicians, pharmacists and nurses. . . . Without passports, without country, these useful and highly cultured refugees presented one of the most tragic spectacles of modern times. No ambassador, no consul spoke up for them to demand the rights and privileges enjoyed by the lowliest citizen of the smallest country.

This is the Jewish situation; and there is no guarantee whatever against the persistence or recurrence of anti-Semitic outbreaks everywhere after this war. Even if we put aside the spiritual, religious and cultural ties making Palestine the only place in the world which persecuted Jews could consider their home and develop with all the devotion a homeland inspires—there is not even any other country acceptable to human beings which the numerous refugee conferences were able to offer to this hounded people. The Jews are prepared for extreme sacrifices and hardest work to convert this narrow strip which is Palestine into a prosperous country and model civilization.

What Jewish youth has already achieved in the few decades of Zionist settlement may be gathered from Dr. Lowdermilk's book. They took over from the period of Arabian predominance deserts and rocks and barren soil and turned them into flowering farms and plantations, into forests and modern cities. They created new forms of cooperative settlements and raised the living standard of the Arabian and the Jewish population alike. The Jews are willing and ready to give any guarantee of protection for the holy places and the civil rights, indeed the autonomy, of Arabs and Christians, a guarantee safeguarded by the overwhelming power of their neighbors on whose cooperation they depend. They offer their assistance and their experience for the economic and scientific advancement of the Arab countries, for the lifting of their population to a modern standard of living.

But this, unfortunately, is just what the Arab leaders do not want. For the true source of Arab resistance and hostility toward a Jewish Palestine is neither religious nor political, but social and economic. The Arabian population of Palestine is negligible in comparison with the vast number of Arab elements in the European provinces of North Africa and Asia. The Arabian chieftains did not arouse the Moslem world against Mussolini's regime in Lybia; most of them were on splendid

terms with him. The Mufti of Jerusalem and other Arab leaders were greatly honored guests in Rome. The rich Arabian
landowners did nothing to improve the nature, the civilization,
or the living standards of their countries. The large Arabian
states are under-populated, the masses of the people are held
in a backward and inferior condition. "Life in the Damascus
of the eighth century was not greatly different from what it is
today," says Professor Hitti in his book about the Arabs. But
the big effendis fear the example and the impulse which the
Jewish colonization of Palestine presents to the peoples of the
Near East, they resent the social and economic uplift of the
Arabian workers in Palestine. They act as all fascist forces
have acted: they screen their fear of social reform behind nationalistic slogans and demagoguery. If it were not for these
leaders and instigators perfect agreement and cooperation could
be achieved between the Arab and the Jewish people.

The purpose of this statement is not a nationalistic one.
We do not, and the vast majority of the Jews does not, advocate the establishment of a state for the sake of national
greed and self-glorification, which would run counter to all the
traditional values of Judaism and which we consider obsolete
everywhere. In speaking up for a Jewish Palestine, we want
to promote the establishment of a place of refuge where persecuted human beings may find security and peace and the un-
disputed right to live under a law and order of their making.
The experience of many centuries have taught us that this can
be provided only by home rule and not by a foreign administration. This is why we stand for a Jewish-controlled Palestine,
be it ever so modest and small. We do not refer to historic
rights, although if there is anything like a historic right to a
country, the Jews can claim it in Palestine, at least as well as
the Arabs. We do not resort to threats of power, for the Jews
have no power; they are, in fact, the most powerless group on
earth. If they had had any power they should have been able
to prevent the annihilation of millions of their people and the
closing of the last door to the helpless victims of the Nazi.
What we appeal to is an elementary sense of justice and humanity. We know how weak such a position is, but we also know

that if the arguments of threats of power, of sacred egoisms and holy wars continue to prevail in the future world order, not only the Jews but the whole of humanity will be doomed.

BEFORE THE BAR OF HISTORY [6]

What are the arguments of the Arabs against Zionism? They can be summarized by the following three statements: "First, Zionism is unfair to the Arabs who now own and occupy Palestine. Second, Zionism, if encouraged by Great Britain and the United States, will be the means of disturbing the friendship which exists between the Arab peoples and the United Nations. Third, there simply is not enough room in little Palestine for the Arabs who are there and the Jews who want to go there."

First, Arab leaders say that Zionism is unfair to the Arabs who own the land. Now as a matter of fact and of history, who *does* own the land? I am not speaking of the private owner of a private plot of land who is able to buy or sell land at will to anyone. I speak of ownership in the larger sense: to whom does the whole land of Palestine belong? Let us go back in history, not to ancient history when the Jews were identified with the land, but back to 1517. The land which we now call Palestine then became part of the Turkish Ottoman Empire. It remained in Turkish hands for four hundred years. Then, during the First World War, Turkey and Great Britain became potential enemies. Before long Britain and Sherif Hussein of Mecca found that it would be mutually beneficial for them to join forces. Britain would gain an ally in Sherif Hussein and as many other Arab leaders as could be persuaded to revolt against their Turkish overlords, and in return the Arabs would gain certain important benefits.

As an inducement to revolt, Britain offered the Arab peoples freedom from the Turkish Empire. They were to have their independence: all the Arabs from the Mediterranean to the

[6] By Wendell Phillips, Rector, Christ Church, Rye, New York; formerly Assistant Chaplain at Columbia University; taught at the American University, Cairo, 1926 to 1929. From an address delivered in Toronto, March 22, 1945.

Persian Gulf, from the Caspian Sea to the Indian Ocean. With only one exception! For a small portion of that vast territory Britain had other plans. That portion was called Syria and included what we of the western world commonly call Palestine. Syria proper was to go to France after the war, and Palestine was to become a Jewish homeland. This arrangement was agreeable to the Arabs who were receiving a generous reward for what was to prove a very feeble effort of revolt against Turkey. . . .

There were no objections raised. . . . In 1922 the rest of the civilized world, in the form of the League of Nations, added its blessing to all that had been done, and gave Great Britain the mandate for Palestine. Great Britain was to assist .he Jews in the establishment of their national homeland. During the same year the Congress of the United States added its approval.

There were, however, certain individuals and forces in England, in Palestine, in the Arab states which had never approved of the whole plan. They did not want a Jewish homeland. They had been fairly defeated, but now they began to sabotage the whole plan. Whispers began. Perhaps Great Britain was not so eager after all to establish this homeland. Perhaps the Arabs could have the whole territory including tiny Palestine. Arab voices began to rise: "We want Palestine. We live here. It belongs to us. What right have these Jews to come in here and take it away from us." The clamor grew. Sincere Britishers, alarmed by this insidious propaganda tried to remind the world of the fact that the Arabs had agreed to have the Zionists take Palestine so long as they could maintain Arab independence in other lands. As Sir Henry McMahon, negotiator of the deal with the Arabs, said much later in 1937, "It was not intended by me to include Palestine in the area in which Arab independence was promised. I also had every reason to believe at the time that the fact that Palestine was not included in my pledge was well understood by King Hussein."

In the light of history, documentary evidence and the action of the civilized world, the Jews are the only rightful owners of Palestine. . . .

The second argument against Zionism is that if it is encouraged by Britain and the United States, it will disturb Arab friendship for the United Nations. "What friendship?" one may ask. The kind of friendship that declares war on Germany when the fighting is all but over!

Three years ago, in 1942, the Arab nations had a magnificent opportunity to show any friendship they might have had for the Allied cause. The Allies needed help. Indeed it looked as if they were almost beyond the need of help. . . . At that time Britain was looking for a friend in the Arab world. Someone, anyone, who could help, who could supply some planes, some men, some supplies, even a word of cheer. From the Arab world came only silence and treachery. Arab rebellions were put down. Peace had to be maintained behind the British lines. It has been said that there were as many British soldiers policing the Arab world to keep order as there were British soldiers facing Rommel on the field of battle. Was that Arab friendship for the Allies?

Meanwhile who were Britain's friends? They were the Jews of Palestine who fought and died for the Allied cause. Thirty thousand fighting men. It has been estimated that one quarter of the army which turned back Rommel was made up of Palestinian Jews. But about these facts there has been a conspiracy of silence. We do not hear about the suicide squads composed of Palestinian Jews who put themselves at the disposal of the British army and navy. We do not hear of the twenty-three Jewish boys who volunteered to slip quietly into Vichy Syria in an attempt to destroy oil installations in the port of Tripoli. They understood that if they were discovered Britain would have to repudiate and disown them. Their families could not receive pensions. But they went, began their destruction and met death.

This story could be multiplied many times over. Take the case of the five hundred Jewish engineers given the task of laying a mine-field on the southern tip of Montgomery's battle line as he faced Rommel in North Africa. They had hardly begun their task when they were spotted by German planes. Within three days they were surrounded by 110 German tanks.

Refusing surrender they waited for the tanks to close in before they let go with their anti-tank guns. The Germans faltered, stopped, turned around. Then up out of fox-holes sprang Jews who climbed on the tanks and threw grenades into openings, increasing the devastation begun by the anti-tank guns and mines. Twenty-six tanks were knocked out in that final attack. Then for one long week the Germans subjected the spot to air attack. Dive-bombers dropped their loads over the spot so that no resistance would be left. Then the tanks came back. This time forty-one were left wrecked on the battle field. Then came more dive bombers, more tanks, more bombers, day after day. The five hundred engineers were reduced to four hundred, then three hundred, then two hundred, then to ninety. When the water supply received a direct hit, the real misery began. Men drank gasoline and ran off screaming mad into the desert. At the end of a month forty-three were left alive, and these forty-three kept the enemy from turning the flank of the British army.

That is friendship. . . . Jewish friendship. Not unselfish friendship, perhaps. They may not have died because they loved Great Britain, but they died in order that other Jews might live, might live in honor and freedom in the land of Palestine as a fitting reward for their contribution to the cause of the Allies, the cause of decency, the cause of humanity. . . .

The third argument against Zionism is that there is not enough room in little Palestine for the Arabs who are already there and the Jews who want to go there. It is suggested that there are far roomier and more fertile places in Europe and America. Why can't Jews go to Arizona or Texas?

In answer it might be said that the Jews of Europe do not want to go to Arizona or Texas, but if they did, and if the League of Nations plus the United States had promised them that they could go to Texas, I believe that promise would have been kept. But the Jews want to go to Palestine, and they are satisfied that there is plenty of room there for everyone who has any intention of going.

It happened that in 1938 the government of the United States sent the assistant chief of its Soil Conservation Service to various spots on the globe to study soil conditions. While he was on this mission Dr. Walter Clay Lowdermilk became fascinated with Palestine. Here is land that has fallen into decay because men have moved away leaving the country to nomads. This part of the world desperately needs new man-power, a larger population. The Arabs have too much rather than too little land. They have a few million people moving on a stage that once held great civilizations, and could again. Think of the life-giving powers in the Tigris and Euphrates valley alone! When an irrigation dam was opened there Dr. Lowdermilk asked a high official: "I suppose this is just the first of a series of such projects?" He replied, "No, this is the last one. We don't have enough manpower to handle any more." In 1926, the then Prime Minister of Iraq had said with real wisdom: "What Iraq wants above everything else is more population."

The same is true, only on a smaller scale, of Palestine. It may be admitted that Palestine is not naturally as fertile as some other parts of the world, but it is fertile enough. The ancient canals can once more be put into use, new ones built, water brought once more to the parched land. The land is still there. The water is still there. The climate is the same as it was when the land was blessed with milk and honey. It has been compared favorably with the present climate of South-ern California where an artificial water supply has given birth to such a miracle as Los Angeles. Only a few decades ago prophets of doom visualized the dry death which would surely close in upon those intrepid souls who first settled Los Angeles.

Palestine has the added advantage of having once proved that it is a productive spot. But soil erosion, lack of care, and grazing animals have brought it to poverty. Where are the Cedars of Lebanon now? They are all gone, except for a few enclosed in a wall which surrounded a shrine. The wall kept out the grazing animals who fed upon the small shoots spring-ing up from the ground. Only within the wall did the shoots grow to be new cedars of Lebanon. Outside the herds de-stroyed trees, plants, and soil alike. And no one cared.

But now comes a new kind of person. A man who cares. A Jew who loves the land of his forefathers. He plants new cedars. He irrigates the land. He works with his own hands. He asks the Arab to work, too, if he wishes to work. This new man has already created new centers of life: over three hundred communities are now witness to his labors. This new man has already created new cities: Tel Aviv the crown of his efforts. He has increased the fruits of the earth. He has created a new economy. He has built factories which during wartime have contributed immeasurably to the Allied cause. He has created hospitals, schools, universities. He does not want to stop. The desert is there waiting to be massaged back to life. Today the waters from the Sea of Galilee run largely wasted down the Jordan only to be lost forever in the salt pit of the Dead Sea. This new man would channel off those waters into fields and vineyards and orchards. Then, by a simple feat of engineering, he would dig a channel to bring the salt waters of the Mediterranean to the top of the Jordan Valley, letting them then fall down the valley into the Dead Sea. This virtual waterfall would total a drop of 1,300 feet, supplying enough water power to bring light and manufacturing power to the land of Palestine. This new man would create a new civilization in Palestine, and in the entire Arab Near East. The land cries out to be saved. It cries out for another three or four million people who could save it. But Arab leaders say there is no more room in Palestine.

We have now considered the three arguments which Arab leaders have used against Zionism. We have seen that these arguments are not so valid as some have supposed. But now let us go a step further, and consider the *real* reasons why Arab leaders are opposed to Zionism. I believe that there are probably three. The first is a certain psychological attitude which we might call Arab exclusiveness; the second is the economic situation which Zionism is likely to introduce into the Arab world; the third is the political aspect of the whole problem.

. The first of these three, Arab exclusiveness, is the least important. How many non-Moslems have ever been to Mecca, ever taken a Cook's tour into the heart of Arabia? No non-Moslem has, except in disguise.

An article on Arabia in *Life Magazine* in 1943 began with these words: "For all practical purposes Saudi Arabia is a closed country to the Christian world. Fewer than one hundred Europeans or Americans have visited its desert fortresses in modern times. No non-Moslem journalist has ever been officially permitted to visit its capital at Riad." This is one illustration of the attitude of mind which looks with disfavor upon the intrusion of any outsider into the Arab world.

Moreover, it is an attitude which is encouraged in the people by their leaders. The average Arab is a miserable creature judged by our standards, and perhaps by any standards. He is poor, badly housed, often desperately sick. He turns to his leaders and asks why. His leaders, unwilling to bestir themselves to better his lot, may simply say that such is the will of Allah. They may go a step further and say that all the ills of the Arab are the result of foreign interference in Arab affairs. It has been said, with some accuracy, that this sort of attitude has developed into the only national policy the Arabs have, a policy of anti-foreignism, directed at the outside world and Zionism alike.

The second and more important reason why Arab leaders are against Zionism is economic. We must remember that Arabia proper is a feudal state, or perhaps more accurately a mediaeval absolute monarchy. The small group in power have everything; the rest have nothing. The leaders—the emirs and feudal owners, the professional classes and clergy who benefit by serving them—are the recipients of whatever fruit the land bears. Between them and the masses there is a great gulf fixed which no one is interested in bridging. Leaders in the Arab world live on a generous scale. A wealthy man in that world is really wealthy, and a poor man is really poor. A poor man has almost literally nothing. Nor is there any concern about the poor. That is the business of Allah. If God wills that a man starve to death, why should mortal man frustrate God's will by feeding him? Thus there is no concern about the welfare of the masses. There is no nonsense about the rights of man, or much less of labor unions. There is no nonsense about democracy. This is the situation, and it suits those on the top very nicely.

You may notice that I differentiate between Arabs and Arab leaders. Whenever anyone says to me "But the Arabs don't want the Jews in Palestine," I automatically ask, "What Arabs?" There is no such thing as "The Arabs." I suppose the nearest thing to an Arab is the person who lives in Arabia. He is the poverty-stricken fellow we have just been considering. He is not against Zionism. He does not know what Zionism is. This is true of the millions of Arabs in most of the Arab world. Then there is the second group whom we might refer to as "The Arabs." These are the masses of Moslems in Palestine itself. We have seen how these have been blessed by the Jews, but we hear, "The Arabs don't want the Jews in Palestine." "What Arabs?" The Arab leaders all over the Arab world, the privileged group who have held all the economic power for centuries, and intend to continue to hold it.

But a danger to their status has loomed up. That danger is Zionism! For Zionism is improving the lot of the average man in Palestine. Zionism is concerned about a man's inherent rights, about his body, his soul, his education, his health, his home, his family, his present and his future. Zionism is interested in the land and the people who live in the land. Zionism is interested in democracy. It is even interested in the rights of labor.

These unorthodox ideas cannot be confined within the limits of Palestine, for such a gospel ignores geographic borders. Unless this heresy is stopped at birth, it may spread over the whole Arab world, with the result that feudalism would begin to disintegrate, and the privileged classes to topple. The privileged classes are not scheming, not doing anything base in their own eyes. They are simply obeying the rules of the game as it is played in that part of the world.

I remember the time when, some years ago, I entertained several of my Moslem friends who came on a visit to the United States. They stayed with me for some weeks. We toured New England, visited Washington and New York. They saw the skyscrapers and the material wonders of our civilization. At the end of the tour I said, "Tell me, what has interested you most about our country?" One of them answered: "We have both been interested in the same thing. Wherever we go we find great buildings, perhaps hospitals, schools, or some other public building. On the corner of each structure there is usually a tablet with the inscription 'This building was given by Mr. So and So.' What we want to know is, why did he give it? What did he get out of it? Surely he must have had some motive beyond generosity. In our land you could not find a single man who would do such a thing unless he was rewarded by the King with a title or some other tangible return."

They simply do not understand our concern for others. We must remember that it has taken us centuries of Judaic-Christian culture to learn the lesson ourselves. We cannot expect others to learn it in a few years.

The truth remains that Arab leaders are indeed against Zionism. The question is how much concern we should show for a few Arab leaders as opposed to the manifest welfare of the great masses of Arabs and all the Jews?

We come now to the third real reason why Arab leaders are opposed to Zionism: the political reason. Almost every really important Arab leader hopes to become the head of Pan-Arabia. He wants to have the backing of every Arab as he continues to grow in power. To do this he must have a program, a rallying cry. "Down with Zionism" is a very convenient program. Hitler faced the same problem in Germany. He had to stir his people and move them with some magic formula. So he shouted, "Down with the Jews." It is a simple and effective formula which demagogues have used in the past and may well use in the future.

Ultimate political opposition to Zionism stems from still another source: Certain important powers in Great Britain are against Zionism. All the facts we have discussed so far are insignificant compared to this one. The wishes of Arab leaders, the rights of the Jews, the productivity of the land, all these count as nothing beside the simple statement that certain important powers in Great Britain are against Zionism. Nor should we too easily condemn these obstructionists. They are convinced that they are working for the best interests of the Empire.

Why is Zionism a challenge to the Empire? For the same reason that it is a challenge to the privileged Arab leaders. Arab labor is cheap, whether it is building roads or airfields. Arab leaders are willing to give up their oil if paid liberally. The eastern end of the Mediterranean is a moderately friendly place. Why should this nice balance be disturbed? Who can tell what might result if a highly developed state is allowed to come to life in the Near East? Who can tell what might result in the economic field for example? Suppose the Zionists set up a state that produces and manufactures. Suppose they show the way to the rest of the Arab world. Suppose the virus spreads around the life-line to Egypt, Iran, Iraq, India and China.

So it is that certain powers in the British Colonial Office look at Zionism and say: "You have performed miracles there in Palestine. You have transformed the desert into a garden. You have built forests and cities. You have lifted a country from desolation. You have improved the lot of the inhabitants. You have performed a miracle . . . *but we don't like it!* We believe it is not to our best interests."

Fortunately, there are other powers in England and in the Empire who believe just as strongly that it is to England's benefit to take the generous course in Palestine. The friends of the Jewish national home in Palestine appreciate the contribution which has been made by the British Government and the British people. Jewish people themselves never forget that Britain has been their traditional friend. Had not British interests and sympathy given strong support to the Balfour Declaration and the mandate, there would not even be the substantial framework of a Jewish national home to discuss. It must be appreciated that Britain set up conditions in Palestine of enormous benefit both to Jews and Arabs; in the interval between wars the Jewish population increased half a million and the Arab population slightly more than half a million. In the same period in Tripolitania Mussolini annihilated the Moslem population to the tune of half a million from an original population of a million. The credit due to the British Government and people for an achievement of benefit both to Jews and Arabs, should be rendered in this age of radical criticisms of all governments, should be recognized and never forgotten.

Let me conclude with this thought. You and I and the members of the civilized world have a moral obligation. It is our duty to allow the Jews to settle Palestine without any restrictions on immigration. We have promised it to them. We have given it to them. And then we have snatched it away! As the result of a legal agreement the Arabs received a territory as large as one third of the United States. The Jews were to receive about one per cent of that amount of land: the little country of Palestine. The Arabs got their land. The Jews got a promise: The Promised Land. We allowed them to go ahead with their plans. We allowed them to pour their lives, their efforts, their money, their dreams, their future into Palestine. We allowed them to begin to build . . . and then we closed the doors, dooming their hopes and dreams. We have a moral obligation to Zionism.

In an effort to excuse our unfaithfulness and immoral action we have sometimes said with Lord Halifax that at times moral considerations must give way to imperial policy. That is a dangerous statement. It is the sort of slogan that once brought us to Munich. It is the sort of slogan which Hitler used. It is a false doctrine which can only lead its followers to ultimate destruction. Rather, let us listen to the words of the late Archbishop of Canterbury, speaking in the House of Lords: "In the matter of Palestine, Britain stands before the bar of God, of history, and of humanity!"

JEWISH PALESTINE IN THE POSTWAR WORLD [7]

During medieval times, despite many discriminations, the Jews could maintain an autonomous organization and a distinc-

[7] By Isaac B. Berkson, Director, Research Department, American Zionist Emergency Council; formerly Director of Jewish Education for the Jewish Agency in Palestine. *Journal of Educational Sociology.* 18:287-94. January 1945.

tive Jewish life: the Jewish community was ruled by Jewish law and its cultural life was nourished by religious and educational institutions. The rise of the modern democratic state made impossible the continuance of the distinctive Jewish way of life in any genuine sense. Theoretically based on the rights of the individual, the democratic state was erected on the foundation of the national history, language, and legal system of each people. Inevitably, this meant the end of Jewish legal and cultural autonomy and a reduction of the Jewish association to matters of belief and practice; indeed, the demands of the modern state made a genuine fulfillment of the Jewish religion impossible, since traditional Judaism required a basis in Jewish law, a background of Hebrew literature, and the support of a system of Hebrew education. It is of the essence of the Zionist analysis to point out that this denial of Jewish autonomy in the modern state was not the result of any arbitrary decision unfriendly to the Jews, but resulted from the need of maintaining a homogeneous culture and education as the basis for the national life. . . .

However complete the victory of the United Nations will be, [Zionists hold that] a Jewish homeland in Palestine will be indispensable, with three great functions to perform: (1) to serve as a Jewish spiritual and cultural center; (2) to make a contribution to the solution of anti-Semitism; (3) to provide a haven for refugees.

Palestine as a Jewish spiritual and cultural center. If the Jewish cultural and religious tradition is to be carried forward, a center of Jewish life is needed where Jews can organize their own social forms, speak a language which they choose, and educate their children in the traditions which they hold sacred. Palestine, for historical reasons, is the only place where such a cultural and spiritual center in the full sense of the term could be developed. It would offer a spiritual haven for those Jews who wish to live a full Jewish life, speaking in Hebrew, studying Jewish literature, keeping the Sabbath and the holidays, and practising the religious precepts in a congenial environment. That this is one of the main functions of Zionism is demonstrated by the conspicuous cultural achievements of Jewish Palestine—the resurrection of Hebrew as a spoken language, the renascence of Hebrew literature, the establishment of the Hebrew University, and many another manifestation of a revitalized national culture, such as the revival of the communal observance of the Sabbath and various festivals. The existence of a flourishing center of the national culture would not only serve the Jews who live in Palestine, but would exercise a strengthening influence on the attenuated forms of Judaism and Jewish life still possible in each country, in conformity with its own conditions.

Palestine as an answer to anti-Semitism. Though obviously incompatible in theory with democracy, anti-Semitism evidently is not easily uprooted even in the democratic countries. Despite the genuine belief of the majority of the American people in equality of rights without reference to race, color, and creed, anti-Semitism has been on the increase here in recent decades. We cannot complacently explain this away by reference to Nazi propaganda, for the quotas in our universities, discrimination against Jews in employment, and restrictions of hotel accommodations to "selective clientele" existed long before the rise of fascism in Europe.

The degree and forms of discrimination practised in the United States may seem unimportant in comparison with the persecution that Jews have experienced throughout the world. But psychologically speaking the subtler forms of anti-Semitism may be cruel enough. They may have a lasting effect on the personality of youth, leading possibly to serious psychic maladjustment, and may bring about a sense of inferiority, cynicism, or rebellion. For some of the victims of these subtler effects of anti-Semitism Palestine may offer a release from psychological tension, since in Palestine Jews can feel themselves as fully acceptable persons. However, such a purpose Palestine can serve only for comparatively few. For the far larger number of Jews who do not return to Palestine, Zionism as a philosophy and conception of Jewish life may provide morale enhancing and character integrating values, since it involves self-knowledge and self-respect and a sense of participation in the destinies and creative achievements of the Jewish people.

A permanent home for the refugees. Palestine thus has a contribution to make in solving the problem of anti-Semitism which might be called the problem of "potential refugees." It also has an important function to perform for those who are already refugees, those who have not been able to, or have not been permitted to, adjust themselves in the country where they have found temporary shelter, and those who will find it impossible to readjust themselves in their home countries after the war. During the last dozen years Palestine has demonstrated its ability to absorb a large number of refugees fleeing from the threat of fascism in Central Europe and economic attrition in Eastern Europe.

Despite the many restrictions, Palestine took care of over 250,000 Jews, counting both legal and illegal entrants during the decade from 1933 to 1943. Thus, despite its relatively tiny size, it absorbed more Jewish refugees than any other country in the world, including the United States—the second largest haven for Jewish refugees—which permitted some 165,000 Jews to enter in the same decade. The Jewish refugees have adjusted themselves well to Palestine, particularly the younger people who have been helped to rebuild their lives by the Youth Aliyah organization under the remarkable Henrietta Szold. A significant feature in the Palestine situation is the fact that the Yishuv, as the Jewish community of Palestine is known, welcomes the refugees; the Histadrut (Labor Federation) and the Va'ad Leumi (Jewish National Council) have expended much effort in assisting the refugees to become a useful and organic part of Jewish Palestine.

The spirit with which the Jewish community welcomes the refugees is in marked contrast with the attitude toward them in other countries. The investigation committees of every nation are ready to send the Jews everywhere except where they are wanted and needed, namely Palestine. As to the desire of the Jews to go there, Mr. David Schweitzer of the American Hias-Ica Emigration Association (Hicem), the largest non-Zionist Jewish emigration agency, recently declared: "Jews of Europe do not engage in debates for or against Palestine, but only think of possibilities of reaching it." . . .

As is well known, there are great political difficulties involved in the establishment of the Jewish national home in Palestine; despite economic advantages the Arab political leaders have steadily opposed Jewish immigration and land purchases, and the creation of the Jewish home. Palestine is only a tiny area of ten thousand square miles in a vast realm of more than two million square miles dominated by Arabs. Nevertheless, they regard it as a Moslem land and have continuously refused to share government with the Jews, let alone to agree to Jewish predominance. Whatever may be the solution of the political question . . . it is clear that there are no inherent economic difficulties in making Palestine a great center of Jewish life that would provide a focus for religious, spiritual, and cultural aspirations and at the same time make a major contribution to the refugee problem.

Palestine, an indispensable factor in the solution of the Jewish problem. Needless to say, Zionism does not envisage an evacuation of Jews from all over the world to Palestine. There are, perhaps, some extremists who entertain such a notion, but this represents neither the desire of the Jews nor the potentialities of Palestine. Moreover, no Jews should be forced to go to Palestine; Zionists are united with all other Jews in insisting on equal rights for Jews in every country. What Zionism proposes is that the doors of Palestine be kept open so that all Jews who need to, or who choose to, may find there a haven of refuge, where they may live the type of life that is for them spiritually and culturally most satisfying; and where they will be liberated from the disabilities and suppressions attaching to the status of a minority, even a "tolerated" minority. While not a total solution of the Jewish problem, Zionism may be regarded as an indispensable factor in any solution, in the sense that no real attack on the Jewish problem, in its spiritual and material phases, can be made without a Jewish Palestine. Moreover, the solution which it contemplates might well be called an integrated solution of the Jewish problem, since it aims to create unified personalities, to satisfy at once material needs and spiritual strivings.

ZIONIST VIEWS [8]

Zionists maintain that the Jews constitute a people or nationality, possessing all the attributes of nationhood, except for the fact that since their exile from Palestine they have lacked a national homeland. While there is much disagreement among them as to the use of the term "Jewish nationalism," they nevertheless insist that Jews should once again assert their nationhood by concentrating in Palestine to form either a Jewish state, a commonwealth, or an independent community in a binational state. All branches of Zionism, including the religious and cultural wings, are influenced by this "nationalist" approach to Jewish life and Judaism.

Zionists deny the charge sometimes leveled against them that their interest in rebuilding the Jewish homeland impugns or might impugn their patriotism or loyalty to the country of which they are citizens. They do not share the fears of the Reformist anti-Zionists in this respect. In refutation of this argument they point to the activities of the Irish in the United States in helping to obtain independence for Ireland, and to the activities of the Polish and Czech Americans in helping to reconstitute Poland and Czechoslovakia as independent states. The patriotism of these citizens, Zionists point out, has never been questioned.

Zionists point out also that just as the valiant resistance of the Greeks in the present war has contributed to the dignity of citizens of Greek descent, and just as the democratic record of independent Czechoslovakia has contributed immeasurably to the pride and dignity of citizens of Czech descent, so have Jewish achievements in Palestine done much to enhance Jewish pride and dignity everywhere, besides helping to dispel many a prejudiced notion about Jews.

Zionists contend, furthermore, that the universalism and the ideals of democracy which the prophets of Israel preached imply not a narrow patriotism or isolationism but a sense of brotherhood with all mankind. A concern for the welfare of one's

[8] American Jewish Committee. Research Institute on Peace and Post-War Problems. "Palestine in the New World." (Jewish Post-War Problems. Unit 6) p. 29-33. 1943.

oppressed brethren abroad and the desire to establish a Jewish national home in Palestine, they hold, are the true expressions of genuine loyalty to the principles of democracy and to the universal teachings of religion. No one is less the patriot because in his enlarged vision of a democratic world he insists that justice be done to a stricken, wandering people, uprooted and homeless.

Zionists assert that characterizing the Jews as a people or nationality does not have any political implications for Jews outside of Palestine; that this definition or characterization in no way implies that the Jews of America or Britain or any other country should become citizens of Palestine. They point out that the connection of the Jews of the world with Palestine is cultural, religious and sentimental in nature, not political. . . .

With reference to the place of Palestine in the solution of Jewish postwar problems, Zionists believe that the Jewish national home is capable of answering some or all of the following needs in Jewish life: Palestine can serve (1) as a physical haven of refuge; (2) as a religious and cultural center for the Jews of the world, and as a guarantee for Jewish group survival; and (3) as a normalizing agency for the Jews in and outside of Palestine. Let us proceed to describe briefly these contentions of the Zionists. . . .

Zionists are among the major proponents of the emigrationist point of view. They . . . believe that a large number of European Jews would prefer to live in Palestine regardless of improved conditions in their own countries or the possibilities for emigration elsewhere. They doubt whether the restrictions on immigration, now operative in the overseas countries, will be relaxed. They say that the achievements of the Jews in Palestine have created the possibilities for increased mass settlement of Jews both in agriculture and industry, and that Palestine should therefore receive primacy in any consideration of Jewish resettlement after the war.

Zionists view the Jewish refugee problem as being more than one of narrow philanthropy—of establishing homeless Jews on secure economic foundations. From a larger humanitarian viewpoint, they say, homelessness implies more than the lack of a place where one can enjoy physical security. A true home for

Jews implies also a place where they may be able to satisfy their individual and collective spiritual needs in an atmosphere suffused with Jewish values.

They point out that even in the democracies, where religious freedom prevails, the wide dispersion of Jews among non-Jews and the primary claims of the dominant culture tend to discourage many Jews from the diligent observance of their religion or from its full transmission to their children. Only in Palestine can Jews observe the seventh-day Sabbath and the Jewish holidays without experiencing grave inconveniences. There, those who wish can observe the Jewish dietary laws (*Kashrut*) without any difficulty or social embarrassment. Moreover, only in Palestine can their children normally acquire a thorough religious training, and study the Bible and other Jewish subjects in the daily schools as part of their regular education.

Zionists are pessimistic about the future of general Jewish culture in the Diaspora without a Jewish cultural center in Palestine. They maintain that to Jews dwelling in democratic countries, Jewish culture must inevitably take second place to the culture of their own land; that few Jews today outside of Palestine have mastered the Hebrew language sufficiently to use it as a living tongue or even as a medium of Jewish scholarship. In the western democratic countries, Jewish scholarship has found it necessary to draw upon immigrants from Eastern Europe for spiritual sustenance and replenishment. But the East-European centers of Jewish culture and learning have been destroyed by the war and, even prior to the war, there was a strong assimilationist trend in many parts of Eastern Europe, leading to a spiritual decline. Zionists point out, furthermore, that even the policy of the Soviet Union in giving Jews full opportunity and state support for cultural expression in Yiddish, has been of little avail in face of the stronger influences of Russian culture.

A more extreme variation of the pessimistic approach to the future of Jewish life in the Diaspora is the view held by a group of adherents of the so-called Shlilat Hagalut ("Negation of the Diaspora") theory—that the Jews are bound to disappear as a distinctive cultural, national and even religious entity unless a sizable number of them is concentrated in one territorial center, in the mind of most, Palestine. Nor is it because of anti-Semitic prejudice or persecution that the sociologists (such as Arthur Ruppin, Ezekiel Kaufman and Jacob Klatzkin), who hold this view, have come to this conclusion. On the contrary, they maintain that persecution has had a tendency, on the whole, to enhance Jewish group solidarity, but democracy and tolerance make for a loosening of Jewish ties and a gradual disappearance of Jewish group loyalty. They believe that because of the economic and cultural opportunities which equality offers, Jews will increasingly relax their specifically Jewish religious and cultural ties, drift away from the anchorage to their historic past, and become assimilated to the point of losing their identity as Jews.

Basing their views on the assumption that persecution will not last forever, these scholars point to past experiences in countries where Jews had been emancipated. The forces of the environment under such conditions of freedom are too strong, they contend, to keep Jewish group life intact and culturally creative.

Those who share the view of these scholars—whether prompted by motives of cultural perpetuation, religious continuation, nationalist sentiment or the normal urge for group survival common to all healthy groups of people, or a combination of these factors—look to a strong Jewish center in Palestine as the only guarantee for Jewish group survival in a world which will become increasingly democratic.

Nor is this belief in eventual Jewish group disappearance held only by Zionists and protagonists of Hebrew culture. Many secular Yiddishists and even some non-Jews share this view. It is this view which prompted many Jews who wish to see Jewish culture in the Yiddish language perpetuated to seek a territory where Jews can live as a free national group. In this connection, it is interesting to note that one of the reasons advanced by Mikhail Kalinin, President of the Soviet Union, for establishing Biro-Bidjan as an autonomous Jewish territory, was to offset the increasing assimilation of Soviet Jews to Great Russian culture. Christian Zionists too, among them such men as the Reverend John Haynes Holmes and Professor Reinhold Niebuhr, have expressed the opinion that the need for preserving Jews and Judaism is one of the reasons why Palestine should be restored to the Jewish people.

Zionists hold, furthermore, that a Jewish national home in Palestine will increasingly help to normalize Jewish life everywhere: (a) by providing an answer to the taunt that Jews are eternal wanderers without a home-country; (b) by providing an answer to the charge regarding Jewish "unproductiveness"; and (c) by providing a population-absorbing safety valve against anti-Semitism.

a. *As an answer to the taunt that Jews are eternal wanderers without a home-country.* Most Zionists hold that anti-Semitism is partly conditioned by the feeling which is quite prevalent in many quarters, that Jews are not like all people in that they are eternal wanderers without a home-country of their own, who depend for their livelihood and cultural expression on the good will and bounty of others. In our own time, Nazi anti-Semitic propaganda has widely disseminated this view about the Jews, and it is a fact that many Jews have developed a feeling of inferiority—of "not belonging." In answer to this problem, Zionists maintain that a flourishing Jewish national home in Palestine will give the Jews of the world a sense of dignity and pride. By being able to point to the social, economic and cultural achievement of their kinsfolk and coreligionists in Palestine, Jews will not only refute thereby the anti-Semitic allegation about Jewish homelessness, but will themselves derive a spiritual satisfaction and a moral courage which no anti-Semite will be able to destroy. Already, it is pointed out, the small Yishuv (Jewish community) in Palestine has become a beacon of light and warmth to the harassed Jews in many parts of the world. Thus, the very existence of a thriving Jewish homeland, it is contended, will be of inestimable value in normalizing Jewish life everywhere.

b. *As an answer to the charge regarding Jewish "unproductiveness."* There is a widely held belief that one of the causes of anti-Semitism is the so-called abnormal economic structure of the Jewish people—the alleged tendency of Jews to concentrate in commercial and professional occupations. Zionists who hold this view have unceasingly urged that Jews should become a "productive" people of farmers and workers. Moreover, they say that Palestine is the place where the abnormality of the Jewish economic structure can be overcome. In fact, one of the major contributions of the Jewish national home to date, they claim, has been its absorption into agriculture and industry of thousands of Jews who formerly were members of the middle class, such as businessmen, storekeepers, professionals and white collar workers. As a result, prevalent notions about Jewish "unproductiveness" are being dispelled, and Jewish security and dignity everywhere are thereby enhanced.

c. *As a population-absorbing safety valve against anti-Semitism.* There are some Zionists who hold that anti-Semitism is caused primarily by the heavy concentration of the Jews in a few localities. With Palestine open to all Jews who desire to enter it, the population pressure, real or imaginary, which has been a factor making for anti-Semitism, will be eased. Zionists point out that it was concern with this type of anti-Semitism in Russia and other countries which originally led Theodor Herzl and his followers to seek an immediate place of refuge for Jews either in Palestine or in some other available country.

While many people today would stress economic and social factors as the more basic contributing factors making for anti-Semitism, the problem raised by Jewish population concentration has not been answered satisfactorily—at least to those who consider it a root-cause of anti-Semitism. It is believed, however, that a Jewish national home in Palestine will help normalize Jewish life in the Diaspora by helping to reduce the areas of Jewish population concentration.

JEWISH STATE OPPOSED [9]

Our Jewish fellow-Americans, Zionist and non-Zionist as well, must realize that such pressures now are ill-advised, will increase tension in Palestine and may precipitate violence and bloodshed there. Furthermore, such pressures embarrass those

[9] Letter by Rabbi Morris S. Lazaron, member Boards of Directors, American-Jewish Joint Distribution Committee and the League of Nations Association; member Executive Committee, National Conference of Christians and Jews. *New York Times.* p. 8E. September 30, 1945.

responsible for the conduct of our international relations and complicate delicate negotiations now being conducted with Britain on many other important issues.

Under these conditions, Jews and Christians should consider long and seriously before associating themselves with any effort which might indeed destroy magnificent achievements in Palestine which the labor and sacrifice of the last quarter century have established, which might deprive thousands of their one hope for a home and precipitate religious and racial warfare in the Near East.

It is hard to believe that any man or group of men would so act as to bring upon themselves responsibility for such dire eventualities. It should be clearly understood here in our own country that the Palestine Jewish community is divided on the issue; at least 25 per cent, according to a recent estimate, are opposed to extremist action.

Let us keep in mind the larger issues. On some things there can be no compromise. The right of Jews, as of all men, to live anywhere and enjoy the privileges of citizenship as long as they obey the laws of the land is not a question of debate. The need to find homes for the stateless and dispossessed, the ability of Palestine to absorb a large proportion of such unfortunates, their desire to go there and the justice of the claim that Palestine should be opened to such immigration within the limits of the complex situation are facts in the picture, supported by the profoundest considerations of justice and humanity among Jews and Christians, American and British.

I believe the British and our own governments appreciate the tragic conditions and are inclined to use their best endeavors to find a practical solution. Propaganda pressure will not better things. It will make them worse. It will involve the American Jewish community in Zionist pressure politics to the detriment of relations between Jewish and Gentile Americans.

Over and above the immediate crisis is the basic question: What shall be the future of the Jewish citizens of America and the world? The effect of Jewish nationalism will be to secularize the Jews of the world, make them people like other peoples, with Judaism a national religion.

If the philosophy of Jewish nationalism dominates Jewish life in America all sorts of emotional and psychological bars will ipso facto be created between Jews and their fellow-citizens, the normal processes of integration in American life will be either delayed or stopped, Jews will form an enclave within the American scene and many of the bridges of understanding which have been built between Jew and Christian will be barred up or destroyed. But Judaism is a universal religion. To make it a national religion is to return to the past. To set us apart from our fellow-Americans in any sense other than religious is to ghettoize this great, free community.

The Zionist philosophy and program impose upon us the necessity to choose between these two propositions. There can be no compromise on this issue which involves the future of Jews here and everywhere.

It is too often forgotten in the heat of controversy that more than two thirds of the Jews of the world now live in lands of freedom. The citizenship enjoyed by them should not be endangered by setting up a Jewish state, which at best could offer a home to several millions, which would always be surrounded by Arab peoples, which would be too small to protect even its own nationals and which would always be the football of international politics.

It was on the assumption that the Jew could and would integrate himself in the land where he lived that the ghetto walls were broken down and Jews achieved complete political emancipation and were granted the rights of citizenship. That principle presumed the renunciation of Jewish nationality by the Jew in exchange for full citizenship. It was on this basis that Jews obtained French citizenship September 28, 1791. It was a presumption with which America started. No national test for Jews! No religious test for Americans! Nationality and religion are independent conceptions, separate and distinct. The bond that unites Jews is a religious bond, not a national one. Jews are politically and nationally an integral portion of the people among whom they live—American, British, French, German, Italian, etc. I venture to suggest that it is only by frank, unqualified acceptance of this cardinal principle that Jews can continue to enjoy full rights of citizenship where they now enjoy them, or claim them where they are now denied.

Let us determine, first of all, how many Jews wish to go to Palestine and let us all unite behind the appeal to open the doors of Palestine to as wide an extent as conditions permit. Let us have done with making irresponsible public demands which can end only in disillusionment, disappointment and possibly bloodshed. Palestine the refuge, the cultural center—yes! But not Palestine the Jewish state. I believe more can be done in Washington, London, Moscow, Paris and with the Arab League and leaders through quiet conversations, pointing out the desperate need, than resolutions, mass meetings and persistent irritating public pressure.

A key to what might be an American approach to the complex Palestine problem was contained in the King-Crane Commission set up during the peace conference by President Wilson to make an objective appraisal of the Palestine situation. On its return from first-hand investigation in Palestine, it delivered its report to the American Commission to Negotiate Peace, the end of August 1919. The report was not made public till December 2, 1922. It recommended "serious modification of the extreme Zionist programs for Palestine of unlimited immigration of Jews, looking finally to making Palestine distinctly a Jewish state." Little attention seems to have been paid to this important document which obviously suggested compromise.

If bloodshed is to be avoided, neither a final decision nor a long-range solution is possible at the present time. The issues are too involved and feeling is too intense. The element of time is needed, plus a wise and just administration of the picture. It should be possible, however, to mitigate the fears of the Arabs by international guarantee against Jewish domination, and to satisfy the demands of Jewish nationalists by a more generous immigration policy with local autonomy guaranteed to each community. It should be possible to protect British imperial interests and to secure to other interested countries, including the United States, ultimate and effective joint responsibility for Palestine by tightening up international supervision over the mandatory group.

Certainly with international guarantee of the integrity of their position, with the threat of Jewish dominance removed, the Arabs in the light of Jewish need and desire, should agree to open the country to reasonable Jewish immigration and to extensive economic development. The mandatory and supervising international authority will see to it that "nothing shall be done which may prejudice the civil and religious rights of existing non-Jewish communities in Palestine," even as the international organization will see to it that "the rights and political status enjoyed by Jews in any other country are not prejudiced or jeopardized."

Through complete autonomy in cultural and measurable autonomy in fiscal affairs, the growing Palestine Jewish community will achieve in Palestine a homeland. The land will expand its economy and with its expanding economy its capacity to absorb immigration will increase. The various communities working together to build up the country they claim as their own may, under statesmanlike guidance and restrained leadership, develop habits of cooperation which can only come naturally through living and laboring together. Until they do, a continuance of the British mandate under the new international authority seems the only practical possibility.

Enduring states are not born mature. They evolve as their inhabitants strive and sacrifice, labor and create together. Britain, Russia, the United States and other countries and peoples have vital and important interests there. Christian, Moslem and Jew draw inspiration from what is to all of them the Holy Land. The political future of Palestine must be built in the unfolding years through peaceful compromise of all these national, racial, religious and international factors.

Meanwhile, international authority must repress the extremist, encourage the moderate and give the land a chance. They who say they love Palestine should not insist on any other way. They who seek "the peace of Jerusalem" will find it only in the way of honorable compromise.

LETTER TO PRESIDENT HARRY S. TRUMAN [10]

Ever since we introduced Senate Joint Resolution No. 112 on Palestine, a continuous campaign, both open and covert, has been conducted against the bill, and more particularly against its basic proposition—that the Jews shall have the right of free entry into Palestine so that they may reconstitute it as a democratic commonwealth. Whoever may be behind this opposition and whatever their motives, their campaign has taken the form of a gross misrepresentation of our position and of the intentions of all who support Jewish aspirations in Palestine. The misrepresentation centers in the astounding and baseless charge that it is proposed to establish in Palestine a "theocratic" state or a state based upon religious or racial discrimination. This insidious campaign has now been carried to the White House in an obvious attempt to influence the Administration. We, therefore, find it necessary to make a full statement of our position in order to dispel such fantastic misconceptions so assiduously fostered.

In drafting our Resolution we had before us the Palestine planks of the Republican and Democratic platforms adopted by the national conventions of the two parties in Chicago, 1944. The relevant words in the Republican platform are as follows:

In order to give refuge to millions of distressed Jewish men, women and children driven from their homes by tyranny, we call for the opening of Palestine to their unrestricted immigration and land ownership, so that in accordance with the full intent and purpose of the Balfour Declaration of 1917 and the resolution of a Republican Congress in 1922, Palestine may be constituted as a free and democratic commonwealth.

The corresponding language in the Democratic platform is as follows:

We favor the opening of Palestine to unrestricted Jewish immigration and colonization, and such a policy as to result in the establishment there of a free and democratic Jewish commonwealth.

[10] By United States Senators Robert A. Taft and Robert F. Wagner. Text of letter sent to President Truman, December 6, 1945. Palestine. 2:4-6. November-December 1945.

Our Resolution is, therefore, no more than a restatement of the position taken by both major parties representing, as they do, the great majority of American citizens.

The expression, "Jewish commonwealth," is not novel. It was not recently invented to represent a new idea. It antedates the Palestine mandate and was used repeatedly by the leading statesmen of Great Britain and the United States in the crucial years preceding and following the Peace Conference at Versailles when the territorial settlements were in the making.

That this was the sense in which the British Government had understood its commitment was stated by David Lloyd George, Prime Minister at the time of the Balfour Declaration, who testified before the British Royal Commission on Palestine as follows: "It was contemplated that when the time arrived for according representative institutions to Palestine, if the Jews had meanwhile responded to the opportunity afforded them by the idea of a national home and had become a definite majority of the inhabitants, then Palestine would thus become a Jewish commonwealth."

General Smuts, Prime Minister of the Union of South Africa, on November 3, 1919, spoke of "an increasing stream of Jewish immigration" and of "a great Jewish state rising there once more."

Mr. Winston Churchill spoke in the same vein: "If, as may well happen, there should be created in our lifetime on the banks of the Jordan a Jewish state under the protection of the British Crown which might comprise three or four millions of Jews, an event will have occurred in the history of the world which would from every point of view be beneficial."

The British Royal Commission attested that "Lord Robert Cecil, in 1917, Sir Herbert Samuel, in 1919, and Mr. Winston Churchill, in 1920, spoke or wrote in terms that could only mean that they contemplated the eventual establishment of a Jewish state."

The position of the United States in favor of the evolution of Palestine into a Jewish state was equally clear. That this was the understanding of the American Delegation at the Peace Conference appears explicitly from the *Outline of Report and Rec-*

ommendations prepared by the Intelligence Section of that Delegation, in accordance with instructions, for the American Plenipotentiaries. This report, dated January 21, 1919, summarized the American attitude in the following recommendation:

That the Jews be invited to return to Palestine and settle there, being assured by the (Peace) Conference of all proper assistance in so doing that may be consistent with the protection of the personal (especially the religious) and property rights of the non-Jewish population, and being further assured that it will be the policy of the League of Nations to recognize Palestine as a Jewish state as soon as it is a Jewish state in fact.

In harmony with this position, President Woodrow Wilson on March 3, 1919, declared: "I am persuaded that the Allied nations with the fullest concurrence of our own government and people are agreed that in Palestine shall be laid the foundations of a Jewish commonwealth."

It cannot be suggested that the statesmen we have quoted, from Lloyd George to Woodrow Wilson, lacked the capacity to express themselves in clear and precise terms. Each of them was a master of the English tongue. Nor would anyone in his senses impute to those enlightened statesmen the advocacy of a "racial state" or a "theocracy" when they used the term "Jewish commonwealth" so freely. What they obviously intended and stated in so many words was that in Palestine, their ancestral land, the Jews should be free to grow into a majority and not be kept down artificially to the position of a minority in which they find themselves in every other country in the world. This is the core and essence of the proposal.

It is clear from the foregoing that our resolution does no more than give renewed expression to the purposes of the British and American statesmen who framed the policies of the Allied nations. Their statements are, if anything, more explicit than the terms of our resolution. The objective remains simple and clear: to ensure that all Jews who desire to settle in Palestine shall be guaranteed the right of entry so that they may develop and repopulate their ancestral land and so that Palestine may become a Jewish state in the sense that Jews will constitute the majority. Our resolution adds the proviso that the commonwealth thus to be created shall be one in which "all men, regardless of race or creed, shall enjoy equal rights."

This is also the official position of the Zionist movement repeatedly expressed. Time and again, on countless occasions, the Zionist Organization made it crystal clear that it contemplates a democratic state in which complete equality of rights and status shall obtain between all citizens, irrespective of race or faith, and between all religious groups within the state.

Under the circumstances, it should be impossible for any well-informed person to maintain in good faith the fantastic notion that the formula "Jewish commonwealth" implies any domination of the Jewish religion over the adherents of other faiths.

Millions of Jews in the Old World regard themselves and are regarded by their neighbors not merely as a religious denomination, such as Moslems or Baptists, but also as a people with a distinctive culture, characteristics and traditions. By the Balfour Declaration and the mandate the nations of the world recognized that just as the Czechs, the Greeks, the Magyars, and the Irish, or any other recognized nationality, are entitled each to a homeland of its own, so the Jewish people was likewise entitled to its national home. The mandate, therefore, speaks of the recognition "given to the historical connection of the Jewish people with Palestine and to the ground for reconstituting their national home in that country."

We are reluctantly driven to the conclusion that the misrepresentations to which we have referred and the false issues raised with regard to the projected Jewish commonwealth are intended to confuse the public, to deprive the Jewish people of their established rights, and to assist the British Government in evading its obligations under binding international agreements. Neither we, nor other Senators who share our views, nor the American people will be deceived by these tactics.

Finally, Mr. President, it is our conviction that the passage of such a resolution is more urgently required now than ever before, in view of the joint Anglo-American Committee of Inquiry. . . . Our country can only proceed on the assumption that the pledges given to the Jewish people and embodied in international covenants shall be honored. If the joint Committee proceeds on that assumption, its hands will be strengthened by the passage of the resolution. If the Committee is not instructed to proceed on that assumption, it is the more necessary that the traditional and basic position of the United States with regard to the Palestine question should be reaffirmed so far as it lies in the power of Congress.

We trust, Mr. President, that this statement will contribute to a clarification of this question touching an important aspect of our foreign policy.

EXCERPTS

Most of the land in areas now denied to the Jews has been uncultivated for hundreds of years, and Arab representatives have gone on record as saying that they can do nothing with such terrain. At the Palestine Round Table Conference in London in 1939, the Arab delegation asserted that 19,000,000 dunams in Western Palestine (which comprises, in all, 27,000,-000 dunams) were not and could not be cultivated by the Arabs. This area, withdrawn from the Jewish land market, is thus condemned to remain waste as long as the White Paper Regulations are in force. In the Negeb, or south country, which is today mostly desert, there are, as unbiased experts have stated, vast possibilities, if modern methods of land development by means of irrigation are applied. In the hill country, which comprises one third of Palestine and which is also excluded from Jewish land purchase operations, it has been demonstrated by Jewish settlements in the past decade that room exists for a larger population. . . .

The restrictive land regulations are a breach of that common law which insists upon equal rights for all citizens; they undermine the normal economy of the country by artificially freezing ownership of land; and they are a flagrant breach of Britain's obligations under the mandate entrusted to it to facilitate the establishment of a Jewish National Home.—*"Nuremburg in*

Palestine," by Elias M. Epstein, head of the Overseas Department, Jerusalem Headquarters of the Jewish National Fund. Palestine. O. '45. p. 9-10.

A unique approach to the Palestine problem has been suggested by ex-President Hoover in a recent statement to the *New York World-Telegram.* Mr. Hoover suggests as a "constructive humanitarian solution" based on careful study of the engineering problems involved, that the Arabs of Palestine be resettled on the fertile soil of under-populated Iraq. Iraq should be given financial assistance in restoring the old irrigation systems which made possible its ancient prosperity.

Mr. Hoover believes that the times are propitious for such a development, since today millions of people are being moved from one land to another. This particular movement could be made the model migration of history. It would be a solution by engineering instead of by conflict.

Commenting on this proposal, the American Zionist Emergency Council issued a formal statement to the effect that the Zionist movement has never advocated the transfer of Palestine's Arab population, but has always maintained that Palestine has "room enough for its present population, Jew and Arab, and for several million more of Jewish settlers." The developments of the last twenty years have amply proved this; nevertheless "when all the long accepted remedies seem to fail, it is time to consider new approaches."

The Hoover plan, the Emergency Council states, represents an important new approach, in the realization of which Zionists would be happy to cooperate with the great powers and the Arabs.—*"Notes on the Palestine Situation." Palestine. N.-D. '45. p. 16.*

I can end only by telling you of a little report from Palestine I saw the other day, which left an indelible impression on my mind. It was written by a woman who had gone to meet a train bringing some 1300 new refugee immigrants to Palestine. She stood with an old man waiting with tears in his eyes for a granddaughter, the only living member of the large family he had left behind him in Europe; with a physician whose wife had been gassed to death in Germany but whose son had somehow escaped and was coming to him; with hundreds of other tremulous, bereft human beings, waiting for some one miraculously rescued relative. Then the newcomers began to descend from the train—an orphaned girl from Italy, an orphaned lad from France, a youth who when asked from where he came, replied: "What difference does that make? What matters is where I have come to, not where I've come from. I've come home."

He stretched out his hands in joy—and the woman saw the number scorched into his flesh—108,223—his slave number in a labor camp. There were such numbers on the hands of all the 1300 newcomers, on the hands, too, of a little boy of six, who came shyly up to the woman and told her, in reply to her question, that he had come originally from a town in Poland. He was six years old and his eight year old sister was with him. "She and I," he said simply, "are the only Jews left of all the thousands in our town. Just she and I."

And to help to give new life to these tragic children in the land to their people's beginnings is without question an integral part of our responsibility as Christian Americans dedicated to the building of a better world.—*Helen Gahagan Douglas, Congresswoman from California. In "To Christian Youth." The American Christian Palestine Committee. New York. '45. p. 7-8.*

By a Jewish commonwealth we certainly do not mean a state which is exclusively Jewish. We do not mean to drive the existing Arab population into the desert or cast it into the sea. On the contrary, those who choose to do so are to remain. Moreover, their civic and personal rights shall be inviolate. There shall be a full and complete equality before the law. Not only that, but the Arabs shall have every right and possibility to preserve and develop their cultural and religious heritage. Their language shall be recognized and their traditions respected. And in addition they shall share fully in the economic advantages and opportunities and the prosperity which will come with the modernization of the country and the development of its resources.

Indeed, this has already been the case in a substantial measure. If, then, we are asked what do we mean by the adjective "Jewish" as applied to the future commonwealth of Palestine my answer is that it is a short and abbreviated way of saying that through the repatriation of large numbers of European and other Jews, the Jewish people will attain a numerical majority in Palestine and thereby permanently guarantee the open door for others who may follow; so that Palestine shall never cease to serve as a sanctuary and homeland for any and all Jews from whatever part of the world who may choose to go there in the future. It will also be a Jewish commonwealth in the vital sense that in that country, in that little corner of the world, the Jewish people, no longer living under minority conditions but as a majority, will be free to apply their talent, their industry, their genius and leave the intangible impress of their civilization upon their ancestral land as in the days of the kings and the prophets.

But the development of this Jewish commonwealth shall take place under democratic institutions and in a democratic spirit. The Jews will preponderate and lead in the development of the country without dominating or oppressing the minority. Jew and Arab devoted to their respective cultures and traditions shall cooperate as free and equal citizens and jointly contribute to the prosperity and welfare of a common single unitary state. The Arab citizens of the Jewish commonwealth will be as favorably situated as are the French-speaking citizens of the British Dominion of Canada. It will be a free and democratic Jewish state composed of Jews, Moslems, Christians and, if there are any, Buddhists, as well—compatriots, all. All shall be eligible to public office, even the highest.—*Emanuel Neumann, Attorney, New York. Address before National Convention of Junior Hadassah, Cleveland, O., November 27, 1943. U.S. House Committee on Foreign Affairs. Hearings, February 16, 1944. p. 315.*

South of the line [drawn from Auja on the Sinai border to Asluj and thence to the Dead Sea in the Negeb] there is . . .

practically no population at all. . . . It is in this area that the greater portion of the Roman settlement existed, and the argument is that as some hundred thousand people managed to live on the land here thirteen hundred years ago there is no reason why a few thousand should not make the attempt today. There would appear to be no valid objections to the scheme provided Jewish organizations and not the British tax-payer find the capital for the enterprise. If the Jews think they can make a success of a settlement here and are willing to foot the bill, there is no reason why they should not be allowed to try. There will be no hardship inflicted on the existing population, for to all intents and purposes they do not exist, and the few nomads who wander through the land at the present time would benefit from any exploitation of the area. They are existing today on the brink of starvation, and a little casual labor on the land, together with wages for camel hire, would just enable them to balance their private budgets—a thing that the Bedouin seldom succeeds in doing without going short of food.

There is, of course, no question of a rich and fruitful land awaiting exploitation. It is an exceedingly barren and harsh country, subjected to sand-storms and high winds; but it has a healthy hot climate, and in this respect it is preferable in every way to the low-lying land around Tiberius or Jericho. The would-be settler will have an exceedingly hard and disappointing time to start with, and one would not suggest an immigration scheme here for any European race but for the fact that necessity leaves no choice. There are, however, today thousands of Jews who are denied the right to exist elsewhere, and this constitutes an incentive to win a living at all costs that is calculated to provide a very exceptional settler who will not easily admit defeat. The fact remains, . . . despite every argument as to change of weather and local conditions, that in this quarter of Southern Palestine some hundred thousand people existed until the seventh century, and that they found sufficient water in this barren region for themselves, their flocks and their orchards. This being the case, one may reasonably expect that some ten thousand might as a beginning find a bare existence there today; and as there are hundreds of thousands of Jews looking for nothing more than a bare existence, the scheme would appear to be at least worth a trial.—*From article "Settlement in Southern Palestine" by Major C. S. Jarvis, Governor of Sinai for fourteen years. National Review. (London). Je. '39. p. 770-3.*

A national Jewish state carries with it . . . dangers to Jews now living outside of Palestine and particularly to those located in central European countries. Should such a state ever prevail, both Palestine and Jewish residents of these European countries would be between the upper and nether millstones. Migration pressures would militate against both. On the one hand, Palestine may be called upon to accept more Jews and at a faster rate than the land can possibly accommodate. Confusion and suffering would inevitably result, with the probability that such a Jewish state itself would be forced to stop or limit immigration. On the other hand, pressures may be placed upon these Central European Jews to force them, against their will, to migrate to Palestine. Being unable to do so, they would be left in a deplorable condition, without status, without assistance and without hope.

Many Americans of Jewish faith oppose the establishment of a national Jewish state upon still another consideration. Such a state would always be a small nation and could never hope to be a decisive force in the diplomacies of the world. It would forever be in one bloc or another. Jewish citizens of other nations of the world would forever be embarrassed either by its decisions or by its neutrality upon issues of world politics. Men of Jewish faith in some nation or group of nations of the world would be, of a necessity, either opposed to or called upon to defend secular, political action. The result must inevitably be that here in America, or for Jews elsewhere, the question of dual allegiances will be raised by men who, in critical times, lack discrimination and understanding. This would be particularly unfortunate in America, where the Jew has found a security greater than has ever been known in all the long history of Israel. The only sure way to avoid such a misunderstanding is to avoid the creation of a national Jewish state.

Palestine has made a great record. Palestine's achievement should not be wasted. Palestine should be *one* of the countries selected for resettlement. But a national Jewish state not only is not essential to such a purpose; it will be a detriment to such a service. In all probability, little if any difference of opinion exists regarding the desirability of considering Palestine as a place of settlement. It is very likely that it is the demand for a national Jewish state in Palestine that engenders the opposition of King Ibn Saud and many others.

It is hoped that Palestine can look forward to the ultimate establishment of a democratic, autonomous government wherein Jews, Moslems and Christians shall be justly represented; every man enjoying equal rights and sharing equal responsibilities; a democratic government in which Jews will be free Palestinians whose religion is Judaism, even as we in this country are Americans whose religion is Judaism. It is further hoped that such a program, embodying the spirit of the Atlantic Charter and the Four Freedoms, would be one to which Moslem and Christian would subscribe together with the Jew, and that Palestine might be another demonstration to the world that men of all faiths can live together in mutual respect for one another, and that such high regard of man for man is the cornerstone of lasting peace. —*Lessing Julius Rosenwald, Chairman Board of Directors, Sears, Roebuck and Company, 1932-1939; Chairman of Trustees of his father's philanthropy, the Rosenwald Fund. Life. Je. 28, '43. p. 11.*

I want to make a few more positive suggestions toward the solution of this question. We must constantly stress the fact that the Arabs need the Jews and they need them terribly. In this world of ours we must all share a common economic and industrial background of interest or we will all go down together because we have first of all to eat. We must farm our land properly, according to the methods which Dr. Lowdermilk so ably presented; we must develop our industries and our natural resources, as Mr. Ziff emphasized. In short, we must build a European civilization in the backward regions of the earth. Unless the Arabs are Europeanized in these fundamental respects they will also go down to destruction. Now the Jews are ideally suited to become the teachers of the Arabs in future, as they are already today. Jewish engineers and agronomists, as well as many other technologists and scientists, are being called as advisers throughout the lands of the Near and Middle East; in future they will be called upon even more.

Jewish Palestine has been physically transformed. Having been there before the transformation began, having as an archaeologist traversed all sections of the country and seen how desolate they were, and having come back to them years afterward in my constant travels, I know what miracles have been accomplished, and that the same miracles can be accomplished elsewhere in the Near East. . . .

The Arabs are learning fast to improve their poultry and their breeds of cattle; they are learning to plant citrus fruits, as well as all sorts of other crops which were at first planted only by the Jews. The Arabs are a teachable people, though they may resist westernization for a long time under the influence of misguided leaders who do not want the country to develop unless they themselves can rule it as they please. Under the influence of these same leaders they were for years before the present World War engaged in a program of destroying forests and irrigation works, destroying as much as possible, because the Arab revolt was really directed against European progress as a whole, not only against Zionism and British domination.

The lands of Palestine now settled by Jews were settled by less than 10,000 to 15,000 Arabs before the Jews moved in. There are now nearly 600,000 Jews in Palestine settled in areas where there had been at most 10,000 to 15,000 Arabs! Jewish immigration has not deprived the Arabs of their rights and privileges in a land where they have been settled for centuries.

It is true . . . that some Arab tribes have been only settled for a generation or two, but other groups have been settled for more than a thousand years, and the lands of the Near East, including Palestine, have been Arab with few intermissions for over 1300 years. The Arabs undoubtedly have a prior right in Palestine but that does not give them a right to deny the Jews their right to come and settle the waste places. Do the Arab propagandists in this country, some of whom are among my personal friends—claim for themselves the right to come with their compatriots and settle in America and do they with the same breath deny the same right of migration into their own homeland to oppressed European Jews?—*From article "The Arabs and the Jews" by Prof. William Foxwell Albright, Department of Oriental Studies, Johns Hopkins University. The Voice of Christian America; Proceedings of the National Conference on Palestine. American Palestine Committee. N.Y. '44. p. 18-22.*

To understand [the] high regard for the Palestine Foundation Fund we have but to consider the record. In the single year of 1944, in spite of many difficulties, more than fifteen thousand refugees were settled on the land. During the five years of war, $7,605,685 were expended on agricultural settlements, of which there are now more than three hundred. Over six million [dollars] went to aid the armed forces and for security, nearly five million to immigration and relief to refugees, nearly three million to labor and housing, nearly two to trade and industry, well over a million to education and culture, and more than a quarter of a million to religious affairs. In a period of fifteen years the Keren Hayesod expended five million dollars on Palestine's remarkable school system, which is a justifiable source of pride to all of the Yishuv.

Money is needed for such enterprises, but it is not money alone which has built up the Land of Promise. A pride in Zion has grown strong in the land, as the forests have grown tall in what was once desert, as the wheat waves proudly where once the crop was stone and sand. Although only 7 per cent of the land in Palestine is owned by Jews, last year Jewish farmers produced 24 per cent of all the wheat, 17 per cent of all the oats, and 9 per cent of all the durum and other grains grown in Palestine. During the war, a 400 per cent increase in the potato crop, an 80 per cent vegetable crop and 50 per cent more milk have been realized by patriotic, industrious Jewish farmers and dairymen.

The Jewish fishing industry, valued at $1,620,000 in 1944, is another enterprise fathered by Keren Hayesod. Workers were trained, ponds built, picturesque villages built. At present in the communal villages of Athlit and Caesaria, two hundred villagers earn a living chiefly by fishing. Eventually it is expected that fifteen hundred families will find employment in the proposed fishing base between Haifa and Tel Aviv.

It is perhaps in its record of help to refugees that the Keren Hayesod has latterly written the most dramatic part of its story. The Foundation Fund financed rescue from concentration camps of thousands of Jews who otherwise would have met death after being subjected to the death-in-life meted out to their less fortunate brethren. Underground workers, many of whom lost their own lives, accomplished the rescue of Jews from many prison camps. Utterly destitute, at the lowest ebb of physical and mental health, these captives were freed and brought to Palestine. They found rest and health in hostels there, were trained to earn a livelihood, and were given loans to help them get started. All of this came out of Keren Hayesod funds . . . at an expense of eight times as much as these services cost before the war. If you have children whom you love and for whom you are providing in your will, you will be glad to hear that thirteen thousand children have been saved from the Nazi death-piles since the ill-omened year of 1933.

Keren Hayesod has made wise use of the skills and knowledge of castaway European Jews. It has equipped factories to which refugees from Poland have brought their experience of modern machines. It has diverted the skill of the Yemenite Jews, craftsmen in silver, leather and wood, to the more essential needs of farming. It has enriched the economy of Palestine by loans to industry, such as the loan of about $125 in 1939 to an impoverished refugee who now employs ninety men and turns out a product for the army which no other factory in the Middle East produces. Keren Hayesod has blazed the trail for new industries, especially since the start of the war. In 1939, eleven loans totalling in all $35,000 were distributed among diamond-working units in Palestine. In 1943 the industry had grown to thirty-two factories, with thirty-five hundred workers, and an output worth over $3,000,000.

Arab-Jewish relations, important to Jewish security, have been strengthened by the Keren Hayesod program. An institute has been established to teach Arabic to Jewish Mukhtars, heads of villages near Arab villages. Courses for children, in Arabic and on Arabian folkways, make for better understanding. Bulletins are issued in Arabic so that Arabs may become acquainted with Jewish projects, may see how Jews benefit their Arabian neighbors.—*From pamphlet "Where There's a Will; Your Share in the Story of Keren Hayesod," Palestine Foundation Fund (Keren Hayesod), Inc. New York. n.d. p. 7-15.*

In general, it is desired to protest against a procedure which seems to accord a right to the various Arab states to be consulted in the affairs of Palestine. The right of our own government as one of the principal allied and associated powers in the First World War as well as by virtue of the United States-British convention above mentioned, to participate in the future disposition of Palestine is obvious and unquestioned. The right of the Jewish people to be consulted is likewise clear and undeniable and is legally confirmed by the League of Nations mandate which, in recognizing the right of the Jewish people to reconstitute their national home in Palestine, authorized also the recognition of the Jewish Agency for Palestine as representing the interest of all Jews in the establishment of the national home. The Arab states are in this matter without legal standing of any kind and we submit that their attitude in recent years is certainly far from giving them a moral voice in this issue.

We feel constrained, at the same time, to make a frank statement of our views with regard to the course of action pursued by the executive branch of the government and the State Department in particular, over a period of years. Despite the unbroken chain of pro-Zionist acts, promises, and pronouncements to which we have referred, the policy they express has not been translated into action. On the contrary, numerous acts and omissions have emboldened the Arab leaders to allege that the American Government was, in fact, withholding its support from the Zionist cause, and that the pronouncements made here from time to time were meant for home consumption. We have consistently disregarded these allegations as unwarranted aspersions upon the good faith and political integrity of our government.

We are now compelled to review the situation in the light of the recent correspondence. We must recall that so far as we are aware, the government took no effective action to protect the interests of the Jewish national home, at the time of the issuance of the British White Paper in 1939, or to rectify that wrong in the years which followed. The government did not energetically intervene even when opening the doors of Palestine became an urgent humanitarian necessity because of the wholesale slaughter of the Jews of Europe. It appears further that our government failed to advise its representatives abroad, particularly in the Near East, that it was definitely committed to the policy of the Jewish national home and to instruct them to be guided accordingly. The State Department has on various occasions appointed to positions of importance in the Near East persons known as avowed opponents of this policy and has had to rely in turn upon reports and advices emanating from them. On two occasions the executive branch exerted its influence to prevent the adoption by Congress of a resolution reaffirming the traditional American policy on this subject. Above all, our government has failed to utilize the fluid political conditions created by the war and the process of political reorientation and reorganization under way in the Near East, for the purpose of insuring the status of the Jewish national home in the context of its Near East policies.

On the other hand, our country has given generous support to Arab aspirations. It was among the first to recognize the independence of Syria and Lebanon. It has encouraged Arab states to make last-minute declarations of war against Germany on the eve of the San Francisco Conference, assuring them places of honor among the United Nations, irrespective of their war records. Nor has it withheld its support from the Arab League despite the fact that the League has declared its opposition to Jewish aspirations and has proclaimed the liquidation of the Jewish national home as one of its major objectives.

The one gratifying positive act in relation to Palestine has been President Truman's recent request to Prime Minister Attlee, the outcome of which, however, is still uncertain. . . . The point has now been reached, at which ambiguity and delay are no longer feasible. Millions of American citizens, who have a strong moral and humanitarian interest in this problem, look to the Administration for immediate and forthright action, which will once and for all dispel any possible uncertainty regarding its present position and future intentions.—*From Memorandum submitted by the American Zionist Emergency Council to the State Department on occasion of the meeting of Dr. Abba Hillel Silver and Dr. Stephen S. Wise with Secretary James F. Byrnes, October 23, 7945. Congressional Record. O. 29, '45. p. A4920.*

Suppose that a few hundred thousand of the million Arabs at present in Palestine would consider life in a Jewish common-wealth impossible. The evidence, it is true, is all, as we have seen, the other way: for the Jewish settlements have actually *attracted* the Arabs like a magnet. But, in the worst case, is there no way out? Surely there is, and a very simple one. The world has recently been discussing the project of moving great hordes of men and women—not a few hundred thousand, but ten or twelve million—from their old homes to a new environ-ment: Germans from East Prussia, Silesia and the Sudetenland to West of the Oder, Poles to Germany, Russians to Poland. It is a cruel proposal, for the migration is to be compulsory, and, in view of the economic misery which must follow the European war, it is likely to be effected in the harshest conditions. But suppose the United Nations said to the Arab statesmen: "We desire to establish, by the necessary stages, a Jewish common-wealth in Palestine, for we believe a settlement of the Jewish question on lines such as these to be an indispensable part of the world settlement. We give our guarantee that every Arab in Palestine shall have complete civic equality and religious free-dom. But if, in spite of this guarantee, any Arab should wish to leave Palestine and settle elsewhere we will make it easy for him to do so; we will see to it that the change takes place in the best conditions, and we will provide ample funds, in each case, for the secure establishment of a new home." If even some hundreds of thousands of Arabs availed themselves of the offer, the cost would be a trifle in the budget of Great

Britain alone, and infinitesimal in that of the United Nations. Would not the money be well spent? Is the tiny sacrifice it represents—were it ever necessary, as it never would be—too much to ask?

Where, it may be asked, are these Arabs to go, if they should indeed wish to leave their present homes? Not very far; for bordering on Palestine are Arab countries which are crying out for a larger population. It is, indeed, a bitter paradox that, while the Jewish people as such has not one square foot of territory, and Palestine is denied them, the agricultural and industrial development of the Arab lands is fatally hampered by shortage of population. In a paper prepared for the Royal Central Asian Society in 1926, Ja'far Pasha al Askari, then Prime Minister of Iraq, stated:

> What Iraq wants above everything else is more population. This is a necessary condition of progress. The size of the country is 150,000 square miles, which is about three times that of England and Wales, whilst its population is only three millions. In the Nile Valley, from Aswan to the sea, where you have a riverain population living upon irrigated lands, there are some thirteen million inhabitants. The possible irrigable area in Iraq is certainly not less than that of Egypt.

The British Government's Ten Years' Report on Progress in Iraq, 1920-1931, speaks of the "gravely insufficient agricultural population" which is a hindrance to the development of irrigated farming, and states:

> Real agricultural development in Iraq will come through an increase of agricultural population . . . for land brought within schemes of irrigation extension.

And here is a more recent view of a Middle East expert:

> Iraq's paramount requirement is an increase of population. With from three and a half to four million inhabitants she cannot do justice to the potentialities of the land—the lack of labor is a constant problem—and she is at a disadvantage against Turkey and Iran with their far larger populations. The settlement of the nomads on the land may add to her wealth, but any substantial increase of population in the near future must come from outside.

Somewhat similar conditions prevail in Syria. Dr. Bonné of the Jewish Agency Economic Research Institute in Jerusalem states on the basis of estimates given to him by the French Mandatory Government that of the 78,000 square miles of Syria, about 23,500 are cultivable, but only about 6,000 are really cultivated. Of the 2,300 square miles of irrigable land, only one third is irrigated. He concludes that the present population of about three millions could easily be doubled.

With regard to Transjordan we have the cautious view of the Palestine Royal Commission:

The area of Transjordan is about 34,000 square miles and its present population is estimated at about 320,000. Thus while the country is almost two and a half times as big as Palestine it contains only about a quarter of its population. That population, moreover, includes a large number of Bedouin, whose pastoral life requires more land than would be needed if in course of time they were to settle down to agriculture. . . . We are not in a position to fix even an approximate figure for the possibilities of new settlement in Transjordania; but, in view of the evidence given by some of those who are acquainted with the country and from what we saw, we consider the hope to be justified that, if fully developed, it could hold a much larger population than it does at present.

The whole position has been summed up in the Report of the Permanent Mandates Commission of the League of Nations, 1937:

It should also be remembered that the collective sufferings of Arabs and Jews are not comparable, since vast spaces in the Near East, formerly the abode of a numerous population and the home of a brilliant civilization, are open to the former, whereas the world is increasingly being closed to settlement by the latter.

—*Victor Gollancz, Chairman and Governing Director, Victor Gollancz, Ltd. London. In "Nowhere to Lay Their Heads." Victor Gollancz. London. '45. p. 32-4.*

I have not been unmindful of the probability that the treaties at the end of the war will contain special provisions requiring the governments of the former enemy states to guarantee equality of rights and opportunities to their citizens without discrimination on the basis of race or religion. I cannot have confidence, however, that these treaties will be effective.

Nor have I more faith in the efficacy of the several proposals for a universal Bill of Rights. Of course, a Bill of Rights should be proclaimed as a part of the peace settlement. The enforcement of its provisions should be one of the avowed and firmly maintained purposes of the victors. Nonetheless, I cannot share the optimism of Lessing J. Rosenwald and his colleagues of the American Council for Judaism when they declare that the solution to the problem of Jews "rests on recognition of the inalienable rights of the individual" and that "once that concept of human freedom is unqualifiedly accepted Jews will require no special measures."

This dictum ignores or glosses over the very special and acutely urgent problem of Jewish postwar refugees. Very respectfully, therefore, I urge the leaders of the American Council for Judaism to take account of the terrible realities of the hundreds of thousands of homeless Jews who at the end of the war can only hope to reestablish themselves outside of Europe.

Where can Jewish refugees expect to go after the war?

To the United States? Unhappily there is no present prospect for the liberalization of the admission of Jewish refugees to this country. We shall do well if we succeed in blocking those exclusionists who would reduce or eliminate the existing quotas or who, failing to change the law, would through changes in administration regulations close the doors against refugees.

Alaska? This potentially very rich territory is nearly empty; but as a territory of the United States, the immigration limitations which apply to the rest of the country apply also to Alaska.

Countries of Central and South America? They need now and will need for some time in the future mostly agricultural immigrants; and there are few farmers among the Jewish refugees. In some of the Latin American countries it is true there is a more rapid pace of industrialization but the opportunities for urban refugees will during the next years remain comparatively slight.

Africa? Angola, for example? It is the same threadbare tale, ambitious plans but no prospects of being carried out within any period which can be of help to Jewish refugees immediately after the war.

Kenya? It was in the highland area of that rich colony that Lord Winterton, British representative at the Evian Conference, first suggested Jewish refugee colonization. But in the face of opposition from the few Hindu inhabitants of the colony, the project was discouraged by the British Government and almost nothing has been done there.

Tanganyika? At first refugees from Hitler Germany were welcomed in this former German East Africa. But when the number of refugees had grown to 7,000, the anti-alien and anti-Jewish propaganda was followed by a decision of the British Government to close the doors of Tanganyika to Jewish refugees.

Ethiopia? This is but the latest of several African schemes. It like the others is so remote from realization as to give no hope of being of value during the next years.

Australia? The latest land settlement scheme for Jews in that comparatively empty continent can be expected to result in the admission of hundreds, perhaps a few thousand, not more, Jewish refugees.

Biro-Bidjan? Do you recall how only a few years ago this rich but difficult virgin territory in eastern Siberia in the Amur region on the border of Manchuria was to become such a haven of Jewish refugees as to solve the Jewish problem! For months in this country anti-Zionists seized upon Biro-Bidjan as a saving alternative. Now, thirteen years later, that is in 1941, the latest time for which we have figures, Biro-Bidjan contains not more than twenty-five thousand Jews and few of these from outside of the Soviet Union. Thus one more substitute for Palestine proves an illusion.

On the record Palestine offers incontestably the primary hope for the solution of the problem of Jewish refugees. The conclusion which emerges inescapably from a realistic résumé of twenty-five years of intergovernmental dealings with refugees and from a realistic appraisal of the world situation is that in Palestine and only there can the mass of Jewish refugees hope to be welcome and to be assisted to integrate themselves in the life of the community. Only in Palestine will most of them feel that they have returned home.—*James G. McDonald, League of Nations High Commissioner for German Refugees; Chairman of President Roosevelt's Advisory Committee for Political Refugees. Palestine. D. '45. p. 4-5.*

I shall not attempt to estimate the final absorptive capacity of Palestine. That would be impossible, for the absorptive capacity of any country is a dynamic and expanding conception. It changes with the ability of the population to make the maximum use of its land, and to put its economy on a scientific and productive basis. It is clear, however, that there is ample proof of the assertion made in our chapter on the Jordan Valley Authority, that full utilization of the Jordan Valley depression for reclamation and power will in time make possible the absorption of at least 4,000,000 Jewish refugees from Europe, in addition to the 1,800,000 Arabs and Jews already in Palestine and Transjordan.

It is interesting to note that British scholars of the Palestine Exploration Fund who explored Palestine during the second half of the nineteenth century had a very high estimate of the country's capacity. That group of valiant explorers—General Charles Warren, General Sir Charles William Wilson, Colonel Claude Rainier Condor and Lieutenant, subsequently Field Marshall Kitchener—were all enthusiastic about the possibilities of further development in Palestine. Sir Charles Warren expressed their common opinion in a book on Palestine issued as early as 1875, before even the earliest modern Jewish settlements were founded:

Give Palestine a good government and increase the commercial life of the people and they may increase tenfold and yet there is room. The soil is so rich, the climate so varied, that within ordinary limits it may be said that the more people it contains, the more it may accept. Its productiveness will increase in proportion to labor bestowed on the soil until a population of 15,000,000 may be accommodated there.

Warren had in mind the historic extent of Palestine which is much larger than the present mandated area. Applying his figures to present-day Palestine and Transjordan, we may say that he and his colleagues appraised the country's absorptive capacity at 12,000,000. What has been done by Jewish settlers in the last six decades would have seemed to Warren and his colleagues merely confirmation of their vision.

On 14 per cent of the cultivated area and 6 per cent of the total area of mandated Palestine, a people with faith and devotion born of long tradition has changed desolation into fertile fields, fruitful orchards and reforested slopes. Ancient cities have been rebuilt and the commerce on their streets quickened, long-unknown resources have been brought into the light of day and sent to the distant marts of the world. After centuries of darkness which crushed the hopes of Palestine's miserable inhabitants, a new force has come into the land and made it live again. The possibility of a new day for the entire Near East is hidden in the fertile lands, the flourishing villages and cities, the cooperatives and the factories of Jewish Palestine.

If the forces of reclamation and progress Jewish settlers have introduced are permitted to continue, Palestine may well be the leaven that will transform the other lands of the Near East. Once the great undeveloped resources of these countries are properly exploited, twenty to thirty million people may live decent, prosperous lives where a few million now struggle for a bare existence. Palestine can serve as the example, the demonstration, the lever, that will lift the entire Near East from its present desolate condition to a dignified place in a free world.— *Walter Clay Lowdermilk, Assistant Chief of the U.S. Soil Conservation Service. In his "Palestine, Land of Promise." Harper and Brothers. New York. '44, p.227-9. The views expressed are those of the author, not of any government department.*

The man who escaped with his life from the anteroom of the gas chamber because its capacity happened to be exhausted, told me: "When I stood there in the corridor, naked, awaiting my fate, I knew that I was being led to death for one single reason only—because I had no homeland of my own." He added, "For you, this may be ideology—for me it is reality."

Today on German soil, soaked with Jewish blood, training farms are being established for Chalutzim—pioneers for Palestine. Two have already been set up. Jews live there with one hope only—to go to Palestine.

It is perhaps no accident that so many of those who survived are either Zionists or religious—people of faith! A young man told me, "Most of what I ate came from the dustbin. But, do you know what is the best remedy against hunger? The hope of Palestine!" . . .

Only five days ago I was with some of the leaders of these people from the camps in the famous Munich beer-cellar where Hitler started on his campaign of polluting the world. There and then they adopted a resolution which spoke of the impossibility of returning to their old homes, and added: "Should the gates of Palestine continue to be closed against immigration, we shall be forced to fight for our right to live with all the means at our disposal."

And let there be no mistake about it. These people mean what they say. Nothing in the world can stand in their way and separate them from their one goal, which is Palestine. A new spirit is abroad among the survivors—a conviction that *this time* the solution must be final. All Jewish communities worthy of the name must do their utmost to bind the wounds of the victims and to prepare their way for the Return, the final Return. It would be a sad day for humanity if it should betray the last and only hope of these tortured souls. *Humanity must not fail them.* —*Eliahu Dobkin, head of Immigration Department, Jewish Agency for Palestine. Palestine. O. '45. p. 7-8.*

The assertion that Jews as a rule do not employ Arabs on their farms and in their factories deserves detailed consideration. During my visits to Jewish cooperative and collective villages, I saw no Arab workers, although I did see a considerable number on privately owned Jewish farms. When I asked the members of a cooperative village whether they accepted Arab labor, they told me that in their case the question was purely theoretical. All these so-called "labor settlements" are based on the principle of what they call "self-labor": in other words, all work is done by the members of the settlement, so no outside laborers, whether Jewish or Arab, are employed.

In industry there is an undeniable tendency to employ Jews in factories built by Jewish capital, and Arabs in factories belonging to Arabs. We found, however, that Jewish owners willingly employ Arab as well as Jewish labor in cases where the undertaking serves both sections of the population. The outstanding instances of this are the Palestine Electric Corporation and the Potash Syndicate, both organized and managed by Jews. The latter in particular employs Arabs in great numbers. In public works, harbors, etc., Arabs are always the majority of the workers, though Jews pay more of the taxes which make these projects possible.

The leaders of the Jewish labor movement in Palestine are genuinely sympathetic with Arab labor, but believe that Arab workers should for the time being be employed not in the Jewish but in the Arab and governmental sectors of Palestine's economy. They point to the economic benefits which Jewish activities have brought the Arab population, and they are ready to help the Arabs modernize their agriculture and industry. The Jewish labor leaders insist, however, that since Jewish work in Palestine aims to create a Jewish commonwealth for the persecuted masses of European Jewry, all hopes for such a commonwealth would be frustrated if Palestine were built by Jewish capital but predominantly Arab labor.

To Palestine's Jewish labor leaders the development of two parallel economic structures seems the best way to assure the general prosperity of the country. When Arab workers become accustomed to unions and the Arab standard of living is raised to higher levels, these parallel economies will, they feel, gradually merge with each other. It is with this general goal in mind that Jewish labor unions cooperate with, and aid, groups of Arabs who wish to organize themselves and improve their working conditions.—*Walter C. Lowdermilk, Soil conservation and forestry expert of the United States Department of Agriculture. From his "Palestine, Land of Promise." p. 162-3. Harper and Brothers. New York. 1944.*

The Jewish investments in Palestine are fundamentally investments in the rehabilitation of men. The investors are content— it is even sound business—to sink large sums of capital in this effort. Comparable perhaps are the investments of the Farm

Resettlement Administration in this country. Societies which undertake to rehabilitate shipwrecked men must build communities which are solvent in the sense that current income exceeds current expenditures plus upkeep, but not necessarily in an amount which permits interest and amortization of the investment at rates currently obtainable in other investment markets.

There is another angle of the high prices paid for land which has to do with the very heavy imports into Palestine in recent years. This money paid for land goes both to large and to small landholders. Much of what the latter receive is handed over to the effendis in payment of debts. Thus, in one way or another, most of the sums invested by Jews in land finds its way as spendable cash in the hands of Arab landowners and money lenders. Much of it is spent for better living (current consumption or better housing) and some at least for improvement of remaining lands. Arabs in this way developed citrus plantations amounting to about 50 per cent of the total. In either case, however, these payments result in a *temporary* spurt of imports.

All the foregoing can mean only that the "deficit colonization" of Palestine is normal to a developing country, and by no means indicative of an unsound economy.—*Clarence W. Efroymson, Associate Professor of Economics, Butler University. Palestine. D. '44. p. 9.*

THE ARAB CLAIM TO PALESTINE

THE ARAB WORLD AND THE ARAB LEAGUE [1]

Most people in England, when they hear the word "Arab" or the phrase "The Arab World," imagine a Bedouin living in a tent or riding on a camel in the desert. This misapprehension is due to several causes. It is due in the first place to the influence of early British writers on the Arab world, like Burton and Doughty, who were chiefly interested in the picturesque life and primitive virtues of the desert dwellers. Lawrence followed in the same tradition, which even today is still eloquently represented by explorers like Philby and Bertran Thomas. Secondly, there has been the influence of Hollywood, which, with its preference for glamour against reality, has gone in heavily for the tent and the camel, the Sheik and the Son of the Sheik seen in the image of Rudolf Valentino or Douglas Fairbanks. Thirdly, the word Arab has, in fact, two meanings, only one of which is commonly understood in England. Originally the word did mean the inhabitants of the desert, the Arab tribes that lived in and came out of the Arabian Peninsula itself, and to this day it has retained this specific meaning not only here, but in the Arab world itself. At the same time, however, the word, following the amazing fortunes of the desert warriors when they left their Peninsula and founded a world empire, has acquired a different and much larger meaning. The Arab conquests of the seventh and eighth centuries were not only military adventures. They were also cultural and racial conquests, as enduring in their results as they were swift and brilliant in their accomplishment. In a large part of the Byzantine world the conquerors settled down, inter-married with the local population, converted the majority to Islam and gave their language to the whole people. In this way, all that part of the world which lies along South and East of the Mediterranean from

[1] Arab Office. London. 12p. October 1945.

the Straits of Gibraltar to the Persian Gulf became Arabized and remained permanently so even after the Arab Empire passed away. This is the Arab world today. It includes Morocco, Tunis, Algeria, Libya, Egypt, the Sudan, Transjordan, Palestine, Syria, Iraq and the Lebanon, as well as the Arabian Peninsula itself. It includes sophiscated city dwellers, among them an educated class speaking English or French and in close contact with European thought, as well as picturesque nomads, and comprises Christians as well as Moslems. It has its roots in a great civilization which flourished in Damascus and Baghdad, in Cairo and Cordova, a civilization which led the world for three centuries when the West was plunged in the night of the Dark Ages, and which, before it decayed, transmitted to Europe through the Arab universities in Spain, the thought of Greece together with a notable contribution from itself five hundred years before the Renaissance.

This civilization was a brilliant achievement which resulted from the blending of Arab and Byzantine thought. With them from the desert the Arabs brought their magnificent language and their new religion in all its first purity and fervor. In the Byzantine world they found the thought of Greece and the laws of Rome; and they found Christianity. The impact of these influences on each other produced Arab civilization, which thus was not something entirely foreign to the West but a foster brother, brought up in the European family. Even Islam, the new religion of the Arabs, was a near relation of the other two great religions on which the spiritual life of Europe and the Mediterranean peoples was founded. Its God was the same as the God of the Jews and the Christians, and its founder, the Prophet Mohammed, did not deny the Hebrew prophets or Christ. On the contrary, he recognized and venerated them all as the bearers of God's word, and merely claimed that he was the last of them and that his message completed theirs.

The influence of Arab civilization on the subsequent development of human thought was considerable. In science its greatest achievements were in mathematics, astronomy and medicine. It is not certain whether the Arabs themselves invented the numerals which bear their name and on which all modern mathematics is founded, or learned them from an Indian source, but one thing is certain, the Arabs invented the zero or cipher—the word cipher comes from the Arabic—and taught the use of the Arabic numerals to the world. They also improved and expanded algebra, first invented by the Greeks. Again, the word algebra itself, as well as the word logarithm, comes from the Arabic. In astronomy their work left a permanent mark in the names of many stars—Betelgeuse, Rigel, Sirius, Aldebaran— which English people pronounce today in an English manner without knowing that they are Arabic words. In medicine the Arabs, basing themselves on the teachings of Galen and Hippocrates, did some admirable research and made discoveries which lie at the basis of a good deal of our knowledge today. Last but not least, they translated Plato and Aristotle into Arabic, and taught them to the European scholars who came from as far away as Oxford to study at the famous centres of Arab learning in Spain. Debarred from painting and sculpture as a precaution against any reversion to idolatry, the Arabs expressed their artistic instincts superbly in architecture; in the rounded domes, circular arches and plain slender pillars of their beautiful mosques and palaces which still attract tourists from all over the world to Cairo, Jerusalem, Damascus and Spain.

Arab civilization disintegrated as mysteriously as it had sprung. The only visible cause was the political disruption of the Arab Empire. Conflicts and divisions arose in it and what was begun by internal schism was completed by foreign conquest and domination. First came the Mongol invasions, then the conquest and occupation of the whole Arab world by the Ottoman Turks for a period of four centuries. The Ottoman genius, purely military and political, did not impart to the Arabs any of those spiritual qualities which, though carried on the point of the sword, had often fertilized a conquered people and, by the impact of one race on another, caused a new civilization to grow out of conquest—as, indeed, had happened when the Arabs conquered their Empire; nor were the Ottomans themselves fertilized by the Arab heritage as the Romans had been fertilized by Greece or as the Goths were fertilized by Rome. The Arab world was reduced to extreme poverty, and poverty begot ignorance and spiritual aridity. For nearly four hundred years the Arab world slumbered in an intellectual night. But even in its slumber it never lost its essential oneness. The Arabs sharing in the Ottoman empire remained a community, speaking one language, descended partly at least from the same ancestors and living in many ways a traditional life inherited from a civilization that had belonged to them all.

This long night came to an end in the nineteenth century. Under the impact of influences coming from Europe and America the Arab mind began to stir. First came Napolean's invasion of Egypt. His expedition was more than just a military attack on an Ottoman province. It was a cultural incursion from Western Europe into the Arab world, the first external stimulus to touch the Arab mind since the sixteenth century. Its results were seen in the amazing career of Mohammed Ali, the founder of modern Egypt. After the evacuation of Egypt by the French, Mohammed Ali became at once the military master and titular governor of Egypt under the Sultan. Eventually, he won virtual independence for himself as hereditary ruler of that country, overthrew Turkish rule in Syria, and with the help of his son and commander-in-chief, Ibrahim, tried to lead a movement for Arab revival and all but succeeded in founding a new Arab Empire stretching to the very gates of Constantinople.

His failure in this attempt was due both to internal and external reasons. The external reasons were the opposition of the European powers, who were alarmed at the prospect of the collapse of the passive Ottoman Empire and the rise in its place of a new and vigorous power which might not be so accommodating, and would certainly disturb the comfortably established equilibrium of forces in the Near East. The internal reasons were many, but foremost among them was the fact that the time was not yet ripe.

Despite his failure, however, Mohammed Ali, both by his rule in Egypt and his adventures outside it, administered a powerful stimulus to the Arab world. His regime in Egypt was the first attempt to create a modern state in that world; and to achieve this end he sought the advice and help of Europeans, particularly Frenchmen, of whom he employed a large number in the various branches of his administration. Under Mohammed Ali's son and viceroy Ibrahim, Syria experienced a spell of eight years' freedom from Turkish rule. Ibrahim identified himself with the Arab tradition and tried hard to create an Arab national movement; and although under pressure from the European powers Mohammed Ali was forced to withdraw from Syria, the experience which the Syrian Arabs had had under his rule left behind new ideas and the suggestion of possibilities undreamed of before.

But Mohammed Ali's was not the only challenge to Ottoman power that came from the Arab world in the early nineteenth century. Another challenge had come from the Peninsula itself, when a chief of the House of Saud (an ancestor of the present King Ibn Saud), championing the cause of the religious Wahhabi sect, to which he had been converted, repudiated the authority of the Sultan and delivered a serious blow at it not only in Arabia itself, but also in Syria and Iraq.

Both these challenges, however, had come too soon to lead to a general movement. It was only later in the century that Arab national consciousness began to awaken, called to life not by the individual exploits of a military leader, but by the message of a rediscovered culture.

For the revival of the Arabic language in its classical form and the intellectual renascence that accompanied it, the Arabs are largely indebted to the American and European teachers that came into Syria and the Lebanon in the middle of the nineteenth century. These brought with them printing presses and started a number of schools. A generation educated in the modern sense grew up. Books were printed, newspapers appeared and a cultural movement was born which drew its inspiration from old Arabic literature and Arab history, while at the same time receiving an immediate stimulus from the impact of contemporary European thought. Gradually the movement spread throughout the Arab world and began to express itself in political nationalism. The aims of this nationalism were two: independence of Turkey and Arab unity. The reawakened Arab mind, exhilarated by the rediscovered glories of Arab civilization, wished to recreate the Arab world as a whole and give it the structure of a modern state. A number of political societies were formed, some secretly inside the Arab world and some openly in Europe, to organize this national movement. The movement included Christians and Moslems who derived the inspiration of their common nationalism from the Arabic language.

The emergence of this national consciousness among the Syrian Arabs coincided with the new despotism of the Sultan Abdul Hamid (1876-1908) and the growth in Turkey itself of a movement for emancipation and constitutional reform. The Turkish reformers did not envisage independence for the Arab world, but merely equality of rights and active participation in a reborn and democratic Turkish Empire. The ferment created by their movement, however (in which for some time the Arab nationalists joined hopefully, only to be disappointed), coupled with the growing evils of the existing rule, the increasing interest of the European powers in the affairs of the Ottoman Empire and the general belief that the "Sick Man of Europe" was nearing the end of his days—all these combined to stimulate Arab nationalism. Encouraged by a tangible hope of liberation from Turkey in the near future, the movement made decisive strides and the seeds which had taken root in Syria threw out shoots into the neighboring Arab countries and finally, after the deposition of Abdul Hamid in 1908, blossomed out into a deliberate and widespread agitation.

Meanwhile, another strand of Arab culture and political consciousness was developing in Egypt under different influences and along separate, though parallel, lines. The first of the Arab countries to achieve virtual independence, Egypt, had been developing as a self-contained nation-state. Under the Khedive Ismail who, like Mohammed Ali before him, turned to the West for help and inspiration, there was another large influx of European ideas into Egyptian life. But although Egypt had become independent of Constantinople in her internal affairs, the Egyptian Government and the Egyptian army remained in complexion largely Turkish. The emerging national consciousness of the Egyptian people resented this state of things, and this resentment, sharpened by other causes, found expression, in the reign of Ismail's successor, in a serious revolt led by an Arab officer. The revolt was suppressed by British intervention and eventual occupation of the country.

The British occupation of Egypt stimulated Egyptian nationalism and the Arab movement in general in two ways: one positive, the other negative. On the positive side, it was another incursion of European influence, this time organized on the political plane. French influence had been mainly cultural and technical. With the British came new ideas about the forms and machinery of political life, financial and judicial administration, the rule of law and democratic evolution. There also came a period of stability and a greater opportunity for free intellectual enterprize, from which not only the Egyptians, but also the Arabs of the surrounding countries benefited. Syrians flocked to Egypt in the last years of the nineteenth and the early years of the twentieth centuries in search of work under the new regime. There they were able to develop in an atmosphere of greater freedom and security than they had ever enjoyed in their own country, and the influence of their vitalized thought seeped back to Beirut and Damascus, acting as a stimulus on their countrymen whom they had left behind. On the negative side the British occupation was a challenge to nascent Egyptian nationalism. It provoked a reaction of resistence and gradually called into being a widespread national movement inspired by the ideal of independence, and invigorated by the cultural renascence that was going on at the same time. A vigorous Arabic press grew up, whose influence was felt throughout the Arab world and whose columns, in addition to the rising sentiment of political nationalism, carried the voice of daring reformers preaching a rational reinterpretation of religious dogma, the emancipation of women and the general readjustment of national life to modern conditions. The number of schools, foreign and native, governmental and private, missionary and secular, increased enormously and, as in Syria, an educated class began to emerge which, apart from Arabic, knew either French or English and so came into direct contact with European thought.

When the First World War broke out the whole African part of the Arab world had been either completely torn away or virtually detached from the Turkish Empire: Egypt by Mohammed Ali, and further still by the British occupation; Tripolitania by Italy in 1912 and Tunis, Algeria and Morocco by France at an earlier time. The nominal suzerainty of Turkey over Egypt was abolished by British action in 1914 when Turkey came into the war on the German side, and a British Protectorate declared in its place. Greater Syria (i.e., Syria, Palestine, Transjordan and the Lebanon), Iraq and the Arabian Peninsula were the only parts of the Arab world that still remained under Ottoman rule.

Arab nationalism in this Eastern part of the Arab world saw in the war its chance of liberation from Turkey. The British Government, for its part, was anxious to secure the help of the Arabs against the Turks and their German allies. The Middle East was in that war as it again proved to be in this, a vital theatre. The Turco-German forces in it not only threatened the Suez Canal and Egypt, but also the approaches to India by the overland route. Britain's position in that theatre was in 1915 and 1916 a critical one. The Arabs lying on the flank of the Turkish position could play a role that might prove decisive one way or the other. Nor was the service which the Arabs had it in their power to render only a military one. The Sultan of Turkey as Caliph had issued a call to all the Moslem subjects of the British Empire to rise in a Holy War against England and her allies. He was very anxious to have this call endorsed by the Sherif of Mecca, Hussein Ibn Ali, who, as a descendant of the Prophet and Custodian of the Holy Places of Islam, held a position of unique prestige in Moslem eyes. With Hussein's endorsement the call to a Holy War might become a formidable weapon against England; without it, and more particularly if he openly defied the Caliph, it would lose most of its sting.

Negotiations were, therefore, opened between the British Government and the Arabs. In return for joining the British and making war on Turkey, the Arabs asked for Britain's recognition after the war of an independent Arab kingdom comprising all the Arab lands East of the Mediterranean and Red Sea. The British Government made a reservation in respect of that part of Syria lying west of the districts of Aleppo, Hama, Homs and Damascus on the twofold grounds that the majority of the population there were not Arabs, and that Britain could not act in respect of that region without detriment to the interests of her ally France, who was known to have certain ambitions in it. The Arab negotiators did not accept this reservation, but agreed to postpone the issue till the end of the war in order not to disturb Anglo-French concord at that moment. On this basis the agreement was concluded and the Arabs revolted against Turkey and fought under Amir Faisel's leadership side by side with Allenby's troops in the Desert Campaign, which ended with the fall of Damascus. In that campaign the Arabs, according to the testimony of Lawrence, Allenby and Lloyd George, rendered invaluable service to the Allied cause and so, in Lawrence's own words, "their bond was heavily honored." They had carried out their part of the bargain and they were entitled to receive the reward they had been promised. But they did not receive it. . . . Instead of achieving the independence and unity they had fought for, the Arab countries, with the exception of Hejaz, were divided into British and French spheres of influence and put under tutelage. France obtained a mandate for Syria and the Lebanon, and Britain mandates for Palestine, Transjordan and Iraq. This meant that the Arabs were now less united than they had ever been. Ottoman rule, with all its faults, had preserved the political unity of the Arab world by holding it all under one sovereign and one administrative system. Under that rule all Arabs were Ottoman subjects; they could, as far as communications allowed in those days, travel from one part of the Arab world to another without let or hindrance, and trade flowed in every direction unimpeded by tariffs. The 1919 Peace Settlement, by establishing French and British spheres of influence and setting up a number of mandates in each, erected a number of artificial barriers that split the Arab world into several small, unreal and isolated units. Syria alone (i.e., that part of the Arab world which had always till then been known as Syria) was now fragmented into three separate states, Syria, Palestine and Transjordan, and in the first of these the French set up five separate administrations.

In this new situation each of the Arab countries concerned became for a time completely preoccupied with its own relationship with the mandatory power and the local problems which this relationship brought into being. A new struggle for freedom had to be waged; independence became the immediate goal. But all the time the idea of unity, as the ultimate goal to be reached after independence, remained alive and throughout the period between the two wars all the Arab countries felt as one and, whenever they could, acted as one on all major issues and at every crisis in their several lives. The wireless, air travel and the enormous growth of the Arabic press helped to strengthen and quicken their corporate consciousness. Through these agencies the Arab world acquired a central nervous system, along which a continuous stream of impulses and reactions flowed between Cairo and Beirut and Damascus and Baghdad and Jerusalem, and right into the very heart of the Arabian Peninsula.

With the exception of Palestine, one after another the Arab countries of the Eastern Arab world won their freedom. The first to do so was Iraq, with whom Britain concluded a treaty in 1930, recognising its independence and undertaking to sponsor its admission to the League of Nations. In return Iraq agreed to the maintenance by Britain of a few military bases in her territory. The next was Egypt, with whom Britain concluded a similar treaty in 1936. In the same year the French, prompted by the British example, negotiated analogous treaties with Syria and the Lebanon. The French Senate and Chamber of Deputies, however, failed to ratify them and they never came into force. Eventually the two countries obtained their independence in 1941 through a declaration made by General de Gaulle and countersigned by Britain at the moment the British forces, with a contingent of Free French troops, crossed their frontiers to liberate them from the Vichy regime.

At this point it was felt that the moment had come to think of the next step: unity. It also happened that several factors at that moment combined to favor the idea. First, the war had amply demonstrated the strategic and economic unity of the Middle East. Secondly, the idea that the postwar world order might be based on regional groupings was very much in the air, and here in the Arab world was a group of nations numbering some 40 millions altogether, occupying a vital region and possessing, in their own heritage, all the factors that make for union. If a regional grouping could be formed anywhere in the world, surely it was here. The British Government, for its part, was anxious to regain the good-will of the Arabs which she had largely lost in 1919. She had gone some way towards doing this by recognizing the independence of Iraq, Egypt, Syria and the Lebanon. She knew, however, that the Arabs wanted not only independence, but unity, and thus in 1941 Mr. Eden made a declaration on behalf of the British Government, expressing sympathy with any move which the Arab leaders might make towards the formation of an Arab union.

Circumstances, however, had changed somewhat since the leaders of the Arab revolt against Turkey had planned one Arab state comprising all the Arab countries in Asia. These countries had developed as separate states since 1919. The division imposed on them at that time had resulted in the growth of local interests and local allegiances which could not now be immediately submerged in a complete union. Neither a unitary state nor a full federation could now be achieved with one stroke. What has been achieved is a league of sovereign states comprising Egypt, Iraq, Saudi Arabia, Syria, Lebanon, Transjordan and Yemen—seven states with a total population of about 40,-000,000 whose object in the wording of the Pact that was signed in Cairo on March 22nd, 1945, is "To draw closer the relations between them to coordinate their political action, to safeguard their independence and sovereignty . . . . to interest itself in general in all questions concerning the Arab countries and their welfare . . . . and to achieve a close cooperation in economic, cultural, social and health matters."

The League is thus, in the first place, a symbol and a moral expression of the oneness of the Arab world. It is, secondly, a serious attempt to give a structure and direction to this spirit of oneness; to provide the machinery by which practical co-operation can be achieved and, in its turn, lead to a greater unity. The more ardent spirits in the various Arab countries, especially among the younger generation, would have liked a much closer union in constitutional form, a union with a federal parliament at least, and they regard the League as only a step in the process of unification. It is a fact, however, which the example of the British Commonwealth has time and again demonstrated, that the strength of a union resides not in its constitution or machinery, but in the spirit that animates its members. The Arab League is to be something like the British Commonwealth, and the ties that bind the Arab countries together are very much the same as those that bind England and the Dominions to one another: a common origin, a common way of life, a common speech and a strong sense of kinship and of pride in belonging to the same family.

Membership of the League is according to its constitution open to all Arab states that have achieved their independence. The only Arab country in this Eastern part of the Arab world that has not yet achieved its independence is Palestine. The reason for this is to be found in the Balfour Declaration and the consequent sponsoring of Zionism by the British Government. The truth of the matter is that in 1919 Britain undertook two obligations in her mandate for Palestine which were, in fact, mutually incompatible. She undertook (for that was the very essence of the mandatory system in regard to an "A" mandate which was the mandate she obtained for Palestine) to help the indigenous inhabitants of the country to reach full independence in the shortest possible time. On the other hand, she undertook by the Balfour Declaration, which was subsequently incorporated in the mandate to facilitate the establishment of a national home for the Jews in Palestine. Although in theory and according to the strict wording of the Declaration, there was nothing in the second obligation to debar Britain from honoring the first, in practice she decided not to do so until the communal problem was settled. The Zionist, who from the beginning intended that Palestine should become a Jewish state, were bitterly opposed to the country becoming independent as long as they were in a minority. Their policy was to prevent independence for a Palestinian state in which the Arabs would be the dominant element, and therefore to oppose the development of self-governing institutions until they had become the majority and could have an independent Jewish state. Thus, while all the surrounding Arab countries achieved their independence in gradual stages between the two wars, Palestine remains to this day under what amounts, in fact, to Crown Colony rule. She could not therefore become a member of the Arab League like the others because she had no national government to represent her. As, however, Palestine is regarded by all the Arab countries in the League and outside it as one of them and an essential part of the Arab world, the League was determined that she should be associated with it. It adopted, therefore, a special procedure, which was to nominate itself, a Palestinan Arab to represent Palestine on the Council of the League, until such time as Palestine could exercise all the effective attributes of an independent Arab state. This procedure and the reasons for it were explained in the following special resolution given in the Annex to the Covenant of the League:

At the end of the last war Palestine, like the other Arab states detached from the Ottoman Empire, was liberated from Ottoman domination. Having become autonomous, she was no longer dependent on any other state.

The Treaty of Lausanne proclaimed that her fate would be settled by the interested parties.

But if Palestine has not been able to order her own destiny, it is no less true that it was on the basis or recognition of her independence that the Covenant of the League of Nations in 1919 settled her status. Her international existence and independence cannot therefore be questioned any more than can the independence of any other Arab country.

If, for reasons independent of her will, this existence has failed to materialize, this circumstance does not constitute an obstacle to the participation of Palestine in the work of the Council of the League. The signatory States of the Present Pact consider that, under these conditions and by reason of the special circumstances involving Palestine, until that country can exercise all the effective attributes of her independence, it behoves the Council of the League to designate an Arab representative from Palestine who will participate in the work of the Council.

In certain quarters the League has been misunderstood and attacked on two counts. In the first place, it is suspected of being a British-engineered organization designed to serve British imperialist interests. This accusation is entirely groundless. As the foregoing pages will have shown, the Arab Unity movement is neither new nor British-born. It existed and asserted itself long before the First World War. It demanded of Britain recognition at the end of that war, and obtained a promise of it, which was not fulfilled. What Britain has done now, therefore, is to help the Arabs achieve what she promised before but failed to give them. Naturally, she hopes to benefit by this gesture. She hopes that by this belated compensation she will regain the confidence and good-will of the Arabs, which she had in considerable measure lost as a result of the wrong done them in 1919. She hopes that by swimming with the stream of Arab aspirations, instead of against it, she will win the cooperation of the Arabs in insuring her interests in their lands. The date at which Mr. Eden made his declaration giving the British Government's blessings to the idea of Arab union, and the circumstances in which he made it are a sufficient indication of why it was made. It was in 1941. Britain was fighting for her life. Her position in the Middle East was critical and she desperately needed the good-will of the Arabs. She knew that what the Arabs wanted was independence and unity. As far as Egypt and Iraq were concerned, the desire for independence had been fundamentally satisfied. There remained Syria and the Lebanon and Palestine. The White Paper, issued in 1939, had, in principle established the basis of an independent and mainly Arab state there within ten years. The independence of Syria and the Lebanon was proclaimed (by the French, but at the instance of Britain and with her guarantee) at the moment of the entry of British troops into those countries in 1941. Thus Britain felt that for the moment she had done everything she could to satisfy the Arab desire for independence. There remained the desire for unity: hence the Eden declaration.

The other score on which the League has been attacked is that the principle of its being is negative and not positive, or in plainer language, that the real purpose and sole *raison d'etre* of the League is to combat Zionism. Here again, the foregoing pages will have disproved this accusation by showing that the oneness of the Arab world and the desire to express it in political structure and action existed long before the appearance of political Zionism in Palestine, and was, indeed, the principal inspiration and feature of the Arab awakening from its first dawn. It is true that one of the chief and most urgent concerns of the League is to ensure that Palestine, an essentially Arab country and an integral part of the Arab world, shall remain an Arab country, become independent and join its sisters in the League. But this is only a means to an end. The end is the reintegration of the Arab community as a living, constructive unit in the human family, fit to play a part worthy of its past and to make another contribution to civilization. The Arab League is not a reactionary or retrogressive move, but a healthy step on the road of evolution, a new synthesis in the process of world integration which will only end when all the nations have become one. It was so designed as to fit into the new World Order and be a useful part in the machinery of international cooperation for security and welfare.

DILEMMA IN PALESTINE [2]

There is a dilemma in Palestine. A national state seems to have been an innate Arab desire of long standing. Faint glimmerings of it have been seen through the years. Prior to 1850 there were feeble attempts at organizing an Arab movement. One of the earliest was in 1847 in Beirut by Arab Christians. Later there were similar attempts among Moslems. But all were premature. The first organized movement seems to have been in 1875, when a secret society was formed by five young Syrians who had been educated at the Syrian Protestant College, under American missionary auspices, in Beirut. Soon Moslems, Christians and Druzes were enrolled in this society. A secret society which played an important part in the development of Arab nationalism was al-Fatat, founded in 1911 in Paris by Moslem Arabs. On June 18, 1913, an Arab congress was held in Paris. The delegates were for the most part Syrian and Lebanese.

[2] By Dr. Glora M. Wysner, Secretary, Committee on Work Among Moslems. *Committee on Work Among Moslems. Bulletin.* No. 6. p. 1-8. November 1944.

Their numbers were about equally divided between Moslems and Christians. At that time the Arab world was under Turkish rule.

The aspirations and claims of the Arab peoples were voiced by the Arab congress when it laid "emphasis on the Arab claim to full political rights and to an effective share in the administration of the affairs of the Ottoman Empire. Throughout the proceedings references were made—prudently veiled, since they related to French ambitions—to the possibility of foreign intervention as a danger to be resolutely warded off."

On November 7, 1914, a call to a "jihad" (holy war) was issued to the Moslem world by the Shaikh al-Islam in Constantinople, the highest religious official in the Ottoman Empire. He called upon Moslems to assist Turkey and Germany in their war against Great Britain, France and Russia. This was followed on November 23 by a manifesto calling upon all Moslems to take their place in the defense of Islam and the holy places.

Great Britain needed desperately the cooperation and help of the Arabs in order to defeat Turkey and Germany. The Suez Canal was threatened and the situation in the whole Middle East was critical. Conversations were held between Great Britain and the Sherif Hussein of Mecca with reference to an Arab revolt against Turkey.

Early in 1915 negotiations between the British through Sir Henry McMahon and the Arabs through Sherif Hussein began. This resulted in the McMahon correspondence in which the British sought the aid of the Arabs in the prosecution of the war against Turkey, against whom the Arabs were being urged to revolt. However, the Arabs insisted upon assurance that in exchange for Arab assistance Great Britain would recognize and uphold Arab independence in a certain area.

Members of two of the nationalistic groups met in Damascus and on May 23, 1915, drew up a protocol stating the conditions on which the Arab leaders would be willing to cooperate with Great Britain against Turkey. The conditions were:

The recognition by Great Britain of the independence of the Arab countries lying within the following frontiers:

North: The line Mersin-Adana to parallel 37° N. and thence along the line Birejik-Urfa-Mardin-Midiat-Jazirat (Ibn 'Umar)-Amadia to the Persian frontier;

East: The Persian frontier down to the Persian Gulf;

South: The Indian Ocean (with the exclusion of Aden, whose status was to be maintained);

West: The Red Sea and the Mediterranean Sea back to Mersin.

The abolition of all exceptional privileges granted to foreigners under the capitulations.

The conclusion of a defensive alliance between Great Britain and the future independent Arab states.

The grant of economic preference to Great Britain.

The crux of the dispute to this day has hinged on whether or not Palestine was included in the Arab territory. The Sherif Hussein claimed as Arab territory what had been outlined in the Damascus protocol of May 23, 1915. Great Britain agreed to this, subject to this modification:

> The districts of Mersin and Alexandretta, and portions of Syria lying to the west of the districts of Damascus, Homs, Hama and Aleppo, cannot be said to be purely Arab and must on that account be excepted from the proposed delimitation.

Hussein consented to the exclusion of Mersin but never accepted the exclusion of Alexandretta, nor the portions of Syria lying to the west of the districts of Damascus, Homs, Hama and Aleppo which Hussein claimed were purely Arab. Great Britain also called attention to the fact that her pledge held good in regions in which she was free to act without detriment to the interests of her ally France.

In order to get a complete picture of this controversy one needs to read all the McMahon correspondence, but until published in Antonius' book *The Arab Awakening,* much of the Arabic text was not available in English. The Arab text was known all over the Arab world, while English speaking people were attempting to form their unbiased opinion of this important matter with only partial material available.

The whole question in Palestine has been complicated by counter pledges. An important one was the Sykes-Picot Agreement concluded in London on May 16, 1916. This was a secret agreement, unknown to the Arabs, between Great Britain,

France and Russia as to the disposal of the Ottoman Empire
and the portion to be claimed by each. The part dealing with
Arab territories was made between Great Britain and France.
France reserved the greater part of Syria, a considerable portion
of southern Anatolia and the Mosul district in Iraq. Great
Britain was to have a strip of territory running from the extreme southern tip of Syria across to Iraq and including all the
country between the Persian Gulf and that claimed by France.
A small area around Jerusalem and Haifa was to be placed
under an international regime. In parts of these areas France
and Great Britain would be free to establish their own administration; in other parts Arab supremacy was to be recognized.
This agreement was made less than six months after the last
note between Sir Henry McMahon and Sherif Hussein was
exchanged. It deliberately carved up that portion of the Arab
world to which Great Britain had given her pledge for independence. Antonius says of this pledge:

> It is a shocking document. It is not only the product of greed at its
> worst, that is to say, of greed allied to suspicion and so leading to
> stupidity; it also stands out as a startling piece of double-dealing.

This agreement, a tragic breach of faith, was negotiated and
concluded without the knowledge of Sherif Hussein. In fact,
it was concealed from him and from all concerned. Unfortunately he first learned of the agreement through an enemy
source, and this eighteen months after it had been made. When
the Bolshevik party seized power in Russia in November 1919,
they published some of the secret documents, which they found
in the archives of the Imperial Ministry of Foreign Affairs. The
Sykes-Picot Agreement was one of the documents they published. The Turks sent this agreement to Hussein and proposed a Turco-Arab peace. This peace gesture to the Arabs
was unsuccessful. Sherif Hussein turned to the British for an
explanation. King Hussein was assured that the Turks' version
of the agreement was another instance of Turkish intrigue and
should be disregarded.

The next important move in this life drama was the well
known and oft quoted Balfour Declaration, issued November 2,
1917. . . .

Upon the interpretation of the phrase "a national home in Palestine" has hinged great misunderstanding. Arab fears have focused on this. For the political Zionist a national home means eventually Palestine as a "national state" with the Jews in control of the country. The Arab looks upon this as a planned effort to deprive him of his inherent rights in Palestine and to make of him a minority people, and this without his consent. Cultural Zionists interpret a national home as a place where the Jew may develop his cultural interests and to which he may look as the center of his Jewish life. Cultural Zionism had been developing slowly in Palestine through the centuries preceding the first World War, encountering little difficulty from the Arabs. It was when political Zionism began to press its claims and its interpretations that real trouble began. A national home in Palestine would have the support of some Arabs, although perhaps not the majority, but all Arabs would oppose Palestine becoming a national Jewish state.

Needless to say this declaration caused confusion and dismay among the Arabs. King Hussein immediately asked for an explanation. This was carried to him by Commander Hogarth in January 1918. King Hussein was assured that the "Jewish settlement in Palestine would only be allowed insofar as would be consistent with the political and economic freedom of the Arab population." King Hussein was willing to give refuge to persecuted Jews in Palestine, but never entertained any thought of surrendering Arab sovereignty there. He continually reiterated this.

Although King Hussein accepted in all sincerity and good faith the explanations and assurances of Great Britain regarding the Sykes-Picot Agreement and the Balfour Declaration, the fears of the Arabs were not easily calmed. Consequently seven influential Arabs in Cairo who had been lending their help to the Arab revolt expressed their apprehensions in a memorial submitted to the Foreign Office through the Arab Bureau in Cairo, in the spring of 1918, asking for a clear and comprehensive definition of British policy for the future of Arab countries. Elucidation was especially asked regarding Syria, Palestine and Iraq.

The British answer to the seven Arabs, a copy of which was sent to King Hussein, is a very important and yet little known document in this whole picture. The British made clear their policy in all the area for which Sherif Hussein had claimed Arab independence. In the territory comprising Palestine the policy was declared to be "that the future government of those territories should be based upon the principle of the consent of the governed." ' This declaration did much to encourage the Arabs and to build up their hopes for Arab independence.

This hope was further strengthened by the words of President Wilson in his address delivered July 4, 1918, at Mount Vernon when he said that the postwar settlement would be based upon "the free acceptance of that settlement by the people immediately concerned."

The fears of the Arabs were dispelled by these declarations of Great Britain and the United States and their faith in these pledges was further strengthened when an official communique was issued to the press in Palestine, Syria and Iraq by the British, November 7, 1918, declaring that France and England aimed at the final liberation of the peoples living under Turkish rule and would aid these people to set up national governments chosen by the people themselves in the free exercise of the popular will. This is known as the Anglo-French Declaration.

The Arabs, by their sustained revolt and their cooperation with Great Britain, aided very materially in the final defeat of Turkey. Arab soldiers gave their lives in the cause and Arab troops were with General Allenby when they entered Jerusalem. Many Syrian and Lebanese leaders were hanged or exiled by the Turks for their disloyalty to the Turkish cause.

In speaking of the revolt of the Arabs against the Turks, T. E. Lawrence said they "kept faith with the British authorities throughout a war history which teemed with doubtful and hazardous situations."

But when the matter came before the Peace Conference, the powers were unwilling to go as far with the Arabs as they had pledged. General Smuts issued a pamphlet, December 16, 1918, in which he suggested that for some time to come in Palestine, because of the heterogeneous character of the population and their incapacity for administrative cooperation, autonomy there would be out of the question and an external power would need to undertake to a large extent the administration. It is to be noted that the heterogeneous character of Palestine was stressed, although at that time nine tenths of the population was Arab and one tenth Jewish. To a certain extent the Jewish group had been Arabized also.

The Emir Feisal, son of King Hussein, with T. E. Lawrence, leader of Arab contingents which cooperated with General Allenby, headed the Hejaz delegation as a representative of his father at the Peace Conference. He found himself powerless in the face of Zionist pressure and imperialistic interests.

Pressed to come to an agreement with the Zionists, Emir Feisal in January 1919, with Dr. Chaim Weizmann signed what is known as the Feisal-Weizmann Agreement which would allow measures to be taken to "encourage and stimulate immigration of Jews into Palestine on a large scale and as quickly as possible to settle Jewish immigrants upon the land through closer settlement and intensive cultivation of the soil."

The condition upon which the fulfillment of this agreement was contingent was attached to the agreement in Feisal's own handwriting in Arabic. This is scarcely known but it reads:

Provided the Arabs obtain their independence as demanded in my Memorandum dated the 4th of January 1919, to the Foreign Office of the Government of Great Britain, I shall concur in the above articles. But if the slightest modification or departure were to be made (sc. in relation to the demands in the Memorandum) I shall not then be bound by a single word of the present Agreement which shall be deemed void and of no account or validity, and I shall not be answerable in any way whatsoever.

Emir Feisal was sympathetic to the aspirations of the Jews and willing to go at great length to cooperate, but he always insisted on Arab rights of independence. At that time the political aspirations of the Zionists were not clearly defined.

For a wholly disinterested picture of the Palestinian situation it is well to read carefully the Report of the King-Crane Commission. President Wilson sent Dr. Henry Churchill King, President of Oberlin College, and Charles R. Crane, manufacturer from Chicago and United States Minister to China, May

1920-June 1921, to study the situation in the Near East in 1919. Their report was signed, sealed and delivered to the American Commission to Negotiate Peace, August 28, 1919. Two days later Mr. Crane advised President Wilson by cable of the essence of the official recommendations of the Commission. This report was not made public until December 2, 1922, when it was published in *Editor and Publisher,* New York, as a "Suppressed Official Document of the United States Government." It was republished in the *New York Times,* December 3, 4, 1922. After amassing and weighing carefully all the evidence, the King-Crane Commission recommended "serious modification of the extreme Zionist program for Palestine of unlimited immigration of Jews, looking, finally to making Palestine distinctly a Jewish state."

This same report continues:

The Commissioners began their study of Zionism with minds predisposed in its favor, but the actual facts in Palestine, coupled with the force of the general principles proclaimed by the Allies and accepted by the Syrians have driven them to the recommendation here made.

The Commission was abundantly supplied with literature on the Zionist program by the Zionist Commission to Palestine; heard in conferences much concerning the Zionist colonies and their claims; and personally saw something of what had been accomplished. They found much to approve in the aspirations and plans of the Zionists, and had warm appreciation for the devotion of many of the colonists, and for their success, by modern methods, in overcoming great natural obstacles.

The Commission recognized also that definite encouragement had been given to the Zionists by the Allies in Mr. Balfour's often-quoted statement, in its approval by other representatives of the Allies. If, however, the strict terms of the Balfour Statement are adhered to—favoring "the establishment in Palestine of a national home for the Jewish people," "it being clearly understood that nothing shall be done which may prejudice the civil and religious rights of existing non-Jewish communities in Palestine"—it can hardly be doubted that the extreme Zionist program must be greatly modified.

But the findings of this Commission seem never to have been given serious consideration by those dealing with the Palestinian problem.

Article 22 of the Covenant of the League of Nations provided that "certain communities, formerly belonging to the

Turkish Empire, have reached a stage of development where their existence as independent nations can be provisionally recognized subject to their receiving mandatory tutelage, in the way of administrative advice and assistance, until such time as they would be able to stand alone." The wishes of these communities were held to be the principal consideration in the selection of the mandatory.

France and Great Britain in the scheme of mandates, imposed upon the Arabs a settlement which violated the promises made to them. Naturally the Arabs thought they had been betrayed and let down by their trusted friend, Great Britain.

The final blow to the Arabs in this long chain of events seemed to come when the Supreme Council met on April 25, 1920, at San Remo and placed the whole Arab rectangle between the Mediterranean Sea and the frontiers of Persia under mandatory rule, part going to Great Britain and part to France. These decisions were made public, May 5, 1920.

The immediate repercussion in the Arab world was one of contempt for the Western Powers, a feeling of complete frustration and bafflement at such a breach of faith. Fear and despair gripped them and the upheavals which followed were outbursts of these feelings.

On June 30, 1922, the United States Congress unanimously passed the following resolution:

that the United States of America favors the establishment in Palestine of a national home for the Jewish people, it being clearly understood that nothing shall be done which may prejudice the civil and religious rights of Christian and all other non-Jewish communities in Palestine, and that the holy places and religious buildings and sites in Palestine shall be adequately protected.

Since 1921 there have been at times serious riots in Palestine. These led to several investigations being made by visiting commissions to Palestine and resulted in the issuance of several White Papers.

The first White Paper, issued June 3, 1922, attempted to explain the Balfour Declaration. It pointed out that it was not contemplated to convert all of Palestine into a Jewish national home but that within Palestine such a home should be founded.

Jewish immigration was not to exceed in volume the economic capacity of the country to absorb it.

In 1929 the Shaw Commission investigated conditions in Palestine following the Arab riots of that year. This resulted in the Passfield White Paper issued October 1930. It sought to regulate Jewish immigration into Palestine by declaring there was no land available for this. Not only was the absorptive capacity of the land considered, but also the unemployment situation among both Jews and Arabs at that time.

The Royal Commission, under Lord Peel, visited Palestine in 1936 and made its report in 1937. This Commission found that one of the causes of the riots was: "the pressure on Palestine exerted by the heavy immigration into Palestine of Jews following the persecutions in Europe and the Arab fear of Jewish domination over Palestine."

In May 1939, the British Government published as a White Paper its final proposals for Palestine. This proposed that within ten years an independent state be created in Palestine. It limited immigration of Jews into Palestine for the ensuing five years to a maximum of 75,000, following which Arab consent would be necessary for further immigration, and provided that land purchase by Jews would be prohibited in certain districts and restricted in others. Strong protests have been made against this White Paper because it limits immigration of Jews into Palestine.

An attempt was made in February 1944 to get the United States Government to register its protest against the White Paper. To this end resolutions were introduced into the House of Representatives by Congressmen Wright and Compton and into the Senate by Senators Taft and Wagner asking

that the United States shall use its good offices and take appropriate measures to the end that the doors of Palestine shall be opened for free entry of Jews into that country, and that there shall be full opportunity for colonization, so that the Jewish people may ultimately reconstitute Palestine as a free and democratic Jewish commonwealth.

Most thoughtful people seem to feel that the White Paper should be abrogated because it discriminates against one group of people—the Jews. But the issues must not be confused.

Discrimination to eliminate immigration is one thing, while to open the doors of Palestine for free entry of the Jews for colonization and in order that the Jewish people may establish a commonwealth there is an entirely different question. The question immediately arises—should such action be taken without the consent of the majority group in Palestine which happens to be the Arab?

A number of Arab countries registered their protests against the Taft-Wagner resolution. Arab groups in this country also raised their voices and their pens against it. General Marshall also advised against the passing of such a resolution.

In an editorial appearing in the *Christian Century*, March 15, 1944, under the title, "How to Make Enemies for the United States," the editor comments upon this and then goes on to say,

> It is to be hoped that the Senate committee will heed the General's request, which has undoubtedly been caused by fear of the effect on the Arab World. The fact is that the whole consideration of this resolution has been conducted in such a way as to make enemies for the United States all over the Near and Middle East. When, one after another, Iraq, Transjordan, Egypt, Yemen, Syria, Lebanon and Saudi Arabia protested, Senator Wagner had the incredibly bad manners, in a message to the Iraqi Parliament, to reply that the United States has been able for more than a century "to reach its own conclusions without advice from foreign officials." This despite the fact that in this very affair the Senate was being asked to tell the British Government what it should do about one of its mandates! . . .

Many seem to think that only a small part of the Arab world is involved in this problem in Palestine. It has far wider implications. The Arab leaders of Syria, Iraq and other countries in the Middle East feel that their welfare in threatened, too. They see the possibility of an ever widening sphere of influence and perhaps later even control of their countries if a national Jewish state is established in Palestine. The whole Middle East feels itself concerned in the eventual solution of the Palestinian problem.

The Christian Arabs stand with the Moslem Arabs for recognition of Palestine as Arab territory. . . .

The Arabs of Palestine have contributed more than their share toward the rehabilitation of Jewish refugees from Europe, since they have already accepted more than half a million of them in a country about the size of Vermont.

In 1920 the Jews represented one ninth of the population in Palestine, while in 1943 they represented one third. During a decade of tragic Jewish history, 1933-1942, Palestine absorbed some 280,000 Jewish immigrants. If the United States had accepted as many Jewish immigrants according to our population as Palestine accepted we would have admitted more than 22,000,000 during this period. The 1942 population of Palestine was 1,605,816. Of this number 1,114,329 were Arabs (987,985 Moslems, 126,344 Christians) and 478,449 were Jews. At the present time the population of Palestine is 152 per square mile, while that of Vermont, about equal in size to Palestine, is 39 per square mile. Had the United States accepted into this country Jewish refugees in the same proportion per square mile that Palestine has accepted them we would have welcomed to our shores in the last ten years some 80,920,000 Jewish refugees.

Authorities are in sharp disagreement as to the absorptive capacity of Palestine. Dr. W. C. Lowdermilk in *Palestine, Land of Promise* feels that several more million could be cared for there by the development of a "Tennessee Valley Authority" in Palestine. Such a scheme would need to be largely financed from America over a period of years for development.

The Arabs note that some American Christians feel it their Christian duty to assist the Jews in their aspirations for a national home in Palestine, but they also note that these same Christians have not been so vocal in attempting to open the doors of America to the persecuted Jews of Europe. It appears to many that we are asking the Moslem Arab to assume a more Christian attitude than Christians are willing to take.

In the face of the bitter and unprecedented persecutions of the Jews in Europe Christians in America have been deeply moved, but perhaps not enough to take wise and concerted action. Are we only deeply enough moved to urge that the doors of another country be opened without the consent of the majority of the people of that country without opening our own doors to save the terrible holocaust to the Jews of Europe? . . .

J. M. N. Jeffries in *Palestine: The Reality* discusses the return of the Jews to Palestine as it relates to prophecy. Many people have given their approval of political Zionism feeling it is a fulfillment of prophecy. The Jews have already returned in such numbers to Palestine that they are now "more numerous than their fathers" (Deuteronomy 30:5). Jeffries says, "These prophecies today are accomplished. The four hundred thousand inmates of the Holy Land form a full remnant of the Jews in the world whose numbers are variously estimated from fourteen to sixteen millions. Only a remnant of these millions *can* return to Palestine."

A Jewish national home does exist in Palestine where an all-Jewish education is possible. If this continues to develop the cultural and spiritual life of the Jewish people, it will fulfill a great need in the life of the Jew and will make a distinct contribution to world progress. But if the national home seeks to be a political power, trouble with the Arabs would seem to be the inevitable result.

A number of reports have reached America recently of the preparations already under way by Jews in Palestine to return to the countries from which they came. In a letter from Dr. Charles R. Watson, American University at Cairo, written April 21, 1944, we read:

> Another of our minor excitements has to do with Palestine where plots against the police have cost a number of lives. The newspapers here have spoken of 70,000 armed revolutionists in training to support Jewish claims in the Holy Land. The reason given for these disturbances at this time is that as soon as Europe is open to a return of the new exiled Jews, there will be a mass exodus of Jews from Palestine back to their homes in Europe, which will weaken seriously the Zionist cause and support. The time to strike is therefore now.

Frederick C. Painton, writing in *The Reader's Digest,* May 1944, points out these same trends when he says,

> The Jewish Agency people fear that the skilled refugees who make many of these products (he was speaking of the Palestine industrial products exhibit at Tel Aviv) will return to their native lands when war is over. The Czech Jews were being absorbed in their nation until the war; they knew no persecutions, no bars. They look upon themselves

(they told me) as Czechs, not as Jews, and are anxious to go home. The Dutch diamond cutter intends to go home to Holland. Strangely enough, scores of the German Jews want to go back to Germany. This failure to sink roots deeply applies equally to Americans; of the 5,500 American Jews in Palestine fewer than 100 have given up their American passports. The other Jews in Palestine know this and fear it; it is one reason why the extremists are making this gesture now. Many leading Jews told me they feared they would lose their main argument at war's end by having no immigrants.

The Jews themselves are very much divided on the Palestinian question. The political Zionists and the cultural Zionists do not seek the same ends. Christians have been drawn into the activities of the Zionist movement without realizing all the implications. This has been well analyzed in the *Information Bulletin* of the American Council of Judaism, Inc., issue for April 30, 1944, published in Philadelphia, Pennsylvania.

It is important that we recognize the painful dilemma in which our Christian friends found themselves. Moved by broad human considerations, by devotion to democratic tenets, and by their religious compulsion of Christian charity and human brotherhood, they have been eager to speak up for the Jews and to help in every way. Because of the heretofore unchallenged Zionist claims, they were led to believe that friendship for the Jews necessitated the acceptance of the Zionist formulas and so they made that acceptance—although with misgivings. They signed statements; gave endorsements; joined organizations; embarked upon activities—all for the purpose of helping persecuted Jews. And, in so doing, they found themselves taking part in the Jewish nationalist struggle for political objectives. The misgivings were muted but they remained nonetheless; and they constituted a barrier to a full, forthright and completely integrated participation in the efforts to solve the problems.

There were misgivings on the chauvinistic character of the Zionist program; on its troublesome implications to American life; on its racialism; on its political manipulations; on the embittered relations with the Arabs.

It must be kept in mind that there are serious divisions among the Arabs as well as among the Jews. The Husseinis are the radical Arabs who demand that Palestine must be given complete independence as an Arab state. The Mufti, [recently] in Berlin with the Nazis, belongs to this party. The Nashashibis are the moderates who are willing to abide by the "White Paper" policy of Great Britain. The extremists, both Jews and Arabs, have resorted to measures that are regretted by the majority of both groups. It is doubtful if a solution can ever be found within the extremist groups. It will need to come from among the moderates.

The Arabs seem to have been handicapped because they have had no official party representing them when negotiating with the British Government. The Jewish Agency is the official party of the Jews to speak and act for them with Great Britain.

Not only is the Palestinian problem of interest to the Arab Moslems, but it has attracted the attention and sympathy of their fellow Moslems around the world. This is having repercussions in the various presses, both Moslem and non-Moslem. This comes from India:

> The shocking twaddle spoken and written by United States publicists and the press about Palestine contains more than one danger. . . . The more the strongest and most democratic existing nation undertakes permanent responsibilities on peace-loving humanity's behalf outside the American continent the better we shall be pleased. But if that participation and acceptance of responsibilities happens, there is already danger that it will have initially to contend with widespread Moslem suspicion. Owing to the much publicized American comments of recent years on the Palestine problem, which are presumed to reflect the general view of the American people, many Moslems now suppose the U.S.A. to be anti-Islamic . . . For that reason comments such as have lately come from the U.S.A. on the very delicate and complex problem of Palestine which excites Moslem interest everywhere, appear to us deplorable. . . .

More and more Christians today are seeking to understand world problems and to wield a Christian influence in their solution. Palestine is a significant part of the world picture. The facts in regard to Palestine must be faced courageously and fearlessly, and with as great an attempt toward Christian understanding as [are] the problems in any other part of the world. It is well to remember certain Christian obligations, such as: to defend the inalienable rights of a people to make their own choices; to protect minority groups; to seek to provide places of refuge for persecuted peoples, and to help them preserve their cultural and religious heritage. These obligations must be fulfilled without wronging some other group who loves freedom, but whose leadership as yet is weak and whose people have not had equal educational, economic and social opportunities for development.

ARAB RIGHTS AND THE BRITISH LEFT [3]

It is true that the majority of the people in the Arab world are backward peasants, it is true that the percentage of illiteracy is still high in some Arab countries, though not in all (in the Lebanon for instance it is no more than about 20 per cent), and it is true that some politicians of the old school are more interested in inter-party manoeuvring and the preservation of their own power than in social reform or economic development. But while all this is true, it is only one side of the picture, the side that the Arab world is still carrying on from the past, but a side that is definitely shrinking as the other side, representing modern tendencies, and new achievement, grows almost day by day.

A young country or a new situation should be judged not by its actual condition at a given moment but by the tendencies visible in it and the way it is moving. The most significant fact about the Arab world today is not that it is still this or that, but that it is *becoming* something else; that there is already a considerable and rapidly growing commercial and industrial middle class, a professional intelligentsia and the beginnings of a labor movement; that side by side with the still high rate of illiteracy there is a great demand for education which is being met on an ever-increasing scale, and finally that interest in social reform and economic development is becoming active and articulate enough to make its impact on the old order felt.

The significance of these facts become all the greater when it is realized that it is only a hundred years since education in the modern sense started in the Arab world and that it is only in the last 25 years that most of the Arab countries have achieved self-government: in 1919 these countries did not emerge into the full freedom of unrestricted opportunity, but into a situa-

[3] By Edward Atiyah, General Secretary, Arab Office, London. 8p. Arab Office. London.

tion bristling with new and artificial problems imposed upon them by the peace settlement of that year and the imperialist policies of Britain and France in the years following. In Syria and the Lebanon, in Iraq and Palestine, the Arabs found themselves striving all over again for the independence and unity they had hoped to win out of the last war. In Palestine they also had to meet a new and, as they saw it, deadly challenge to their very existence as a nation. Instead of being able to concentrate all their newly liberated energies on education, social reform, and economic development they were forced by a natural reaction of self-defense to engage in a long and bitter political struggle involving at times general strikes, armed rebellion, the banishment of their leaders and all the destruction and waste, both physical and psychological, attendant on such a conflict.

The main hope of the Arab world today lies in its commercial and professional middle class and its emergent labor movement, and particularly in the educated men and women of the younger generation. In every Arab country these young men and women are leading movements for social reform, adult education, improvement of agriculture and village life, economic development and the opening of dispensaries, welfare centres and maternity clinics.

Thus the Arab movement is essentially a popular movement. It is an expression of the new and progressive forces in the Arab world, not a manifestation of the old order of privilege, nor an instrument of reaction. It expresses defensive and constructive aspirations, the aspirations of small and young nations that have long been oppressed and prevented from developing, and that now only seek to be free and to develop their latent possibilities, as a part of the progressive world. It has no predatory intentions; it is not aimed against any other nation. Above all it is genuinely indigenous, and not, as many here believe, a spurious product created by British imperialism to serve its own ends. For the major portion of the period between the two wars it was in conflict with western imperialism, British as well as French, struggling for freedom in Iraq, and Egypt and Palestine as well as in Syria and the Lebanon. Nor was the part played by Britain in regard to the formation of the Arab League more than one of belated and sympathetic recognition for something which the Arabs themselves had always desired and striven for. . . .

Arab nationalism has not had to struggle against British and French imperialism only. It has also had to struggle against Zionism, which to the Arabs is a more insidious form of imperialism than either of those two, because it threatens them with the loss of their land and with a subjection more complete and permanent than anything implied in the political and economic imperialism of Britain or France. Indeed, the struggle with British imperialism is now substantially over, and that with French imperialism in its last phase. But the Zionist challenge remains, a challenge which the Arabs, not only of Palestine but of all the Arab lands represented in the League, are determined to resist.

In this struggle between Zionism and the Arabs the sympathies of the British Left have been almost entirely enlisted on the Zionist side. The reasons for this are not difficult to understand. In the first place the Zionists are here, as British citizens, to plead their cause in person. Many of them are to be found in Fleet Street, in Parliament and in the Left movement itself. They are a part of the British people in daily contact with the public and possessing every facility they need to put their case to their compatriots. The Arabs have very few representatives in England, and these are not English. They cannot speak to Englishmen as members of the family but only as foreigners. It follows from all this that people here know much more about the Zionist case than about the Arab and so come to be more in sympathy with it.

In the second place, the Socialists in particular tend, very rightly and properly, to champion the Jewish cause in general. For in addition to the decent humanitarian feelings of a civilized people which they share with Englishmen of other political persuasions, they have in the internationalism of their creed and its emphatic stand against any kind of racial or national discrimination, a consciously formulated political and moral motive for befriending the Jews and combating anti-Semitism. The strength and urgency of this motive have been greatly reinforced during the last ten or twelve years by the Nazi challenge. In the fight against Nazism a natural alliance developed between the Left movement as its chief opponent and the Jews as its chief victims. Sympathy with the Jews increased in proportion to the outrages inflicted upon them; and as anti-Semitism spread in the countries that fell into the Nazi orbit, the champions of freedom in the rest of the world and particularly in England strained every nerve to prevent it rearing its ugly head in their lands. This was the retort of chivalry and humanity to barbarism. At the same time and for the same reasons an inhibition developed against any criticism of Zionism. Zionism was accepted as the natural solution of the Jewish problem and support for it increased in proportion to the growing urgency of the anti-Semitic challenge. To criticise Zionism, to admit the arguments against it, to speak up for the Arabs became almost impossible in Left circles, for it was feared that to do so would smack of anti-Semitism or at least encourage it in others. And so Zionism acquired a kind of sacrosanct immunity to criticism and its advocates were free to press their case without fear of opposition and with the tide of sympathy, which Jewish suffering in Europe had evoked, swelling up behind them.

This attitude, which does credit to the heart of the Left movement, rests on three fallacies. The first is the failure to distinguish between Jews and Zionists and between anti-Zionism and anti-Semitism. The second is the belief that only Zionism can solve the Jewish refugee problem and the transference of the humanitarian sympathy evoked by the latter to the specific political aims of the former. The third is the conviction that Zionism is a good thing for the world and not a bad thing for the Arabs.

All these are questions fraught with the gravest moral and political issues, not only for the Arabs but also for the Jews themselves and for the world, and no member of the Left should subscribe to Zionism without at least trying to understand them. The first thing he should understand is that anti-Zionism is not anti-Semitism and that not all Jews are Zionists. Political Zionism (and this is the Zionism in question) is the attempt to establish in Palestine a Jewish national state and either reduce the indigenous Arab population of the country to a minority in their own land or drive them away altogether. Anti-Zionism is the opposition to this attempt. To be anti-Zionist is therefore something quite different from being anti-Jewish. Indeed, there are many anti-Zionists among the Jews themselves, in England and the U.S.A. Edwin Montague, the only Jewish member of the British Cabinet in whose name the Balfour Declaration was issued, was, in the interests of the Jewish people as he conceived them, a stern opponent of Zionism and resisted the Declaration with all his might. In this he was supported by several other distinguished Jews and by a representative Jewish organization. . . . To [the] anti-Zionist Jews the only solution of the Jewish problem is complete political assimilation and equal rights of citizenship with the rest of the population in every country where Jews may happen to live. In their view the attempt to revive Judaism as a nationality and to establish a Jewish state is bound to prejudice the status of the Jews as citizens of other countries, where many of them are permanently established as Englishmen or Americans or Frenchmen and have no intention of giving up this citizenship and going to the national state. The harm they fear is that the existence of a Jewish national state might seem to encourage a divided allegiance in the Jewish mind and revive the old suspicion that the Jew can never become assimilated to the country in which he lives and will always remain a Jew first whatever his nationality may be. They also fear that the existence of a Jewish national state would, by offering a convenient dumping ground to which Jews might be sent from any country in the world, encourage anti-Semitism and provide it with a plausible excuse for the expulsion from their present homes of Jews who may not wish to leave them.

Lastly, they cannot believe that a movement which has aroused and is bound to go on arousing the bitterest hostility and opposition of the Arab world; a movement whose aims cannot be realized except through the coercion of the Arabs, can be a healthy thing for the Jews. In this they are absolutely right. The supporters of Zionism must understand that there is not the slightest hope of the Arabs, not only of Palestine but of all the countries represented in the League, ever acquiescing in Zionism and that therefore the attempt to enforce it has the effect of rousing the fierce resentment of 40,000,000 Arabs against the Jews and will, if persisted in, end by converting the whole Middle East area into a violently anti-Jewish bloc and so depriving the Jews, as individuals, of all friendship and hospitality in a region which until the appearance of Zionism had always afforded them a secure home. For the Arab world has a clean record with regard to anti-Semitism. Neither in Palestine itself nor in any of the other Arab countries have the Jews ever been persecuted. Indeed, when they were being massacred in Europe and hounded by the Inquisition out of Spain, they always found a refuge in the Middle East, and those of them who before the days of political Zionism had come into Palestine as individuals to settle down in the Holy Land were allowed to do so, accepted as a part of the native population and never molested. The opposition to Zionism therefore does not spring from anti-Semitism. It springs from the natural and powerful instinct of self-defense against an aggressor. For Zionism is an act of aggression against the Arabs; and while anti-Zionism does not derive from anti-Semitism, it is bound, if persisted in, to lead to it, and so prejudice the position of all Jews in the Middle East and render a great disservice to world Jewry.

There are two aspirations in Zionism, a negative and a positive, the second being largely the product of the first. The negative aspiration is to have a secure refuge to which the Jews can go as a matter of right from the lands where they are persecuted, a home of their own in which they will be either alone or the majority so that they will escape from their minority status and be permanently free from fear of persecution. The positive aspiration is to recreate in this home the Jewish community as a nation on the basis of its traditional culture. As for the first aspiration it has never been contemplated even by the Zionists themselves that this national home or state would include the whole of world Jewry. From the beginning it was realized that the vast majority of Jews in the countries of the West (England, France, the United States, Belgium and Holland) were happy in their position as citizens of these countries and would not want to go to Palestine or wherever else the Jewish state might be established. Zionism was therefore intended to solve the problem of the Jews in Eastern Europe (mainly those of Poland and Russia) whose plight there was indeed grievous and who were desperately eager to get away. It was thus admitted that the Jewish problem was capable of another solution than the creation of a national state and that indeed it had been so solved in the countries of the West. It was admitted that the Jews living in these countries had a security and equality which enabled them to live not as a minority but as full citizens like the rest of the population. It was also realized that no national state in Palestine, even if the Jews had the whole country to themselves, could absorb the whole of world Jewry. It is, therefore, impossible to argue that the creation of a Jewish national state is essential to the solution of the Jewish problem. If assimilation and equality of rights is to be the main solution it is entirely arbitrary to contend that it cannot be the whole solution. If there are still countries in which the Jews are persecuted or feel insecure, the remedy is either to alter the conditions in these countries and so insure for the Jews the same security and equality of rights they enjoy in the West or enable them to migrate to the other countries in which these conditions already exist and have provided a solution for the Jewish problem. Thus seen the problem becomes a refugee problem to be solved on the humanitarian plane. Towards this solution Arab Palestine has contributed a larger share in proportion to its size than any other country in the world. It has received and accepted as a permanent part of its population 600,000 Jews against an Arab population of 1,200,000 and it should not in fairness be asked to take any more. The United Nations, now that Nazism has been completely destroyed in Europe and a World Charter has been formulated, have it in their power to solve the Jewish problem in the only way it can and should be solved, that is to say by guaranteeing for the Jews wherever they may be found the same human, civil and political rights as everybody else enjoys; and by the rigorous prevention of all persecution or discrimination on grounds of race. For the United Nations to support Zionism as a necessary solution of the Jewish problem is to admit defeat and declare the bankruptcy of the principles for which this war has been fought and which are supposed to have been vindicated and safeguarded in their victory. It is a reasonable hope that the penetration of Eastern and Central Europe by Russian influence will greatly help in providing the conditions that will solve the Jewish problem in its original home on this sound basis.

As for the positive Zionist aspiration, that is to say the recreation of the Jewish community as a nation on the basis of its traditional culture, there are two comments to be made on this. The first is that here again world Jewry is of divided opinion. Many Jews consider that their race has made its contribution to the world as a community and cannot do so again; that the contribution which the Jews can make to civilization today can only be made by them as individuals, as citizens of England or America or France, or the Soviet Union, as members of the world community and exponents of a civilization that has become essentially international. For these reasons they do not believe that either they themselves or the world has anything special to gain from the revival of Hebrew culture as such, still less from its expression through a national state. The second comment is that if a section of world Jewry is impelled by the Hebrew inspiration and strongly desires to rebuild its own culture, it is welcome to do so but only on condition that it does not trespass in this attempt on the rights of any existing nation or culture. To attempt to recreate Jewish culture through the establishment of a Jewish national state in somebody else's country is an intolerable trespass on the rights of that country and should not be allowed. In Palestine, as it is today and without the creation of a Jewish state, the Jews have been able to develop their own culture to a considerable degree and will have the opportunity to continue to do so, since the Arabs do not object to the Jews having in Palestine a spiritual and cultural centre provided it does not threaten to express itself in a political form that would violate the rights and status of the Arab population. That this right and this status will be violated by the creation of a Jewish national state is a truth demonstrable on historical, moral and legal grounds to anybody who has the honesty of mind to see it.

Historical Grounds. The Zionists have by the endless repetition of a specious argument convinced a large section of the British public that they have a historical right to Palestine at least equal to that of the Arabs, if not superior to it. The judgment of the King-Crane Commission (an authoritative body consisting of a number of Americans of the highest integrity and competence appointed by President Wilson in 1919 to investigate conditions on the spot in the Arab world) on this Zionist claim is bluntly that "it cannot be taken seriously." The Arabs have, according to all accepted criteria, a prescriptive right to Palestine resulting from thirteen centuries of continuous occupation and complete Arabization. The Jews' previous occupation of the country came to an end 2,000 years ago. It had never been complete save for a period of 70 years, and did not leave any lasting imprint on the land. How can such a remote and (in the political sense) completely terminated connection take precedence over or even compete for quality with the present stark reality of Arab ownership?

Legal Grounds. Here again the Zionists have by dint of clamor, repetition and the most ingenious casuistic contortions tried to prove that they have an equal, if not superior, right to Palestine arising out of the promise made to them by the British Government in 1917, viz., the Balfour Declaration. The truth of the matter is that the Balfour Declaration (which in any case did not promise the Jews anything more than "the best endeavors" of the British Government "to facilitate" the establishment *in* Palestine of a national *home* for the Jewish people) was itself incompatible with a solemn promise previously made to the Arabs. In 1916 Britain concluded an agreement with the Arabs whereby, in return for their participation in the war against Turkey, she promised to recognize at the end of the war an independent Arab Kingdom East of the Mediterranean and Red Sea, and by no acrobatics of interpretation can it be shown that Palestine was excluded from this area. There was no mention of Palestine whatever in that agreement. There was only one reservation referring, on any honest and straightforward reading of the text, to the Northern coastal strip of Syria which no more included Palestine than Scotland includes England.

Moral Grounds. But even if the British Government had not concluded any treaty with the Arabs it still would not have had the right to issue the Balfour Declaration, by which it promised somebody's property to somebody else. The Balfour Declaration was morally invalid because Palestine was not Britain's property so that she could promise it to the Zionists or anybody else. According to all the principles enunciated by the Allies during the 1914-1918 war, and notably President Wilson's Fourteen Points and the Covenant of the League of Nations, Palestine belonged to its people. The British Army did not conquer Palestine from the Arabs so that Britain might dispose of it by right of conquest (even if the right of conquest had not been repudiated by the Allies); it conquered it from the Turks and liberated it for its rightful owners, the Arabs, who themselves participated in the campaign of liberation.

Lastly, the Zionists appeal to the Left movement on ideological and practical grounds. They claim that they are a civilizing force in the Arab world, that they are the spearhead of socialism assaulting feudalism and that they are developing Palestine economically in a manner which the Arabs could not develop it, and bringing to it a prosperity from which the Arabs themselves are benefiting. These claims are a tissue of fallacies. . . . Far from Zionism being able to act as a bridge for Western civilization to the Arab world it is prejudicing that world against the West and breeding in it a resistance to Western civilization, and this is a matter of the gravest danger. For the progress of the Arab world, for the peace of the Mediterranean basin and for the development of harmonious and fruitful relations between the Arabs and the peoples of the West towards a world synthesis, it is essential that the Arabs should understand and assimilate the basic values of European civilization. Their leading thinkers are alive to this and are doing much to bring about this understanding. Nor is the Arab mind unreceptive to the Western message. Unfortunately however the message first reached the Arab world through a relationship of power. It came with imperialism and so could not evoke an unalloyed welcome. Today it is being further prejudiced by Zionism, which is widening, not bridging the gulf.

The Jewish Communist settlements in Palestine are indeed admirable in themselves, but it is completely wrong to imagine either that they can become the spearhead of socialism in Palestine, or that they represent the whole of Zionist enterprise. They are mere enclaves and have no general significance. They are, like monastic orders, isolated from their surroundings, and can no more lead to the socialization of the Middle East than did Robert Owen's colonies lead to the socialization of Canada. Many of them existed under Turkish rule long before Zionism appeared and they could continue to exist irrespective of whether a Jewish state is formed in Palestine or not. Only 18 per cent of the Jews in Palestine live in these settlements; the remainder are building up an industrial capitalist order in the cities.

It is true that the Zionists, coming from Europe with superior education, technique and organization, and disposing of enormous funds contributed by world Jewry, have been able to achieve a greater measure of economic development in these twenty-five years than the Arabs, but it would be extremely immoral to argue that this gives them a right to take the country away from its people. This was the argument used by the Italians to justify their conquest of Abyssinia. This is the argument which imperialists have always put forward to justify colonization. But civilized world opinion, and particularly socialist opinion, has rejected it as being immoral and has substituted in its place the new and moral principle that the less technically advanced countries of the world should be helped by the more advanced nations to develop their land for their own benefit and for the benefit of the world at large. If the Arabs of Palestine were not as advanced as the Jews in 1918, the moral remedy was that they should be helped by the mandatory power to develop as quickly as possible and not condemned to lose their land to somebody else. The economic development which the Jews have achieved in Palestine has been almost entirely in their own interest. They are developing the country for themselves with the intention of making it entirely their own, so that any incidental benefit the Arabs may have derived from this development is temporary and entirely offset by the implication of this major political threat. At the same time the Arabs have suffered in many ways as a result of Jewish enterprise and economic development. It is a principle of Jewish enterprise not to employ an Arab unless there is no alternative to doing so. It is a condition of the acquisition of land by the Jewish National Fund that such land shall never again be sold to an Arab and that no Arab laborer may be employed on it. When the Jews buy land the Arab peasants become dispossessed and drift into the cities to seek work as landless proletarians.

This is only one answer to the Zionist claim that they can develop Palestine and the Arabs cannot. The other answer is that the claim itself is not true. The development of Palestine in the last twenty-five years is by no means entirely due to Zionist enterprise. A part of it is due to the action of the mandatory power itself and not a little of it is the result of Arab enterprise. It cannot be too much emphasized that the Arabs started at a grave disadvantage as compared with the Jews. They were only just beginning their new and autonomous life, while the Zionists came with the full apparatus of European education and technical skill and with the financial backing of world Jewry. And all along, the terms on which the mandate was applied to Palestine and the official policy of the British administration have favored the Zionists against the Arabs. The most glaring illustration of this fact is that in the Jewish Agency the Zionists have been allowed to have an organization which amounts to a government of their own, which indeed was described by the Peel Commission as an *imperium in imperio,* while no such body exists for the Arabs, who on the national plane are only represented by the mandatory administration. But the mandatory administration, apart from the fact that it is British and not Arab, is torn between the conflicting obligations of the mandate and is in personnel proportionately more Jewish than Arab. In spite of all these handicaps, however, the Arabs have achieved considerable progress in these twenty-five years and have a number of big undertakings to their credit in finance, commerce, agriculture and industry. In spite of all the economic progress of the last twenty-five years and the creation of many new industries, Palestine is still mainly noted for its citrus growing. But this industry existed before Zionism. It was indeed created by the Arabs themselves in the days of the Ottoman regime more than 200 years ago. It was the Arabs who developed the Jaffa orange and brought it to its present perfection and they have maintained their lead in this industry to this day. The dominant fact of the situation is that the Arabs have proved themselves capable of developing their country if given a reasonable chance. With the creation of the Arab League and the plans now being worked out by it for economic cooperation throughout the Arab world, the Palestine Arabs would be in a much better position to do this. If at the same time they are given the technical help and advice they need either from Britain or in the more general ways which the various Arab countries and the Arab League itself may arrange for, they should be able to perform their task adequately, to develop their country for themselves in the first place and in the interests of the whole world in the second.

But the most formidable answer to the Zionist claim that they have brought prosperity to Palestine from which the Arabs themselves have benefited is to be found on the moral plane. Progress and welfare are not only matters of material wealth; they are also matters of the spirit. More important than money are peace, harmony and happiness, and by this criterion Zionism in Palestine stands condemned. By its attack on the feelings, rights and interests of the people of the country it has brought not welfare but strife and misery; and the chief result of its presence has been to generate in twenty-five years the greatest concentration of hatred and violent nationalism known anywhere in the world outside the Nazi orbit. To the Arabs indeed Zionism seems as hideous as anything the Nazis conceived in the way of racial expansion at the expense of others. The Zionist's claim to have brought prosperity to the country sounds in Arab ears very much like Hitler's talk of the blessings of the New Order, and the historical, legal and moral arguments adduced to support the Zionist case for Palestine appear to them in the same light as those used by the Nazis to justify the spoliation or destruction of the nations they attacked, while the novel contention, put out by some Zionist advocates, that the matter is not one of rights but of the greater need of the Jews for Palestine smacks unmistakably of the *Lebensraum* doctrine. This extraordinary "greater need" argument seeks to justify itself by regarding the whole Arab world as one unit that could well afford to cede to the Jews what is only a very small part of it. The Arab population of this small part, it is contended, could either live as a minority in a Jewish state or preferably be moved to another part of the Arab world. It would be interesting to see how the inhabitants of, say, Scotland or of any American state would react to a similar suggestion if made to them.

This "small part" of the Arab world is holy to all the Christians and all the Moslems of the world. It has in it the third Holy City of the Moslem tradition as well as the most sacred shrines of the Christian religion, and the most important point to bear in mind in this connection is that these Moslem and Christian shrines in Palestine are not sacred to the Jews but positively abhorrent. To hand them over, therefore, to Jewish custody would not only provoke intense resentment in the Moslem world but might easily lead to a growth of anti-Semitic feeling among both Moslems and Christians and so do considerable harm to the Jewish cause in general. On the other hand, the Jewish shrines have also their holy place in the Moslem and Christian traditions, and there should be nothing repugnant to world Jewry in their remaining, as indeed they have been for over a thousand years, in Arab custody.

The only feasible and healthy solution of the Jewish problem, particularly from the socialist point of view, the only solution in line with progressive evolution and democratic ideology, lies in the acceptance of the Jews wherever they may happen to live as full citizens enjoying complete equality of rights with their fellow nationals in a world from which all persecution and discrimination on racial grounds shall have been abolished. This solution has been achieved in the countries of the West, and in the Soviet Union. Progressive people everywhere and in particular members of the Left movement should strive for its application to the whole world. Indeed, the Jewish problem is not an isolated problem; it is part of the general problem of minorities throughout the world and its solution is essentially implied in the triumph of democracy and socialist principles. If at the moment there are Jews in Germany and other parts of Europe, tragic survivors of the Nazi terror, who have no wish to go on living in the land where they have suffered so much, their position presents a human problem that should be solved internationally. Other countries than Palestine, particularly the British Commonwealth and the United States, with their vast territories and great absorptive capacity, should offer to do their share. The admission of fifty or a hundred thousand Jews to these countries would not cause them any inconvenience nor raise awkward political issues. In the case of Palestine the admission of more refugees cannot possibly be regarded in this humanitarian aspect. There it would cause serious prejudice to the Arab population and raise the gravest of political issues. Every Jew that comes to Palestine as a refugee is one more brick in the structure of the national home, one more unit towards a Jewish majority which, if ever attained, would result in the domination of the Arabs as a minority in a Jewish state established forcibly in their own country. By already receiving more than 600,000 Jews against 1,200,000 Arabs, Palestine has surely contributed far more than its just share towards a solution of the Jewish problem. These Jews have come to Palestine against the will of the Arabs and contrary to the pledges made to them. If it be asked what compromise the Arabs are willing to make, the answer is that they are willing to accept those Jews that have come to Palestine and wish to remain in it as Palestinian citizens, and to give them full and equal rights with themselves, provided the pledges of the British Government in the White Paper of 1939 are carried out. But to ask the Arabs to surrender their country entirely to the Jews either in the name of humanitarianism or in order to satisfy the political claims of Zionism is neither reasonable nor moral. Least of all is it compatible with the tenets of the socialist movement.

KING IBN SAUD TO PRESIDENT ROOSEVELT [4]

This is indeed a happy occasion for us to join with you in rejoicing at the triumph of those principles in defense of which war was declared and to remind those great personalities in whose hands, after God, the fate of the world order rests, of a right which has existed unquestioned since the dawn of history.

This right men now seek to destroy by injustice unparalleled and unequaled in history. Such is the right of the Arabs in Palestine, which the spokesmen of Jewish Zionism wish to scorn and abolish. . . .

All people have the natural right to live in their homeland, a right guaranteed to them by natural law established by the principles of humanity which the Allies have proclaimed in the Atlantic Charter and on numerous other occasions.

The Arabs have a natural right in Palestine which needs no explanation. We have on a separate occasion mentioned to Your Excellency, as we have many times to the British Government, that the Arabs have inhabited Palestine since the beginning of history and that they have throughout the ages been its masters and enjoyed an overwhelming numerical superiority.

We would now make a brief reference to Palestine's history, ancient and modern, up to the present day, to make it clear that Zionist claims in Palestine are not based on historical facts.

The earliest recorded history of Palestine begins in the year 3500 B. C., its first inhabitants being the Canaanites, an Arab tribe which emigrated from the Arab peninsula and had its first abode in the lowlands, hence the name Canaanites. In 2000 B. C. a section of the Jews under the leadership of the Prophet Abraham emigrated from Iraq (Ur of the Chaldees), settled in Palestine and then immigrated because of famine into Egypt where they were delivered into bondage by the Pharaohs.

The Jews remained scattered there until their delivery from exile by the Prophet Moses, who brought them back to the land

[4] Letter, March 10, 1945, addressed to the late Franklin D. Roosevelt, President of the United States. *Congressional Record*. 91: (daily) A4912-13. October 29, 1945.

of Canaan by the southeastern route, either in the time of Rameses II, i.e. 1250 B. C., or his son, Munfitah, 1225 B. C.

If we accept the text of the Bible, we find that the conqueror of Palestine was Joshua, the son of Nun, who crossed with his army and captured the city of Jericho from the Canaanites, with great cruelty and barbarity: witness his words to his army:

"Burn ye all that is in the city and slay with the edge of the sword both man and woman, young and old, and ox and sheep, and burn the city with fire and all that is therein." Joshua, chapter 7, verses 21 to 24.

Thereafter the Jews split up into two kingdoms. One, the Kingdom of Israelites with its capital Samaria (Nablus), lasted 250 years and then fell into the hands of Shalmaneser, King of the Assyrians, in the year 722 B. C., and was led into captivity. The other, the Kingdom of Judah, with its capital Jerusalem, lasted 130 years after the Kingdom of Israel had perished.

It was later destroyed by Nebuchadnezzar, King of Babylon, who burned down the city and the temple with fire, and led the people into captivity to Babylon in the year 580 B. C.

The captivity in Babylon lasted 70 years, and then the Jews returned to Palestine by order of Cyrus, King of the Persians.

The Greek conquest followed in 332 B. C., under the command of Alexander the Macedonian, their rule continuing in Palestine for a period of 272 years.

The Roman conquest took place next in the year 63 B. C., under the command of Pompey, their rule lasting in Palestine for 700 years.

In the year A. D. 637 the Arabs occupied Palestine, and their rule lasted continously for 880 years.

The orders of the Caliph to the conqueror were: "You shall not act treacherously, dishonestly, commit any excess or mutilation, kill any child or old man; cut or burn down palms or fruit trees, kill any sheep, cow or camel, and shall leave alone those whom you find devoting themselves to worship in their cells." This was related by Ibn-al-Atheer, the famous historian.

Palestine then passed under the rule of the Turks in A. D. 1517, during the reign of Sultan Saleem the First, and their rule lasted for 400 years. The Arabs were the inhabitants and participated with the Turks in the government and administration of the country. It was then occupied by the British who are still there.

This history of Palestine, an Arab country, shows that the Arabs were its first inhabitants and that they dwelt there for a period of 3,500 years before Christ and have remained there since Christ until the present day.

They ruled it alone or with the Turks for a period of about 1,300 years, whereas the disjointed reign of the Jews did not exceed 380 confused and sporadic years.

No Jewish rule has existed in Palestine since 332 B. C. nor until the British forces entered Palestine in 1918, i.e., for 2,200 years there have been few Jews there and they had no influence. They numbered not more than 80,000 when the British entered Palestine, and lived comfortably, happily, and prosperously in that country with the original inhabitants, the Arabs.

The Jews were merely aliens who had come to Palestine at intervals and had then been turned out over 2,000 years ago.

The permanent rights of the Arabs in Palestine rest on the following:

1. The right to dwell there. This they have done since the year 3500 B. C. without ever leaving the country.

2. The natural right of life.

3. The existence therein of the Holy Land.

4. The Arabs are not aliens in Palestine and there is no intention to bring any of them from other parts of the world to settle there.

The historical claims of the Jews is, however, a fallacy. As already mentioned, their brief and sporadic rule gives them no right to claim that they own the country, for to occupy a country and then leave it entitles no nation to claim and demand ownership thereof. The history of the world is full of such examples.

The solution of the problem of the persecuted Jews in the world differs from the fictitious problem of Zionism. For to provide homes for the scattered Jews is something in which the whole world can cooperate, and here Palestine has borne more than its full share. But to bring these scattered people, put them in countries already occupied, and do away with the original inhabitants is an act unparalleled in human history.

We state frankly and plainly that to help Zionism in Palestine not only means to endanger Palestine but all neighboring countries.

The Zionists have given clear evidence of their intentions in Palestine and in all neighboring countries. They have organized dangerous secret military formations. It would thus be a mistake to say that this was the action of a group of their extremists and that it had met with the disapproval of their assemblies and committees. . . .

If the matter were left to the Arabs and these aggressors, it might perhaps be easy, but they are protected by the British Government, the friends of the Arabs. The Zionists did not respect the sanctity of this protection, but plotted mischief, beginning first with Britain and threatening the Arabs after Britain with similar and more dangerous plots.

Thus, if the Allied governments, whose friendship the Arabs are aware of, wish to see the fires of war break out and bloodshed between Arabs and Jews, their support of the Zionists will surely lead to this result. What we and the Arab countries fear from the Zionsists are:

1. That they will carry out a series of massacres as between themselves and the Arabs.

2. That the Zionists will be one of the main causes of dissension between the Arabs and Allies. . . .

3. That the ambitions of the Jews are not confined to Palestine alone. The preparations they have made show that they intend to take hostile action against neighboring Arab countries.

4. Supposing that the Jews obtain their independence somewhere in Palestine, what is to prevent them from coming to an agreement with any power that may be hostile to the Allies and to the Arabs? As it is, they have begun taking hostile action against Britain while under her protection and mercy.

Such factors should no doubt be taken into consideration in regard to the establishment of peace in the world when the problem of Palestine is discussed. Not only is the gathering of Jews in Palestine based on no historical argument nor on any natural right, and is in fact absolutely unjust, but it constitutes at the same time a danger to peace, to the Arabs and to the Middle East.

The crux of the matter is that the formation of a Jewish state in Palestine will be a deadly blow to the Arabs and a constant threat to peace, for disturbed conditions are bound to prevail between the Jews and the Arabs, and if the patience of the latter is one day exhausted and they despair of their future then they will be obliged to defend themselves and future generations against this aggression. No doubt the Allies, who are working to uphold peace and respect for men's rights, are aware of this. We have no doubt that they are dissatisfied with this uneasy situation which threatens peace in the Middle East. . . .

The Jews should not be permitted to exploit the forebearance of the Arabs or their desire to avoid any embarrassment to the Allies, to obtain concessions to which they are not entitled.

All we ask is that the Allies should fully realize the rights of the Arabs and for the present prevent the Jews going ahead in any new matter which may be considered a threat to the Arabs and to the future of every Arab nation, in order that they, the Arabs, may be assured of justice and equity in their lands.

RECONCILIATION IN PALESTINE [5]

First we face the situation that on all acceptable political grounds Palestine is an Arab country. Quite apart from the reasonable assumption that some of the present population of Palestine must be descended from the Canaanitish tribes who occupied the country before the Hebrew incursions of the fifteenth century before Christ, the Arabs have been the predominating population for 1,000 years. In 1918 they constituted 93 per cent of the population. Allowing for an Arab immigration from surrounding territory of 100,000 or even more, since that time, they have increased to nearly 1,000,000. Now a tenure of 1,000 years constitutes a good claim on even conservative

[5] By E. B. Castle, M.A., Headmaster, Leighton Park School, England. *Hibbert Journal*. 43:140-7. January 1945.

political reckoning; it is as good as that of Anglo-Saxons to England and better than that of Anglo-Saxons to other parts of the world. It is not unnatural, therefore, that Arabs experience a reasonable soreness over the omission of any reference to "Arab" in the Balfour Declaration. That was a regrettable mistake that cannot be remedied and might well be forgotten. The political right of the Palestinian Arab to Palestine, then, must be conceded. He is rooted in its soil. On all historical and political tests Palestine was an Arab country in 1918.

But there are complications. The Palestinian Arab shares in the national aspirations of the Arab world which is part of the urge for independence in subject peoples everywhere. Here he comes up against the mandate which rightly or wrongly delays his independence. He regards it as unfair that he, a Mohammedan, should be forced by Christian powers to solve the Jewish problem which is the special creation of Christian peoples. Moreover, the Arabs are an intelligent people with a great culture and a glorious past, but in Palestine they find themselves frustrated by material and cultural disadvantages. It has been one of the misfortunes of the Palestinian Arab that he has been subjected for 400 years to the sluggish tyranny of the Turkish Empire where material progress and educational opportunity were alike non-existent. He now finds himself confronted with the competition of an able people, reared in the best material and intellectual backgrounds of Europe. This exacerbates his fear of the immigrant Jew whose gifts and skills he will seldom acknowledge but always fears, often without reason. His poverty and the parsimony of British rule have prevented the growth of Arab educational provision which might in time remove his sense of frustration. The Department of Education has done its best with the meager funds at its disposal, but it is sad to record that in 1939, after twenty years of mandatory rule, even on the low plane of very elementary education half the applicants for school places were refused for lack of buildings and teachers. In the school year 1935-36 out of a total Arab school population of 260,000 only 42,000 were in government elementary schools. Of those who applied for school places 48 per cent were "deferred" for lack of accommodation. In towns alone the number refused admission was 62 per cent of total applications. An examination of secondary education reveals a similar position. There is one government Arab secondary school in Palestine which, when I visited it in 1938, housed 100 boys—true, in a splendid building. Other schools have secondary classes (total about 1,000 children). There are two or three private Arab schools, but the major part of secondary education for Arabs is given in several Christian missionary schools. Teachers' training facilities are utterly inadequate to supply the needs. That the Arab wants education is proved by the fact that since 1920 no less than 218 primary schools have been built by the villagers themselves. They only asked for teachers. And the intelligent Palestinian Arab noted that in the neighboring independent state of Iraq the education bill was 10 per cent of the national budget compared with 5 per cent in Palestine. There is no Arab university.

This situation does not serve to give confidence to Arabs who see a highly integrated and highly civilized people with the advantages of Western education behind them making an enormous impact on their lives—often, it is true, a healthy impact. But the Arab is not anti-Jewish. He is anti-Zionist. The clash is not religious but political and economic. Division and feud among the Arabs themselves has not assisted harmony, but behind it all lies a fear of extinction. The Arab is aware that he can look only to the Palestinian Government and his own efforts for release from disadvantages inherent in his position. But he sees opposed to his lack of social and educational opportunity a highly organized system of Jewish education subsidized with admirable sacrifice by faithful Jews all over the world. Indeed, Jewish effort in the educational sphere is one of the noblest and most productive of their activities. Jewish children enjoy a provision that embraces 99 per cent of Jewish children from three to fourteen years of age. There are nineteen secondary schools totalling over 6,000 pupils; six teachers' training colleges, although half the teachers come from abroad; there are nine technical and agricultural schools and, crowning all, on its wonderful site on Mount Scopus, stands the magnificent Hebrew University, which is destined to become one of the greatest seats of learning in the Middle East. This leads us to a consideration of the Jewish background.

Here is a great but persecuted people, bound together by ties of religion and a common sorrow, whose sufferings have evoked the sympathy of all generous minds. Their problem is a world problem, created by the intolerance of peoples who bear the name of Christian; and its final solution must be a world solution, for Palestine can never provide a complete answer. The Jews are heirs of an age-long ideal unique in history—the desire to return to their land of origin. This desire is not universally shared by Jews, but has assumed vital political significance during the last twenty-five years. Basically it is founded on an entirely noble and practicable urge to upbuild the character of the Jewish people and to evolve a culture of their own on soil which has a meaning for the Jewish soul. Quite apart from this ideal which has the sympathy of all right-minded people, persecution of the cruellest kind has made essential some form of political status for some Jews. Reliance on the good-will of Christian nations for fair treatment has so far proved a bitter, a humiliating and a barren thing; and there is much reason in the Jewish claim that statelessness or minority status will always mean persecution when rogues seek scapegoats to flay. Suggestions for settlement in other parts of the world have proved sterile, but in any case such solutions would not satisfy the Zionist idea. The Zionist claims the right to return to the land of his fathers, towards which the mind of the Jewish people has been turned for centuries. He also claims, and with justice, that Jewish endeavor in Palestine during the last twenty years (for which no praise is too high) has brought wealth and energy to the country. But some would go further and maintain that this proof of their creative mission gives them a right to unlimited immigration and to the foundation of a Jewish state in Palestine. The Zionist sees his claim legalized in the Balfour Declaration as embodied in the mandate, a part of international law. But no such legal right exists as far as an "independent Jewish state" is concerned. A "national home in Palestine" has never been acknowledged to mean a Jewish state of Palestine, nor does the mandate imply this.

In spite, therefore, of the strongest claims on other grounds, we have to admit that on all accepted political grounds the Jewish claim is weak. One hundred years ago there were 12,000 Jews in Palestine; in 1918 there were 80,000; today nearly 500,000. It is impossible to concede the principle that primitive occupation of a country, despite vast periods of occupation by another people constitutes a political right to return to it after, say, 1,500 or 1,000 or even 500 years. Fantastic situations the world over would arise if such a claim were admitted. It is, indeed, a delightful exercise for an idle hour to readjust the frontiers of the world on this basis. Furthermore, while admiring the faithful aspiration of the Jew to return to the Promised Land, the claim that this unfading hope constitutes a political right of entry departs from all reality. On this principle we have only to desire Naboth's vineyard long enough to stake out a claim for possession. It is equally dangerous to develop the claim, as many Jews and their American and British supporters have done, that because a certain people have the initiative, equipment and technical ability to develop the material resources of any area of the earth's surface, they have the political right to possess it. That is the basis of Hitler's "New Order" for Europe. It will not in the end help the Zionists, nor will it help their friends to help the Jews, if they continue to claim entry into Palestine as of right.

But political rights are not the only values worthy of recognition in a civilized community. Where a deep wrong has been committed it becomes the privilege of all peoples to put it right. And there can be no doubt at all that the sheer human appeal of the Jewish position in the modern world is of the greatest significance and commands the utmost sympathy. The physical and spiritual needs of the homeless Jews, therefore, must constitute a major part of the background in all our thinking on the problem of Palestine. They have, moreover, done superb pioneering work, in supremely difficult conditions, in good faith and with a high hope. The only spot on earth which satisfies the Zionist's sense of homeland is the land of Abraham. But again, one must urge in their own interests, that this does not constitute a right to majority rule in Palestine, and it can never be a legitimate appeal, even of a persecuted people, that powerful states should support them in a claim to the territory of a weaker people, if that weaker people have a historical right to stay where they are, free from foreign incursions. I cannot forget the unanswerable humanity and wisdom of an old Arab Sheik in a remote village in the Judean hills when referring to this attitude of the Western powers: "When we are sorry for people we ask them to stay in our own home, we do not send them to somebody else's!" We British and American sympathizers with the Jewish sorrow should never forget our own responsibility, for if Palestine is filled to capacity with Jews there would still be 12,000,000 outside for whom our friendship would still be needful. Anyhow, we must be careful, in acknowledging the Jewish claim on ourselves, that we do not ask others to bear the burden of our charitable feelings. But the fact remains that amid the tangle of suffering, feud and unreason, we have yet to find a generous solution to the human claim of the Jew to have a resting place, a spot on the globe where, in so far as it is politically and economically possible, he may pursue in peace the course of a free and unfrustrated existence. And part of this solution must now lie within the borders of the Arabs' Land of Blessing.

So far, then, it has been suggested that the political claim of the Arab to political predominance in Palestine is incontestable and that the political claim of the Jew is weak. We recognize, nevertheless, that the human claim of the Jew is great and that somehow it must be met. But there is a third party in this situation. The British Government is the Mandatory Power responsible for the welfare of both Jew and Arab, and on it rests much, but not all, of the responsibility for so directing the conflicting interests of the two communities as to secure peace and satisfaction to both. Great Britain has not had an easy progress; not merely because she has undertaken the thankless task of reconciling utterly conflicting views and welding into one citizenship two peoples whose traditions and language and immediate ambitions defy reconciliation, but because Great Britain herself has peculiar interests which divide her mind and inhibit disinterested action. The strategic position of Palestine in relation to British imperial sea routes is obvious: the war has amply demonstrated this. And the one word "oil" explains the rest.

With such interests frequently predominating over her international obligations under the mandate, Britain has not been able to avoid the criticism that her enthusiasms in implementing the mandate and using all the persuasive powers at her disposal to ease the situation in Palestine has been less than the demands of her imperial interests. But it must be admitted in fairness that the intransigence of Jew and Arab would have made even a single-minded policy vastly difficult. Nevertheless, out of this tangle of policies one clear duty for Britain emerges. She can no longer allow imperial or economic considerations to divert her from making paramount in her attitudes to Palestine the overriding duty of acting solely in the interests of the two peoples over whose destiny she has been placed by international agreement. That is why Britain rules Palestine. She has no other justification for being there.

I trust that the above estimate of this vexed triangular situation does justice to the three peoples involved in it. I have attempted to separate political rights from what may be called human rights, for until the air is cleared in this way we shall fail to approach any solution from the right background. But having done this we have to admit that anyone who has had any personal experience of the intense passions prevailing on each side, of the obstinate refusal of the zealous Zionist or nationalist Arab to concede an inch of his position in the interests of compromise, will still remain sceptical of any happy ending to the Palestinian problem. Nevertheless, the truth remains that Arab and Jew must live together, and live at peace. We arrive then at a deadlock in the presence of an urgent situation that requires immediate action. When such an impasse occurs in human affairs there is nothing else to do but to lean back, think again, and examine ourselves very carefully to see whether we have always been right all the time. This cannot be done unless in the brief respite for reflection we train our thoughts along a higher level than the level of rights—namely, along the level of moral obligation. If it be humanly possible, and I believe it is, for the leaders of these two noble peoples to consider more fundamentally the reasonable claims of the other side, and if all the persuasive genius and generous propensities of British rule weighed in to make this possible, then we could begin again to make peace in Palestine. There is no other way. That has become evident. No argument on the plane on which the dispute has so far been conducted can now influence opinion on the one side or the other. For years the wrangling has proceeded until bitterness is mountains high and the moderate opinion of serious men has been buried amidst maximalist clamor. It is to this central corpus of moderating thought that appeal must be made. This will be done when each side is capable of saying "What can we give?" For Jews and Arabs have lived together before and they can do so again if the influences that make for reconciliation are placed before those that divide.

What can the Arabs give? First they might tread more softly on the nationalist pedal, especially in their schools; they might give up their fear of being submerged and test out the capacity of the Jews to cooperate by offering cooperation. They might recognize the indisputable fact that the Jews can, indeed, bring to Palestine benefits in which they might share. Their major gift would be to yield up their right to be afraid and to suspect. But beyond this the Arab world beyond Palestine might make a still larger contribution in its plan for Arab federation by considering the feasibility of including a binational Arab-Jewish state within the federation. Can they come to see that such a coordination of Arab and Jewish genius might bring unimaginable benefits to the poverty-stricken area of "the desert and the sown?"

What might the Jews give? They can first yield up their obstinate claim to enter Palestine as an absolute right, for such claims create fear and arouse a spirit of resistence, neither a sentiment on which to base agreement. "We shall not be satisfied until. . ." "We are here by right. . ."—these are not the words to encourage consultation. Can their leaders be more humble and conceding? Can they dispel the impression that they believe themselves always to be 100 per cent right? For they must remember that in the eyes of the Arabs they are invaders, at least newcomers, strangers, utterly unknown to the people of the land until they came. The Jews need not proclaim this to the Arabs, but they might acknowledge it to themselves. Can they forget for one moment that they are the most persecuted people on the globe, and act as free generous agents in a common enterprise with another people? In personal contacts with Zionists in England and Palestine I have not found this conceding spirit as evident as it might be; but I am confident that if the Jews would agree to be united in moderation they would gather to their cause more powerful friends and might win over like-minded Arabs so that together they might pursue their common task. Can they, in short, act up to those noble standards of loving conduct which they, more than any people in the world, have left as the highest heritage of the human race.

The Jews have given much to Palestine. In the nature of their struggle it has been hardly possible for them to do more than develop their own resources and attend to their own needs. What they have given to the Arabs has been incidental, not a deliberate and planned giving. That was perhaps inevitable. But can they now in these quieter times, before the fires of contro-versy again burst forth, *deliberately* plan to use their special gifts and skills on behalf of the less fortunate Arab? I think especially of the educational and medical services. Can they for instance, demand from the Palestinian Government better educa-tional opportunity for Arab children? I know the difficulties; the type of welcome they might receive in some Arab quarters. But they might nevertheless go outward from their own acute problems and seek a solution of them by neglecting them. This may be a counsel of perfection. But a revolutionary situation demands revolutionary methods to direct it. And I am acutely conscious of the moral insecurity of any Englishman who recom-mends such moral solutions to other folk.

To both communities I suggest that documents and barren promises be forgotten, that rights should not be strenuously asserted, that reconciling factors be sought and used, that every agency in school, factory, trade union, farm and office, be utilized for encouraging contacts and common endeavour for the consum-mation of a common task—the peace and prosperity of Palestine.

I have declared more than once in this essay that Jew and Arab have in the end to live together. In political terms this means a union of Jews and Arabs enjoying equal political rights in a binational state. When all claims have been heard, and all human needs considered, there can be no other solution with any hope of success. It is at this point that the role of Great Britain becomes evident, and if necessary the mediation of America and the United Nations. For it is within the power of Great Britain and America to encourage two developments: First to bring into the open the large body of enlightened moderate opinion on both sides; secondly to act quickly in preparing for the common responsibility of Arab and Jew to organize their own country within a wider economic and political federation of Palestine, Transjordan, Syria and Lebanon. This means the rapid devolution of administration into Arab and Jewish hands. To be faced with the task of government is the surest way of securing collaboration between those responsible for it. So far the British official has held far too much of affairs in his own hands. Political and administrative experience must be open on a far larger scale to both Arab and Jew. But the most urgent need of the situation is that preparation for responsible duties in the binational state must begin now.

THE JEWISH NATIONAL HOME IN PALESTINE [6]

To the Arabs, political Zionism is an exotic movement, internationally financed, artificially stimulated and holds no hope of ultimate or permanent success. Not only to the 50,000,000 Arabs, many of whom are descendants of the Canaanites who were in the land long before the Hebrews entered Palestine under Joshua, but to the entire Moslem society, of whom the Arabs form the spearhead, a sovereign Jewish state in Palestine appears as an anachronism. These Moslems constitute a somewhat self-conscious society of about 275,000,000 who dominate a large portion of Africa and Asia. Even if the Zionist political program, supported by British and American diplomacy and bayonets, should some day become a reality, what chance of survival has such an alien state amidst a camp of would-be hostile Arabic and unsympathetic Islamic world? There was a time in

[6] Statement of Philip K. Hitti, Professor of Semitic Literature, Princeton University, before the House Committee on Foreign Affairs, February 15, 1944. United States. House. Committee on Foreign Affairs. Hearings on H.Res. 418 and H.Res. 419. p. 241-5. 1944.

which a foreign state, a Latin one, was established in the Holy
Land; but its memory lives today only in books on the crusades.

For, be it remembered, on no other issue did the Moslems in
modern times seem to manifest such a unanimity. Even on the
question of the restoration of the caliphate, after it was destroyed
by Mustafa Kamal in 1924, there has been more friction and
less solidarity, as evidenced by the proceedings of the Islamic
congresses held in Cairo and Mecca. Verbal protests against
the Zionist political program, which this resolution adopts, and
cash to fight its provisions have poured in the last two decades
from Morocco to Malay. In India a "Palestine day" was celebrated in 1936 and the All India Moslem League passed a
resolution at its annual session on October 18, 1939, and another in its April meeting of 1943 warning the British against
converting Palestine into a Jewish state. Jerusalem in Moslem
eyes is the third haram, the third holy city after Mecca and
Medina. It was the first qiblah, the first direction in which
the early Moslems prayed before they began to turn in prayer
toward Mecca. The land was given by Allah as a result of a
jihad (holy war) and therefore for the Moslems to relinquish
their claim on it constitutes a betrayal of their faith. It is even
more sacred to the Christians, of whom there are today some
one hundred and thirty thousand in Palestine.

This uncompromising, persistent opposition to political Zionism, whose cause the resolution espoused, does not spell anti-
Semitism. Of all the major peoples of the world, the Arabs
perhaps come nearest to being free from race prejudice. Besides, they, like the Jews, are Semites and they know it. They
also know that their two religions are closest of kin, closer than
either of them is to Christianity. Nowhere throughout medieval
and modern times were Jews better treated than in Moslem-
Arab lands. So welcome were American Jewish ambassadors to
the Sublime Porte at Constantinople that our government appointed three of them in a row: Straus, Elkus, and Morgenthau.

These Arabs and Moslems cannot understand why the Jewish
problem, which is not of their making, should be solved at their
expense. They deeply sympathize with the afflicted Jews but are
not convinced that Palestine solves the Jewish problem; Palestine

does not qualify as a country without a people ready to receive a people without a country. They fail to understand why the American legislators, so solicitous for the welfare of the European Jews, should not lift the bars of immigration and admit Jewish refugees, millions of whom could be settled on the unoccupied plains of Arizona or Texas. This certainly falls within their jurisdiction. The word "reconstitute" in the resolution would no doubt interest them and they would like to remake the map of Europe and put up their claim on Spain, which they occupied at a much later date and for a longer period of time. Some of them would raise the question how would the people of the United States react to a suggestion from, say Russia, to reconstitute Oklahoma or Indian Territory. They realize they have no spokesmen in America, no high-pressure groups, no machinery for influencing American public opinion or legislation, but they are willing to rest their case upon its merits and upon America's sense of justice.

Some of them may have forgotten the Anglo-French declaration of November 8, 1918, promising the peoples so long oppressed by the Turks complete and definitive liberation and "the establishment of national governments and administrations drawing their authority from the initiative and free choice of the indigenous population"; or the words of Woodrow Wilson's twelfth point that the non-Turkish nationalities which are now under Turkish rule should be assured an undoubted security of life and an absolute opportunity of autonomous development; or the corresponding provision in the Covenant of the League of Nations, article 22; but they certainly do remember the third article of the Atlantic Charter that Great Britain and the United States, "respect the right of all people to choose the form of government under which they will live."

No Westerner, or Ifranji as called in Arabic, is more highly respected and more implicitly trusted by the Arab and Moslem people than the American. There is a reason for it. For years American teachers, preachers, physicians, archeologists, pilgrims, and philanthropists have frequented the eastern shore of the Mediterranean with the intent of giving rather than taking and with no imperialistic designs. The American press at Beirut, the first well-equipped press in that region, celebrated its hundredth anniversary eight years ago. The American University of Beirut celebrated its seventy-fifth anniversary three years ago. In this institution a large number of the leaders of thought and action throughout the Arab East were trained. In the First World War and the immediate period following, no less than $100,000,000 was raised by the American public to relieve suffering among the people of the Near East and to rehabilitate their land—an unparalleled figure in the history of private philanthropy. No wonder the word "American" has become associated in the minds of Arabs and Moslems with fair play, honorable dealing, and democratic conduct. All this reservoir of good-will accumulated through generations of unselfish and hard working Americans will be threatened with destruction by the passage of the resolution now before this committee. . . .

The people of the United States are not only interested in winning the war but in contributing to the establishment of a postwar world order in which regional stability is somewhat secure and the chances of future conflicts are at least reduced. Nothing, in the judgment of the speaker, is more conducive to a state of perpetual unrest and conflict than the establishment of a Jewish commonwealth at the expense of the Arabs in Palestine. If such a commonwealth were established at the insistence of the United States, we then assume moral responsibility for its preservation. Will the people of the United States be willing to send their navy to protect such a commonwealth if established?

The British never contemplated such an ambitious scheme as the conversion of Palestine into a Jewish commonwealth. Sandwiched in between conflicting promises to the Arabs— which made the once-promised land multi-promised—the Balfour Declaration, which was echoed in the United States Congress resolution of 1922, viewed with favor, "the establishment in Palestine of a national home for the Jewish people"—quite a different thing from converting Palestine into a Jewish state. And that was viewed with a big proviso: "It being understood that nothing shall be done which may prejudice the civil and religious rights of non-Jewish communities in Palestine." The Zionist representatives proposed to the then British Government this text "The reconstitution of Palestine as the national home of the Jewish people," which is practically the same as the resolution before us had it, but that was not the text adopted.

In its White Paper of June 3, 1922, the British Government said:

Unauthorized statements have been made to the effect that the purpose in view is to create a wholly Jewish Palestine. Phrases have been used such as that Palestine is to become as Jewish as England is English. His Majesty's Government regard such expectation as unpracticable and have no such aim in view. . . . They would draw attention to the fact that the terms of the declaration referred to do not contemplate that Palestine as a whole be converted into a Jewish national home but that such a home should be founded in Palestine. When it is asked what is meant by the development of the Jewish national home in Palestine, it may be answered that it is not the imposition of a Jewish nationality upon the inhabitants of Palestine as a whole, but the further development of the existing Jewish community, with the assistance of Jews from other parts of the world, in order that it may become a center in which the Jewish people as a whole may take, on grounds of religion and race, an interest and a pride.

The author of this statement was Winston Churchill, then Colonial Secretary; and the Zionist accepted it.

In its statement of policy of 1937 the British Government declare—

that their obligations to Arabs and Jews, respectively, were not incompatible, on the assumption that in the process of time the two races would so adjust their national aspirations as to render possible the establishment of a single commonwealth under a unitary government.

In the 1939 statement it was again made clear that Palestine shall be constituted a sovereign independent state, a Palestinian state in which all Palestinians—irrespective of race or origin—will be citizens enjoying equal political, civil and religious rights. In that statement the provision was made for limiting Jewish immigration for economic as well as political reasons.

Even then the British administration of Palestine has been confronted throughout its history with a series of strikes and disturbances beginning April 1920 and culminating in the serious revolution of 1936.

ARAB NATIONALISM AND POLITICAL ZIONISM [7]

The cultural progress of the Zionist colonies in Palestine has been remarkable in many ways. The great Hebrew University on Mount Scopus and its Library are monuments to the breadth and wisdom of its founders and builders. The large influx of Jewish capital into Palestine has furnished a basis for taxation (levied on the Arabs as well) which the British Government has used in part for public improvements—roads, public health, etc.—in which the Arabs have a natural share. At the same time, the Arab feels his total economic position less secure than before. Why this is the case, a single item relating to farm labor, will sufficiently illustrate:

It is especially the position of the Arab agricultural laborer that has to be considered, for most Arabs (and this is part of the traditional charm of the land) have gained their livelihood from the soil. What has been happening to him may best appear by quoting from a lease of the Jewish National Fund as to Jewish settlers on Palestinian land:

The lessee undertakes to execute all works connected with the cultivation of the holding only with Jewish labor. Failure to comply with this duty by the employment of non-Jewish labor shall render the lessee liable to the payment of a compensation of ten Palestinian pounds for each default. . . . Where the lessee has contravened the provisions of this Article three times the Fund may apply the right of restitution of the holding, without paying any compensation whatever.

The Jewish Agency provides in its Constitution that

Land is to be acquired as Jewish property . . . title to be taken in the name of the Jewish National Fund, to the end that the same shall be held as the inalienable property of the Jewish people.

On this arrangement, land bought by the Jewish Agency, let us say from an Arab landlord employing Arab labor, ceases automatically to be a place of possible residence or work to those laborers. As Sir John Simpson put the matter in his Report:

It ceases to be land from which the Arab can gain any advantage either now or at any time in the future. . . . He is deprived forever

[7] From pamphlet by William Ernest Hocking, Alford Professor of Philosophy Emeritus, Harvard University. p. 4-7. League of American-Arab Committees for Democracy. Flint, Mich. n.d.

from employment on that land. . . . Nor can anyone help him by purchasing the land and restoring it to common use. The land is in mortmain and inalienable.

There have been good reasons, from the standpoint of providing occupation for more Jewish immigrants, for such policies as these; but it is at least understandable that despite improvements in other ways, despite the fact that every step of the advance of Zionist ownership is legitimate, and paid for at high prices, the Arab masses as a whole have felt their relative position deteriorating. It is not a question of the number of persons dispossessed, and undisposed to accept compensation. It is a question of the attitude of the slowly advancing power. Its strength, intelligence, cash backing, splendid equipment, render it in Arab eyes the more formidable because of this attitude. Hence they have come to face the future with concern.

But why not override these feelings, which after all affect only a relatively few people on a very small piece of land? Why cannot the Arabs give up an insignificant fraction of their "immense domain," and even accept the idea of an exchange of population with, let us say, Iraq, if it will make for the realization of the Jewish dream? This proposal is now being vigorously urged in some quarters and many Americans are impressed by its apparent reasonableness.

Those who are promoting this view do not explain what they propose to do with the extensive religious establishments of Islam in Palestine, including the great mosques and various schools. These establishments are not, like those of the Christians, primarily of a memorial nature: they are important educational and devotional centers for a living religion, within the region of its central activity. To maintain such establishments a considerable local population is required and assumed: to deport the million Arabs to Iraq would be another way of strangling these institutions. They require also a flow of worshippers and pilgrims, both physically and morally free to come and go. The entire Moslem world is concerned in this. If we think the matter unimportant, they do not.

As for the "immense domain" of the Arab peoples, that is largely desert. The cultivable portions are chiefly strewn around the rim, whose northern arch is known as the Fertile Crescent.

The value of Palestine to either Arab or Zionist does not derive from its size but from its situation, and the functions which that situation enables it to carry out.

The material and present-day advantages of Palestine come largely from its position on the Mediterranean coast. Commercially it belongs to the European area. Palestine stands in an important strategic position between Europe and the budding industrial development, not so much of Palestine itself as of the lands behind Palestine, Arab lands which are entering on a new economic era. One Zionist proponent estimates the immediate background which Palestine might serve as 40,000,000 in number, with a remoter region of 400,000,000 people. All this region will need is outside financing; whose finance is it to be? And what control will go with the financing? If the future economic importance of Palestine is to be, as I surmise, commercial rather than agricultural or industrial, its prosperity will depend to a large extent on its relations to this growingly important hinterland. And vice versa, the prosperity of that hinterland might depend to a considerable extent on its relations with the financial powers, the warehouses, and the commercial lanes centering in Palestine and vicinity.

The significance of these facts is not obscure to the Zionist. It is also not obscure to the Arab, desirous of being master of his own industrial future; desirous therefore of keeping his direct front on the Mediterranean, and access on equal terms to the facilities of Palestinian harbors, roads and air stations. Cultural relations with Europe will also be important for the new life of the Arabian provinces. Surrender of Palestine to exclusive Zionist control would thus amount to acceptance of a barrier between them and Europe at the outset of their newer national career.

And when Zionists plans are extended, as they are by some, to bring Transjordan into the Jewish commonwealth, it must not be forgotten that the Zionist land-bloc would then cut clear through the thin Fertile Crescent to the desert. It would lie directly across the north-and-south lines of land travel and pilgrimage, including the railroad built chiefly for the convenience of pilgrims between the northern Moslem lands and Mecca. This would revive, within Arabian territory, that nightmare of

European politics, the Corridor. To ask for Palestine and Trans-jordan as a minute percentage of the total Arab territory is thus like asking for a microscopic section across one wrist.

The disconcerting thing about these proposals, to which the United States is asked to become a party, is not so much the rivalry of interests, which is a usual thing in the world, as the silence of Zionist spokesmen about the existence of any such Arab interests. They do not mention the Arab political aspirations, which like their own, have the sanction and documentary support of Great Britain. They tend to blackwash the cultural achievements and interests of the Arab peoples, whom they prefer to represent as typified by the Bedouin rather than by members of the Arab Academy at Damascus or the scholars of Beirut, and whom they describe even in literature now being circulated among us as "nomadic," "backward," "half-civilized." Do they not know the new Arab university life, the new literature, the new history, the new economic prowess? Do they forget that it was the Arabs who for six hundred years preserved the classical culture of Greece for a dark Europe?

And do they not know that just as they themselves are making beginnings in Palestine, so the Arab peoples in far greater numbers are making their new beginnings, after four centuries of oppression by the old Turkish regime? Mr. Lowdermilk, who will not be accused of over-enthusiasm for the Arab future, testifies to the rapid progress of an *unsubsidized* Arab agriculture (*Palestine, Land of Promise,* p. 158f.) and industry, about 2000 industrial plants having been started by them in recent years in Palestine alone. The young Arab world of today is living, as human beings should live, largely in the future. Its nationalism has to win its own steadiness, self-control, and world-responsibility; but its substance is a justified faith in what is to be, rather than fixing its eyes on what is.

If the Zionists do not know of these things, it is high time they learned of them. And if they do know of them, why do they so constantly speak and act as if they were not true? This failure on their part to appreciate what it is that they would push aside gives, I think, the clue to the emotional aspect of the Palestinian problem.

For given this temper of disparagement, can anyone explain to the American public why the Arabs should welcome the prospect of becoming dependent for their own progress in any degree on Zionist understanding and good-will?

It is not the bad effendis—who serve the Zionist spokesmen as the sufficient explanation of all opposition to their plans—it is not the landowners and the moneyed muftis alone, it is the entire Arab population of Palestine and the neighboring territories that cannot accommodate its mind to that prospect.

And we are asked to make a national commitment to the cause of political Zionism, I fear with our eyes half shut, a commitment whose consequences would be not alone an added tension in a situation already strained by the demands of war, but a revulsion against everything Anglo-American on the part of the Moslem world, already half inclined to seek the guarantors of its destiny elsewhere.

I speak with all consideration when I say that I believe the political Zionists at this moment as distinct from the cultural Zionists who have built the noble Hebrew University and who know what a national home must be, I believe the political Zionists to be the chief enemies of the cause of Zionism as well as of the Jewish interests in the world of tomorrow. What can they hope to gain by extricating their brethren from the prejudices of Europe only to build a community in Palestine which has to be protected by western force (and if we intervene, then by American force also) because it is cradled in an environment of distrust and fear cultivated by their own methods of realizing a misplaced nationalistic ambition?

IS ZIONISM A SOLUTION? [8]

The Arabs: The Arabs argue that Palestine is and has been their country for over 1,200 years. They deny the right to Britain or any other foreign power to interfere with their affairs. They point to the pledge of the Allies to recognize their freedom

[8] From article by Michel G. Malti, Professor of Electrical Engineering, Cornell University. *Arab World*. 1, no.2:74-80. Fall 1944.

and to Wilson's 14 points and contend that to impose Zionism on them, against the expressed wishes of the Arabs, is contrary to these declarations.

The Arabs deny that they have derived any benefits from Zionism. On the contrary, they assert that Zionism has ruined their economic life. To prove this assertion they point to the fact that the Constitution of the Jewish Agency provides that "Land is to be acquired as Jewish property . . . title to be taken in the name of the Jewish National Fund, to the end that same shall be held as the inalienable property of the Jewish people." Moreover, a lessee of land thus acquired "undertakes to execute all works connected with the cultivation of the holding only with Jewish labor. . . .

The Arabs further argue that they do not need the Zionists to develop Palestine. They can develop Palestine themselves. As evidence of this they point to the progress already accomplished in Iraq, exclusively by Arab effort, after that country had attained independence.

The Arabs assert that they have long dreamt, fought, and labored for a federation of Arab states. They do not care to have an alien state in the geographical center and at the cross roads of this federation. They have had enough trouble fighting European imperialists. They have suffered enough from clashes of interest over their country. They are sick and tired of being pushed around by Turks, Europeans and Zionists and they will resist as they have already resisted any attempts in this direction. Every freedom loving nation should admire and support them in this stand.

To the Arabs, as to all Moslems, Jews and Christians throughout the world, Palestine is the center of many holy places. The Arabs have guarded these shrines for over 1,200 years and have shown extreme liberalism and lack of fanaticism in allowing all nations and all creeds full and free access to these sacred places. They do not propose to turn over this duty and responsibility to the Zionists. Nor is this all, Palestine is the gateway between North Africa and Arabia. Yearly thousands of Moslem pilgrims cross Palestine to visit the holy cities of Mecca and Medina. Such gateway will never be yielded by the Arabs to the Zionists for obvious reasons.

The Arabs assert that they can never trust the Zionists. This assertion is borne out by the Zionist behavior over the past twenty-five years. The Zionists have propagandized in Europe and America against the Arabs. They have completely disregarded Arab rights and aspirations and have distorted the facts about Arab deeds and Arab help to the Allies during this and the last world war. Their demands for help against the Arabs, from Turkey, Britain and from the United States, their avowed intention of "making Palestine as Jewish as England is English"; all these and many other acts of aggression by the Zionists are matters that the Arabs can never condone. If trust and friendship does not exist between two peoples, it is indeed impossible for them to live as neighbors, let alone side by side in the same country. As Palestine is an Arab country, there is but one solution. The Zionists must get out.

History reveals that when a nation covets the land of another nation, the aggressor attempts to acquire that land by conquest. The Zionists apparently do not believe in the lessons of history. They think that they can acquire Palestine by a mixture of Zionist propaganda with non-Zionist blood. They propagandized their formulae in Britain during the First World War and got the Balfour Declaration. Britain realized its error only after it had lost British lives and British prestige. Thereupon it issued the White Paper giving up the whole Zionist scheme as too costly, too impracticable, too fantastic, and too futile. Now the Zionists have turned their vitriolic propaganda machine against their erstwhile benefactor—Britain—and are propagandizing their worthless formulae in the United States. The Arabs ask whether the Americans will be wise enough to profit by the experience of their British cousins over a period of twenty years and turn a deaf ear to all Zionist propaganda and Zionist sentimentalism.

The Arabs again review their own history and that of other nations who have suffered and are still suffering from imperialism. They conclude that no people benefit ultimately by giving up their country or even their civil rights to another nation. Take a country or its civil administration from a people and there is no price high enough that you can pay them in return. This simple lesson is deeply engraved in the mind of every Arab through many decades of suffering under Turkish, British and French imperialism and colonization. The Arabs know that colonization is inimical to their interests and no arguments can convince them to the contrary. Hence, the Arabs assert that Palestine cannot be taken by propaganda. It can be taken only after every one of 90 million Arabs and some 400 million Moslems has died in a holy war for its defense.

The British: The realistic British argue that their pledge to Zionism is contained in the Balfour Declaration and its subsequent interpretation. They assert that there is nothing in this declaration to commit Britain to support the establishment of a Zionist state in Palestine. Hence, Britain has amply fulfilled its obligation to Zionism. They quote figures showing that the Jewish population in Palestine increased by 477 per cent against an increase of only 55 per cent in the Arab population from 1922 to 1939.

The British point to the lamentable disturbances in Palestine as manifestations of intense Arab apprehension that the Zionists will ultimately dominate them. The British assert that Arab acceptance of Zionism is impossible and, hence, two alternatives are left to Britain.

1. To expand Zionist immigration into Palestine against the strongly expressed wish of the Arabs.

2. To permit further immigration only with Arab acquiescence.

The British see no moral obligation on them to adopt the first alternative. Indeed they are sure to point out that their moral obligation lies in the second alternative which they have adopted thereby closing the doors of Palestine to further Jewish immigration as of March 1944.

Britain has other arguments in its favor. In spite of all that Van Passen states in his *The Forgotten Ally* Britain has been the friend of the Jews. She has offered them a tract of land in British East Africa. She has championed their cause whenever they suffered persecution. She even went so far as to grant them Palestine as a refuge subject only to Arab consent. Her experience in Palestine, however, showed that it is extremely costly to meddle with Arab affairs. Britain could not afford to antagonize 90 million Arabs in the Middle East and another 90 million Moslems in India in order to please a few Zionists who have an idea, were allowed to try it under British auspices, and found for themselves that it is neither practical nor workable.

The Center of the Rectangle: Our politicians, aspirants or candidates for office, time-servers and clergymen are bombarded by the very active, highly organized and most efficient Zionist propaganda. To show how successful the Zionists have been, in swaying public opinion to their cause, consider the following resolution introduced in both Senate and House on January 27, 1944, and referred to committee:

> Resolved, that the United States shall use its good offices and take appropriate measures to the end that the doors of Palestine shall be opened for free entry of Jews into that country, and that there shall be full opportunity for colonization, so that the Jewish people may ultimately reconstitute Palestine as a free and democratic Jewish commonwealth.

This resolution was tabled after General Marshall, our Chief of Staff, testified that its effect would be to arouse the animosity of the Arab and Moslem world and thus hamper our war effort. . . . In spite of General Marshall's testimony, [the Zionists] caused to be introduced in both the Democratic and Republican Party's Platforms, planks committing the candidates of these parties, and hence our country, to help the Zionists in their acquisition of Palestine.

The implications of such activities, on the part of the Zionists, to mold the foreign policy of the United States, are very far reaching indeed. Let us pause to consider them.

1. The policy proposed by the Zionists is opposed to that of our British Ally as issued in the White Paper prohibiting further immigration into Palestine. It is consequently most embarrassing to the British and constitutes one more cause of strained relations between us and our Ally.

2. The Zionist policy is in contradiction to our oft-expressed ideals of self-determination of small nations. The average American with his sense of decency and justice, refuses to bully the people of Palestine into accepting Zionist immigration.

3. We have, over the past seventy-five years, established good-will and friendly relations with the Arabs of the Middle and Near East, through our missionary work, our educational institutions and our many humanitarian activities. The Zionist policy brands us as anti-Arab, destroys the good-will and good name we have so carefully built over years of untiring effort and makes us enemies of a block of 90 million Arabs and some 500 million Moslems throughout the world. Nor is our loss only moral. The land inhabited by the Arab Moslems alone, covers an area three times that of the United States and comprises enormous riches, natural resources and trade possibilities. The economic loss to the United States, implied by the adoption of the Zionist policy is enormous.

4. The policy which the Zionists would have us adopt is either not enforceable and, therefore, harmful only in so far as it endangers our moral and economic advantages in Arab lands, or it is enforceable and, therefore, implies the dispatch of American boys to fight the Arab world. As I have already pointed out, the cause of Zionism is anti-American and is contrary to American interests. Hence few, if any, Americans would lay down their lives for Zionism.

5. Turn the picture around and imagine a foreign power passing a resolution or adopting a plank demanding that the United States open up New Hampshire, New Mexico or Arizona to unrestricted immigration of the Jews to the end that one of these states shall become a Zionist state. It cannot be contended that there is less room here than there is in Palestine nor that the need of the Jews is less effectively served through such action. How would we, Americans, react to such a proposal? We would justly consider it as the height of insolence! Yet here are the Zionists forcing our Congress and our political parties to interfere with the internal affairs of a foreign people. Those in politics, who support such Zionist policy, should know that the American people realize that we have no right to interfere with the internal affairs of other people. The American people also have enough common sense and common decency to know that if we want other nations to respects our right to the control of our internal affairs, we must be willing and ready to reciprocate. . . .

These, then, are the arguments of . . . the parties concerned. Obviously Palestine and Zionism are no solution of the Jewish problem. Is there a solution? I think there is!

The first step in arriving at a solution is to abandon the idea of Zionism. It has been tried under British auspices and proved unworkable. It obviously does not solve the Jewish problem. It beclouds the issue and diverts energies from the real problem at hand—namely, the minority problem. It behooves the Jews, therefore, and especially the Zionists among them to face the facts, throw away sentimentality and be realistic.

The second step is to admit that the problem of the Jew is that of any minority. Its solution consists in educating the public to a better understanding not only of the Jewish problem but also of all minority problems. The Zionists are quite adept along these lines. Let them use their efforts and energies in profitable pursuits.

JEWISH NATIONAL HOME INADVISABLE [9]

For the following reasons the claims of the Zionists cannot be maintained:

1. The most important element in this whole controversy which is being lost sight of is that Palestine has been an integral part of Syria for 25 centuries. The fact that international chicanery and Zionist-British schemes separated it from its motherland does not make it a separate country. Syria is determined that the Balfour Declaration and Congressional resolutions based upon it shall not be the final chapter in the history of Palestine or binding on either Syria or Palestine.

2. At the time Lord Balfour made this declaration, November 2, 1917, Palestine was not a part of the British Empire, nor was it in possession of the Jews, whose population in Palestine was only 55,000 as against 800,000 Arabs, and England had no right to make any promises in respect thereto.

[9] From statement of Faris S. Malouf, President, Syrian and Lebanese American Federation of the Eastern States, Boston, Mass., before the House Committee on Foreign Affairs, February 16, 1944. United States. House. Committee on Foreign Affairs. Hearings on H.Res. 418 and H.Res. 419. p. 284-92. 1944.

3. At the time Balfour made his declaration, Britain had through Sir Henry McMahon already entered into a solemn agreement with King Hussein in behalf of the Arabs, October 25, 1915, that England would recognize and assist in the establishment of an independent Arab state, including Palestine. The Arabs were then in complete possession of Palestine and were about to declare their independence and revolt against the Turkish Empire. In consideration of this agreement on the part of England the Arabs revolted against Turkey and shed their blood for three years with the armies of the Allies against the combined forces of the central powers and Turkey.

4. Lord Balfour's declaration was made secretly to a private English gentleman, Lord Rothschild, and it was more than a year later that the Arabs learned of it. One cannot help asking what right had England to give somebody else's country to a people who were disunited, unorganized, and scattered among the nations of the world, without consulting the people who are immediately concerned and who have occupied that land as its natives from time immemorial and certainly owned it and inhabited it exclusively for the last thirteen centuries?

5. In view of the clear binding agreement between England and King Hussein, the Balfour Declaration, secretly issued and intentionally concealed from the Arabs, was dishonest, insincere, ambiguous and impossible of enforcement.

It was dishonest because the Arabs who were the primary party in interest were not consulted; it was insincere because it does not purport to give the Jews any definite or specific rights, for careful study and consideration of the wording of the declaration will show that the establishment of a Jewish homeland in Palestine is subordinated to and conditioned upon a statement which reveals conscious guilt on the part of England. That statement is found in the second half of the declaration as follows:

It being clearly understood that nothing shall be done which may prejudice the civil or religious rights of existing non-Jewish communities in Palestine.

One wonders what does the phrase "A home for the Jewish people in Palestine" mean.

Does it mean an independent Jewish state?

Does it mean the superimposition of a Jewish majority upon the Arab people in Palestine?

Does it mean unrestricted Jewish immigration into Palestine?

And if it does not mean any one of these three propositions, what else can it mean?

And if it means any one of these propositions, how could that be obtained without "prejudicing the civil or religious rights of existing non-Jewish communities in Palestine."

With the Balfour Declaration and the efforts of the Zionists to establish their Jewish national home in Palestine in disregard of the Arabs' wishes, a revolution was begun. Concerning this revolution the Royal Commission reported the following findings of facts:

It is, indeed, one of the most unhappy aspects of the present situation—this opening of a breach between the Jewry and the Arab world. We believe that in ordinary circumstances the Arabs would be ready enough to permit a measure of Jewish immigration under their own conditions and control, but the creation of a national home has been neither conditioned nor controlled by the Arabs of Palestine. It has been established directly against their will. . . . The reasons of this breach are:

First. The establishment of a national home involved at the outset a blank negation of the right implied in the principle of national self-government;

Second. It soon proved to be not merely an obstacle to the development of national self-government, but apparently the only serious obstacle;

Third. As the home has grown, the fear has grown with it, that if and when self-government is conceded, it may not be national in the Arab sense, but government by a Jewish majority.

I should make this distinction. I should say to the Zionists: Your resolution is based upon the Balfour Declaration and if the Balfour Declaration is weak and invalid in any respect . . . it is my duty to say that it ill behooves the United States to support that declaration.

There are countless reasons why this resolution ought not to pass. I shall deal with only a few of these reasons.

1. All three documents, the Balfour Declaration, the Lodge-Fish resolution and the present resolution, are full of inconsistencies. If these inconsistencies could be removed or someone could reconcile them perhaps it would go a long way toward solving the problem, for each one of them provides that nothing shall be done to prejudice the rights of the people in Palestine. Here the reference is to the people who were in Palistine prior to the Balfour Declaration. Then the language of these documents goes on to provide for a national home and now a Jewish commonwealth. How can anyone establish a political state composed of people who are recently gathered and more of them are to be gathered from the four corners of the globe and put them in Palestine and wait until such a time as they become the majority before self-government can be established? This certainly prejudices the rights of the Arabs in Palestine.

The next inconsistency is the establishment of a Jewish commonwealth which is a religious state. How can you establish a Jewish state after the Jews have become the majority in Palestine and still call it a democratic state as against the people who profess different religions? Our understanding of democracy is a complete separation of the state and the church.

2. It took Great Britain 22 years, from November 1917 to the spring of 1939, to discover its grave mistake at the cost of several uprisings in Palestine which culminated in the Arabs' war for independence from 1936 to 1939, resulting in the destruction of thousands of Arab homes and the shedding of much Arab, Jewish, and English blood, and also after endangering the relations of Great Britain with the Arab and Moslem world.

In 1939, England sought to rectify the wrong by issuing the White Paper, after long conferences with representatives of the Arabs and Jews and after recommendations of several royal commissions appointed by His Majesty's Government to study the situation. Therefore the White Paper is not an appeasement measure. Rather, it is a solemn pledge and a binding "open covenant openly arrived at" after exhaustive study and consultations by the British Government with both the Arabs and the Zionists. Now, after all of this, we find the Zionist influence at work in these United States to get Congress to adopt this resolution as if the lesson learned by Great Britain after a quarter of a century of struggle and bloodshed has been of no value to the Zionists in the United States who would advocate a Jewish commonwealth in Palestine at the expense of the Arabs. Great Britain is now seeking to rectify this wrong. Shall we go on to aggravate it? Do we want Great Britain to break a promise?

3. Passage of this resolution makes imperative the continuation of the British mandate over Palestine until such a time as the Jews shall become the majority there, and not even then, but until both the Jews and Arabs have been forced by the sword to live together in peace. Is there anything in your experience or in history to show that such a thing is possible if the Arabs are forced to remember forever that they were denied their independence and self-government for the sole purpose of imposing upon them a Jewish state in which they shall become the minority?

4. In order to make the mandate of this resolution effective, force must be used. If Great Britain rejects our good offices does the Congress want the United States Government to war upon our friends, the Arabs? Will the American people sanction the use of force upon the Arabs so that they may give way to the establishment of a Jewish commonwealth in Palestine? If this is not contemplated by this resolution, is it then our purpose simply to give the Jews lip service without any genuine conviction behind it? Or is it simply a nice expression of sympathy which might be all right to please the Zionists among us, but which will gain for us the suspicions and the lack of confidence on the part of the Arabs?

If you entertain the possibility of subduing and silencing the Arabs of Palestine by some magic and because they are not a strong nation, what about the 50,000,000 Arabs in the Near and Middle East? What about the 300,000,000 more Mohammedans in Asia and Africa? Great Britain has heard from them and has seen the injustice of their cause.

5. The passage of this resolution strikes at the foundation and the principles for which our men and women are dying on every battle field and on every continent today. Its passage will strike at the confidence the United States enjoys throughout the world. . . .

Is it humane to drive the Arabs out of their homes and country in order to give them to others who by all the legal and moral codes have lost any claim to them for more than 2,000 years?

Is it humane to reduce the Arabs to a minority in their land which the Royal Peel Commission described in its report to the British Government in July 1937 as follows: "Palestine or, more strictly speaking, Syria, of which Palestine had been a part since the days of Nebuchadnezzar (605-562 B. C.), was to the Arabs their country, their home, the land in which their people for centuries past had lived and left their graves."

6. The passage of this resolution will strike at the principles for which we are fighting this war as declared in the Atlantic Charter, because it tends to withhold self-government from the Arabs of Palestine until such a time as the Jews have become the majority when they and not the Arabs will be in control.

7. The passage of this resolution broadcasts to the willing ears of our enemies as well as to India, the Balkans, eastern Europe, and all of the countries whose future will need to be influenced either by their confidence in us and our way of life or to be influenced by some other theories and alignments if their confidence in us is undermined. So if this resolution is passed it will weaken their confidence and make us just another nation whose pronounced fundamental theories of what is politically true and right are not controlling in the fact of organized racial, religious, and sectional pressures.

9. It is very important for the molding of the United States policy toward the Near East to take into consideration the fact that Palestine is the southern part of Syria and has been a part of Syria for 25 centuries, that Syria and Lebanon inspired, I believe, by the United States and Great Britain have just attained their full independence and Syria has never relinquished her right to Palestine as its natural southern part, nor do the people of Palestine wish to be separated from Syria.

10. The passage of this resolution is an interference with the affairs of Great Britain. We have just witnessed the indignation of a great allied nation when one of our prominent citizens unofficially expressed an opinion concerning Poland. Let us not do too much interference.

11. The passage of this resolution will be the greatest disservice to innocent Jews everywhere. Those who have succeeded in getting into Palestine in the last twenty years and who number 500,000 may, if further immigration is stopped and the establishment of a political Jewish state, is given up, live in Palestine in peace and participate in its affairs on equal footing with the Arabs. If this resolution is passed and if our government and the government of Great Britain undertake to enforce its provisions, you will have endangered not only the interest but the very lives of the Jews in Palestine and consequently placed them in an unenviable position throughout the world.

Proposals for solution of the Jewish problem:

I wish to say with the most sincere conviction that history cannot justly attribute to any distinct element of mankind greater, continuous, or more lasting contributions to civilization, than those made and being made by the Jews. Those of us who are opposing this resolution do condemn and abhor their persecution as repulsive to human conscience and we do not attempt to ignore the existence of a Jewish problem or the urgency for its just solution. The solution, however, requires frankness and courage to face the truth.

If the Jews are really seeking a refuge and a homeland where they can live in peace and develop their distinct abilities, Palestine can never become that refuge and it can never solve their problem, certainly not through political Zionism. Palestine, however, will welcome the establishment within its gates of spiritual and cultural Zionism which will revive for the benefit of the entire world the idealism which marked the ancient Hebrews and Jews as a distinct people.

This can be accomplished by a restricted and moderate immigration into Palestine of the type of Jewish people who desire to revive for themselves and the world a spiritual and cultural Zionism in the same manner as that of the American missionaries and educational groups who have gone to work in the Near East and in other parts of the world.

It is not for me and it is doubtful whether it is for anybody else but the Jews themselves to determine their future course. I will, however, say that if the great and able leaders of thought among the Jews insist that they should have a political state, then it would seem to be the sacred duty and the happy privilege of the United States and Great Britain to offer out of their vast, and practically vacant territories, a suitable place for the establishment of a Jewish state, where they can enjoy self-government without losing the sentimental and religious values which they entertain for Palestine, and let Palestine be their missionary home.

A Jewish state can be an economic as well as social blessing to the British Empire or the United States if it could be established in some territory where the present population is so thin that racial adjustments could be made without inflicting injustice as it is in the case of Palestine.

I cannot conceive of any Jewish state with a greater population than anywhere from 1,000,000 to 5,000,000 for many generations to come, and certainly that number compared to the vast territories in question cannot constitute inconvenience to any part of the British Empire or the United States. Any statesman or organization of leaders who can reason this proposition to the acceptance of the Jews and the English speaking people will have rendered the greatest service to the world which history may record.

Insofar as the present Jewish population in Palestine is concerned, the Arabs intend, provided immigration is stopped and a proportionate representative government is created, to afford them protection with all the privileges of the land which are enjoyed by the Arabs themselves, and to guaranty their majority rights by constitutional provisions and proper international obligations. This the Arabs will consider their sacred obligation for a world trust.

Finally, as the Jewish problem calls for a just solution, it ill behooves the Jews who are rightly clamoring for their minority rights, and who are protesting against Hitler's methods, to disregard the rights of the great majority in Palestine, and to urge and advocate a policy which requires the use of force against the Arabs.

PALESTINE, AN ARAB VIEW [10]

Whatever may have been the original aims of Zionism, during the First World War its leaders made it a movement for the conquest of Palestine after the method of Joshua. If they had desired only to find a refuge and cultural center among the Arabs of Palestine, they would have sought an understanding with them. Instead, while Arabs were dying in battle for their own independence and the victory of the Allies, Zionist leaders were bargaining with British politicians. Out of that unholy partnership came the Balfour Declaration, according to which Palestine was to become a Jewish state under the mask of a national home and at the same time a second Ulster for use as a military base to defend the British empire. The fact that the League of Nations approved this declaration cannot legitimize Britain's act in giving away the property of other people nor the Zionists' act in accepting it.

Zionists, of course, lay claim to Palestine on two main grounds, neither of which has legal or moral standing. There is the claim based on the ancient historical connection between the Jews and Palestine—a connection which ended two thousand years ago. If this claim is valid, then the Greeks have a right to Asia Minor, the Arabs to Spain, the Germans to Holland and the Mexicans to Texas and California. . . . Again Zionists say, the Jews have a right to Palestine because it is their holy land. But it is also the Moslem holy land and the Christian holy land. The rights in it of all these groups are moral and spiritual, not political, for the land belongs to its citizens of all faiths.

Since their entry into Palestine the Zionist zealots have added other arguments. Thus they try to justify their enterprise by advertising widely that the Arabs have greatly benefited by it. Some landowners have certainly become prosperous by selling their land to Zionists at high prices. But what became of the thousands of farmers who had been living on these estates for generations? Some of them went to less fertile farms, but most of them drifted to Haifa and other cities to swell the already

[10] From article by Jabir Shibli, Professor of Mathematics, Pennsylvania State College. *Christian Century.* 60:359-61. March 24, 1943.

crowded market of day laborers. And while Zionist capital and enterprise have led to a rise in the wage of Arab labor, they have led also to an abnormal rise in the cost of living, so that the standard of living for the common man has not really improved. Besides, Zionism has aimed to organize in Palestine a closed community where only Jews will produce and only Jews will profit. The labor unions are all-Jewish unions; Jewish children must go to 100 per cent Jewish schools; Jews must employ only Jewish workers, patronize only Jewish hotels, Jewish taxis, Jewish stores: all land bought can never be sold back to the Arabs, nor may Arabs be employed on it (so the lease states). Even the great Hebrew University is only for those who speak Hebrew. Any benefit that reaches the Arabs is merely incidental to the Jewish development, and the Zionist policy insures that such benefit shall be slight.

Zionists emphasize their ability to redeem the land. They have built roads, improved agriculture and built irrigation systems on a small scale. The land so redeemed, however, is but a small fraction of their holdings, the major part being well developed farms from which they dislodged Arab farmers. The Jews own 350,000 acres, which is about one sixth of the land suitable for cultivation, and nearly all of it is situated in the most fertile areas. Moreover, while two thirds of the Arabs are engaged in agriculture, less than one fifth of the Jews live in agricultural settlements, the majority of which would collapse without constant aid from abroad. That the Jews have the wealth and the ability to develop Palestine is obvious. But their claim to Palestine on the ground that they can rebuild it is on the same level with Hitler's claim to Europe on the ground that he can give it a new order of prosperity.

Zionists take special pride in the industrialization of Palestine. In two decades Jewish capitalists have built half a dozen large industries and some four thousand minor ones. Most of these were created not because they were required for the normal development of the country, but in order to get as many Jews as possible into Palestine to attain a Jewish majority in the population. This mad rush to modernize Palestine has already disfigured its landscape and secularized its life in a manner offensive to the Arab inhabitants. Furthermore, all the economic situations controling the future—the fertile valleys and coastal plains, the electric power, the streams for irrigation, the potash development of the Dead sea—are in the hands of Zionists. The Lord Melchetts and Lord Readings of British Jewry and other Zionist capitalists and speculators have a large stake in the economic exploitation of Palestine. The Arabs were not asked to cooperate in the development of the natural resources of their own country.

Whatever real progress has been made is due to British skill in colonial administration. Imperialism is only the bad side of Britain. The marked improvement in Palestine in communications, agriculture, education, health and sanitation, in the conservation of antiquities and the upholding of justice in the courts shows what the British genius for government can do even under hampering circumstances. If, instead of being compelled to organize for defense against Zionist aggression, the Arabs had been free to cooperate with Britain, the results would be a thousand times what they are.

A final plea made in behalf of the Zionists is that Christendom, which has persecuted the Jews, owes them a home of their own in Palestine. But Christendom cannot undo its wrong against the Jews by committing a wrong against the Arabs. The persecution of the Jews is a disgrace to civilization. The problem of relieving their distress is a world problem and any country that refuses to make the sacrifices necessary to solve it is shirking a moral responsibility. But now that half a million Jews have found refuge in Palestine, that little country, which is smaller than Vermont, has clearly done more than its share.

For twenty-five years the world has ignored Arab protests. A British administration and a British military force have straitjacketed the Arabs while an army of 500,000 Zionists entered Palestine as conquerors. Misrepresented and misunderstood abroad, and pressed hard by a pitiless alliance of military and financial powers at home, the Arabs in despair resorted to violence. The latest riots were the beginning of a people's revolt which, because of Arab sympathy with the democracies, has been brought to a standstill for the duration. But it will be resumed after the war unless justice is done. For the Arabs would rather die fighting for their homes and native land than go elsewhere to live.

Now that Britain has recognized that the Balfour Declaration is self-contradictory and has decided against the establishment of a Jewish state in Palestine, Zionists have turned to America for support. Already their lobbyists have organized the American Palestine Committee, most of whose three hundred members are politicians. Zionist propaganda is so clever and widespread that there is real danger that America will look at Palestine through Zionist spectacles, especially since the Arab case is practically without a voice either in the press or on the radio. But justice is on the side of the Arabs, and they have faith in American integrity. Through their half million countrymen who have become American citizens, through the work of American missionaries and the great American University of Beirut, they have come to know and admire the American spirit of democracy and justice. Surely their faith will not be betrayed.

What then is the solution of the Palestine problem? The first step is a change of Jewish leadership. So long as the present leaders of Zionism remain in power, the gulf they have created between Jew and Arab cannot be bridged. Let them be replaced by men like Dr. Magnes, Professor Einstein, Rabbi Lazaron, Mr. Sulzberger and other exponents of cultural Zionism who respect the rights of the Arab. The next step would be a termination of the mandate and the establishment of an independent, democratic Palestinian state—not two states or cantons, one Jewish and one Arab, but a single state. For Palestine is indivisible. The Jews are interested in all of it, and so are the Moslems and the Christians.

As one united people with a common citizenship and equal rights, mingling together as good neighbors, Jews and Arabs will be fully able to constitute a government capable of determining the future of Palestine and dealing with all subjects, including immigration. Then, since the interests of Britain are consistent with those of the Arab countries, a freely negotiated treaty between Britain and an independent Palestine, similar to the treaties with Egypt and Iraq, would be of mutual helpfulness As to the holy places, a national interreligious committee, with representatives from other countries, would have the oversight of them. I submit that such a plan would provide a center in which Jewish faith and culture will find inspiration in the land of their birth and their ancient glory. It would be stable because based on justice and Arab consent; and it would have ever larger possibilities of development as Arab and Jewish interests meet and interpenetrate.

There is a new spirit abroad in the Arab world, quick with the promise of revival of Arab greatness. The Arabs of today have the same vitality and capacity as the Arabs who built a world empire and carried civilization to the whole world. They have the natural resources, the brains and the manpower. The unification of Arab countries is on the way; no imperialist or financiers can prevent it. Before the end of the present century there will be a United States of the Arabs with a hundred million people, extending from the Indian Ocean across Western Asia and the northern half of Africa to the Atlantic. The Arabs would welcome the aid of a friendly Jewish people as partners in building the new civilization.

The time has come to restore peace to the Holy Land. In a world torn by hate and force, let it become the symbol of peace for Jew, Moslem and Christian. "Let peace roll down as a river and justice as a mighty stream."

EXCERPTS

One of the things that struck me in Palestine was that Arab industry there does not constitute a threat, in the competitive sense, to Egyptian industry, but Zionist industry does so. For it is backed by the Jewish Agency which, in turn, is backed by the incessant flow of foreign contributions.—*Fuad Abaza Pasha, President, Egyptian Royal Agricultural Society, in al-Ithnayn (Cairo Arabic weekly). Quoted in Institute of Arab American Affairs. Bulletin. D. 15, '45. p. [3].*

Your Majesty will recall that on previous occasions I communicated to you the attitude of the American Government toward Palestine and made clear our desire that no decision be taken with respect to the basic situation in that country without full consultation with both Arabs and Jews.

Your Majesty will also doubtless recall that during our recent conversation I assured you that I would take no action, in my capacity as Chief of the executive branch of this Government, which might prove hostile to the Arab people.—*From letter of former President Franklin D. Roosevelt to King Ibn Saud of Arabia, April 5, 1945. Congressional Record. O. 29, '45. (daily) p. A4913.*

If it is true that President Truman sent a letter to Prime Minister Clement Attlee demanding the entry of 100,000 Jews into Palestine, then it is contrary to all oral and written promises and undertakings to the effect that the United States would not move in the matter before consulting the Arabs.

Arabs in general and Iraqis in particular do not believe Zionism is the means of solving the world-wide Jewish problem. The Palestine Arabs have the right to determine their fate without intervention by other nations.

Iraq protests strongly against any attempt to admit strangers to Palestine without the consent of the Arabs who are the legitimate owners of Palestine. The Iraq Government regards it as its duty to inform the United States Government that it deems any support given Zionism to be an act directed against Iraq in particular and against the Arab peoples in general.—*From text of note sent the United States by the Government of Iraq. Released in Baghdad October 3, 1945. New York Times. O. 4, '45. p. 4.*

The Arab world has been undergoing a tremendous change during the past few years. The presence of huge Allied expeditionary forces on its soil, the new contacts made between the people of the land and the Allied representatives, coupled with war necessity, spurred the movement for progress and industrial activity. As evidence we may cite the formation of two corporations which might have far-reaching effect on the economic life of the Arab countries. A recent Jerusalem report has it that an Arab Transport Company, with a capital of one million pounds

($4,000,000) is being formed. Promoters and stockholders are nationals of Egypt, Palestine, Transjordan, Syria and Lebanon. The company will link these countries by a network of bus, taxi and freight services. Another report from Bethlehem states that an Arab diamond cutting and polishing company had been formed in that city. About three hundred workmen who had been employed in the mother-of-pearl industry are to operate the new plant. The company plans to engage an expert diamond cutter to supervise the work.—*Institute of Arab American Affairs. Bulletin. S. 15, '45. p. [4].*

One of the major developments of World War II is the emergence of the Arab nations as an important factor in the world of tomorrow. More than ever before, the natural resources of the Arab countries and their strategic position make them either a cockpit of contending powers or a secure link between peaceful nations.

This is heightened by the discovery that almost unlimited quantities of petroleum are stored under the surface of Arab countries. The rapid progress of aviation and the nature of the Arab terrain, with its vast stretches of level lands and constant climatic conditions, have made of the Arab lands "an interminable air base," a bridge between continents—more so than in the days of the caravans or in the days of the train and steamship. In the meantime, the latent spiritual forces of the Arab countries have come to the surface in these days of intensive industrialization and closer community of nations. The Arab world is projected by world events into the focal point of interest more than ever before.

It is therefore natural for the United States, a leading industrial country and a pioneer in aviation, to take increasing interest in the Arab world. This interest, however, is free of the sordid greed and political machinations which have marred the relations of some other powers. Long before its interest in the resources and position of the Arab countries, the United States founded schools, publishing houses and hospitals in those countries. American institutions of learning there won the confidence of the Arab people long before there was even any conjecture of petroleum under the sandy dunes of Arabia or in the rugged country of ancient Assyria. These American institutions have been an important factor in the Arab renaissance and the awakening of the national spirit of the people.—*Institute of Arab American Affairs. Bulletin. Jl. 15, '45. p. [1].*

At the outset, I wish to emphasize that it is not only the 1,000,000 or less Arabs which are concerned in Palestine, but that 300,000,000 Moslems throughout the Near East and India are vitally interested in this matter.

Supposing the recommendation I have seen advertised in one of the great newspapers were adopted for the removal of Arabs from Palestine to Iraq? Who would finance such a removal and the development of new farms and homes? Would not the average American taxpayer resent any such thought and consequently become perhaps anti-Semitic? I am afraid there would be the following results:

First. Recent history indicates there would be a great deal of resistance and bloodshed in Palestine itself as it is well known that both Arabs and Jews have considerable amounts of arms;

Second. The Moslems in Yemen, Arabia, might annihilate the 40,000 Jews now there. I wonder if they might not be viewed as hostages and in a similar manner the 100,000 Jews now in Iraq and who have lived there peacefully for over 1,300 years.

Third. In Egypt there might be great riots and anti-non-Moslem reactions which could result in the greatly handicapping of the large non-Moslem interest in education, the American University, and so forth, and in businesses.

Fourth. In Turkey the non-Moslems might be treated in a manner similar to the Arabs from Palestine and be deported— in this case, Jews (70,000) and Christian Armenians would, perhaps, suffer most.

Fifth. In India the 90,000,000 Moslems who have upheld the British Government when the Hindu Indian Congress was making passive resistance, would very probably voice great opposition to a removal of Arab Moslems and might cause great disturbance and trouble which would interfere with our war against Japan in that sphere.

Sixth. There are many Moslems in Java, China, and the Philippines to whom this matter would undoubtedly be broadcast by the Japs and Germans so might cause a great antagonism toward the Allies as these people might fear similar removals after the war.

Seventh. Along the African routes of our air transport, most of the countries traversed are Moslem inhabited; could not there be many acts of sabotage by angry Moslems all along both the north African and central African routes?

Eighth. If the proposed pipe line for bringing American-controlled oil from the Persian Gulf eventuates, an unfriendly Arab people along this line would be a constant menace and might involve American troops.

Do you believe the American public would wish their sons to be sent to the many points in Moslem countries on police duty and possibly lose their lives in a matter entirely aside from our fight for the four freedoms? Might this not cause anti-Semitic feeling?. . . The British Government can tell you what it has cost in lives and money to keep their Palestine mandate. Does the American Government wish to assume such liabilities?

Now for the other side. The United States Department of Agriculture can confirm, or not, my statement that Palestine has now been developed to nearly its maximum productivity under present conditions. The Palestine Government Partition Report to the British Government, 1938, Command 5854, tends to confirm this statement. Only if the irrigation project to bring water from Syria to Palestine eventuates, can any very considerable additional acreage be cultivated. But in Palestine there are great areas, which are steep limestone mountains with very thin soil and able only to support grazing—and not very much of that during the hottest parts of the summer seasons. My first trip from Jerusalem to Jericho was in July 1929. The progress made to date in agriculture is a very great achievement and a credit to the energy of the present population and Jewish financing.

To add greatly to the present population would not seem to be sound economy and would not attain the aims of those of Jewish faith for the above reasons.—*K. S. Twitchell, Consulting Engineer, Saudi Arabia Mining Syndicate; former Chief of*

United States Agricultural Mission to Saudi Arabia, before U.S. House Committee on Foreign Affairs, February 16, 1944. Hearings on H.Res. 418 *and H.Res.* 419. '44. *p.* 280-1.

Long before the Second World War, German and Italian propaganda had made inroads in the Arab area. Bitterness and disappointment had made the Arab mind fruitful soil for such Axis efforts. Then, too, the successful fighter holds a very high place in Arab esteem. The growing military might of the Nazis and their successive diplomatic triumphs gave Germany tremendous prestige in the Near East, particularly when contrasted with the appeasement tactics of France and Great Britain. Above all the Arabs had no experience of cooperation with Germany by which to judge Nazi promises. There were a few nasty brushes between Arabs and Turkey's German allies during the last war but they were largely forgotten; the horrors of the last war were blamed on the Turks rather than on the Germans. At any rate the French and British were close at hand and the Nazis were far away.

In these matters the Arabs showed all the naïveté of a rural-pastoral people, inexperienced in the conduct of their own and of international affairs, unknowing about the world yet moved by certain deep emotions which drove them on, to wit, nationalism. It is hard to believe that they could have hoped to end French and British rule with the help of the Nazis and the Fascists and then expect their helpers to leave them serenely free. We need hardly remind ourselves however that there were others than Arabs who believed the promises of the Nazis. The Arabs were never quite so sure of the Italians whom they disliked and distrusted for of them they had some knowledge through contacts in North Africa, but even Fascist propaganda had considerable success, particularly in Palestine and Arabia proper.

The measures of the success of Axis propaganda amongst the Arabs was to be seen in those two dangerous events of the spring of 1941, the pro-Axis *coup d'etat* in Iraq and the Syrian campaign. The Germans came uncomfortably close to establishing themselves in Iraq and Syria. The damage which would have been done to the British and the United Nations cause is self-evident. The Iraq *coup* was nipped in the bud just in time. It might not have been had the pro-Nazi puppet not jumped the gun before the Nazis were ready. In Syria the fighting was bitter. The native population there would have been happy enough to see the Vichy French ousted, but they had no intention of helping de Gaullist French replace the Vichy French. What they wanted was to get rid of the French completely and they were not sure the British would help them do it. The result was that they took little part in the fighting, thus making it much harder to oust the Vichyites and their German associates.—*Richard Merrill Saunders, History Department, University of Toronto. From his pamphlet "Whither the Near East?" p. 24-6. (Behind the Headlines. Vol. 4, no. 4.) Canadian Institute of International Affairs. Toronto. 1944. The views expressed are those of the author and not of the publishing organization.*

The attempt to compel the Arabic-speaking peoples of Palestine (still two thirds of the population, even after 25 years of Jewish immigration) to open their country to unlimited Jewish immigration and allow their country to be made into a Jewish state is the rankest imperialism and the most undemocratic proposition one can imagine. The nations of the world are asked to use their united strength to override the protests of the majority population in Palestine. Because the majority of Jews (of whom only 650,000 of the total 12,000,000 are in Palestine) want Palestine opened for settlement by such of their co-religionists as wish to go there, we are told that "democracy" demands the Jews be given Palestine. This is to ignore the rights and protests of the majority population in Palestine. This sort of "democracy" makes nonsense of the name, and the whole outlook resembles that which was used to justify Hitler's Germany in adding helpless Czechoslovakia to the Germany's *Lebensraum*.

Palestine is too small a country to afford a solution of the numerical aspect of the world Jewish problem. The national home for the Jewish people already in existence there provides a well based religious, cultural, and diversified communal life for Jews where they have full opportunity to work out their special contribution to the life of Jews everywhere and to international life. But when it comes to thinking of Palestine as a potential place where even a majority of the 12,000,000 Jews left in the world might migrate and establish themselves, the very size and overcrowded character of the tiny land make it impossible. No matter what is done with Palestine, the "Jewish problem," which Zionists define as fundamentally their "homelessness," will remain exactly what it is: there will be Jews in great numbers in every country willing to have them. To attempt to justify the sacrifice of the rights and feelings of the Arabic-speaking peoples of Palestine on the grounds that it will solve this international Jewish problem "once and for all" is vain. . . .

For Christians to propose that the Arabic-speaking peoples of Palestine open their gates to Jews, when they themselves in the U.S.A. and the British Empire argue that they cannot accept more Jewish immigration is plain hypocricy and a travesty of Christian charity. If we with a country of 131,669,000 square miles and a population of only 44 to the square mile think we cannot receive more without threatening our economic life or our American ways of living, how do we think it will affect the life of a country of 10,000 square miles, half of which is almost waterless desert, with a population density of 156 to the square mile?—*Rev. Charles T. Bridgeman, for 20 years the American Church's representative in Jerusalem. Living Church. O. 21, '45. p. 15.*

My sympathies are all with the Jews. I have known them intimately in South Africa, . . . but my sympathy does not blind me to the requirements of justice. The cry for a national home for the Jews does not make much of an appeal to me. The sanction for it is sought in the Bible and the tenacity with which the Jews have hankered after Palestine. Why should they not, like other peoples of the earth, make that country their home where they are born and where they earn their livelihood?

Palestine belongs to the Arabs in the same sense that England belongs to the English or France to the French. It is wrong and inhuman to impose Jews on the Arabs. What is going on in

Palestine today cannot be justified by any moral code of conduct. The mandates have no sanction but that of the last war. Surely it would be a crime against humanity to reduce the proud Arabs so that Palestine can be restored to the Jews, partly or wholly as their national home.

The nobler course would be to insist on a just treatment of the Jews wherever they are born and bred. . . .

This cry for the national home affords a colorable justification for the German expulsion of the Jews. . . .

And now a word to the Jews in Palestine. I have no doubt that they are going about it the wrong way. The Palestine of the Biblical conception is not a geographical tract. It is in their hearts. But if they must look to the Palestine of geography as their national home, it is wrong to enter it under the shadow of the British gun.

A religious act cannot be performed with the aid of the bayonet or the bomb. They can settle in Palestine only by the goodness of the Arabs.

They should seek to convert the Arab heart. The same God rules the Arab heart who rules the Jewish heart. . . .

I am not defending the Arab excesses. I wish they had chosen the way of non-violence in resisting what they rightly regard as an unwarrantable encroachment upon their country. But according to the accepted canons of right and wrong, nothing can be said against the Arab resistance in the face of overwhelming odds.

Let the Jews who claim to be the chosen race prove their title by choosing the way of non-violence for vindicating their position on earth. Every country is their home, including Palestine, not by aggression but by loving service.—*Mohandas K. Gandhi, as quoted by a Staff Reporter in an article in the Christian Science Monitor, Mr. 3, '39.*

The thing that gives me most concern is the fact that our Jewish fellow citizens and their friends are participating in a movement to create a Jewish pressure group in our country for the purpose of bringing about changes in the policy of other nations. It is my view that the American people have nothing to do with the internal affairs of other nations. We have no rights in the matter of immigration in Palestine nor do we have rights with respect to the White Paper.

We have nothing to do whatever with the immigration policy in Palestine or in any other country except our own. We deny the right of other countries to bring pressure upon us with respect to immigration and it is our duty to refrain from doing so with respect to other nations what we would not have other nations do to us. It is a matter for the British to determine. So far as the present controversy is concerned, we are not parties to the White Paper nor are we parties to the Treaty of Versailles.

I have been greatly concerned by evidence of a rising tide of antipathy to the Jews in our country. I wish to avoid anything like an anti-Jewish movement here. I defended the Jews against the Ku Klux and I do not wish to see Ku Klux persecution or any other sort of persecution started here. But if the Jews put forward a group movement they may rest assured that there will be a counter movement and it will be quite fearful.

The Jews should not set the example nor provide the provocation for a counter Jewish movement in this country. If they should do this the situation for them would be much worse than they now imagine. We ought not to have racial or religious pressure groups of any sort in this country. The Jew is an American citizen. He has the right of petition. But in the absence of a wrong by this country to the Jews as a race or group, a Jewish movement ought not be formed, for the reason that such a movement will be the provocation for a counter movement, if for no other reason. . . .

The object in view with respect to the Wagner resolution and the movement to abrogate the White Paper is the same. Should the White Paper be abrogated . . . there will be a migration to Palestine, which would upset the balance there. I agree that the movement to abrogate the White Paper is not as definite as the Wagner resolution but they are a part of one whole. I might say that if there is a difference it is a difference between the camel's nose and the camel and at any rate each group contemplates a Jewish group for purposes of propaganda and agitation in this country concerning foreign policy and relating to the rights of other nations.—*From letter by Josiah W. Bailey, Senator from North Carolina, to Fred G. Rypins of the Greensboro Committee for the Abrogation of the White Paper, March 18, 1944. League of American-Arab Committee for Democracy. Flint, Mich.*

Apart from the general offensive against the White Paper in principle, a subsidiary agitation is being conducted on ostensibly *ad hoc* humanitarian grounds for the settlement in Palestine of Jewish survivors of Nazi brutality in Europe. This demand is being put forward as a humanitarian appeal for the solution of the immediate Jewish refugee problem and as such it may seem reasonable and win support even from some of those who are opposed to the basic aim of Zionism, viz., unlimited immigration and the conversion of Palestine into a Jewish national state. It may win support on the grounds that the admission of another 100,000 Jews or so to Palestine, as a measure of relief, would be only a slight modification in detail of the White Paper necessitated by the unforeseen complication of the war, and that as such it would not affect the fundamental policy of the White Paper or the ultimate position of the Arabs. The answer to this line of argument is that when the White Paper was issued in May 1939, the proportions of the Jewish refugee problem in Europe were far more formidable than they are today. The White Paper however laid down that only 75,000 more Jews should enter the country over a period of five years. The Nazi regime has now been destroyed, and the United Nations have it in their power to afford the Jews in Europe complete security and equality with everybody else. Indeed this solution of the Jewish problem is essentially implied in the triumph of democracy, and for the United Nations to seek any other would be a confession of bankruptcy and an admission of the defeat of the very principles for which they have fought this war. It cannot therefore be argued that a modification in the terms of the White Paper is necessary because the plight of the Jews in Europe has become more serious than it was in 1939. If, however, there are many Jews left in Germany and Austria who do not wish to go on living in the land where they had their terrible experience, the humanitarian duty of providing them with new homes devolves on the civilized world collectively. The Arabs . . . are at one with the rest of the civilized world in condemning those responsible for these horrors and in desiring to see their victims humanely succored. But it should be emphasized that although the problem is essentially a humanitarian one, its solution at the expense of Palestine would involve the gravest political issues. Every Jew that arrives in Palestine is one more brick in the structure of the proposed Zionist state, one more unit towards a Jewish majority against the Arabs, so that it is impossible for the Arabs to regard the matter only in its humanitarian aspect.— *"Statement of Present Arab Attitude Over the Palestine Question." Arab Office. London. Jl. 30, '45. p.3.*

The attitude of the Arab League towards the Palestine question is clearly expressed both in the Alexandria Protocol and the League Covenant which grew out of it. The following is the text of the paragraph dealing with the question in the Alexandria Protocol:

> The Committee considers that Palestine constitutes an important element in the structure of the Arab nations and that the rights of the Arabs in it could not be encroached upon without the peace and stability of the Arab world being affected. The Committee also considers that the promises made by Great Britain about the ending of immigration, the safeguarding of Arab lands and the leading of Palestine towards independence represent nothing but a recognition of fundamental Arab rights and that their execution will be a step to the end sought and towards ensuring peace and stability in the Arab world. The Arab nations pledge their full support to the cause of the Arabs of Palestine. They deplore the horror undergone by the Jews at the hands of certain dictatorship states in Europe but point out that their condemnation of the persecution suffered by the Jews does not connote approval of Zionism. It would be a great injustice to attempt to settle the Jewish problem by creating a new problem in Palestine from which both Arabs and Jews would suffer.

This was a declaration of principle and attitude. In the League Covenant signed in Cairo on the 24th March of this year this attitude took concrete shape in a special resolution concerning Palestine of which the following is the text:

> At the end of the last war Palestine, like the other Arab states detached from the Ottoman empire, was liberated from Ottoman domina-

tion. Having become autonomous, she was no longer dependent on any other state. The Treaty of Lausanne proclaimed that her fate would be settled by the interested parties. But if Palestine has not been able to order her own destiny, it is no less true that it was on the basis of the recognition of her independence that the Covenant of the League of Nations of 1919 settled her status. Her international existence and independence cannot therefore *de jure* be questioned any more than can the independence of any other Arab country. If, for reasons independent of her will, this existence has failed to materialize, this circumstance does not constitute an obstacle to the participation of Palestine in the work of the Council of the League. The signatory states of the present Pact consider that, under these conditions and until that country can exercise all the effective attributes of her independence, it behooves the Council of the League to designate an Arab representative from Palestine who will participate in the work of the Council.

Thus Palestine is now officially associated with the Arab League.—*"Statement of Present Arab Attitude Over the Palestine Question." Arab Office, London, Jl. 30, '45. p. 2-3.*

A newly awakened America, deeply conscious of its heightened responsibilities as a world leader, can no longer afford to be indifferent to the strategic and economic importance of the Arab lands, nor to the implications of the intellectual and political reawakening of its seventy million peoples.

These Arab territories, connecting as they do three continents and two oceans, and now looming as one of the world's largest producers of petroleum, are becoming more than ever, the focus of world attention.

The intellectual stimulus, provided nearly a century ago by contact with your own American educational establishments, was one of the chief factors contributing to the tremendous spiritual and cultural reawakening which fired the imagination of the Arab peoples, and spurred them on in their forward surge towards the attainment of their final goal of complete freedom.

The world must recognize the cold hard fact that all of the Arab peoples are indissolubly united in their determination to achieve their final and complete freedom from all foreign domination. In writing about the prospects for world peace, one of your most able Americans recently to occupy a post of importance in the Arab World, Mr. James M. Landis, former Minister of State in Cairo, has publicly urged American support to Arab aspirations, by frankly stating that, "It is the continued acceptance of the Middle East as the pawn of empires that is the real danger."

The major problem facing the Arab world today is that of Palestine. It is our conviction that Americans are being propagandized to take a stand on an issue, only one side of which has been presented to them.

Let no one mistake our attitude on the Zionist issue. For it is one which will shake the whole Arab-Moslem world to its foundations. All are united as one against political Zionism, Christians and Moslems alike.

The Arab countries are determined to resist with all the resources at their command, the Zionist scheme for establishing a political state in Palestine. They are equally determined to resist any move to force further Jewish immigration to Palestine. For they believe that the continuous flow of immigrants into Palestine and the demand for the establishment of a Jewish state there amount to one and the same thing.

Furthermore, Arab opinion is convinced that the real motive behind the present drive to open up the doors of Palestine, is a political rather than a humanitarian one; and that the real objective is the implementation of the Zionist scheme of achieving Jewish sovereignty by building up a Jewish majority.

The only reasonable solution that will safeguard the peace of that area, and perhaps that of the whole world, would be one which would give full recognition to the wishes of the majority of the people of the country, who desire the immediate establishment of a democratic Arab state, which will become a part of the growing family of independent Arab states, joined together in the Arab League.—*From "A Statement on Objectives of the Arab Office" delivered at a press conference October 4, 1945. mim. Arab Office. Washington, D.C. p.2-4.*

The Arab claim that only in Palestine was there importation of foreigners to run the country is a valid one. The idea of importing foreigners from the four corners of the earth to rule the land against the specific will of its inhabitants is indeed

unique. It was never the original intention of those who drafted
the Balfour Declaration or the League of Nations mandate. Dr.
Weizmann, the man who made the greatest single contribution
toward the Balfour Declaration, was until 1931 vehemently
against a Jewish majority in Palestine. He was apprehensive
that Zionism would turn political and military, thus exposing
to serious dangers the great ideals of the social, religious and
cultural regeneration of Judaism.

Zionism did turn political and military. In 1943 young
Jewish nationalists embarked on a reign of terror in order to
force the British to abrogate pledges embodied in the White
Paper of 1939. Sabotage and destructive activities continue to
the present day. Moreover, it is no longer a secret that the
Jewish community in Palestine, numbering a little over half a
million, has been able to organize a secret army estimated officially at 30,000 strong and equipped with arms. . . .

It is true that Zionism has introduced large-scale development and prosperity. But for whose benefit? What indirect
advantages the Arabs have had, they paid for dearly in blood,
in painful anxiety, in loss of liberty and, last but not least, the
economic enslavement to Jewish capital monopoly. Almost one
third of the total agricultural area has passed into the hands
of Zionists, where Arabs can no longer be employed either as
tenants or as ordinary agricultural laborers. Seventy per cent
of the total economic wealth is now in the hands of Jewish
capital monopolies.

Today the desire for more freedom, more social, cultural
and economic development, dominates the minds of the younger
generation of Arabs and drives governments in independent Arab
states, as well as in mandated territories, to work feverishly to
provide funds for large-scale reconstruction and development. In
Iraq, despite the shortages of the war, a scheme to provide
hygienic dwellings for workers in the vicinity of Baghdad has
been carried out. Legislation to protect the interest of the working classes has been promulgated Similar steps have been taken
by Egypt, Syria and the Lebanon. The estimates for 1945-1946
contain larger appropriations for these schemes. In Palestine
and in the Arab town of Jaffa alone, development schemes

which involve the expenditure of some eight million dollars have recently been approved. Zionists in Palestine have openly expressed themselves against these schemes. It is curious, but nevertheless true, that Zionism seems to dread nothing more than those same ideas which it claims to foster.—*Khulusy Khairy, The Arab Office, Washington, D.C. Asia and the Americas. D. '45. p. 607.*

How many want to go to Palestine? Who knows? In the past the majority of those who have gone to Palestine have done so under pressure and to escape from continuing persecution. The whole movement has been heavily subsidized. In the end, those who cannot find a home in Europe—probably much less than a million—must be helped to go to various countries on other continents where opportunities for a livelihood can be found. Some should certainly be permitted to go to Palestine. Some should come to America (whether the existing immigration quotas would need reconsideration is not yet evident). Some will wish to seek their destiny in South America and in other lands.

So it is an absurdly false plea that free or large immigration to Palestine is necessary to save the persecuted Jews in Europe. The fact is that Zionists are now actually issuing pleas, both in America and in Great Britain, for Jewish volunteers to emigrate to Palestine to help make up the desired quotas to be admitted there, because they cannot find enough Jews in Europe who are willing to go. . . .

The Jews must decide for themselves whether Judaism is a nation or a religion. They cannot eat their cake and have it too. If Judaism is a nation that must have a geographic location, then the Jews in America (and in other lands) must either choose to be resident aliens or forswear their Jewish nationalism and become citizens in the lands where they live. The insistence upon the establishment of a Jewish national state in Palestine compels them to make that choice. The alternative recognition of Judaism as a religion should mean that Palestine can be a nation in which Moslems, Christians and Jews can live together as Palestinians. If the Zionistic insistence that Palestine must be a Jewish national state with a majority of Jewish citizens could be dropped, then there would be real hope that a solution, satisfactory to all, could be found for the problems of government in that land.

The relation of Zionism to world peace is too often overlooked. The Arab countries of the Middle East fear they can expect little or nothing from Great Britain. France is not in good repute among them. The United States seems to them to be dominated by Zionists, so far as political developments in the Middle East are concerned. So the Arab world is naturally turning to Russia for support and help. Zionism thus becomes an issue that has an important bearing upon America's good relations with Russia. Are we presently to discover that America is backing the Jews and Russia the Arabs? Some officials in the Department of State in Washington seem to be aware of this aspect of Zionism, but the fear of arousing the antagonism of some political supporters of the administration has prevented them from making any public statements. They have ventured to do no more than to use some influence to prevent the adoption of the pro-Zionist resolutions that have been introduced in Congress.—*"Christians and Zionism," by A. L. Warnshuis, Secretary Emeritus of the International Missionary Council. Christian Century. N. 21, '45. p. 1285.*

The Jewish settlements in Palestine have been a remarkable achievement. Most attention has been drawn to the agricultural settlements. These have been widely advertised, possibly in view of the insistence in Article 6 of the mandate that close settlement by Jews on the land should be encouraged, possibly also, in part, because the romance and adventure inherent in these settlements are a stimulus to generous support of the movement. The emphasis placed on this branch of the work of the Zionist organization is, however, disproportionate. As is pointed out in the Report of the Royal Commission, "the proportion of workers on the land (earners) to the Jewish population . . . today is 6.4 per cent." The great mass of the Jewish immigrants are not workers on the land, but residents of the towns. The population of one town, Tel Aviv, far exceeds in number the total population of all the agricultural settlements. This is not to say that the Jewish settlements are unimportant. They are the very remarkable result of the combined application of outstanding technical skill, abounding energy and practically unlimited resources provided by the generosity of Jewish communities in many lands. But the great majority of the Jewish population of Palestine today consists of skilled and unskilled workers in industry and on public works, industrialists, tradesmen, persons living on their private resources and professional men of all types. The number in these last two classes is very large, and in some directions that of professional men is out of all proportion to the needs of the community. Evidence was tendered to the Royal Commission that in Tel Aviv there was one doctor to every 161 persons, in Palestine as a whole one doctor for every 560 persons, while in the United Kingdom there is one doctor for about 1,085 persons.

Industrial development is an essential to the prosperity of the Jewish section of the population, which has grown from 55,000 in 1918 to at least 500,000 at the present time. In 1942 the value of the output of industrial workers was £30,000,000. Apart from war supplies, iron and steel articles, textiles, leather goods, foodstuffs, chemicals and pharmaceutical preparations, drainage pipes and glass, essential oils and lorries were produced by Jewish industry in Palestine. This phenomenal development has been due to three main causes—the provision of cheap capital by what Professor Bentwich describes as "philanthropic-capitalist instruments," protection of industry by carefully regulated tariffs, and the important monopoly for the production of electric power and light granted by the government to Mr. Pinhas Rutenberg, a Russian Jewish engineer, and now exploited by the Palestine Electric Corporation. Some of the conditions of this monopolistic concession are remarkable, not least the postponement of payment of customs duty on imported material "until the profits of the company, after writing off amortization, depreciation and reserve, are first sufficient to enable the company to pay a dividend of at least 8 per cent per annum tax free."—*Sir James Hope Simpson, appointed by British Government, 1930, to report on immigration and land settlement in Palestine. Fortnightly (London). D. '44. p. 344-5.*

We ask you Americans:

Would you want to give the so-called homeless and stateless Jews a sovereign homeland within your borders?

Would you tolerate constant outside interference and dictation in your internal affairs?

Would you permit foreign governments to control your immigration policy?

Zionist claims and Arab refutations:

1. Zionists rest their claim to Palestine on historical grounds.

So do the Arabs. The fact is that the Arabs have been there for centuries and are there now. Jews left Palestine in A. D. 71.

2. Zionists claim Palestine on religious grounds.

So do 300,000,000 Moslems, to whom it is the second holiest land.

3. Zionists claim that the Arabs cannot be entrusted with the rights of minorities.

When Christendom was persecuting Jews, the Arabs tolerated them and gave them refuge. Christian Arabs are one with their Moslem brethren in opposing Zionism.

4. Zionists claim that the Arabs cannot be entrusted with the protection of the holy places.

A Moslem family, the Nusaibehs, of Jerusalem, have been entrusted by the Christians with the custody of the keys of the Holy Sepulcher for several generations.

5. Zionists claim that since Palestine constitutes less than 1 per cent of the Arab world, the Arabs should concede this "notch" to their Jewish cousins.

Most of the Arab world consists of deserts. The State of Vermont is less than 1 per cent of the area of the United States. Would the people of Vermont be willing to vacate it and move into other parts of the United States upon an order from a foreign power or group of powers?

6. Zionists claim that the Arabs benefit from their colonization of Palestine.

With reference to Jewish colonization of Arab land, Sir John Hope Simpson, in his report (Cmd. 3680), said: "It ceases to be land from which the Arab can gain any advantage whether now or at any other time in the future. . . . He is deprived forever from employment on that land. . . . Nor can anyone help him by purchasing the land and restoring it to common use. The land is in mortmain and inalienable."

7. Zionists claim they brought the benefits of western civilization to the Arabs of Palestine.

Syria, Lebanon, Egypt, Iraq, and Turkey have prospered and made remarkable progress without benefit of Zionist immigration. In the last 60 years the population of Egypt has tripled.

The Arabs have not benefited at all from Jewish education because the language of instruction in all Jewish schools is Hebrew.

As to medical facilities Arabs do not frequent Zionist hospitals. According to the last report of the Palestine Government to the League of Nations, out of 11,800 patients admitted to Zionist hospitals, four were Moslems, seven were Christians, and . . . [the rest] were Jews.

8. Zionist claim that with intensive industrialization a large Jewish population is possible in Palestine.

According to Mr. Paintor, of the Reader's Digest, Jewish enterprises in Palestine are only 40 per cent self-supporting. Thus far, Zionist intensive industrialization in Palestine has been possible only through charity and discriminatory tariff.—*Statement by Arab Office, Washington, D.C. New York Times. N. 7, '45. p. 16. Reprint, Congressional Record. D. 20, '45. p. A6139.*

The immigration of the Jews into Palestine has been conducted with outstanding ability. The Jewish Agency and the National Federation of Labor (*Histadrut*) have organized the recruitment, transport and settlement of those admitted on the Labor schedule, with amazing success. Criticism has been made in the past by the orthodox section of Jewry in Palestine that politics rather than religious devotion have been considered by the recruiting authorities, and it is, in fact, remarkable that, whereas in the older settlements which were founded before the time of the Balfour Declaration the synagogue was the center of the village life, in the later settlements that position is occupied by the village school. Politics are now far more obvious than religious enthusiasm, and, to quote Dr. Toynbee, Zionism is "in essence a secular, economico-political expression of Jewish national aspirations." The Zionist movement today is definitely an urge of political nationalism, and the Jewish settlement is no longer regarded as a settlement of Palestinian Jews in Palestine—if it were ever so regarded—but of national Jews in Eretz Israel. Therein lies the tragic impossibility of reconciliation between immigrant Jew and aboriginal Arab.

Judging by recorded statements of Zionist leaders it is fair to conclude that, at the outset, the policy of Zionism did not aim at political dominance in Palestine. At the tenth Zionist Congress, held at Basle in August 1911, the President made a statement, from which the following is extracted:

> Only those suffering from gross ignorance or actuated by malice, could accuse us of the desire of establishing an independent Jewish kingdom. . . . *The aim of Zionism is the erection for the Jewish people of a publicly recognized, legally secured home in Palestine.* Not a Jewish state, but a home in the ancient land of our forefathers where we can live a Jewish life without oppression and persecution. What we demand is that the Jewish immigrant to Palestine be given the opportunity of naturalizing as a citizen without limitation and that he can live unhindered in accordance with Jewish customs . . . that and nothing else is our aim.

Dr. Weizmann in an address to the Zionist organization in 1931, of which he was then President, said:

> The Arabs must be made to feel, by deed as well as word, that, whatever the future numerical relationships of the two nations in Palestine, we on our part contemplate no political domination. But they must also remember that we on our side will never submit to any political domination.

That principle was also adopted by the British Government, and was announced, before the mandate was actually granted by the Council of the League of Nations, in the Churchill Memorandum of June 3, 1922. It included the following sentences:

> Unauthorized statements have been made to the effect that the purpose in view is to create a wholly Jewish Palestine. Phrases have been used such as that Palestine is to become "as Jewish as England is English." His Majesty's Government regard any such expectation as impracticable and have no such aim in view. Nor have they at any time

contemplated . . . the disappearance or the subordination of the Arabic population, language or culture in Palestine. They would draw attention to the fact that the terms of the [Balfour] Declaration referred to do not contemplate that Palestine as a whole should be converted into a Jewish National Home, but that such a home should be founded in Palestine.

Had the Jewish authorities been content with the original object of settlement in Palestine—"a Jewish life without oppression and persecution" in accordance with Jewish customs, the national home would have presented no difficulty. The Jews could have entered and settled as so many did in the Palestine Jewish Colonization Association settlements—founded in many cases long before the Balfour Declaration—in friendly relationship with their Arab fellow-citizens, and themselves loyal citizens of Palestine. The unfortunate fact is that the Jewish immigration today is not composed of Jews who, on religious grounds, wish to return to the land of Zion, in order to lead a Jewish life, without oppression and persecution, in accordance with Jewish customs. Rather is it composed of Jews, largely devoid of religious conviction, animated by a spirit of political nationalism, and determined to secure domination in Palestine, the homeland of the Arab for at least 1,300 years. No effort has been made to coalesce with the existing population. On the contrary, there is extreme divergence between the virile occidentalism of the immigrant and the conservative orientalism of the mass of the resident population. After its description of the organization of Jewish policy in Palestine the Royal Commission writes: "it would be difficult to find in history a precedent for the establishment of so distinct an *imperium in imperio*." . . .

Though Palestine may properly be regarded as the spiritual home of every devout Jew, there is no proper ground to conclude that it is the haven of refuge for Jews unjustly persecuted. The solution to persecution in Europe is to prevent it. If that be impossible, the havens of refuge should be in those countries, such as Great Britain, the United States of America, and the U.S.S.R., among others, who sympathize with the sufferers and have a sense of the dignity of man as man. It is unfair and indeed hypocritical to express sympathy, while refusing to accept the sufferers into one's own country and compelling their acceptance in Palestine, where they are not welcomed. Were the doors of Great Britain, the United States, the U.S.S.R. and France thrown open, the problem of persecuted Jewry would be immediately solved.—*Sir John Hope Simpson, appointed by British Government, 1930, to report on immigration and land settlement in Palestine. Fortnightly (London). D. '44. p. 346-9.*

BIBLIOGRAPHY

An asterisk (*) preceding a reference indicates that the article or a part of it has been reprinted in this book.

BIBLIOGRAPHIES

British Information Services. Selected list of British official publications on the Palestine mandate. 9p. mim. The Services. 30 Rockefeller Plaza. New York 20. Mr. '44.

Cohen, Iva G. comp. American Jewish bibliography, July 1943-June 1944. 15p. American Jewish Committee. 386 4th Ave. New York 16. '44.
Reprinted from American Jewish Year Book Vol. 46.

Woolbert, Robert G. Foreign affairs bibliography; a selected and annotated list of books on international relations, 1932-1942. Palestine, p. 550-4. (Published for Council on Foreign Relations). Harper & Bros. New York. '45.

Zionist Archives and Library. Articles on Zionism and Palestine in current periodicals. Vol. 3, no. 5. 13p. mim. The Library. 41 E. 42d St. New York 17. Ag.-S. '45.
Issued bimonthly.

Zionist Archives and Library. Recent material on Zionism and Palestine. Vol. 3, no. 5. 4p. mim. The Library. 41 E. 42d St. New York 17. S-O. '45.
Issued bimonthly.

GENERAL REFERENCES

Addleson, Abraham. Epic of a people; the story of the Jews. 359p. Bloch Publishing Co. New York. '43.

American Jewish Conference. Jewish position at the United Nations Conference on International Organization; report to the delegates of the American Jewish Conference. 127p. The Conference. 521 5th Ave. New York 17. Je. 25, '45.

American Jewish Conference. Jews in liberated Europe. 54p. mim. The Conference. 521 5th Ave. New York 17. '45.

American Jewish Conference. Proceedings of the second session, December 3-5, 1944, Pittsburgh, Pa. Alexander S. Kohanski, ed. 390p. The Conference. 521 5th Ave. New York 17. '45.
See index.

American Jewish Conference. Report of the Interim Committee and the Commission on Rescue, Commission on Palestine, Commission on Post-War, November 1, 1944. 128p. The Conference. 521 5th Ave. New York 17. '44.

Andrews, Fanny Fern. Holy land under mandate. 2 vols. Houghton, Mifflin & Co. Boston. '31.

Apenszlak, Jacob, ed. Black book of Polish Jewry. 343p. Roy Publishers. New York. '43.

Baker, Robert L. Oil, blood and sand. 300p. D. Appleton-Century Co. New York. '42.

Baron, Salo W. Social and religious history of the Jews. 3 vols. Columbia University Press. New York. '37.

Ben-Horin, Eliahu. Middle East, crossroads of history. 248p. W. W. Norton & Co. New York. '43.

Ben-Jacob, Jeremiah. Jewish struggle. 232p. George Allen & Unwin. London. '42.

Bentwich, Norman De M. Fulfilment in the promised land, 1917-1937. 246p. Soncino Press. Hindhead, Surrey, England. '38.

Bentwich, Norman De M. Jewish youth comes home; the story of the Youth Aliyah, 1933-1943. 159p. Victor Gollancz. London. '44.

Bentwich, Norman De M. Judaea lives again. 191p. Victor Gollancz. London. '44.

Bentwich, Norman De M. Palestine. 302p. Ernest Benn. London. '34.
Bibliography, p. 294-6.

Berger, Elmer. Jewish dilemma. 257p. Devin-Adair Co. New York. '45.

Brand, Howard B. Who shall possess Palestine? a search of the record reveals the rightful heir. 15p. Destiny Publishers. Haverhill, Mass. '44.
Reprint from Destiny, February 1944.

British Information Services. Britain's mandate for Palestine. (ID 497) 12p. The Services. 30 Rockefeller Plaza. New York 20. Mr. '44.

British Information Services. 50 facts about the Middle East. 31p. The Services. 30 Rockefeller Plaza. New York 20. Je. '44.

*British Information Services. Palestine inquiry; statement by Ernest Bevin, Secretary of State for Foreign Affairs, in House of Commons, November 13, 1945. 5p. mim. The Services. 30 Rockefeller Plaza. New York 20. '45.

British Library of Information. Extracts from the White Paper on Palestine issued May 17th, 1939. 15p. mim. The Library. 50 Rockefeller Plaza. New York 20. '39.

Brodetsky, S. Jewish problem. 15p. Jewish Agency for Palestine. 77 Great Russell St. London W.C. 1. N. '44.

Broido, Ephraim. Jews, Arabs and the Middle East. 22p. American Zionist Emergency Council. 342 Madison Ave. New York 17. n.d.

Chambers, Frank P.; Grant, Christina P.; and Bayley, Charles C. This age of conflict; a contemporary world history, 1914-1943. 856p. Harcourt, Brace & Co. New York. '43.
See index.

Churchill, Winston. What Mr. Churchill said in 1939 about the White Paper. 12p. British Association for the Jewish National Home in Palestine. 18 Manchester Sq. London W. 1.

Cohen, Israel. Britain's nameless ally. 48p. W. H. Allen & Co. London. '42. Distributed by Universal Distributors Co. 38 Union Square. New York 3.

Cranborne, Viscount. Extracts from speech in House of Lords, March 23, 1943. In British speeches of the day. No. 3. p. 28-32. British Information Services. 30 Rockefeller Plaza. New York. My. '43.

De Haas, Jacob. History of Palestine; the last thousand years. 523p. Macmillan Co. New York. '34.

Dugdale, Blanche E. C. Balfour declaration; origins and background. 32p. Jewish Agency for Palestine. 77 Great Russell St. London W.C. 1. Mr. '40.

Duker, Samuel, ed. New social forms and cooperative Palestine. 96p. League for . . . Palestine. 1140 Broadway, New York 1. '44.

Edidin, Ben M. . . . Palestine. 264p. Behrman's Jewish Book House. New . . . '39.
Bibliography, p. . . . 60.

Elbogen, Ismar. Jewish national home in Palestine. In his Century of Jewish life. p. 589-635. Jewish Publication Society. Philadelphia. '44.

Erdaily, Joseph. Jewish world problem solved. 41p. The Author. Twain Harte, Calif. '45.

Erskine, Beatrice C. Palestine of the Arabs. 256p. George C. Harrap & Co. London. '35.

Feiwel, T. R. No ease in Zion. 365p. Alfred A. Knopf. New York. '39.

Fink, Reuben, comp. America and Palestine; the attitude of official America and of the American people toward the rebuilding of Palestine as a free democratic Jewish commonwealth. 2d rev. ed. 538p. American Zionist Emergency Council. 342 Madison Ave. New York 17. '45.

*Foreign Missions Conference of North America. Palestine question, a Christian position. 8p. mim. The Conference. 156 5th Ave. New York 10. O. '45.
    Summary. Information Service (Federal Council of the Churches of Christ in America). 34:[1-3]. O. 27, '45. Official church body speaks on Palestine.

Friedrich, Carl J. American policy toward Palestine. 106p. American Council on Public Affairs. 2153 Florida Ave. Washington 8, D.C. '44.

Gathorne-Hardy, Geoffrey M. Short history of international affairs, 1920-1938. 487p. [Issued under the auspices of the Royal Institute of International Affairs]. Oxford University Press. London. '38.
See index.

Gittelsohn, Roland B. Modern Jewish problems; a textbook for high school classes and Jewish youth groups. 267p. Union of American Hebrew Congregations. Cincinnati. '43.

Golding, Louis, Jewish problem. 213p. Penguin Books. London. '39.

Gollancz, Victor. Nowhere to lay their heads; the Jewish tragedy in Europe and its solution. Victor Gollancz. London.
Reprint. 37p. American Palestine Commission. 41 E. 42d St. New York 17. '45.

Goodman, Paul. History of the Jews. rev ed. 169p. World Publishing Co. Cleveland. '43.

Goodman, Paul, ed. Jewish national home; the second November, 1917-1942. 296p. J. M. Dent. London. '43.

Gottschalk, Max and Duker, Abraham G. Jews in the post-war world. 224p. Dryden Press. New York. '45.
Based on a study by the Research Institute on Peace and Post-War Problems of the American Jewish Committee.

Granovsky, Abraham. Land policy in Palestine. 208p. Bloch Publishing Co. New York. '40.

Great Britain. Colonial Office. Palestine; correspondence with the Palestine Arab delegation and the Zionist Organi ı, (Cmd.1700) 31p. H.M. Stationery Office. London. Je

Great Britain. Colonial Office. Palestine: rep   mmigration, land settlement and development. J. H. Simpson.   5p. (Cmd.3686) H.M. Stationery Office. London. '30.

Gunther, John. Land of Israel. *In his* Inside Asia. rev. ed. p. 573-89. Harper & Bros. New York. '42.

Hanna, Paul L. British policy in Palestine. 214p. American Council on Public Affairs. 2153 Florida Ave. Washington 8, D.C. '42.
Bibliography, p. 196-205.

Harrison, Earl G. Report to President Truman; the plight of the displaced Jews. 16p. United Jewish Appeal for Refugees, Overseas Needs and Palestine. 342 Madison Ave. New York 17. S. 29, '45.

Heline, Theodore. Palestine, the restoration of the Holy land. rev. & enl. ed. 35p. New Age Press. Los Angeles. '42.

Hocking, William E. Mandates: the burden of Palestine. *In his* Spirit of world politics. p. 333-92. Macmillan Co. New York. '32.

Hyamson, Albert M. ed. British consulate in Jerusalem in relation to the Jews of Palestine, 1838-1914. 2 vols. Edward Goldston. London. '39-'41.

Hyamson, Albert M. Palestine old and new. 287p. Robert M. McBride & Co. New York. '38.
English edition: Palestine: a policy. Methuen and Company. London. '42.

Ireland, Philip W. ed. Near East; problems and prospects. 265p. University of Chicago Press. Chicago. '42.

Janowsky, Oscar I. Nationalities and national minorities (with special reference to East-Central Europe). 232p. Macmillan Co. New York. '45.

Jewish Agency for Palestine. Documents and correspondence relating to Palestine, August 1939 to March 1940. 28p. The Agency. 77 Great Russell St. London W.C. 1. Mr. '40.

Jewish Agency for Palestine. Documents relating to the Balfour Declaration and the Palestine Mandate. 53p. The Agency. 77 Great Russell St. London W.C. 1. My. '39.

Jewish Agency for Palestine. Documents relating to the McMahon letters. 20p. The Agency. 77 Great Russell St. London W.C. 1. Mr. '39.

Jewish Encyclopedia. 12 vols. Funk & Wagnalls Co. New York. '25. Palestine. Vol. 9, p. 479-504; Zionism. Vol. 12, p. 666-86.

Jewish National Fund and the Palestine Foundation Fund. Jewish Jerusalem past and present. The Fund. Jerusalem. '39.

Joint Palestine Survey Commission. Reports of the experts submitted to the Joint Palestine Survey Commission. 741p. Daniels Printing Co. Boston. '28.

Kisch, Frederick H. Palestine diary. 465p. Victor Gollancz. London. '38.

Kurland, Samuel. Biluim, pioneers of Zionist colonization. 78p. Hechalutz Organization of America. 1140 Broadway, New York. '43.

Laski, Neville J. Jewish rights and Jewish wrongs. 156p. Soncino Press. Hindhead, Surrey, England. '39.

Lazaron, Morris S. Palestine and Jewish nationalism. *In his* Common ground. p. 61-131. Liveright Publishing Corporation. New York. '38.

Lowdermilk, Walter C. Palestine, land of promise. 236p. Harper & Bros. New York. '44.

McDonald, James G. Where can the refugees go? 12p. Jewish Agency for Palestine. 77 Great Russell St. London W. C. 1. '44?

McDonough, Randolph P. and Kinney, Dorothy W. Challenges to the UNO; Palestine, an international trusteeship. (Journeys behind the news. '45, no. 15) 8p. mim. Social Science Foundation. University of Denver. Denver. D. 15, '45.

Main, Ernest. Palestine at the crossroads. 309p. George Allen & Unwin. London. '37. W. W. Norton Co. New York. Distributors.

Mendelsohn, Morris J. and others. American-British convention on Palestine. 36p. New Zionist Organization of America. 55 W. 42d St. New York 18. '44.

Morgenstern, Julian. Nation, people, religion, what are we? address, October 16, 1943. 30p. The Author. Hebrew Union College. Cincinnati, O. '43.

Naiditch, Isaac. Edmond de Rothschild. 114p. Zionist Organization of America. 1720 16th St. Washington 9, D.C. '45.

Namier, Lewis B. Numbers and exodus. *In his* Conflicts; studies in contemporary history. p. 137-62. Macmillan & Co. London. '42.

Nehru, Jawaharlal. Palestine and Trans-Jordan. *In his* Glimpses of world history. p. 762-7. John Day Co. New York. '42.

Neumann, Emanuel. Alignments in the Near East. 15p. American Palestine Committee. 41 E. 42d St. New York 17. '42.

Nunberg, Ralph. Fighting Jew. 295p. Creative Age Press. New York. '45.

Palestine Economic Corporation. Report for the calendar years 1940, 1941, and 1942. 74p. The Corporation. 570 Lexington Ave. New York. N. 3, '43.

Parkes, James. Palestine yesterday and to-morrow. 19p. British Association for the Jewish National Home in Palestine. 18 Manchester Sq. London W. 1. My. '45.

Pinsker, Leo. Auto-emancipation. 28p. Zionist Organization of America. 1720 16th St. Washington 9, D.C. '44.

Popper, David H. Puzzle of Palestine. (Headline Books no. 14) 111p. Foreign Policy Association. 22 E. 38th St. New York 16. '38.
Bibliography, p. 111.

Questions and answers on Palestine. 12p. American Christian Palestine Committee. 41 E. 42d St. New York 17. '45.

Revusky, Abraham. Jews in Palestine. 3d ed. rev. 383p. Vanguard Press. New York. '45.
Bibliography, p. 349-51.

Rosenblatt, Bernard A. Palestine's national capital. 5p. Palestine Foundation Fund (Keren Hayesod). 41 E. 42d St. New York 17. n.d.

Roth, Cecil. Short history of the Jewish people. rev. ed. 448p. East & West, Ltd. London. '43.

Royal Institute of International Affairs. Information Department. Great Britain and Palestine, 1915-1936. (Papers, no. 20) 109p. The Institute. London; Oxford University Press. New York. '37.

Ruppin, Arthur. Jewish fate and future. tr. by E. W. Dickes. 386p. Macmillan & Co. London. '40.

Samuel, Edwin. Handbook of the Jewish communal villages in Palestine. 92p. Zionist Organization Youth Department. Jerusalem. '45.
Bibliography, p. 81-5.

Samuel, Herbert L. S. 1st viscount. Memoirs. 304p. Cresset Press. London. '45.

Samuel, Maurice. Harvest in the desert. 316p. Alfred A. Knopf. New York. '44.
Review. Saturday Review of Literature. 27:20-2. Ag. 19, '44. W. H. Hindle.

Samuel, Maurice. On the rim of the wilderness; the conflict in Palestine. 247p. Horace Liveright. New York. '31.

Sereni, Enzo and Ashery, R. E. eds. Jews and Arabs in Palestine. 416p. Hechalutz Organization. New York. '36.

Sidebotham, Herbert. British policy and the Zionist mandate: our proud privilege; a memorandum. 36p. Ernest Benn. London. '29.

Sidebotham, Herbert. Great Britain and Palestine. 310p. Macmillan and Co. London. '37.

Silver, Abba H. Zionism: what it is—what it is not. 32p. Zionist Archives and Library. 41 E. 42d St. New York 17. n.d.

Simson, H. J. British rule and rebellion. 331p. William Blackwood and Sons. London. '37.

Stein, Leonard J. Memorandum; the Palestine White Paper of October, 1930. 89p. Jewish Agency for Palestine. 77 Great Russell St. London W.C. 1. N. '30.

Stein, Leonard J. Promises and afterthoughts; notes on certain White Papers relating to the Palestine conferences. 34p. Jewish Agency for Palestine. 77 Great Russell St. London W.C. 1. My. '39.

Steinberg, Milton. Partisan guide to the Jewish problem. 308p. Bobbs-Merrill Co. Indianapolis. '45.
Bibliography, p. 297-9.

Szold, Robert. War time Palestine. 12p. Zionist Organization of America. 1720 16th St. Washington 9, D.C. D. '43.
Reprint from New Palestine. February 4, 18, 1944.

*Taylor, William R. Near East: yesterday and today. In Anderson, Violet, ed. United Nations today and tomorrow; addresses at Canadian Institute on Public Affairs, August 21-28, 1943. p. 83-100. Ryerson Press. Toronto. '43.

Tulin, Abraham. Analysis of British policy in Palestine. 30p. (Toward a Jewish Commonwealth. Unit no. 1) 30p. Hadassah. Political and Education Committees. 1819 Broadway. New York 23. '43.

Udin, Sophie A. ed. Palestine year book, 5706; review of events July 1944 to July 1945. 531p. Zionist Organization of America. 1720 16th St. Washington 9, D.C. '45.

United States. Department of State. Near Eastern Affairs. Mandate for Palestine. (Near Eastern ser. no. 1) 115p. Washington, D.C. '31.

United States. House. Committee on Foreign Affairs. Establishment of a national home in Palestine; hearings, April 18-21, 1922 on H.Con.Res. 52. 170p. 67th Cong. 2d Sess. Supt. of Doc. Washington, D.C. '22.

*United States. House. Committee on Foreign Affairs. Jewish national home in Palestine; hearings on H.Res. 418 and H.Res. 419, February 8, 9, 15 and 16, 1944. 512p. Supt. of Doc. Washington, D.C. '44.
Includes appendix of documents relating to the Jewish national home in Palestine; Remarks of British statesmen in opposition to the White Paper, and Memorandum of the Jewish Agency for Palestine on the legal aspects of the British White Paper.

Universal Jewish Encyclopedia. Isaac Landman and Louis Rittenberg, eds. 10 vols. Universal Jewish Encyclopedia, Inc. 50 Court St. Brooklyn, N.Y. '39-'43.

Visson, Andre. Coming struggle for peace. 301p. Viking Press. New York. '44.
Arab aspirations and world politics, p. 190-201; Palestine, p. 228-41.

Viteles, Harry. Post war problems of Palestine. 20p. American Zionist Emergency Council. 342 Madison Ave. New York 17. '45.

Warhaftig, Zorah. Relief and rehabilitation; implications of the UNRRA program for Jewish needs. (From War to Peace. no. 1) 223p. Institute of Jewish Affairs. 330 W. 42d St. New York. '44.
Bibliography, p. 171-213.

Welles, Sumner. Time for decision. p. 257-71. Harper & Bros. New York. '44.

Wurm, Shalom. Palestine and the Arab world. 14p. mim. Habonim Labor Zionist Youth. 45 E. 17th St. New York 3. '44.

Zeligs, Dorothy. Story of modern Palestine. 227p. Bloch Publishing Co. New York. '40.

Ziff, William B. Rape of Palestine. 612p. Longmans, Green and Co. New York. '38.
Bibliography, p. 580-93.

Zionist Organization of America. Annual report for the 46th annual convention, September 11-13, 1943. 62p. The Organization. 1720 16th St. Washington 9, D.C. '43.

Zionist Organization of America. Report to the 48th annual convention, November 16-20, 1945. 114p. The Organization. 1720 16th St. Washington 9, D.C. '45.
Also separate. Goldstein, Israel. Zionist program and implementation; presidential report. 23p. The Organization.

PERIODICALS

American Economic Review. 34:538-60. S. '44. Palestine: a problem in economic evaluation. A. E. Kahn.

American Forum of the Air. 7, no. 30:1-14. Jl. 24, '45. How can we solve the troubles of the Near East? Willmott Lewis and others.

American Magazine. 140:34-5+. N. '45. New lands for Europe's uprooted millions. G. T. Renner.

American Mercury. 58:326-32. Mr. '44. Palestine and British policy. Eliahu Ben-Horin.

American Mercury. 61:685-92. D. '45. Fact and legend about Palestine. Gerold Frank.

Annals of the American Academy. 237:94-106. Ja. '45. Peoples of the Mohammedan world. Ernest Jurat and L. K. Kiser.

Annals of the American Academy. 240:75-6. Jl. '45. British foreign policy in Europe: the Palestine tangle. Michael Wright.

Arab World. 1, no. 1:5-9. Summer '44. Arabian oil. Orlo Truesdale.

*Arab World. 1, no.3:19-22+. '45. Soviet Russia, the Jews, and Palestine. J. G. Hazam.

Asia. 38:39-42. Ja. '38. Realities in Palestine. Pierre Van Paassen.

Asia. 41:223-7. My. '41. Withering of a mandate. Albert Viton.
Reply, with rejoinder. Asia. 41:327. Jl. '41. N. A. Faris.

Asia. 42:271-4. My. '42. Solution for Palestine. John Van Ess.

Asia and the Americas. 42:692-4. D. '42. Japheth in the tents of Shem; Jewish and Christian minorities of postwar Palestine and Syria must be protected. W. F. Albright.
Reply, with rejoinder. Asia and the Americas. 43:261. My. '43. Neville Barbour.

Asia and the Americas. 43:235-9. Ap. '43. Dynamic Palestine policy. Albert Viton.

Asiatic Review. n.s. 33:858-68. O. '37. Before and after the Palestine report. Archer Cust.

Catholic World. 155:268-75. Je. '42. Moslem holy land. J. E. Uhler.

Catholic World. 159:166-8. My. '44. Palestine puzzle. N. O. Rush.

Christian Century. 62:1309-11. N. 28, '45. Sorry story of Palestine.

Christian Century. 62:1405. D. 19, '45. President Truman's position on Zionism defined.

Christian Science Monitor Weekly Magazine Section. p. 4. S. 16, '44. Whither Palestine? W. H. Stringer.

Collier's. 116:24+. Ag. 11, '45. Terror in Palestine; Stern gang and the UMO. Frank Gervasi.

Collier's. 117:23+. Ja. 12, '46. No peace in Palestine. Frank Gervasi.

*Commentary. 1, no. 2:9-16. D. '45. Must the Jews quit Europe? an appraisal of the propaganda for exodus. Zachariah Shuster.

Commercial and Financial Chronicle. 152:3079-82. My. 17, '41. Palestine.

Commercial and Financial Chronicle. 162:2500. N. 22, '45. Joint Palestine study planned by U.S. & Britain.

Congressional Record. 91:(daily) A4680. O. 16, '45. Jew—Gentile—Arab; editorial from the Christian Science Monitor.

Congressional Record. 91:(daily) A4856-7. O. 25, '45. Signs of trouble are seen abroad. K. E. Mundt.

Congressional Record. 91:(daily) A5601. N. 30, '45. One more difficult problem. H. B. Snyder.

Congressional Record. 91:(daily) 12316-21. D. 17, '45. Restoration of Palestine as a homeland for the Jewish people; Senate debate on S.Con.Res. 44.

Congressional Record. 91:(daily) 12352-67. D. 17, '45. Reports of Hearst Unofficial Senatorial Commission.

Congressional Record. 91:(daily) 12560-72. D. 19, '45. Palestine Jewish homeland; House debate on H.Res. 466.

Congressional Record. 91:(daily) A6136-9. D. 20, '45. Palestine—Jewish homeland. L. H. Smith.

Contemporary Jewish Record. 5:547-51. O. '42. British policy in Palestine. Eleazer Lipsky.

Contemporary Jewish Record. 5:597-617. D. '42. Arab politics in Palestine. J. C. Hurewitz.

Contemporary Jewish Record. 6:381-5. Ag. '43. Postwar economy and Palestine. E. A. Norman.

Contemporary Jewish Record. 6:563-78. D. '43. Jewish right, Christian power. H. M. Kallen.

Contemporary Jewish Record. 7:64. F. '44. Zionism and Palestine; nationwide campaign to marshall American public opinion against the White Paper.

Contemporary Jewish Record. 7:80-4. F. '44. Memorandum on the 1939 White Paper on Palestine; text of a communication submitted by the American Jewish Committee to Viscount Halifax, January 17, 1944.

Contemporary Jewish Record. 7:127-45. Ap. '44. Palestine and the future of the Jews, a pragmatic approach. Mordecai Grossman.

Contemporary Jewish Record. 7:177-8. Ap. '44. Zionism and Palestine; Congressional resolutions and hearings.

Contemporary Jewish Record. 7:339-52. Ag. '44. Unpromised land; possible Jewish settlement in the Kimberley region of Australia. I. N. Steinberg.

Reply. Contemporary Jewish Record. 7:646-7. D. '44; *Rejoinder.* Contemporary Jewish Record. 8:80-2. F. '45.

Contemporary Jewish Record. 7:375-84. Ag. '44. Socio-economic relations of Arabs and Jews in Palestine. B. D. Weinryb.

Contemporary Jewish Record. 7:487-96. O. '44. Jewish political parties in Palestine. Robert Weltsch.

Contemporary Jewish Record. 8:53-61. F. '45. Jews and Arabs: a case study in political understanding. Bernice Kaufman.

Contemporary Jewish Record. 8:115-28. Ap. '45. Palestine in the changing Middle East. B. D. Weinryb.

Contemporary Jewish Record. 8:301-7. Je. '45. Palestine: an economic appraisal. B. B. Seligman.

Contemporary Review. 152:257-69. S. '37. Palestine problem. Norman Bentwich; H. St. J. P. Philby.

Contemporary Review. 162:292-6. N. '42. Balfour declaration: 25 years after. Israel Cohen.

Contemporary Review. 165:229-34. Ap. '44. Communal villages of Palestine. Edwin Samuel.

Contemporary Review. 167:221-6. Ap. '45. Problem of Palestine. A. M. Hyamson.

Contemporary Review. 167:369-73. Je. '45. Britain and the Arab world. U. P. Mayer.

Current History. n.s. 8:398-402. My. '45. New Arab federation. S. B. Fay.

Current History. n.s. 9:121-5. Ag. '45. Criticism of Professor Fay's New Arab federation; reply with rejoinder. Elisha Friedman.

Current History. n.s. 10:48-55. Ja. '46. Middle East in the post-war world. P. L. Hanna.

Current Thought (Calcutta). 1:69-90. Jl. '39. Palestine tangle. A. R. Siddiqui.

Current Thought (Calcutta). 1:91-8. Jl. '39. Palestine. Peter Krieger.

Department of State Bulletin. 13:455-63. S. 30, '45. Displaced persons in Germany; letter from President Truman to General Eisenhower transmitting report of Earl G. Harrison.

Department of State Bulletin. 13:623. O. 21, '45. Attitude of American government toward Palestine; with text of letter of April 5, 1945, by President Roosevelt. J. F. Byrnes.

Department of State Bulletin. 13:790-1. N. 18, '45. Situation of Jews in Europe. H. S. Truman.

Dublin Review. 205:32-60. Jl. '39. Pledge betrayed. D. V. Duff.

Economic Geography. 13:235-59. Jl. '37. Economic geography of Palestine. E. R. Casto.

Economist (London). 146:328-9. Mr. 11, '44. America in the Middle East.

Economist (London). 146:422-4. Ap. 1, '44. Deadlock in Palestine?

Economist (London). 146:430-1. Ap. 1, '44. Right of asylum; admission of Jews escaping from South Eastern Europe to Palestine.

Economist (London). 147:631-2. N. 11, '44. Spotlight on Palestine.

Economist (London). 148:105-6. Ja. 27, '45. Middle Eastern unity.

Economist (London). 149:222-3. Ag. 18, '45. Zionist issue.

Economist (London). 149:324-6. S. 8, '45. New start in the Middle East?

Economist (London). 149:708-10. N. 17, '45. Postponement in Palestine; question of Jewish immigration.

Editorial Research Reports. 1, no. 6:107-20. F. 9, '45. Immigration to Palestine. F. M. Brewer.

Empire Review (London). 74:117-20. S. '41. Palestine, a crown colony? E. M. E. Blyth.

English Review. 61:529-39. N. '35. Palestine problem reviewed after ten years. C. R. Ashbee.

Far Eastern Survey. 13:120-2. Je. 28, '44. Refugee settlement in Australia. Shirley Jenkins.

Foreign Affairs. 16:143-55. O. '37. Palestine report; alternatives to partition. Viscount Samuel.

Foreign Affairs. 16:156-66. O. '37. Arabs and the future of Palestine. H. St. J. B. Philby.

Foreign Affairs. 20:324-38. Ja. '42. Palestine's role in the solution of the Jewish problem. Chaim Weizmann.
  Same separate. 14p. Jewish Agency for Palestine. 77 Great Russell St. London W.C. 1; *Condensed.* Contemporary Jewish Record. 6:155-62. Ap. '43.

Foreign Affairs. 24:119-29. O. '45. Toward Arab unity. H. A. R. Gibb.

Foreign Commerce Weekly. 13:3-9+. D. 4, '43. Arabia—royal visits, war strategy, questions of oil, trade-route factors, turn businessmen's eyes toward the ancient, picturesque peninsula. M. A. Neilan.

Foreign Commerce Weekly. 17:12-15+. O. 7, '44. Post-war Palestine. R. J. Barr.

Foreign Policy Reports. 10:158-68. Ag. 29, '34. Great Britain and the race problem in Palestine. E. P. MacCallum.

Foreign Policy Reports. 11:50-6. My. 8, '35. Arab nationalist movement. E. P. MacCallum.

Foreign Policy Reports. 13:194-204. N. 1, '37. Liquidating the Palestine mandate. D. H. Popper.

Foreign Policy Reports. 21:98-107. Jl. 1, '45. Palestine and America's role in the Middle East. G. S. McClellan.

Foreign Policy Reports. 21:108. Jl. 1, '45. American organizations interested in Palestine. O. K. D. Ringwood and G. S. McClellan.

Fortnightly. 158(n.s. 152):373-81. D. '42. Bridge of Asia. Rosita Forbes.

Fortnightly. 162(n.s. 156):341-9. D. '44. Palestine mandate. J. H. Simpson.

Fortnightly. 164(n.s. 158):97-103. Ag. '45. Great Britain and the Levant. Norman Bentwich.

Fortnightly. 165 (n.s.159):21-7. Ja. '46. Palestine statement. J. H. Simpson.

Fortune. 26:90-5+. N. '42. Middle East: its power politics.

Fortune. 30:112-17+. S. '44. Explosive Middle East. F. L. Babcock.

Fortune. 30:166-72+. O. '44. Much promised land. F. L. Babcock.

Fortune. 32:160-4+. S. '45. Middle East challenge; a vast market likes our goods. J. M. Landis.

Forum. 104:353-4. D. '45. Problem: Palestine. W. K. Kelsey.

Free World. 3:219-25. Ag. '42. Arab alignments in the Near East. Emanuel Neumann.

Geographical Journal. 92:259-66. S. '38. Natural resources of Palestine. A. Bonné.

Geographical Review. 17:75-88. Ja. '27. New Palestine. Andrée Choveaux.

Geographical Review. 27:550-65. O. '37. Pioneer fringe in Palestine; settlement possibilities south and east of the Holy Land. Jean Gottmann.

Geographical Review. 27:566-73. O. '37. Problem of Palestine; note on the report of the Royal Commission.

*Geographical Review. 29:61-80. Ja. '39. Geographical regions of Palestine. D. H. Kallner and E. Rosenau.

Great Britain and the East. 56:275. Ap. 10, '41. Raising standards in Palestine.

Harper's Magazine. 188:413-18. Ap. '44. Soviet wooing of Palestine; Russian-British competition in the Middle East. Eliahu Ben-Horin.

Harper's Magazine. 190:82-90. D. '44. Future of the Middle East; political problems. Eliahu Ben-Horin.

*Hibbert Journal. 43:140-7. Ja. '45. Reconciliation in Palestine. E. B. Castle.
    Reply. Hibbert Journal. 43:265-9. Ap. '45. Wyndham Deedes.

*Information Service (Federal Council of the Churches of Christ in America). 33:1-8. O. 7, '44. Conflict over Palestine.

Institute of World Affairs. Proceedings. 16:225-31. '38. Situation in the Near East. S. Hossain.

International Affairs. 14:369-88. My. '35. Palestine's progress and problems; with discussion. Norman Bentwich.

International Affairs. 18:171-93. Mr. '39. Report of the Palestine partition commission; with discussion. John Woodhead.

International Affairs. 20:458-72. O. '44. Middle Eastern perplexities; with discussion. H. A. R. Gibb.

International Affairs. 21:87-105. Ja. '45. Jewish world since 1939. James Parkes; J. H. Simpson.
  Same. Menorah Journal. 33:11-37. Ap. '45. Europe and Palestine; two Christian views of the Jewish future. James Parkes; J. H. Simpson. *Comment.* International Affairs. 21:294. Ap. '45.
International Conciliation. 352:426-33. S. '39. Palestine: the present situation. Viscount Samuel.
International Labour Review. 30:623-35, 797-819. N.-D. '34. Jewish colonization in Palestine. M. Berenstein.
International Review of Missions. 34:406-11. O. '45. Missionary to the Jews in Palestine to-day. G. L. B. Sloan.
Iowa Law Review. 25:32-77. N. '39. Palestine mandate in practice. Benjamin Akzin.
Jewish Affairs. 1, no.4:1-15. N. '41. Projects for Jewish mass colonization.
Jewish Frontier. 7:13-18. Ja. '40. More homelands for the Jews? H. J. Jonas.
Jewish Frontier. 10:12-14. Je. '43. Conditions for Zionist success. Norman Angell.
Jewish Frontier. 10:4-77. O. '43. White Paper; documents, discussion.
Jewish Frontier. 11:11-15. My. '44. Jordan Valley authority. Alexander Lurie.
Jewish Frontier. 12:6-8. Ap. '45. Palestine question since Yalta.
Jewish Frontier. 12:9-14. Ap. '45. New problems of Palestine immigration. Eliyahu Dobkin.
Jewish Frontier. 12:8-10. Je. '45. Trusteeship issue. Benjamin Akzin.
Jewish Frontier. 12:4-7. Jl. '45. Palestine and the trusteeship charter.
Jewish Frontier. 12:3-6. Ag. '45. America's role in Palestine.
Jewish Review. 2:5-40. Ap. '44. Jewish community in Palestine. B. D. Weinryb.
Jewish Review. 2:141-76, Jl.-O. '44. Economic and social forms in Palestine. B. D. Weinryb.
Jewish Social Service Quarterly. 14:304-19. Mr. '38. Partition of Palestine and its consequences. M. J. Karpf.
Jewish Social Service Quarterly. 19:56-66. S. '42. Political and cultural aspects of Jewish post-war problems. A. G. Duker.
  Also separate. American Jewish Conference. Research Institute on Peace and Post-War Problems. (Reprint series no. 3) 15p. The Conference. 521 5th Ave. New York 17. '43.
Jewish Social Studies. 5:327-54. O. '43. Palestine as a colonial enterprise. Raphael Straus.
Jewish Social Studies. 6:123-54. Ap. '44. Chapters of Arab-Jewish diplomacy, 1918-22. M. Perlman.
Labour Monthly (London). 18:409-17. Jl. '36. Events in Palestine. British Resident.
League of Nations Monthly Summary. 19:328-36. Ag.-S. '39. Palestine: observations on the policy laid down in the White Paper of May 1939.

Life. 15:93-101. O. 11, '43. Jewish homeland; Palestine wants a million more Jews.

Life. 19:32. D. 10, '45. Dream in which the UNO goes to Palestine.

Living Age. 360:68-73. Mr. '41. Jews' stake in Palestine. Arthur Settel.

Living Church. 111:15. O. 21, '45. Is Palestine the answer to the Jewish problem? C. T. Bridgeman.

London Quarterly of World Affairs. 11:124-30. Jl. '45. Arab world today. H. St. J. B. Philby.

London Quarterly of World Affairs. 11:131-7. Jl. '45. Palestine mandate and the League of Arab states. Norman Bentwich.

Menorah Journal. 25:236-41. Ap. '37. After the Royal Commission. Norman Bentwich.

Menorah Journal. 25:289-304. O. '37. Palestine partition proposal; an objective analysis. Leonard Stein.

Menorah Journal. 26:89-93. Ja. '38. Alternatives to Palestine partition. Norman Bentwich.

Menorah Journal. 26:139-50. Ap. '38. For and against a Jewish state; a survey of Jewish attitudes. William Zukerman.

Menorah Journal. 28:311-25; 29:104-10. O. '40; Ja. '41. Jewish colonization in Palestine. W. C. Lowdermilk.

Menorah Journal. 31:227-58. O. '43. Zionism today; a clarification. O. I. Janowsky.

Menorah Journal. 32:102-12. Ap. '44. Arab problem in Palestine. W. C. Lowdermilk.

Menorah Journal. 33:162-96. O.-D. '45. Zionism reconsidered. Hannah Arendt.

Michigan Academy of Science, Arts and Letters. Papers. 28:597-612. '42. Origin of the Balfour declaration. W. I. Cargo.

Milbank Memorial Fund Quarterly. 23:307-52. O. '45. Population problems of Palestine. F. W. Notestein and Ernest Jurkat.

Moslem World. 32:122-46. Ap. '42. American experiment in peace: the King-Crane Commission. H. N. Howard.

Moslem World. 33:239-53. O. '43. Palestine, Mohammedan holy land. C. D. Matthews.

Nation. 156:196-200. F. 6, '43. Jews of Europe; case for Zionism. P. S. Bernstein.

Nation. 158:92-4. Ja. 22, '44. Guns in Palestine. Jesse Lurie.

Nation. 158:326-8. Mr. 18, '44. Palestine run-around. I. F. Stone.

Nation. 158:589-91. My. 20, '44. TVA on the Jordan. G. W. Norris.

Nation. 159:685-6. D. 2, '44. Truth about the terrorists. Gerold Frank.

Nation. 159:783-4. D. 23, '44. Compromise for Palestine. J. L. Magnes.
  Reply. Nation. 160:138-9. F. 3, '45. Bernard Joseph.

Nation. 154:214-16, 253-5. F. 21-28, '45. Jews after the war. Reinhold Niebuhr.

Nation. 160:357-8. Mr. 31, '45. Two were hanged. Gerold Frank.

Nation. 160:413-14. Ap. 14, '45. Pan-Arabia deserta. Hal Lehrman.

Nation. 160:511-13. My. 5, '45. New hope for the Jewish people. Sumner Welles.

Nation. 161:449. N. 3, '45. Poulos and Palestine. Freda Kirchwey.

Nation. 161:543-4. N. 24, '45. Jewry in a blind alley. I. F. Stone.

Nation. 161:726-8. D. 29, '45. Middle Eastern tories. I. F. Stone.

Nation. 162:33. Ja. 12, '46. Palestine inquiry. Freda Kirchwey.

National Review (London). 112:247-50. F. '39. Arab rebellion. Troy McCormick.

National Review (London). 112:767-73. Je. '39. Settlement in southern Palestine. C. S. Jarvis.

National Review (London). 124:161-2. F. '45. Future of the Jews. J. Brander.

New Europe. 4:3-25. N. '44. Jews after the war, the test of security; special issue presenting symposium on the Jewish question.

New Palestine. 33:14-15. D. 4, '42. Principles of non-Zionism. J. J. Weinstein.

New Republic. 108:303-4. Mr. 8, '43. New Zionism.
  Discussion. New Republic. 108:448-9. Ap. 5, '43.

New Republic. 108:554-6. Ap. 26, '43. What hope for the Jews? P. S. Bernstein.
  Discussion. New Republic. 108:735-6. My. 31, '43.

New Republic. 112:667-70. My. 14, '45. Which way Zionism? J. M. Read.

New Republic. 113:692-3. N. 26, '45. Interim policy for Palestine.

New Republic. 113:831-3. D. 17, '45. Oil, blood and sand. Inge Kaiser.

New Statesman and Nation. 11:890-1. Je. 6, '36. Arabs and Jews. C. R. Ashbee and others.

New Statesman and Nation. 30:276-7. O. 27, '45. Plan for Palestine. H. N. Brailsford.

New York Times. p. 16. Ja. 22, '45. Palestine settlement must come from outside. A. O'H. McCormick.

New York Times. p. E5. O. 21, '45. Palestine crisis troubles Britain. Sydney Gruson.

New York Times. p. 12. N. 14, '45. Texts of statements on Jews and Palestine. Ernest Bevin; H. S. Truman.

New York Times. p. 13. N. 14, '45. Truman discloses U.S. Palestine role. J. H. Crider.

New York Times. p. 4. N. 15, '45. U.S. in British trap, Zionists here say; American Zionist Emergency Council charges Truman errs in accepting joint inquiry, issue called prejudiced.

New York Times. p. 14. D. 5, '45. Truman held firm on open Palestine.

New York Times. p. 1+. D. 11, '45. Palestine inquiry board is named.

New York Times Magazine. p. 9+. N. 18, '45. Two worlds meet in tense Palestine. Gene Currivan.

Newsweek. 26:54. N. 12, '45. Palestine: hate day.

Newsweek. 26:49-50. N. 26, '45. **Fire in Zion.**

Northwestern University on the Air: The Reviewing Stand. 5, no. 3: 1-12. Je 24, '45. Conflict in the Middle East. Louis Gottschalk and others.

Palestine. 2:7-8. Mr. '45. Will the Arabs accept a Palestine solution?

Palestine. 2:9-10. Mr. '45. British public opinion and Palestine. Selig Brodetsky.

Palestine. 2:1-2. S. '45. What is America's Palestine policy?

Palestine. 2:3-6. S. '45. American interest in a sound Palestine solution. C. J. Friedrich.

PM. 6:3. N. 14, '45. Palestine Jews strike to protest Anglo-U.S. plan.

Political Affairs. p. 918-34. O. '45. What is the outlook for the Jewish people? Alexander Bittelman.

Political Quarterly. 7:509-21. O. '36. Palestine before the commission. G. T. Garratt.

Political Quarterly. 13:91-9. Ja. '42. Palestine and colonial economic development. Rita Hinden.

*Political Quarterly. 16:297-306. O. '45. Jewish-Arab co-operation in Palestine. J. L. Magnes.

Political Science Quarterly. 41:384-412. S. '26. Palestine problem. Quincy Wright.

Quarterly Review. 269:341-58. O. '37. Palestine report. E. M. E. Blyth.

Quarterly Review. 282:269-84. Jl. '44. Palestine and the Jewish future; the Balfour declaration, the 1939 White Paper, and the promised Jewish state. Israel Cohen.

Queen's Quarterly. 37, no. 4:679-97. [O.] '30. Britain and Palestine. A. E. Prince.

Reader's Digest. 44:21-6. My. '44. Report on Palestine. F. C. Painton.

Round Table (London). 27:740-54. S. '37. Palestine report and after.

Round Table (London). 28:31-43. D. '37. Palestine and the Arab world.

Round Table (London). 29:252-77. Mr. '39. Palestine: the wider hope.

Round Table (London). 29:457-75. Je. '39. Palestine: a leaf turned; with text of British promises to the Arabs.

Round Table (London). 31:698-708. S. '41. Arab nationalism and the war.

Round Table (London). 35:137-42. Mr. '45. Empire and the Arab East.

Royal Philosophical Society of Glasgow. Proceedings. 50:64-78. '20. Future of Palestine. T. H. Weir.

New Republic. 112:357-8. Mr. 12, '45. New pan-Arabism. Heinz Eulau.

Rural Sociology. 5:327-44. S. '40. Jewish agricultural colonization in Palestine: a sociological experiment in collectivism. J. W. Eaton.

Saturday Evening Post. 218:18-19+. Ag. 18, '45. Middle East explodes. Harold Lamb.

Scottish Geographical Magazine. 53:380-7. N. '37. Palestine report: its geographical background. Archer Cust.

Senior Scholastic. 46:5-6. F. 12, '45. Palestine: two ways of life in conflict.

Senior Scholastic. 47:6-7. D. 3, '45. Palestine, much promised land.

Sociological Review. 32:29-49. Ja. '40. Fertility and mortality of the population of Palestine. Rita Hinden.

Spectator (London). 174:6-7. Ja. 5, '45. Palestine today. Eustace Gordon.
    Discussion. Spectator. 174:57, 80. 128. Ja. 19, 26, F. 9, '45.

Spectator (London). 174:567-8. Je. 22, '45. Arab world: proposed conference and Arab League. Nevill Barbour.
    Discussion. Spectator. 174:595; 175:12. Je. 29, Jl. 6, '45.

Spectator (London). 175:327-8. O. 12, '45. Mr. Bevin's problems.

Spectator (London). 175:353-4. O. 19, '45. Palestine plan. G. R. Driver.

Survey Graphic. 34:190-4+. My. '45. Europe and the Mediterranean. V. M. Dean.

Survey Graphic. 34:195-8+. My. '45. Palestine, as a refuge from fascism. I. A. Hirschmann.

Time. 44:38. N. 13, '44. Stern gangsters.

Time. 46:40. N. 12, '45. Eruption.

Town Meeting (Bulletin of America's Town Meeting of the Air). 11, no. 28:1-21. N. 8, '45. Should we support the establishment of a Jewish state in Palestine now? S. S. Wise and others.

United States News. 19:27-8. O. 26, '45. U.S. issue on Palestine: how far to back the Jews' cause.

University of Chicago Round Table. No. 224:1-16. Je. 28, '42. Near East. H. A. R. Gibb and others.

University of Chicago Round Table. No. 383:1-17. Jl. 22, '45. Middle East: zone of conflict. Carl Friedrich and others.

University of Chicago Round Table. No. 397:1-29. O. 28, '45. Palestine question: is there an answer? W. E. Hocking and others.

University of Toronto Quarterly. 13:207-20. Ja. '44. Near East today and tomorrow. W. R. Taylor.

Victoria Institute (London). Journal of the Transactions. 62:96-116. '30. Arabs and Jews in Palestine. W. M. Christie.

Victoria Institute (London). Journal of the Transactions. 62:241-65. '30. Jews under the Palestine mandate; with discussion. Israel Cohen.

PALESTINE AS A JEWISH HOMELAND

BOOKS AND PAMPHLETS

Alpert, Carl. Palestine between two wars. 38p. Zionist Organization of America. 1720 16th St. Washington 9, D.C. '44.

American Emergency Committee for Zionist Affairs. Balfour declaration and American interest in Palestine. 20p. The Committee. 41 E. 42d St. New York 17. ['42].

American Jewish Committee. Research Institute on Peace and Post-War Problems. Palestine in the new world. (Jewish post-war problems; a study course. Unit 6) 71p. The Committee. 386 4th Ave. New York 16. '43.
Bibliography, p. 69-71.

American Jewish Committee. Research Institute on Peace and Post-War Problems. Position of the Jews in the post-war world. (Jewish post-war problems; a study course. Unit 5) 64p. The Committee. 386 4th Ave. New York 16. '43.
Bibliography, p. 59-64.

American Jewish Conference. Program for postwar Jewish reconstruction. 16p. The Conference. 521 5th Ave. New York 17. Ap. '45.

American Jewish Conference. Statement of organization and a summary of resolutions adopted. 31p. The Conference. 521 5th Ave. New York 17. '43.

*American Jewish Conference. Committee on Preliminary Studies. Survey of facts and opinions on problems of post-war Jewry in Europe and Palestine. 143p. The Conference. 521 5th Ave. New York 17. Ag. '43.
Documents, resolutions and statements issued by national organizations participating in the American Jewish Conference, p. 111-43.

American Zionist Emergency Council. America speaks on Palestine; editorials from American newspapers condemning White Paper policy and demanding reconstruction of free and democratic Jewish commonwealth in Palestine. The Council. 342 Madison Ave. New York 17. '44.

American Zionist Emergency Council. British labor and Zionism. 24p. The Council. 342 Madison Ave. New York 17. ['45]

American Zionist Emergency Council. Jewish case; the place of Palestine in the solution of the Jewish question. 30p. The Council. 342 Madison Ave. New York 17. n.d.

American Zionist Emergency Council. Palestine day, November second, nineteen hundred forty-four. 44p. The Council. 342 Madison Ave. New York 17. '45.

Assaf, Michael. Arab movement in Palestine. 73p. Masada Youth Zionist Organization of America. 381 4th Ave. New York. Jl. '37.

Avniel, B. Jewish industry in the rebuilding of Palestine. 4p. Jewish Forum. 305 Broadway. New York 7. '45.
Reprint from the Jewish Forum. S. '45.

Ben-Gurion, David. ABC of Zionist policy. 20p. Habonim Labor Zionist Youth. 45 E. 17th St. New York 3. '44.

Ben-Gurion, David. Palestine in the post-war world. 23p. Jewish Agency for Palestine. 77 Great Russell St. London. W.C.1 '42.

Board of Deputies of British Jews. Jews in Europe; their martyrdom and their future. 64p. The Board. Woburn House, Upper Woburn Place. London W.C.1. '45.

Brandeis, Louis D. Brandeis on Zionism; a collection of addresses and statements. ed. by Solomon Goldman. 156p. Zionist Organization of America. 1720 16th St. Washington 9, D.C. '42.

Christian Council on Palestine. Truth about Palestine. 28p. The Council. 70 5th Ave. New York 11. '46.

Cohen, Israel. Progress of Zionism. 5th rev. ed. Central Office of the Zionist Organisation. 77 Great Russell St. London W.C.1. '39.

Deedes, Wyndham. Palestine shapes its future. 16p. Jewish Agency for Palestine. 77 Great Russell St. London W.C.1. My '45.

Douglas, Helen G. Christian youth; address, New York, October 14, 1945. 8p. American Christian Palestine Committee. 41 E. 42d St. New York 17. '45.

*Einstein, Albert and Kahler, Eric. Arabs and Palestine. 12p. American Palestine Committee. 41 E. 42nd St. New York 17. '45.

Emergency Committee to Save the Jewish People of Europe. White paper in Palestine and the problem of saving the Jewish people of Europe. 18p. mim. The Committee. 25 W. 45th St. New York 19. Jl '45.

Feuer, Leon I. Why a Jewish state. 94p. Richard R. Smith. New York. '42.

Frankenstein, Ernst. Justice for my people. 208p. Dial Press. New York. '44.
  Review. Saturday Review of Literature. 28:17. D. 29, '45.

Gervasi, Frank. To whom Palestine? 213p. D. Appleton-Century Co. New York. '46.

Goldstein, Israel. Road ahead; a program for American Zionism. 22p. Zionist Organization of America. 1720 16th St. Washington 9, D.C. '44.

Goldstein, Israel. Zionist program and implementation. 23p. Zionist Organization of America. 1720 16th St. Washington 9, D.C. '45.

Greenstein, Joseph. Redeem the people, rebuild the homeland. 32p. Palestine Foundation Fund, 41 E. 42d St. New York 17. S. '45.

Hebrew Committee of National Liberation. Statement of policy pertaining to the entry of Hebrews into Palestine. 24p. The Committee. 2315 Massachusetts Ave. Washington 8, D.C. Ja. '45.

Herzl, Theodor. Jewish state; an attempt at a modern solution of the Jewish question. rev. ed. 111p. Scopus Publishing Co. N.Y. '43.

Holmes, John Haynes. Jews and the Christian conscience: a plea for Palestine. 20p. Community Church. Church Office. 40 E. 35th St. New York 16. '45.

Jabotinsky, Vladimir. Answer to Ernest Bevin; evidence submitted to the Palestine Royal Commission, (House of Lords, London, February 11, 1937). 32p. Bernard Ackerman, Inc. New York. '46.

Jewish Agency for Palestine. Development of the Jewish national home in Palestine; memorandum submittted to His Majesty's Government, May, 1930. 99p. The Agency. 77 Great Russell St. London W.C.1. '30.

Jewish Agency for Palestine. Jewish case against the Palestine White Paper. 35p. The Agency. 77 Great Russell St. London W.C.1. Je. '39.

Jewish Agency for Palestine. Memorandum submitted to the Palestine Royal Commission. 324p. The Agency. 77 Great Russell St. London W.C.1. N. '36.

Jewish Frontier Association. Broken pledge; the case against the White Paper on Palestine. 96p. The Association. 45 E. 17th St. New York 3. n.d.

Lewisohn, Ludwig and others. Jewish commonwealth in Palestine. 28p. Zionist Organization of America. 1720 16th St. Washington 9, D.C. '44.

Lindeman, Eduard C. Palestine, test of democracy. 8p. American Christian Palestine Committee. 41 E. 42d St. New York 17. '45.

Lipsky, Louis. End of a tragic failure. 3p. mim. Independent Jewish Press Service. 207 4th Ave. New York 3. Ag. 4, '44.

Lipsky, Louis. Rally for Jewish rights; speech at Lewisohn Stadium, New York. 4p. mim. American Jewish Conference. 521 5th Ave. New York 17. Ap. 29, '45.

Lourie, Arthur. Britain and Palestine; an examination of present British policy in the light of the mandate for Palestine. 19p. American Zionist Emergency Council. 342 Madison Ave. New York 17. n.d.

Lourie, Arthur. Facts about Palestine. 17p. Zionist Archives and Library. 41 E. 42d St. New York 17. n.d.

Maclean, Norman. His terrible swift sword. 126p. Christian Council on Palestine. 70 5th Ave. New York. ['42]

Mendelsohn, Morris J. and others. Jewish legion and the Palestine question. 43p. New Zionist Organization of America. 55 W. 42nd St. New York 18. Ap. '45.

National Conference on Palestine. Voice of Christian America; proceedings, March 9, 1944. 48p. Zionist Archives and Library. 41 E. 42nd St. New York 17. '44.

Neumann, Emanuel. Zionism and the Arab world; testimony submitted to the Committee on Foreign Affairs of the House of Representatives, February 15, 1944. 14p. American Zionist Emergency Council. 342 Madison Ave. New York 17. '44.

Palestine Foundation Fund (Keren Hayesod) Inc. Where there's a will; your share in the story of Keren Hayesod. 19p. The Fund. 41 E. 42d St. New York 17. n.d.

Perry, Silas S. Britain opens a gateway. 96p. Museum Press. London. '44.

Petition to the President of the United States respectfully submitted by members of the faculties of American schools of higher learning. 17p. American Zionist Emergency Council. 342 Madison Ave. New York 17. '44.

*Phillips, Wendell. Arabs and the Jews in Palestine. 17p. Canadian Palestine Committee. 2 Bloor St. E. Toronto 5. '45.
   Same slightly abridged. Before the bar of history. [15]p. Club Program Service. 41 E. 42d St. New York 17.

Revusky, Abraham. Absorptive capacity of Palestine. (Toward a Jewish Commonwealth. Unit no. 2) 16p. Hadassah. 1819 Broadway 23. New York. '44.

Revusky, Abraham. Looking forward. 28p. Palestine Foundation Fund (Keren Hayesod). 41 E. 42d St. New York 17. n.d.

Ruffman, Louis L. Modern Palestine, the makings of a Jewish national home. 40p. mim. Hadassah. 1819 Broadway. New York 23. '39.

Smelansky, Moses. Jewish colonization and the fellah. 56p. Mischar w' Taasia Publishing Co. Tel-Aviv. '30.

Some facts on the Palestine situation. 9p. mim. American Palestine Committee, 41 E. 42d St. New York 17. S. '45

Syrkin, Marie. Why a Jewish commonwealth? (Toward a Jewish Commonwealth. Unit no. 3) 31p. Hadassah. 1819 Broadway 23. '44.

Thompson, Dorothy. I speak again as a Christian. 14p. American Zionist Emergency Council. 342 Madison Ave. New York 17. '45.

Van Paassen, Pierre. Forgotten ally. 343p. Dial Press. New York. '43.
   Review. Saturday Review of Literature. 26:12. N. 6, '43. Frederick Gruin.

Weizmann, Chaim. Jewish people and Palestine; statement made before the Palestine Royal Commission in Jerusalem on November 25th, 1936. 2d ed. 31p. Zionist Organization (Central Office). 77 Great Russell St. London W.C.1. '39.

Wise, Stephen S. Zion, homeland and hope. *In his* As I see it. p. 135-65. Jewish Opinion Publishing Corporation. New York. '44.

PERIODICALS

American Jewish Chronicle. 1:8-10. D. 1; 6-9+. D. 15, '39; 7-11. Ja. 1, '40. Behind the Palestine betrayal. J. M. Patterson.

American Mercury. 57:339-47. S. '43. Jews who fight Zionism; reply to L. J. Rosenwald. Maurice Samuel.

American Scholar. 13, no. 4:437-47. [O.] '44. Jews: a problem that cannot wait. Robert Gordis.
   Discussion. American Scholar. 14, no.1 and 2:123-6, 252. Ja.-Ap. '45. Ephraim Frisch; V. S. Yarrows.

*Annals of the American Academy. 240:89-98. Jl. '45. Case for a Jewish commonwealth in Palestine. L. E. Levinthal.

Annals of the American Academy. 240:99-108. Jl. '45. Compromise in Palestine. M. S. Lazaron.

Answer. 3:8-9. O.-N. '45. White man's burden, 1945 version. S. Merlin.

> *Answer*; a non-sectarian approach to the problems of the Hebrew people in Europe and Palestine, published by the Answer Publishing Comapny. 25 W. 45th St. New York 19.

Answer. 3:20. O.-N. '45. Great Britain fomenting trouble in Palestine; text of communication to British Government by the Hebrew Committee.

Answer. 3:26. O.-N. '45. Saving Jews or appeasing Arabs. E. A. Mowrer.

> *Reprint* from the New York Post. S. 25, '45.

Atlantic Monthly. 174:85-90. N. '44. Palestine: the dream and the reality; a survey of Jewish nationalism. M. S. Lazaron.

*Atlantic Monthly. 175:101-6. F. '45. Creed of an American Zionist. Milton Steinberg.

Christian Century. 60:196-7. F. 17, '43. Palestine, a decent way out. C. E. Shulman.

Christian Century. 60:548-9. My. 5, '43. Is Zionism fair to the Arabs? S. R. Harlow.

Christian Century. 62:1418-19. D. 19, '45. Sorry story of Palestine; reply. H. M. LeSourd.

Churchman. 159:4-13. N. 1, '45. Palestine as a homeland for the Jews; symposium.

> Discussions by H. A. Atkinson, H. G. Douglas, Nelson Mead, N. L. Goldstein, J. P. Lewis, H. M. LeSourd, Wendell Phillips and C. H. Voss.

Commentary. 1, no. 2:35-42. D. '45. Future of Europe's Jews. Sidney Hertzberg.

Commentary. 1, no. 2:64-71. D. '45. Moyne case: a tragic history. Gerold Frank.

Congressional Record. 91:(daily) A4047-9. S. 5, '45. Palestine and the labor government. Emanuel Celler.

Congressional Record. 91: (daily) A4519. O. 5, '45. Letter from George Berke, chairman of the Chattanooga Zionist Emergency Council.

Congressional Record. 91: (daily) 9831-54. O. 16, '45. Palestine; House debate.

Congressional Record. 91: (daily) A4919-20. O. 29, '45. American policy on Palestine; text of memorandum submitted by the American Zionist Emergency Council to the State Department, October 23, 1945.

Congressional Record. 91: (daily) A5004-5. N. 1, '45. Palestine pledges and policy. Emanuel Celler.

Congressional Record. 91: (daily) A5220-2. N. 14, '45. Resettlement of Palestine. R. F. Wagner.

Congressional Record. 91: (daily) A5317-18. N. 19, '45. Palestine and the Jewish need—1945 summary. C. W. Efroymson.

Congressional Record. 91: (daily) A5431-2. N. 23, '45. Statement on Palestine. G. M. Gillette, A. L. Somers, and J. D. Stern.

Congressional Record. 91: (daily) A5551. N. 28, '45. Palestine situation. Herbert Hoover.

Congressional Record. 91: (daily) 11428-31. N. 30, '45. British military policy in Palestine. Owen Brewster.

Contemporary Jewish Record. 6:151-5. Ap. '43. Commonwealth or binational state? Erich Kahler.

Contemporary Review. 161:158-63. Mr. '42. Palestine, the Jews, and the war. Israel Cohen.

Contemporary Review. 164:337-42. D. '43. Zionism and the Jewish problem. Cecil Roth.

Foreign Affairs. 9:409-34. Ap. '31. Palestine situation restated. Felix Frankfurter.

Foreign Affairs. 21:239-49. Ja. '43. Toward peace in Palestine. J. L. Magnes.
 Condensed. Contemporary Jewish Record. 6:162-7. Ap. '43.

Free World. 9:47-50. Ja. '45. Eye-witness report on Jewish Palestine. Nahum Goldmann.

Free World. 10:41-3. N. '45. Jewish problem must be solved now. Nahum Goldmann.

International Affairs. 15:671-83. S. '36. Palestine to-day; with discussion. Chaim Weizmann.

Jewish Frontier. 9:7-10. Ap. '42. Appeal to the British people. E. C. Johnson.

Jewish Frontier. 9:8-10. D. '42. Jewish Palestine and the United Nations. E. D. Thomas.

Jewish Frontier. 10:6-9. Ap. '43. Palestine—a Jewish commonwealth. Moshe Shertok.

Jewish Frontier. 10:8-15. Ag. '43. This is our reply. David Ben-Gurion.

Jewish Frontier. 11:11-14. Ap. '44. To whom does the earth belong? Dorothy Thompson.

Jewish Frontier. 11:16+. S. '44. Partition, again? Hayim Greenberg.

Jewish Frontier. 11:15-17. D. '44. Sumner Welles on Palestine. Alexander Lurie.

Jewish Frontier. 12:7-12. Ja. '45. Palestine and the problem of refugee rehabilitation. J. G. MacDonald.

Jewish Mirror. 1:12-14. N. '42. Arab-Jewish problem. Nahum Goldmann.

*Jewish Mirror. 1:11-17. D. '42.-Ja. '43. Motives behind the Balfour declaration. A. S. Lyrique.

*Journal of Educational Sociology. 18:287-94. Ja. '45. Jewish Palestine in the postwar world. I. B. Berkson.
 Bibliography, p. 317-20.

Life. 14:37-8+. Je. 21, '43. In reply to King Ibn Saud on Jewish homeland in Palestine. S. S. Wise.

Life. 14:11. Je. 28, '43. Reply to Zionism; Why many Americans of Jewish faith are opposed to the establishment of a Jewish state in Palestine. L. J. Rosenwald.

Menorah Journal. 24:302-4. O. '36. Causes of Arab unrest. Joseph Klausner.

Nation. 161:247-9. S. 15, '45. Palestine, a world responsibility. R. F. Wagner.

Nation. 161:399-401. O. 20, '45. Have the Arabs a case? Eliahu Ben-Horin.

Nation. 161:615-17. D. 8, '45. Palestine pilgrimage. I. F. Stone.

New Palestine. 33:10-12. N. 6, '42. Zionism's cardinal principle. Robert Szold.
    Also separate. 11p. Zionist Organization of America. 1720 16th St. Washington 9, D.C.

New Palestine. 33:13-15. N. 6, '42. Battle of documents. Louis Lipsky.
    Also separate. 8p. Zionist Organization of America. 1720 16th St. Washington 9, D.C.

New Palestine. 33:6-9. D. 18, '42. Atlantic Charter and the Jews. Joseph Dunner.

New Palestine. 34:51-3. O. 8, '43. Camouflage of a tragedy. Louis Lipsky.

New Palestine. 34:284-6. Mr. 3, '44. Zionist case; digest of the hearings before the House Foreign Affairs Committee, Feb. 8, 9, 15, 16. Isidore Cooperman and A. E. Ginsberg.

New Palestine. 34:289-91+. Mr. 3, '44. Arab-Jewish case; from testimony before the Committte on Foreign Affairs of the House of Representative, February 15. Emanuel Neumann.

New Republic. 113:622. N. 12, '45. Blackmail in Palestine.

New Republic. 113:633-5. N. 12, '45. Peace for Palestine. W. H. Stringer.

New Republic. 114:7. Ja. 7, '46. Send them to Palestine.

New Statesman and Nation. 26:229-30. O. 9, '43. On a Jewish soldier's letter. H. J. Laski.
    Same. Contemporary Jewish Record. 7:48-51. F. '44.

New Statesman and Nation. 27:285-6. Ap. 29, '44. Palestine scene. Norman Bentwich.

New York Herald Tribune. O. 31, '45. Commonwealth of Palestine. Sumner Welles.
    Same. Congressional Record. 91:(daily) A5126-7. N. 7, '45.

New York Times. p. 12. F. 17, '45. Compromise for Palestine. J. L. Magnes.

*New York Times. p. 8E. S. 30, '45. Jewish state opposed. M. S. Lazaron.

New York Times. p. 1, 4. O. 1, '45. Dewey backs plea for Jewish state.

New York Times. p. 8E. O. 7, '45. Issues in Palestine; reply to M. Lazaron. Milton Steinberg.

New York Times. p. 12. O. 24, '45. Text of American Zionist Emergency Council memorandum to the State Department, October 23, 1945.

New York Times. p. 8E. Ja. 6, '46. Arab transfer favored; protest against Hoover plan evokes argument. E. M. Friedman.

New York Times. p. 9. Ja. 28, '46. Zionists oppose Trans-Jordan aim.

New York Times Magazine. p. 12+. N. 1, '42. Chemist who created a state; Dr. Weizmann tells of the new day he foresees in Palestine after the war is over. S. J. Woolf.

Palestine. 1:7-9. D. '44. Plymouth and Palestine; a discussion of deficit colonization. C. W. Efroymson.

Palestine. 2:3-6. F. '45. Why the Zionists are right. Dorothy Thompson.

Palestine. 2:3-5. My-Je. '45. To the United Nations; memorandum submittted by the Jewish Agency for Palestine.

Palestine. 2:3-6. Jl.-Ag. '45. What lies ahead in Palestine. David Ben-Gurion.

Palestine. 2:6-8. O. '45. Face to face with the survivors. Eliahu Dobkin.

Palestine. 2:8-10. O. '45. Nuremburg in Palestine; crucial land problem. E. M. Epstein.

*Palestine. 2:4-6. N.-D. '45. Letter to President Harry S. Truman. R. A. Taft and R. F. Wagner.

Reader's Digest. 45:113-15. Jl. '44. Dissenting reports on Palestine; reply to F. C. Painton.

THE ARAB CLAIM TO PALESTINE

Books and Pamphlets

Antonius, George. Arab awakening; the story of the Arab national movement. 471p. J. B. Lippincott Co. Philadelphia. '39.

*Arab Office. Arab world and the Arab League. 12p. The Office. 161 St. Stephen's House, Westminster, London W.C. 1. O. '45.

Arab Office. Statement of present Arab attitude over the Palestine question. 4p. The Office. 161 St. Stephen's House. Westminster, London W.C.1. Jl. 30, '45.

Arab Office. Statement on objectives of the Arab Office, delivered at Press Conference, Wardman Park Hotel, October 4, 1945. 4p. mim. The Office. Wardman Park Hotel. Washington, D.C.

Arberry, A. J. and Landau, Rom, eds. Islam today. 258p. Faber & Faber. London. '43.

*Atiyah, Edward. Arab rights and the British left. 8p. Arab Office. 161 St. Stephen's House. Westminster, London W.C.1. n.d.

Bailey, Josiah W. United States Senator from North Carolina replies to the Committee for the Abrogation of the British White Paper, relating to Jewish immigration into Palestine. 3p. League of American-Arab Committees for Democracy. 1907 Detroit St. Flint 5, Mich. '44.

Berger, Elmer. Jewish dilemma. 257p. Devin-Adair Co. New York. '45.

Bustani, W. F. Palestine mandate, invalid and impracticable. 168p. American Press. Beirut. '36.

Byng, Edward J. World of the Arabs. 325p. Little, Brown & Co. Boston. '44.

Canaan, T. Conflict in the land of peace. 118p. [Syrian Orphanage Press.] Jerusalem. N. '36.

Faris, Nabih A. ed. Arab heritage. 279p. Princeton University Press. Princeton. '44.

Hitti, Philip K. Arab claim to Palestine; radio broadcast March 13, 1945. 3p. mim. Institute of Arab American Affairs. 160 Broadway. New York 7.

Hitti, Philip K. Arabs: a short history. 224p. Princeton University Press. Princeton, N.J. '43.
Based on his History of the Arabs.

Hitti, Philip K. History of the Arabs. 3d ed. 767p. Macmillan & Co. London. '44.

*Hocking, William E. Arab nationalism and political Zionism. [7]p. League of American-Arab Committees for Democracy. 1907 Detroit St. Flint 5, Mich. '44(?).
Same. Papers on Palestine. p. 21-8. Institute of Arab American Affairs. 160 Broadway. New York 7. '45; Moslem World. 35:216-23. Jl. '45.

Institute of Arab American Affairs. Manifesto of the Institute of Arab American Affairs on Palestine; submitted to the United Nations Conference on International Organization at San Francisco. 3p. The Institute. 160 Broadway. New York 7. Ap. '45.

*Institute of Arab American Affairs. Papers on Palestine, a collection of statements, articles and letters dealing with the Palestine problem. 54p. The Institute. 160 Broadway. New York. '45.
Bibliography, p. 54.

Jeffries, Joseph M. N. Palestine: the reality. 728p. Longmans, Green & Co. New York. '39.

Katibah, Habeeb I. New spirit in Arab lands. 320p. The Author. 303 5th Ave. New York. '40.

Newton, Frances E. Searchlight on Palestine; fair-play or terrorist methods? some personal investigations. 23p. Arab Centre. 72 Victoria St. London W.C.1. '38.

Palestine Arab Congress. Two memoranda submitted to the Council and Permanent Mandates Commission of the League of Nations respectively through H. E. the High Commissioner for Palestine by the Executive Committee, Palestine Arab Congress. 32p. The Congress. Jerusalem. Ap. 12, '25.

Saunders, R. M. Arab nationalism. *In his* Whither the Near East? (Behind the headlines. Vol. 4, no. 4) p. 17-28. Canadian Institute of International Affairs. 230 Bloor St. W. Toronto. '44.

Stark, Freya. Arab island; the Middle East, 1939-1943. 235p. Alfred A. Knopf. New York. '45.
> *English edition*: East is west. 213p. John Murray. London. '45.

Van Ess, John. Meet the Arab. 229p. John Day Co. '43.
> *Review.* Saturday Review of Literature. 26:12-13. N. 6, '43. Frederick Gruin.

*Wysner, Glora M. Dilemma in Palestine. 8p. (Bulletin no. 6) Committee on Work Among Moslems. 156 5th Ave. New York 10. N. '44.

PERIODICALS

American Historical Review. 48:722-32. Jl. '43. Possibility of union among the Arab states. P. K. Hitti.

American Jewish Chronicle. 1:6-7. Ja. 1, '40. Arab viewpoint. R. J. Longuet.

Arab News Bulletin. 1, no. 2:[1-3]. Ja. 1, '46. Reply of the Arab League to Mr. Bevin's statement on Palestine.
> See also current issues.

*Arab World. 1, no. 1:72-9. Summer '44. Palestine; testimony before the House Foreign Affairs Committee, February 15, 1944. P. K. Hitti.
> Arab World; a quarterly magazine sponsored by American citizens of Arab descent to cement Arab American friendship. G. Kheirallah, ed. 1182 Broadway. New York. Vol. 1, no. 1. Summer '44-date.

Arab World. 1, no. 1:79-82. Summer '44. Letter to F. I. Rypins. J. W. Bailey.

Arab World. 1, no. 1:84-6. Summer '44. Cables from Jamil Al-Madfai, President of Iraq Senate and M. R. Shabibi to Senators Wagner and others.

Arab World. 1, no. 1:87-91. Summer '44. Dispatch from Cairo. Henry Gorrell.

*Arab World. 1, no. 2:41-8+. Fall '44. Is Zionism a solution? M. G. Malti.
> *Also separate.* [16p.] League of American-Arab Committees for Democracy. 1907 Detroit St. Flint 5, Mich. '44.

Arab World. 1, no. 3:7-11. '45. Friends of the Arabs. Martin Sprengling.

Asia. 38:44-6. Ja. '38. Pan-Arab dream. Ameen Rihani.

Asia and the Americas. 44:464-8. O. '44. Vying for Arab favor. J. M. Baroody.
> *Same abridged.* New Statesman and Nation. 28:264. O. 21, '44; *Reply.* J. C. Wild. New Statesman and Nation. 28:304. N. 4, '44.

Asia and the Americas. 45:290-4. Je. '45. Arab upheaval. J. M. Baroody.

Asia and the Americas. 45:438-42. S. '45. Arabs and the world. Dorothy Adelson.

Asia and the Americas. 45:607. D. '45. Arabs and the world; reply. Khulusy Khairy.

Bulletin of International News. 21:799-804. Jl '44. Arab unity; a note on recent developments.

Catholic World. 162:301-10. Ja. '46. Palestine reality. Jabir Shibli.

Christian Century. 59:1187-8. S. 30, '42. Near East—an Arab view. J. Bakhus.

*Christian Century. 60:359-61. Mr. 24, '43. Palestine, an Arab view. Jabir Shibli.
  Discussion. Christian Century. 60:460-1. Ap. 14, '43.

Christian Century. 60:640. My. 26, '43. Is Zionism fair to the Arabs? reply to S. R. Harlow. Jabir Shibli.

Christian Century. 62:1284-6. N. 21, '45. Christians and Zionism. A. L. Warnshuis.
  Also separate. 8p. Institute of Arab American Affairs. 160 Broadway. New York 7. '45. *Discussion.* Christian Century. 62:1419. D. 19, '45.

Christian Science Monitor. Mr. 3, '39. Gandhi's message to Jewry; Palestine belongs to the Arabs.
  Separate. 3p. League of American-Arab Committees for Democracy. 1907 Detroit St. Flint 5, Mich.

Collier's. 114:19+. Jl. 8, '44. Allah's oil. Frank Gervasi.

*Congressional Record. 91: (daily) A4812-13. O. 29, '45. King Ibn Saud's letter to President Roosevelt and the President's reply to the King.
  Same. Congressional Record. 91:(daily) A5179-80. N. 13, '45.

English Review. 63:324-32. O. '36. Has England failed in Palestine? E. M. E. Blyth.

Free World. 10:44-5. N. '45. Arab position as to Jews in Palestine. A. R. Azzam.

Great Britain and the East. 45:430. O. 3, '35. Palestine from the Arab standpoint.

Great Britain and the East. 46:371. Mr. 19, '36. Arab and Jew in Palestine. Z. Zhouri.

Great Britain and the East. 47:15. Jl. 2, '36. Palestine woman's plea. Mrs. Yaqub Tawil.

Great Britain and the East. 47:482. O. 1, '36. Palestine: round table conference. K. A. Ibrahim.

Institute of World Affairs. Proceedings. 16:225-31. '38. Situation in the Near East. Syud Hossain.

International Affairs. 15:684-99. S. '36. Arab view of the situation in Palestine; with discussion. Emile Ghory.

Life. 14:76-7. My. 31, '43. Ibn Saud's pronouncement on the Palestine question.

Moslem World. 25:354-8. O. '35. Islam in Palestine. Alfred Nielsen.

Moslem World. 35:316-23. O. '45. Arab Women's Congress, Cairo, December 10-20, 1944. Louise Fuleihan.

New Statesman and Nation. 12:346-7. S. 12, '36. Palestine. E. A. Ghory.
　　Reply. New Statesman and Nation. 12:387. S. 19, '36.

New York Times. p. 1+. S. 30, '45. Arab League asks Tripolitania rule.

New York Times. p. 4. O. 4, '45. Iraq irked by U.S. on refugee haven.

New York Times. p. 5E. O. 14, '45. Oneness of Arabs cry of new league. Sydney Gruson.

New York Times. p. 4. O. 19, '45. Texts of letters exchanged by Ibn Saud and Roosevelt.

New York Times. p. 25. O. 21, '45. Warning of war bared by Arabs; text of memorandum presented to Secretary of State Byrnes October 12th by representatives of four Arab states, Egypt, Iraq, Lebanon, and Syria.

New York Times. p. 9. O. 23, '45. Arab ruler warns Zionists to desist; Transjordan Emir on the Palestine situation.

New York Times. p. 16. N. 7, '45. Arabs insist on their rights; statement by Arab Office, Washington, D.C.
　　Same. Congressional Record. 91:(daily) A6139. D. 20, '45.

New York Times. p. 6. N. 10, '45. Arab hits Truman on Palestine issue. Gene Currivan.

New York Times. p. 5E. N. 11, '45. Arab League bids for power in Middle East. Clifton Daniel.

New York Times. p. 20. N. 19, '45. Jewish immigration urged. G. A. Oldham.

New York Times. p. 14. D. 24, '45. Hoover Iraq plan opposed. Khalil Totah.

New York Times. p. 12. D. 29, '45. Arabs oppose Welles plan. Samir Shamma.

New York Times Magazine. p. 9+. Je. 17, '45. Fires that flame behind the Arab crisis. C. L. Sulzberger.

Princeton Herald. Ap. 21, '44. Palestinian Arabs descended from natives before Abraham. P. K. Hitti.
　　Also in Papers on Palestine. p. 16-20. Institute of Arab American Affairs. '45.

Saturday Review (London). 162:396-8. S. 26, '36. Trouble in Palestine. Focus.

Saturday Review (London). 162:556-7. O. 31, '36. Selling the Arabs to the Jews. Michael O'Dwyer.

Socialist Commentary (London). 10:235-9. D. '45. British labour and the Arab people. Margaret Pope.

Spectator (London). 155:668. O. 25, '35. Arab rights in Palestine. C. M. Chapman.
　　Discussion. Spectator. 155:723, 779-80, 818. N. 1-15, '35.

Spectator (London). 156:938. My. 22, '36. Palestine, the Arab case. I. Nakhleh.

Spectator (London). 173:60. Jl. 21, '44. Balfour declaration. Louis Rieu.

Discussion. Spectator. 173:81. Jl. 28, '44.

Spectator (London). 175:191-2. Ag. 31, '45. Peril in Palestine. S. H. Longrigg.

Discussion. Spectator. 175:220. S. 7, '45. Israel Cohen.

Spectator (London). 175:329-30. O. 12, '45. Arab League. Edward Atiyah.

Times Educational Supplement (London). 1566:208. My. 5, '45. Arab education in Palestine.

Virginia Quarterly Review. 22, no. 1:32-47. [Ja.] '46. Conflicts in the Arab East. P. K. Hitti.

Also separate. Institute of Arab American Affairs. 160 Broadway. New York 7.

World Dominion and the World To-day. 23:335-8. N. '45. League of Arab nations. S. A. Morrison.

ORGANIZATIONS

American Christian Palestine Committee. 41 E. 42d St. New York 17.
Combines the American Palestine Committee and the Christian Council on Palestine.

American Council for Judaism. 1321 Arch St. Philadelphia.

American Council on Public Affairs. 2153 Florida Ave. Washington 8, D.C.

American Emergency Committee for Zionist Affairs. 41 E. 42d St. New York 17.

American Jewish Committee. 386 4th Ave. New York 16.
Publishes *Commentary* (Vol. 1, no. 1. N. '45) incorporating its former publication *Contemporary Jewish Record.*

American Jewish Conference. 521 5th Ave. New York 17.
Issues *Conference Record.*

American League for a Free Palestine. 25 W. 45th St. New York 19.

American Zionist Emergency Council. 342 Madison Ave. New York 17.
Publishes *Palestine.*

American Zionist Youth Commission. 381 4th Ave. New York 16.

Arab Office. Wardman Park Hotel. Washington, D.C.
Issues *News Bulletin*; and *News Letter* (mim.)

Arab Office. 161 St. Stephens House, Westminster, London W.C. 1.

Arab Office. P.O. Box 431, Muscara Quarter. Jerusalem, Palestine.

British Information Services. 30 Rockefeller Plaza. New York 20.

Canadian Arab Friendship League. Windsor Hotel. Montreal.

Canadian Arab News Service. P.O. Box 116, Station N. Montreal.

Canadian Institute of International Affairs. 230 Bloor St. W. Toronto.

Canadian Palestine Committee. 2 Bloor St. E. Toronto.

Committee on Work Among Moslems. 156 5th Ave. New York 10.

Federal Council of the Churches of Christ in America. 297 4th Ave. New York 10.

Foreign Policy Association. 22 E. 38th St. New York 16.

Habonim Labor Zionist Youth. 45 E. 17th St. New York 3.

Hadassah. 1819 Broadway. New York 23.

Institute of Arab American Affairs. 160 Broadway. New York 7.
    Issues *Bulletin of the Institute of Arab Affairs*. Vol. 1, no. 1. Jl. 15, '45-date.

Jewish Agency of Palestine. 77 Great Russell St. London W.C.1.

Jewish Frontier Association. 45 E. 17th St. New York 3.
    Publishes *Jewish Frontier*.

League of American-Arab Committees for Democracy. 1907 Detroit St. Flint 5, Mich.

New Zionist Organization of America. 55 W. 42d St. New York 18.

Palestine Foundation Fund (Keren Hayesod). 41 E. 42d St. New York 17.

United Jewish Appeal for Refugees, Overseas Needs and Palestine. 342 Madison Ave. New York 17.

Zionist Archives and Library. 41 E. 42d St. New York 17.

Zionist Organization of America. 1720 16th St. Washington 9, D.C.
    Publishes *New Palestine*.

THE REFERENCE SHELF

is published to make available when needed, collections of articles and bibliographies on timely subjects for public discussion. Each number is devoted to a single subject. To make the material available at the time of greatest need, publication is irregular. Each volume contains seven or more separate issues, about 1500 pages in all. Complete volume, $6.00; single numbers as quoted.

The Reference Shelf is listed in the Readers' Guide to Periodical Literature, Education Index, Industrial Arts Index, and Cumulative Book Index.

Future Issues To Be Announced.

Volume XVIII. $4.30

Volume XVII. $3.45

Volume XVI. $6

Volume XV. $5.40